FEMININE SOVEREIGNTY

FEMININE SOVEREIGNTY

8 Pillars for Regenerating Ourselves and Our World

MAGGIE SALE OSTARA, PhD

FEMININE SOVEREIGNTY PRESS

FEMININE SOVEREIGNTY PRESS

ISBN 979-8-9892512-1-6 print edition
ISBN 979-8-9892512-0-9 e-book edition
Cover Illustration: Maggie Ostara
Book and Cover Design: HR Hegnauer
Author Photo by Cristie Kiley Design

Thanks to those artists and institutions that generously granted permission for reprinting their work:
"I Sense Your Presence," lyrics by Shimshai Cook, published by CDBY
Heart Coherence and Entrainment © HeartMath Institute
"Woodland-Cultural-Burn-1" © by Alysha Beck, UC Davis

The names of some of the people mentioned have been changed to protect their anonymity.

Advance Praise

"Broad in scope, deep and rich in understanding, Maggie Ostara's *Feminine Sovereignty* brings a rare level of insight and guidance to our troubling times. Like an oracle sounding a call, this book asks us to wake up to the very real challenges the world faces, and to access the wisdom and power within ourselves and our communities to actively transform the world we inhabit. With the 8 Pillars we are taken on a practical journey to become "sovereign beings, evolving together into compassionate sovereign stewards of our mother, our beautiful planet Earth." Poignant, real, and compelling. An infusion of possibility as we struggle to find our way forward."

—Robin Winn, founder of Human Design Certification
Training for Professionals and author of *Understanding Your Clients Through Human Design: The Breakthrough Technology*

"Feminine Sovereignty is the book I've waited forty-four years to read! During this pivotal time in our human and planetary evolution, we need a powerful yet compassionate resource like this to help us heal our deepest core wounds and integrate from a place of love, strength, vitality, and self-awareness. Maggie is a solid visionary who offers us an empowered, potent voice to navigate the upcoming winds of our time, as an individual and as a collective."

—Shivali Panchal, Clinical Director,
OC Vitality Integrative Health & Wellness

"Maggie Ostara is a powerhouse who has discovered a vehicle for her passion and, within that passion, has found her deeply feminine voice. In *Feminine Sovereignty: 8 Pillars for Regenerating Ourselves and Our World*, she lays out a compassionate plan to support personal awakening while developing alignment with the larger community. Maggie is not just

about change, she is about transformational possibility and the hope that tomorrow can be born from today. This book matters – read it."
—Desda Zuckerman, founder of Sacred Anatomy
Energy Medicine and Sacred Anatomy Academy and
author of *Your Sacred Anatomy: An Owner's Guide
for the Human Energy Structure*

"For anyone interested in shifting the power dynamics in the current world, a deep dive into sovereignty is essential. Through a blend of deep wisdom, practical application, creative firepower, and lived experience, Maggie Ostara walks with readers through building sovereignty on the inner landscape and expressing it through stewardship out in the world.

"Maggie brings together all the realms – mind, body, heart, spirit, individual, systemic, culture – to help you remember how to access your intuition, your co-creative power, and capacity to cause culture – not in theory or in Pollyanna thinking, but instead in grounded, rooted, real, and deeply embodied, heart-led ways. A true guide always takes the journey first, and Maggie Ostara gifts us with a book that comes from her own devotion to this path for many decades. Thank you, Maggie, for showing us the means through which we can live, lead, and succeed differently."
—Christine Arylo, MBA, Transformational Leadership
Advisor, mentor, and teacher, and author of
*Overwhelmed & Over It: Embrace Your Power to Stay
Sustained and Centered in a Chaotic World*

"A comprehensive guide to transforming your life, while supporting people and planet. *Feminine Sovereignty* is more than a book, it is an invitation into a deep exploration of personal and collective truth. As I read the introduction I immediately felt myself being pulled into a portal of transformation.

"Maggie has expertly woven various concepts and modalities from her rich background in academia and personal development into something that is intimate and approachable. I especially loved the interweaving of some deep and complex ideas within the system of Human Design into the very practical pillars of transformation that are the foundation of the book.

"I am delighted that Maggie has captured this wisdom for people around the globe as a jumping off point for a new level of personal sovereignty. Highly recommend!"

  —Darla LeDoux, founder of Sourced and
   author of *Shift the Field*

"I have been in community with Maggie for over fifteen years, and every step of the way her work has been on the emergent edge of transformation! Her perspective and insights through her new book can offer tools that women are seeking to develop the innate guidance we seek. This book's focus on accessing our innate, creative life force as a core source for developing strength from within will be illuminating!"

  —Shiloh Sophia, curator of Musea, co-founder of Intentional
   Creativity, and author of *Tea with the Midnight Muse:*
   Invocations and Inquiries for Awakening

Table of Contents

Foreword: Manda Scott I
Foreword: Kia Miller IV
Foreword: Karen Curry Parker VII
Foreword: Susan Harper IX
Prologue XI

Introduction: Taking Command, Becoming Sovereign

Take Command 3
Sovereignty Is a Force Whose Time Has Come 5
Evolving Power 10
What's Inside 11
A Spiraling Journey 13
My Eclectic Approach 14
This Book Is for You If 16
What This Book Asks of You 20
Primary Evolutionary Tools 26

Pillar One: Co-Creating with the Flow of Life

Exploring the Web of Life 35
We Humans Are Spiritual Beings 36
What Gets in the Way: Isolation, Separation, and an Angry God 40
Accessing Your Intuition and Cultivating Your Creative Power . . 46
Your Turn: Take Time to Assess, Integrate, and Apply What
    You've Learned 63

Pillar Two: Emotional Wisdom

Navigating Emotional Life 75
We Humans Are Emotional Beings 76
Building Your Emotional Wisdom 91
Your Turn: Take Time to Assess, Integrate, and Apply What
    You've Learned 103

Pillar Three: Vitality, Embodiment, and Connection with the Living World

Your Body: Your Most Intimate, Longest-Term Relationship .. 115
We Humans Are Physical Beings 116
Building Your Vitality, Embodiment, and Connection
    with the Living World 128
Your Turn: Take Time to Assess, Integrate, and Apply What
    You've Learned 138

Pillar Four: Radiance and Energetic Adeptness

Understanding Our Personal Energy. 149
We Humans Are Energy Beings 150
Harnessing Energy, Radiating Light, Becoming Magnetic 162
Your Turn: Take Time to Assess, Integrate, and Apply What
    You've Learned 179

Sadhana Practice: Your Daily Date with the Divine

We Humans Are Habitual Beings. 191
My Sadhana Practice Based in Kundalini Yoga 194
Self-Correction and Self-Creation 200
Your Gift to You 209

Introducing Part Two: Spiraling Outward

The Purpose of Feminine Sovereignty. 214
The Fulcrum Point 216

Pillar Five: Know Your Purpose and Your Contribution

Fuel Comes When Feeling on Purpose 221
We Humans Are Purposeful, Contributing Beings 222
Exploring Your Purpose and Building Your Contribution 233
Your Turn: Take Time to Assess, Integrate, and Apply What
    You've Learned 247

Pillar Six: Communication that Connects

The Balm of Attention 257
Growing Your Communication Abilities 274
Your Turn: Take Time to Assess, Integrate, and Apply What
    You've Learned 286
New Desired Capacities 291

Pillar Seven: Mutually Beneficial Collaborations

Being in THIS Together 297
We Humans Are Communal, Collaborative Beings 298
Creating Mutually Beneficial Collaborations 314
Your Turn: Take Time to Assess, Integrate, and Apply What
    You've Learned 329

Pillar Eight: Compassionate Sovereign Stewardship

Helpful Burning, Harmful Burning, Cultural Burning 339
We Humans Are Compassionate, Stewarding Beings 340
Cultivating Your Capacity for Compassionate Stewardship 364
Your Turn: Take Time to Assess, Integrate, and Apply What
    You've Learned 390

What Now, What's Next?

Your Learning Questions 401
Your Self-Assessments 401
Project Invitations 404
You Matter 408

Epilogue 411
Resources 413
Bibliography by Chapter 415
Acknowledgment 427
About the Author 429

For Sam

that you may have a healthier,

more beautiful world in which to blossom.

Foreword: Manda Scott

This book blew me away. It's so profoundly necessary in this time of huge turmoil. Many want to make a difference – but we don't know how and we don't know what to do or where to go. *Feminine Sovereignty* offers us a path to get to the edge of ourselves, from which we might jump off into the unknown of something bigger, stronger, more *alive* than the death cult we've fostered for so many generations.

We're in an urgent time of change when everyone is needed. We're beyond the Great Transition now. We're in the thick of the climate and ecological emergency: wholesale environmental degradation is impacting people across the planet, and though we know we need to act, we still lack the roadmaps and models for how we could step away from the monster we've unwittingly created. Like the worst of all zombies, the market economy (and all that flows from it) knows only how to grow. Its whole mode of being is to extract, consume, and destroy, and we are caught up in the flow even when we know it's killing us as well as the rest of the living web.

But the fact that we're embedded in the system makes it really hard to see how we could create something different. For sure, telling people things are bad and getting worse is not a useful strategy: we can see it failing in real time. What we need are creative ideas for a future built on different principles and values; we need stories of how the world could look and feel and work and be if we weren't being told that we were basically born to pay bills and then die. We need, in fact, a template for a world that works in ways we'd be proud to leave to the generations who come after us.

This may be obvious, but even now most writers are still writing in the old paradigm – largely because we don't have the resources from which to build these new ideas. For years we've run the *Accidental Gods* podcast, showcasing people *who are already* working across the world to help regenerate ourselves and our planet in a variety of ways. Our mainstream media may not yet have caught up, but there are many people all over the world creating radical, revolutionary projects in regenerative agriculture and forestry, decentralized governance, and local green energy systems;

cleaning up toxic waste; creating local, healthy food systems, and so much more. So much is happening – it all just needs to get on people's radar and become the things we talk about, think about, and dream about.

By 2022, three years into the podcast, we decided it was time for something more specifically targeted toward creative writers. We knew it was time to ditch the dystopias; we all know how bad things could be. We also know that where we put our energy and imagination is where we end up, and while nobody wants to end up with the ugly love child where *The Road* meets *The Handmaid's Tale*, that's the course we're all on.

But then again, nobody believes in utopias precisely because they don't feel real; we don't know how to get to the worlds those utopias describe from the ones we're in.

What we need, therefore, are *Thrutopias* – stories of how we get from where we are to where we need to be in ways that feel grounded, plausible, and doable. Above all we want them so badly that getting to those Thrutopias, to feeling the way they show us we could feel, to finding the new values of compassion, decency, integrity, and connectedness, feels like the single most important thing we could do with our time on Earth.

With this in mind, we ran the Thrutopia Writing Masterclass over six months in 2022, specifically to give established writers ideas to spark the new stories we need. We brought a series of presenters to explore ideas of how we might get from exactly where we are to the more beautiful future our hearts know is possible. We looked at writing fiction, screenplays, poetry, songs, blogs, short- and long-form fiction – all the narrative forms we could think of – because we need stories of how we get through this time to the other side.

Maggie Ostara was one of our most committed students. She understood both the urgency and the potential of this time. In *Feminine Sovereignty*, she has taken the Thrutopian themes and made them her own. She's been engaged in transformational work for many years before participating in this course, and now she's drawn on what she's calling the *Thrutopian Imperative* to inform the ways we create purpose, contribution, and how we communicate and collaborate with each other. Certainly we need all of this.

The honesty, integrity, and personal vulnerability Ostara brings to this project is genuinely magical. I am in awe of her capacity to shine light inside and help us face, digest, and integrate what we see. She seamlessly bridges two elements necessary for us to become the changemakers we need to be: our inner resilience and emotional intelligence and our ability to show up in the outer world powerfully, with care and compassion, as we work together to evolve ourselves and our world. Too often we tend to focus on one or the other of these aspects, not fully realizing that they're intimately intertwined. If we keep trying to create change with our old ways of being, we won't get far. We've already tried that. And if we keep focusing solely on personal development and do nothing to contribute to changing our outer world, we're out of touch with reality. We need a holistic approach that honors all of who we are and that is part of the healing that will enable us to do what needs to be done.

This is essential reading for anyone who wants to reclaim their personal sovereignty – wherever they are on the spectrum of gender identity, whatever age or color they are, whatever creed they follow. This is a generous, clear-hearted book and it'll change lives. Not only that but it also just might help us evolve so that we get to total systemic change in time.

—Manda Scott, host of podcast *Accidental Gods*
and author of *The Boudica* series
(*Dreaming the Eagle, Dreaming the Bull,
Dreaming the Hound, Dreaming the Serpent Spear*)

Foreword: Kia Miller

With *Feminine Sovereignty*, Maggie Ostara gives us a profound and timely teaching on reclaiming the aspects of life we very much need to find balance. Through her delineation of 8 Pillars, she lights a path toward the healing of our relationship with the planet, ourselves, each other, and Spirit. Our senses are engaged and the mystic within each of us awakened by her poetic writing and inspiring wisdom, allowing us to connect with the archetypal Goddess who resides in our hearts.

Feminine Sovereignty invites us to access a deeper truth and gives us opportunities to acknowledge patterns of belief and behavior that no longer serve us. Maggie's personal stories inspire us to reflect on our own lives: our traumas and victories alike.

We don't see the world as it is. We see everything through our conditioning, likes and dislikes, beliefs, and perspectives. The habits we live by are largely inherited. Our subconscious mind, programmed by society, family, and memories, influences our behavior without our awareness, keeping us stuck and distanced from our own sovereignty.

Maggie presents the possibility of a new world of dynamic collaboration and connection. *Feminine Sovereignty* offers a form of empowerment training through which you can become responsible and sovereign, queen/king of your own domain, ready to take radical self-responsibility for who you are and how you choose to walk through the world.

If you come to this work with the desire to unlock your evolutionary potential, to source solutions for problems that seemed insurmountable, to access healing power, and to identify new possibilities, then you've arrived in the right place.

The pathway is clearly laid out in the *8 Pillars for Regenerating Ourselves and Our World*. Each pillar presents a relevant and somewhat urgent invitation. Taken as a whole, the message is to develop an understanding of who and what you are: energy, consciousness, illuminated intelligence within a physical form. You have thoughts, emotions, preferences, challenges, and one single calling: to discover, know, and honor yourself.

As a yoga student and teacher, I share along with Maggie an ancient lineage of truth-seekers who took on the challenge of self-realization. They studied the human condition and asked questions such as, *Who am I? What is my purpose? What is the source of life? What does it mean to walk in right relationship in the world?* The ancient yogic texts speak to the idea of oneness. The mantra *Ek Ong Kar* speaks to this: all of creation and the Creator are one. We are each an expression of the *one* creative consciousness. We are all made of the same elements. We share the same world, yet we have unique features and talents. We are sacred sisters and brothers, with nobody higher and nobody lower.

The ancient yogis developed a handbook for the human being, including an understanding that our physical body and mind are just two aspects of us. Ultimately we exist on five different levels: soul or pure consciousness, awareness, mind, energy, and body. To come into a state of integration between all five levels is the true purpose of yoga. Therefore we must engage in a process of awakening that activates all five. This includes moving the physical body, building vital energy, calming the mind, developing discernment, and taking liberating actions that lead toward harmony and peace. Maggie lays this all out beautifully within the 8 Pillars.

One of the most illuminating aspects of this book shows up in Pillar Four, where Maggie teaches about cultivating emotional wisdom and creating "energy adeptness" – the ability to act effectively in the world. Here she shares Kundalini Yoga kriyas (specific yoga sequences) and Human Design, a powerful system to develop one's inner guidance system: intuition.

As a yoga teacher I have experienced the full illuminating power of Kundalini Yoga, known as the Yoga of Awareness. Those who engage in the kind of practices Maggie shares in this book and who dedicate themselves to a daily practice or "daily date with the divine" can successfully unravel layers of unconscious conditioning and access new levels of vitality, creative thinking, emotional freedom, and joy.

Maggie astutely includes moments of self-reflection so that readers can better assimilate what they've learned and see where they connect with each concept. This includes the important illumination of the shadow aspects of our being, and is where we begin to engage consistently with the inner voice of our conscience, where we turn our love inward and recognize the beauty of who and what we are. These moments of self-reflection are where we awaken!

Through an intention to change, coupled with the discipline to implement the teachings of each pillar, you can transcend "normal" and experience "extraordinary." As you do this work, you'll begin to access the outward spiral Maggie speaks of in Pillars Five through Eight. You'll develop a sense of purpose, speak with clarity and compassion, and seek mutually beneficial collaborations.

This book is your opportunity to step into your power, to embody your true essence, to break free and experience true authenticity. We all need to do this. This is how we can serve that which desires to be born: a new era that reflects the values of love, compassion, mutuality, equality, and freedom from suffering. If each one of us commits to our own awakening, we open the potential for everyone else.

As it says in the oldest of the yogic texts, the *Rig Veda*:

"May we learn to walk together, talk together, think together, and co-ordinate our actions. Let there not be disharmony between our actions and others' actions. As a result, you will not become a threat to anyone, and they will not be a threat to you."

May it be so.

—Kia Miller, founder of Radiant Body Yoga

Foreword: Karen Curry Parker

Human Design entered my life many years ago, and when it did, it grabbed hold of me. It hasn't let go since. I was fortunate enough to be among those who discovered and worked with Ra Uru Hu, the founder and original developer of Human Design. As I practiced and taught this system over the years, I realized that what had been gifted to us through Ra was incomplete. I created Quantum Human Design to give voice to what we often call the "higher expression" of an aspect of the system, what I consider a more awakened and empowered expression. In this way, Quantum Human Design evolves the original system in the direction of greater wholeness, possibility, healing, and embracing the true potential that is our birthright as human beings.

You are a once-in-a-lifetime cosmic event – and yet it can be difficult to acknowledge and truly own that for yourself when you're mired in conditioning that tells you otherwise. Partnering the illuminating and affirming character of Human Design with practices and perspectives gleaned from decades of work in human potential creates a potent cauldron for change of the sort we so need in our world today.

Feminine Sovereignty offers a clear path to developing your personal sovereignty, a path that's remarkably layered and complex yet at the same time easy to follow. Maggie acknowledges Human Design as a powerful system for revealing the truth of who we are and includes it here as a key tool in developing sovereignty. Yet cognitive awareness of our truth is only part of the journey. This book brings in powerful energy to complement Human Design, as I have done in my own Quantum Alignment System. We need this support to help us decondition from the behaviors, beliefs, and ways of being that confine us.

The story of Human Design includes a prophecy that we are on the cusp of a massive creative revolution that's already unfolding and influencing all of us. In this book, Maggie speaks to the significance and power of creativity as demonstrated in the Human Design system and in our lives more generally. She helps us understand that we are all creative beings, making the point that creativity isn't the domain of special people but a core aspect of each one of us. Yet certain indicators show that collectively we've been becoming less creative over the last few decades. We need to change this and awaken and express our creative nature to navigate the challenges in our world today.

Human Design shows us ways of knowing that are often not well understood or respected by the culture at large. As we take in and integrate the perspectives and lessons Human Design offers us, we can move out of these confining and inaccurate stories about who we are and create new stories more true to our experience, self-knowing, and aspirations. In this way we become more and more whole, more in alignment with our Human Design, and more aware of our actual strengths, intelligences, and superpowers. As Maggie points out, all of this aids us on our journey of developing our personal sovereignty.

Human Design has become more popular, yet many people still haven't heard of it or don't understand its potential to help them uplift their lives. In *Feminine Sovereignty*, Maggie brings Human Design into broader awareness, making the system's specific concepts and possibilities more accessible to the novice. She shares enough to intrigue the reader and illustrate her point without being overwhelming. As with any sophisticated system, walking this line isn't easy. Yet this is what's needed for the transformative and evolutionary potential of Human Design to continue to make its way into the minds and hearts of more and more people.

If you're new to Human Design, *Feminine Sovereignty* offers you a way in that I hope inspires you to dive in more deeply. You don't need to have experience with this system to enjoy the essence of what's shared here. And if you're already familiar with Human Design, this book will place the system's innate power inside the larger story of human development and evolution.

Feminine Sovereignty reveals just how much is at stake in how we're engaging with life here at this potent time of change. It gives us permission and instructions to look deeply inside and grow ourselves with care and compassion into who we have the potential to become. It encourages us and exhorts us to awaken to our role as sovereign stewards, caring for our planet and each other in addition to ourselves. It will inspire, disrupt, intrigue, challenge, and love you from beginning to end. A rich journey indeed.

—Karen Curry Parker, creator of Quantum Human Design
and author of *The Encyclopedia of Quantum Human Design*

Foreword: Susan Harper

Our living world is so vast and rich. From the tiniest microbes to the largest galaxy, consciousness takes many forms. Yet in our modern world we tend to collapse our perception into feeling and knowing just a small fraction of our reality. We tend to perceive ourselves and our living context as individuated, isolated, solid, and static objects that we can count and manipulate.

Yet the truth is much larger, more dynamic, and continually changing. Consciousness emerges, explores, expands, morphs, contracts, diminishes, rippling and rolling, smelling, and tasting, reaching and falling, moving and shifting always. Continuum helps us tap into and experience this richness through sounds, subtle movement, imagery, breathing, and reaching our perception into the spiraling contours of our living world.

So many feel isolated, alone, and afraid. While there are many social, economic, political, and technological contributors to this, a more fundamental cause lies in feeling disconnected from our Earth and the living world. As Maggie notes in this beautiful offering, I often teach that gravity offers us a force of belonging, which is so supportive and healing when we feel uprooted. We actually have, right here beneath us, a way to feel our wholeness, our aliveness, and our connection with our home, the planetary body. Yet we forget, and when we do, confusion and despair can set in.

Feminine Sovereignty invites readers to pause and wonder, slowing the mental processes that can isolate us and awakening our perception of our place in the planetary body and even in the cosmos. The speed at which we habitually operate inhibits our ability to sense the humming of life within and all around us. As we slow down and go within, we can touch and ride the movement always already happening inside us and reach out to relate to the green ones, the winged and slithering ones, our mineral allies, and those swimming in our ancient waters. Our relatedness simply needs to be noticed in order to be touched and felt.

This book will help you understand the value of cultivating your perception of the living world and the cultural and historical forces that have diminished it. Having a larger context in which to understand and explore our experience relieves the sense of isolation and separateness. Maggie provides many lenses through which to create this larger context, layers of meaning building one upon another. As you read, you'll immerse yourself in different perspectives, some of which will be familiar while others are new to you. You'll build a kaleidoscope of perception through which to cultivate your dynamic sense of sovereignty.

—Susan Harper, creator of Continuum Montage

Prologue

Have you felt the pain of living a life not your own?

Maybe you've achieved success as defined by others, temporarily elated only to discover how quickly the feeling fades. Maybe you're tired of buying new clothes, new jewelry, new electronics, maybe even a new home or a new car, to try to get that feeling back.

And then you stop to listen. Something, someone, somewhere seems to be silently screaming. You cock your head and tune in to an ongoing inner debate. Part of you says: *Better to do what they say, to make yourself useful, to stay focused on the tasks you've been given and not make waves. You know what happens to people who make waves.* Another part is moving her mouth, but you can't hear what she's saying even though you can feel her urgency. She's standing in her own uniqueness, her quirky specialness, her intrinsic value as an expression of the creative intelligence of the Universe. But there hasn't been space or listening for her – for all of her, and all of you.

You ponder as you drag yourself up and out to work at something that may seem okay, even better than okay, from the outside. But inside you can feel your truest self leaning away from, pouring your life force in the direction of conforming. You pull in on the reins and bridle that you put on her, forcing her back onto the path you chose without knowing any better, maybe, or perhaps because it's felt more safe and secure. But you're beginning to realize that the promised or imagined safety and security rest on top of a crumbling foundation, one that requires continued exploitation of the Earth's "natural resources," extracting power lodged deep underground, in moving water, and in forests and mountains, leaving behind poisons and dead places where nothing living flourishes.

Take a few deep breaths now because, yes, turning to face this can be very disturbing and disheartening. Yet as you breathe and allow your awareness to grow you also free yourself from the blinders and bridle your society taught you to wear from your earliest days. These devices turned you away from the singing of the little people and the trees' whispers and the flowers' laughter toward the signs you were told are more important and more real.

And so you learned your numbers and your letters and what they mean when you combine them into sequences. How well you did this indicated how smart you are, or *so you were told*. Of course you did your best. You put that bridle on your life force and wrested your attention away from the call of the forest and the streams and even the birds. You directed it toward squiggles on a page, and then in books, and now screens flickering with light.

You hush the part of you that cannot help but ask: "*This* is what's real? *Really?*"

You learned to hush that part so thoroughly that by the time you get to make more and more choices for yourself you can barely hear her, at least not clearly, not most of the time. She may slip into your dreams on occasion because you can't truly silence her. You can only close your inner ears and ignore the heart that beats in rhythm with this deeper, more ancient, aspect of your being.

Perhaps cracks are showing or being felt in the image you created of yourself, the one in charge who knows how to navigate life's complexities and create the success you were told would bring you happiness. Yet that hollowness inside reverberates louder each day, its echoing dissatisfaction slowly rising to the level of pain. *That's why you picked up this book, isn't it?* Because that silent screaming has become so distracting and disturbing that you can no longer simply ignore it.

I know. I get it. More than once, I've done my own dance with the soul inside me shredding my life from within and trying to get out, to get free.

Because here's the thing: We, all of us, have many, many layers of experience we've inherited from our ancestral line, as well as the myriad other lives on our soul's journey and this one precious life we're living here in this moment. We've gotten really, really good at surviving and expanding our influence as the planet's dominant species. We still carry within us the marks of violent creation that led us to where we are now. What we've learned has made us *successful* as the planet's *primary predator*.

Yet now we stand on the edge of a precipice we didn't realize we were digging, digging, digging with each act of violence against the Earth. The precipice yawns before us. None can tell what will happen were we to teeter off the edge and drop into the depths below. Your soul-self, the one silently screaming inside, has seen the precipice deepening year after year, generation after generation. Yet her warnings have often gone unheeded.

A different part took the blinders and put them on. She submitted to the bridle willingly, closed her inner ears, and focused straight ahead. But oh, now the bridle holds you too tightly, the blinders create distress, and your soul's call finally makes its way into your daily consciousness.

You stand, the precipice in sight, your heart pounding, your ears burning, and your eyes tearing, asking: "Now what?"

Now what indeed?

You reach up and unbuckle the bridle, and off it comes with the blinders. Suddenly light pours in, and what once was narrow becomes incredibly wide. A sudden, sharp intake of breath helps you receive what you're seeing and feeling. And you realize you need to sit down or else you might teeter and fall.

You can feel Spirit within you dancing. While you like the feeling, you also know that the part of you who's been bridled for so long will need time and attention to grow into what you now sense is possible. Like an inmate released from prison, or a wild animal raised in captivity now let go, you need to adjust to your new reality. You ask Spirit inside of you to show you the way, and she says:

If you were to listen in the cool, quiet morning, from around the corner of your mind, you might hear your longed-for future whispering. That possibility is always already here, you see, not just in the imaginings of those who fear what's to come or in the musings of those who long to escape their present experience. Yes, those who are desperate do shape shimmering images of possibility that perhaps they'll live into. Yet alongside these grow visions smelling of rich soil and bursting with new life that expresses humanity's potential as sovereign stewards.

In some places these visions have already taken root and now are reaching into the sky, drinking possibility from the infinite. Released from the bridle of consumer culture, curiosity and commitment unearth connections that have always been lying in wait, eager to be noticed and activated. The people, thus freed, create lavishly, paintbrushes of possibility dripping with vivid colors and configurations not seen in such numbers for millennia.

Their singing rides on the wings of ravens, carried across the inner planes, whispering invitations to those who choose to listen. In a moment or a lifetime you turn and cock your head, opening your inside ear. The scent of freesias wafts your way, pulled along in the wake of whispers, tickling your tastebuds.

You begin to feel that despair isn't necessary even as you face what's most difficult. That dangerous road need not be taken, even though billboards with blinking arrows would send you that way. *No,* you feel choice rising inside you as you wrest it away from the reach of the media, rich with disaster scenarios. *No,* you say quietly to yourself as you place a hand on your forehead and reach inward to grab those stories. Slowly, purposefully, you pull out of your imagination versions of the future to which you refuse to give your lifeforce. You disperse them with three strong claps of your hands.

Ah … Space. Quiet.

Now the whispers, barely heard, slide in, spreading into your heart and belly. Pulsing. Warm. Alive. Their voices rise and fall with a cadence at once new and familiar, as ancient as the mutterings of the gods who created us. The air around you begins to shimmer, luminescent, gold and silver and your favorite colors softly emerging from the ethers. As you watch you feel more than see the way the particles of light swirl and swoosh as if they were still in the wave forms from which they came. As they slow down, the particles drop into form, an exquisite temple of light building itself before you. You realize as you watch that you can participate in shaping its form, co-creating this sacred space of consciousness. One, two, three, four … eight pillars altogether begin to take shape, each with its own shape, color, and tone.

You drift up the stairs that have appeared, moving into a temple designed by your desires. As you step inside, labradorite stretches out before you, offering a foundation of stability and magic. The pillars phase in and out of form, shimmering and translucent one moment, shiny and solid the next. A moment later they appear rough and ridged and you sense, more than see, the way they root down into the Earth, even as they reach, green-tipped, upward into the sky.

"These are your pillars," Future whispers in your ear. "Your longing has called them, and they invite you into this portal of consciousness. Can you feel how their lifeforce responds to your desires?" And yes, indeed you can. Colors shift, movements change direction, shapes form and morph.

You're mesmerized, delight and wonder bubbling inside. "They're here to offer you their support," Future confirms. "But to receive it, you must be willing to grow yourself in ways new to you that may be challenging *and uncomfortable."* You can feel the smile in Future's words. *"Are you willing?"*

Oh yes, you silently murmur. *I've been so confined. I'm very willing if this leads me to freedom.*

"Freedom, yes," Future nods, "and more than freedom too. For you see, this Temple of Sovereignty requires you to use your inner power for the good of all beings, and not just for yourself."

You don't really know what that means, and you feel a bit intimidated by that thought. *Me, what can I do?* you wonder.

"You'll find out, dear one, *if you're willing,*" Future assures.

You move to the pillar closest to you and reach out your hands. It presents a surface to you that feels eerily solid and transient at the same time. It's not cold as you expected but warm and humming with life. As you close your eyes, the pillars' presence becomes magnified, and you feel yourself inside a green-filled space, glittering, gleaming, glorious all around you. *Yes, yes,* you affirm, *very willing.* For an infinite moment all is clear, the temple pure crystalline forms riding waves of potential through the cosmos.

And then a raven calls to her mate in the branches above you, and you suddenly feel again the half-drunk cup of coffee in your hand. As you open your eyes, your perception collapses into sequential moments in time. Yet a patina of that deep knowing still colors all you see, a sense of majestic pillars reverberating inside you. You know you're forever changed, a new path stretching out before you.

You delete the news apps from your devices and turn off notifications for everything but communiques from your most beloved. And you nourish the rich silence within, listening, feeling, imagining, wondering, shimmering, leaning into what's next.

XV

Taking Command, Becoming Sovereign

Growing ourselves into our sovereign selves and our compassionate stewardship in support of the living world.

"You are a Center of Consciousness
within the One Life."

—Sanaya Roman, channel for Orin

"What are you willing to do
if you want a better way?"

—N.K. Jemisen, four-time Hugo Award winner,
MacArthur Genius Award recipient

How sovereign am I?

**How can I fully express myself
and step into my potential?**

Take Command

I'm sitting in a large auditorium filled with several thousand people. On stage a silver-haired, highly polished white man in a $5000 Armani suit is teaching about sales. He's everything I've learned to distrust. I'm sitting, arms crossed, eyes narrowed, barely breathing. I'm committed to being here for the next few hours, so I think, *I might as well listen to what he has to say.*

As I listen my mind slowly begins to open. He's confident and passionate yet surprisingly not egoic, and I'm getting drawn in. He started out talking about his work in the insurance industry and how over time he became a trainer for people in the insurance industry. *Yeah, good at sales,* I think, *getting people to buy life insurance. Huh.*

But now he's shifted, and he's talking about the seminars he's created to help people not just be better at sales but to create lives they really desire. He's talking about having to do what you want in life and not just fill your days with someone else's priorities and then drag yourself home without energy to do what you love.

My ears perk up. I'm at a transition point in my life. I spent the last eight years getting a PhD and then I landed a plum professorship at an Ivy League university. I'd accomplished everything I set out to do – the degree, the job, the book that was about to be published with a major academic press. But I was unhappy, I was getting sick, and I wasn't sure why. I was confused and uncomfortable. My whole life had led me to this place and, astonishingly, I didn't want to be there. I was standing on the edge of the world I'd known, a chasm of uncertainty gaping before me.

Several months earlier I'd been walking down West End Ave in New York, searching for I didn't know what. I'd thrown my arms up into the air, gazing at the splintered clouds and brilliant blue overhead, and out loud I'd said to the Universe:

"I don't know what to do. I'm at the end of what I know. So you have to bring me what's next. I'll do my part. I'll go out and look. But you have to bring it to me because I have no idea what's next or where I'm going. *You have got to bring it to me, okay?*"

This was the first time I'd explicitly put out a request, a prayer, to a higher intelligence. Before I'd always relied on my own strategy and intelligence, and they'd taken me far. But now I knew I needed help and help of an entirely different kind than I'd experienced before.

Not long after, the opportunity to join a network marketing company called Nikken, a health and wellness company from Japan, came to me. I resonated with the company's philosophy of the 5 Pillars of Health, their products had helped me resolve a back issue I'd had for a decade, and I loved and trusted the person who introduced me. Yet it all felt at a distance, just a bit blurry, as if I were in a dream.

The environment couldn't have been more different from what I was used to. Everything about it was foreign to me. I'd grown up in an academic family, and the life of the mind was what I knew. It's what I was good at. I wasn't at all sure where this was going. I'd agreed to come to this event to get a bigger picture of what was possible. That's how I first met the man in the Armani suit, Bob Proctor. Proctor, ironically, caught my attention partly because of how erudite he was. Little did I know at that moment that Proctor would be my first prosperity teacher and a catalyst in my next phase of life.

Back in that auditorium, Proctor is telling a story about inviting a man to his seminar. "I'd really like to go, but I can't," the man says.

"Well, why can't you?" Proctor asks.

"Because I have to work," the man replies as if this were obvious.

"What does having to work have to do with coming to seminar?" Proctor prods.

"I can't just not go to work," the man says, exasperated. "I have a family, a mortgage."

Proctor points his finger out into the audience, and I swear he's pointing directly at me. He says: "When are *you* going to take command of your life?!"

Like an arrow to my heart. I inhale sharply and pause my breath. My eyes dart side to side, seeing nothing. *When are you going to take command of your life?* I repeat quietly to myself. *When am I going to take command of my life? Wait. Aren't I in command of my life?* I pause, considering. *No, actually, I don't think I am. Not anymore anyway.* That is a very uncomfortable admission.

I'm stunned and don't really know why. My mind spins as if in a room of mirrors. Everywhere I look I see myself, yet I seem and feel different in each reflection. For years I'd known who I was and exactly where I was going. I was delighted to go to graduate school. I'd done extremely well, and I'd landed an exceptional job at Columbia University. I'd been totally focused, and I'd created exactly what I wanted. I'd felt very in command until, well, I hadn't. At that moment I was in the void: the old falling away, the new not yet formed.

What does that even mean, I wonder, *to take command of your life?* For Proctor, in this moment, it means not being beholden to a job that would limit your options and control your time. *But what else does it mean, what else?*

I came to really like that phrase "take command," even though it confused and even scared me at first. I liked it so much that fifteen years after my first encounter with Proctor, I named several major three-day events I created "Take Command." I use the term *command* as distinct from control, as stemming from the *power within* that comes with personal sovereignty rather than from fear or the desire to dominate and control others. Of course this contrasts sharply with our common association of "command" being something that kings, queens, emperors, or empresses do to others – *command their people.*

In developing our Feminine Sovereignty, we practice taking command first of our inner landscape, then of our actions and interactions with others in the outer world. What that looks and feels like is the subject of this book.

Sovereignty Is a Force Whose Time Has Come

Sovereignty has been around for thousands of years, and over time has made its way in and out of our ways of understanding power, authority, dominion, responsibility, accountability, and our relationships with the land and with each other. Twenty-plus years ago when I first began using the term, few people knew what I was talking about. Even my business coach at the time dissuaded me from using it, saying, "I don't think you can use it. I'm not sure what that means, and I'm college-educated. Plus no one knows how to spell it."

But ideas circulate, as *Big Magic* author Elizabeth Gilbert points out, until they're received, adopted, expressed, and acted upon. They whisper in ears and shout around corners until someone pays attention.

Sovereignty simply would not be ignored, and I now see myself as an *early adopter*.

My focus with clients has always been on supporting them in developing their personal sovereignty: their ability to develop command of their inner landscape and their inner power and authority. Heeding the words of my coach (for better or for worse), I didn't put sovereignty at the front of my brand until recently. What *sovereignty* means is now being explored and claimed by many people with varying associations and purposes. Often *sovereignty* is invoked to mean self-determination and autonomy, and in defense of individual rights.

People who've been marginalized and suppressed by the *overculture* use *sovereignty* to assert authority over their lives and how they're represented. I borrowed the term *overculture* from mythologist and author Clarissa Pinkola Estes to name the way western culture, also called *modernity*, asserts its superiority, power, and authority over, well, everyone. Groups such as Indigenous Americans use the term sovereignty to assert their dominion over their tribal lands and laws. Individuals use it, such as a woman asserting her right to choose what happens to her body or her independent legal status, or to free herself from misogynist beliefs and behaviors she's internalized. NRA proponents use it in defense of what they call their second amendment right to bear arms. Thought leaders such as Ken Wilbur use "sovereignty" to describe a state of being in contrast to "union" or, in the case of author Francis Weller, in contrast to "community," as if these states were mutually exclusive. Kia Miller, creator of *Radiant Body Yoga* and my yoga mentor, and Desda Zuckerman, creator of *Your Sacred Anatomy*, both speak of the energetic sovereignty one can achieve as the result of the practices they teach.

Sovereignty is a rich word with a complex history, a vibrant and unfolding present, and a very potent and purposeful future. Sovereignty is emerging into a new life at this time, and what that life will consist of is now being developed and debated in the hearts and minds of many. I find this exciting and hopeful. Together we'll explore its depths throughout this book.

Sovereignty: What Does It Mean?

Indulge me for a moment as I dip into an online etymological dictionary to research the history of the terms *sovereign* and *sovereignty*. According to this source, these terms arose in the fourteenth century among European royalty seeking to consolidate their power. This was part of campaigns to elevate the authority of royals, kings in particular, over the Catholic Church, the aristocracy, and of course everyone else. Kings became the representative of God in human form, cast in the tradition of an all-powerful and punishing Christian God. The sovereign is the one destined to rule – the law giver, judge, and ultimate authority.

History, of course, is much messier than that. Rivals among and within royal families abounded, crowns passing from head to head as new hands grasped the objects of power. The story of royal sovereignty served to mask royal battles and often the lack of legitimacy of blood inheritance that was supposed to authorize the rightful king (or occasionally the queen). The mythology of the *rightful rule*r has captured hearts and imaginations for centuries and continues in popular culture today.

Many stories illustrate this point, from our ongoing fascination with the Arthurian legend to Aragorn in *Lord of the Rings*, Ailen in *Throne of Glass*, Princess Leia in the *Star Wars* series, Snow White in *Snow White and the Huntsman*, and Princess Diana in *Wonder Woman*. Our collective imagination continues to be seduced by the underlying premise that there is a rightful ruler. The twist here on history is that this rightful ruler must be recognized not just by their blood, although that's part of it. They must also demonstrate their fundamental goodness, their benevolence, and their higher purpose of acting for the good of all. Notably, J. R. R. Tolkien says that the rightful king will be a *healer* as well as a *warrior*.

A similar mythos can be found in the Celtic *Sovereignty Goddess*. Typically the high priestess, this woman became the Sovereignty Goddess to speak for the land and the people and to choose the king who would protect them. While these pre-Roman peoples were warriors, their role was to protect their communities and the land, not to colonize and exploit others and their land. The Sovereignty Goddess bestowed authority on the one who would be king, and through the rite of *hieros gamos* (in Greek, "sacred marriage") symbolically marrying the king to the land. At times the Sovereignty Goddess ruled with the king as queen, and at others she continued in her role as high priestess. In either case their collaboration honored both masculine and feminine principles garnered and channeled in the service of the greater good for all.

Our modern yet mythic heroic figures must face and overcome what's indisputably evil: Sauron of Mordor in *Lord of the Rings*, the Valg in *Throne of Glass*, the evil Queen in the *Snow White* stories, the Empire and Emperor in *Star Wars*, or the god Ares in *Wonder Woman*. This evil exploits and kills the land as well as the people; the ancient forests of Fangorn, for example, were cut down to feed the fires of Isengard and the pits in which Saruman makes his orcs. In these stories, the rightful sovereign saves the people and the land from this evil rather than fighting with other royals (which would be more historically accurate). In today's world that's a mission we can all get behind, whereas war for conquest is not.

These stories speak to a deep longing within to become more sovereign ourselves.

In the back of our minds and hearts whispers the part of us who knows we've subordinated ourselves to the dictates of the overculture and traded our freedom for *comfort* and *convenience*. We find it difficult to own this desire or to cultivate it within ourselves because we're afraid of what it will cost us, what we'd have to give up in order to experience it. So we project our desire outward onto popular culture, deriving temporary satisfaction from our heroes' and sheroes' journeys. We want to grow into our power. We want to fulfill our destiny and play a vital role in history. But often we don't really know what that means or how to do it. *Maybe you can relate?*

Alongside these initiate stories, queens have been popping up everywhere. Some of these are already familiar: *Prom queens. Beauty queens. Drag queens.* But now I see *queen* being used even more than sovereignty. I first became aware of this when Dana Elaine Owens declared herself Queen Latifa with her debut album, *Hail the Queen*, in 1989. Indeed she is the Queen, blasting open the previously male-dominated genre of rap and opening a path for other female rappers. Two decades later, fans named Beyoncé Queen Bey, dubbing her the queen of entertainment. Black women call each other *queen*, denoting respect, appreciation, and affection.

By its very nature *queen* challenges the ways in which Black women have been denigrated, dehumanized, and commodified inside colonialism ever since the slave trade brought them to the Americas. *Queen* says: "I see you. I acknowledge you. I honor and respect you regardless of any other ways you've been treated or regarded." This witnessing carves out a space of appreciation and care inside an overculture of violence and suppression.

Black women aren't the only ones doing this. I've seen personal branding for the Queen of Transformational Retreats, Evergreen Launch Queens, Queen of the Throne (yes, the toilet!), and the Queen Whisperer. Entertainment features the challenges and triumph of female monarchs (e.g., *The Crown, Reign*, Queen of the Dragons from *Game of Thrones*, and *Elizabeth: The Golden Age*). Amazon includes pages of books with queen in the title. I've participated in a Queen's Council, been part of the Rebel Queens, and often been invited to a Queens' Tea. Women of many races and ethnicities commonly use queen as an honorific – "She's the queen of …. (fill in the blank)" – to denote respect for a woman's area of expertise.

For a country that was founded on throwing off the English monarchy, we certainly continue to be captivated by stories of royalty, and particularly queens. What is it about queens and crowns that keeps drawing us in?

The short version is that we're starved for images of and stories about powerful women. Beyond the majesty and wealth of a queen, which in themselves can be compelling, the mystique of her power captures and intrigues us. We still have so few historical examples of powerful women despite the efforts of feminist scholars over the last fifty years to uncover and represent significant women throughout time. Most people aren't familiar with this kind of academic work and continue to rely on both their outdated education and popular culture. Many more women, particularly white women, are now coming into political and financial power across the globe. Most recently we've also seen more women of color, like Vice President Kamala Harris and political leader and *New York Times* best-selling author Stacey Abrams, rise to political power. At the same time some, disappointingly, simply replicate the power dynamics of the men whose places they've taken.

We need to evolve our political values and actions to stand for the welfare of all people and the living world, not just change the gender of who's in charge. ***This is what Feminine Sovereignty is all about.***

Evolving Power

The purpose of this book is to support you to grow into your fullest potential and become a fully expressed, empowered woman (or man, two-spirited, or gender-fluid person) capable of meeting the challenges of today, not just in your own life but in relation to our world. To do this you'll benefit from exploring your understanding of and relationship with power. You'll continually be invited to dig into the meaning, qualities, and expressions of power as part of your journey to developing your personal sovereignty and your compassionate stewardship. I enter this fray having worked with the concept of sovereignty for twenty-five years both in my own personal development and with hundreds of clients and thousands of students in my online programs.

My intention is to help you better understand the nature of the hierarchical power-over paradigm that we've been living inside of for the last few thousand years and how it continues to influence your perceptions, aspirations, and actions. With this awareness you can evolve your understanding of and relation to power so that you can build your power within and learn to share and rotate power with others (power between and among us).

In the old paradigm under patriarchy, *power* equals the ability to control, manipulate, and dominate. The royal sovereign exemplified this. All resources belonged to – were owned by or were under the dominion of – the crown to do with what *he (almost always a he)* wanted. Patriarchy is a system of domination that relies on a concentration of wealth and resources in the hands of a few very powerful men. This system has harmed everyone, *including most men*. Patriarchy fueled colonialism, genocide, slavery, and the brutal subordination of women of all classes, races, religions, and nationalities. This is the system we're evolving out of, and the system from which we're wresting away the concept of sovereignty to serve very different purposes.

As we evolve ourselves, we're creating energetic templates and pathways that then become available to others. This is influential and vital work.

We're experimenting with ways of being and behaving that move us in the direction of the world we long for. In this we're participating in what

I'm calling the *Thrutopian Imperative*. We're exploring ways of moving from our current dilemmas to a world we'd be proud to leave to future generations. This mirrors the *Seventh Generation Principle* for which indigenous people are known.

I discovered "Thrutopia," a term first coined by philosopher, professor, and activist, Rupert Read, in a seminar I took with Manda Scott in 2022. Scott is the celebrated author of the Boudica series and host of the leading-edge podcast *Accidental Gods*. (The Boudica was the warrior queen who helped hold off the Roman invasion of the British Isles for a generation.) I felt an immediate affinity for this new genre, which is not a utopia, not a dystopia, but a *thrutopia* – a *way through*. Feminine Sovereignty offers ways to grow yourself into the person who can face the big issues of today with purpose, optimism, and vigor with the intent to regenerate yourself and our world. In becoming sovereign, you grow your stamina and your flexibility, your sensitivity and your resilience, your vision and your ability to take right action, all of which gives you stability and agency even in this turbulent time.

What's Inside

I use the term *pillars* in this book because it invokes a sense of stability. As our times become more challenging and uncertain, you need to build your inner strength – your *mettle* – so that your nervous system becomes stronger, and you can handle challenges with more equanimity, creativity, and compassion. Being more resourced and resilient, you can then turn to the outer world to make your contribution to creating the healthy, thriving world you'd be happy to leave to future generations.

Part One (Pillars One through Four), *Spiraling Inward*, dives deep inside your inner landscape. These pillars focus on developing your inner power in the spiritual, emotional, energetic, and physical realms. Part One culminates in *Your Daily Date with the Divine*, which guides you to create a practice that enables you to embody and express the awakened expressions of Pillars One-Four

Part Two (Pillars Five through Eight), *Spiraling Outward*, opens with an introduction that guides you from your inner world to being out in the world with other people. Part Two then spirals out into the world to explore your purpose and contribution, communication that connects, mutually beneficial collaborations, and developing and acting in service to the well-being of all of life. We need to develop new perspectives and skills so that we can interact with each other as sovereign beings and grow ourselves into compassionate sovereign stewards of our planet.

Each pillar begins with a lyrical, narrative section that invites you to enter the pillar's themes *experientially* rather than *conceptually*. While concepts inform, experience teaches. You'll find narrative bits of different kinds sprinkled throughout to encourage you to move out of your analytical mind and into your creative mind and your experiential body. If you enjoy these sections as a guided meditation, you may want to record yourself reading them so you can listen with your eyes closed and fully immerse yourself in the experience. (And yes, I'll create an audio book version before too long.)

Each pillar ends with a section called *Your Turn*. Here I invite you to connect your life experience and current state of consciousness with the themes raised within the pillar. I share more extensively about this section below. Let me say here that this section is, as its name implies, where you get to reflect on what you've been discovering and apply it to your own life and perspective. Use the invitations and exercises to make real this journey in your daily life, so you become the change you want to see in the world, become a *sovereign self* in command of her domain, and a compassionate sovereign steward caring for our living world.

The book culminates in *What Now; What's Next?*, which guides you through pulling together what you've learned and experienced over the course of reading the text and then creating your next steps. The book concludes with a final Coda that mirrors our opening *Prologue*.

You'll also find an extensive bibliography plus a rich array of practices, exercises, and additional materials in our Feminine Sovereignty virtual global community.[1]

---

1 This is a dynamic quantum community of sovereign evolutionaries exploring, growing, and playing together. You're invited to join us to enjoy additional resources related to the book, participate in events and programs, and find a supportive place for yourself inside this virtual Temple of Sovereignty. See the Resources Page to find out how to join us.

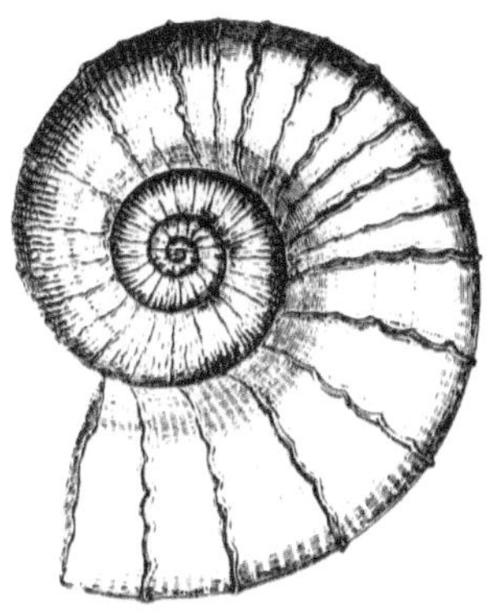

A Spiraling Journey

Because of the nature of two-dimensional writing, the path provided by the 8 Pillars may seem linear. The chapters explore the pillars sequentially and topics do build one upon another. While there's a developmental logic to their presentation, in actual practice you're unlikely to experience these pillars as a linear, logical progression, and I'm not suggesting that you try. Far more likely is that once you've learned the basic content of the pillars, you'll discover that your life experience will spiral inward for a time, then outward as your needs and desires dictate, then inward again as new challenges reveal further demands and opportunities for inner growth, healing, and awareness. This will necessarily be an iterative process.

Growth, development, healing, and transformation aren't linear processes. Spirals and cycles structure the living world and are inherent in our life experience.

Only human-made things such as architecture, the alphabet, calendars, and storylines use lines and right angles. Nature creates and moves through spiraling waves of energy, and we're no different. Anticipate that themes will arise and fall in your awareness, recurring when you're ready to go deeper with your understanding. While we may move calendrically through time, we also always spiral back over memories, traumas, and patterns when we're ready to understand, heal, and grow at a deeper level.

In fact revisiting and revising stories you've created about your past experiences is common to those on a personal growth path. Don't judge yourself when a familiar challenge arises. This doesn't mean you've reverted to an earlier stage in your personal growth, so don't beat yourself up about that as I've heard many do. Instead open your inquiry into what now calls for your attention. What's *new* in this moment? What's possible that wasn't possible before? What's now ready to be revealed, healed, or understood? What wants to be created that couldn't be created before?

Spiraling around may also reveal places where you'd benefit from developing a *new capacity.* Maybe now you're ready to be initiated into a more advanced stage of your emotional wisdom, for example, or your embodiment and vitality. Maybe you're ready to address a past trauma you didn't have the inner strength, stamina, or support for before. Maybe now you're ready to stop eating a food you love but that you know your body doesn't like. Perhaps you now take up a new form of exercise that your body is craving but that you've been resisting. Perhaps you'll forgive someone (or yourself) that you've been holding a grudge against. Or maybe you'll reach out and join a collaborative effort that now inspires and lights you up. Embrace what arises with curiosity. Let your heart lead you into new possibilities and new behaviors.

As we mature, we become more and more able to handle both outside situations and our own inner challenges that would have overwhelmed us before.

In becoming sovereign stewards, we expand our sense of responsibility beyond our individual lives, our families, and even our work situations. For this we need to build new perspectives, new abilities, and new capacities. While that may seem like a lot, this is, step by step, an exciting, inspiring, mind- and heart-opening journey that you can participate in at the rate that's right for you.

My Eclectic Approach

Throughout this book you'll discover insights, teachings, and suggested practices from many wisdom traditions, including traditional Human Design and Quantum Human Design, Kundalini Yoga, regenerative historicism, quantum physics, indigenous wisdom keepers, Nonviolent Communication, Continuum Movement, neuroscientists, and recent developments in psychology and neuroscience. You'll hear different voices and be exposed to different points of view, different kinds of intelligences, and different ways of being, all expressed through different genres. I'll tell many stories and try not to sound too academic (though at heart I'm still a scholar).

This rich and diverse approach represents and expresses the complexity of our lives today. Our range of experiences shouldn't be and can't be without harm, reduced to a simple, singular narrative or a set of action steps: "to dos." We dream over morning coffee. We peruse email and social media. We work, often sitting and gazing at computer screens. We gobble down stories in novels and on television and at the movies. We meditate and breathe and pray. We seek nature while walking on concrete through neighborhoods and city parks. Our perceptions, states of consciousness, embodied experiences, and types of intelligences used all shift through our days. We simultaneously live inside many narratives, employing many ways of being. The form of this book speaks to this complex and shifting inner world and outer reality.

At the risk of stating the obvious, let me say this is a *very personal book*. Everything included comes through the lens of my own experience, my learnings, my values, and my ability to perceive and articulate connections among what may seem to others like disparate elements, my work with clients over the last two-and-a-half decades, and my college students for more than a decade before that. Others would no doubt choose different ways of approaching this material or might argue with some of my interpretations – and that's okay with me. I invite you to walk with me as you will, with a clear mind and open heart. I honor whatever path you choose.

I share and offer from my perspective as a highly educated white woman who grew up in a Black neighborhood in the 1960s and '70s. In my growing up, I had a taste of what it's like to be part of a minority, although I'd never equate it to what people of color experience in this country. I always knew I was, because of my *assigned race*, a welcome member of the larger overculture represented in media of all forms (television, movies, magazines, etc.). Yet this experience of being a minority gives me a certain sensitivity and sensibility that most white people don't have (at least in relation to their race). My academic work in African American studies and Women's and Gender Studies further developed my capacity to see our history and experience from *the margins* of the "Story of Progress."[2] I hope this work speaks to many people of different backgrounds, assigned races, and genders, even as I speak from the authority of my own specific experience.

This Book Is for You If …

I wrote this book for those of us who are now realizing that we stand in the shadow of the *Story of Progress* and can see and feel its breakdown. This story promotes the advance of western civilization, posited as beginning in ancient Greece and Rome, moving into western Europe, and reaching its apex in the United States. This story relies on colonization, slavery, and extractive practices that provide fuel for the growth of technology, cities, and wealth, based in western science. This story has been so ubiquitous that it's been invisible, part of the air we breathe, at least to those who've benefited from it. Only recently have more and more of us come to see this as *a story of power-over* and begun to reckon with its consequences.

The heroine of our *Prologue* newly awakens to the way in which she's been bridled to the Story of Progress. As she removes her bridle and blinders, her perception opens out and she begins to experience her connection with the living world and the Web of Life. My first experience like this came as I was sitting in that auditorium listening to Bob Proctor, when I realized that I really hadn't been in command of my life. I'd been following a trajectory that I knew I could excel at, yet wasn't in the end entirely true to my heart (or my Human Design as it turns out). I was thirty-six years old when I stepped away from what I knew and onto a new timeline. I've had multiple moments of awakening since then when something I'd taken for granted suddenly appeared differently because I was viewing it from a different angle – and my whole world changed.

---

2 This phrase is inspired by Charles Eisenstein in *The More Beautiful World Our Hearts Know Is Possible*, in which he talks about the "Story of the World" and the "Story of the People."

We're here to midwife ourselves and our communities and our very Earth into, Eisenstein again, the "more beautiful world our hearts know is possible." Yet you may not be sure what your role is and what you need to do. The magnitude of what needs to be done can feel overwhelming and confusing. You might feel disempowered as you step away from that shadow narrative. We know that's not how we want to live, inside the allure of the Story of Progress. We're aware of how our culture privileges the left-brain ways of knowing, such as logic, analysis, strategy, categorization, and quantification. This kind of intelligence has brought about much progress in terms of the mass production of goods and building infrastructure (e.g., roads, bridges, housing, sanitation). It has also come at a cost, a much higher cost than the architects of this progress ever imagined.

We're drawn to right-brain intelligences like creativity, intuition, perceiving energy and the unseen world, sensuality and embodiment, the mystery of consciousness and interrelatedness, what Thich Nat Hahn calls "interbeing." **We recognize the dire consequences of left-brained dominance, yet we've felt at a loss as to how to truly shift our world to being more holistic.**

We're interested in and open to ancient wisdom traditions that reveal and express intelligences and ways of knowing that lie outside the lens of western reason, rationality, and logic. Maybe you've been taking yoga classes, singing kirtan, receiving acupuncture, pulling tarot cards, reading your horoscope, collecting crystals, learning your Human Design, or sitting silently on cushions. You're drawn to mythical stories that express essences and truths masked by the Story of Progress, particularly those having to do with strong or nonconforming women.

Having been on a personal and spiritual growth path for a while, we've gained perspective on our personal stories and have some understanding of how they relate to a larger collective story. We've had enough life experience to appreciate the insights of psychology and have already done a significant amount of inner work healing our trauma and dismantling our triggers. We also perceive the limitations of a talking approach and have sought out energetic, creative, and somatic approaches to healing and personal development. We've been actively evolving ourselves and our relationships as best we can with what we know.

We also know that *men aren't the issue.* We're aware that many, even most, men have suffered under patriarchal ideology, as well as most though not all women. We understand that patriarchy is a hierarchical system based in coercion and brutality that is millennia old, what social systems scientist, futurist, and cultural historian Riane Eisler calls a "dominator society." The feminism I embrace seeks to overturn and unravel this brutal ideology that in truth *hurts everyone.* This feminism is in no way man-hating.

Seeing patriarchy as an *ideology* tells us that brutality and hierarchy are not an inherent aspect of human nature, as we've been taught, but part of our collective conditioning. Similarly we see *white body supremacy*[3] as an outgrowth of colonialism, not as an aspect of the living world. Even conceptually knowing all of this, we know we're not yet fully free of the impact and perspectives of these ideologies, and *we want to be.* That's really the key thing.

We're mature enough to face these truths, and we want to be *part of the solution.* Yet we also sometimes feel uncertain and unclear about how to empower ourselves in new ways that are effective, equitable, and sustainable. We don't want to create new versions of power-over strategies in feminine guise as we've seen expressed among some women leaders today. We're very aware of how *insidious* is our conditioning.

---

3 A term I learned from Resmaa Menakem in *My Grandmother's Hands.*

We've already accomplished socially defined versions of success. We're coming to see the enormous personal cost this type of success has demanded. Many of us are exhausted, having not listened to our inner messages and instead adhered to outside standards. We want to powerfully make our contribution, but not at the expense of our own health and well-being. We want to cultivate our leadership potential inside a sustainable, equitable, and compassionate paradigm. We know we need to be stronger – physically, emotionally, energetically, and spiritually – and we're actively engaged in ways to build our capacity.

We want to understand how to cultivate an awakened consciousness, and how to grow ourselves into who we need to be as citizens of the New World we long for and can feel just beyond the horizon. We realize the need to forge new ways of being, engaging with life, engaging with each other, and with our home, the Earth. We're willing, yet uncertain.

This book addresses this desire. It presents a clear path to becoming sovereign of your own self first, then growing yourself into someone who can face and create solutions to the big problems humanity now faces. Compassionate sovereign stewardship requires a level of maturity that collectively we've not yet accomplished. Yet we must if we're to stop our habits of destruction and domination, help our ecosystems heal, and survive as a species.

Many of the qualities we seek are associated with the feminine and with women. This gender assignment is meant to be *descriptive* rather than *deterministic*. Use it or not as it works for you. I focus on women because I have worked with them the most; they are leading in the personal and political development spheres, and women are who I know best. Yet the principles can be embraced, modified, integrated, and implemented by anyone of any gender if it suits them.

It may be that, like me, you and your lineage have benefited from the Story of Progress to some degree with a better lifestyle, higher education, and economic stability. Even though I'm aware of the ways the overculture tries to diminish me as a queer woman, and now as an elder woman, I'm equally aware of the advantages my white privilege and educational background give me. I navigate this complexity with as much awareness as I can.

As the Story of Progress breaks down, women like me may become ter-rified at the potential loss of our privilege and have to face the coerciveness of the entitlement to which we've become accustomed. We may simul-taneously feel elated at the fissures we see in heteronormative, patriarchal white supremacy and the possibilities becoming visible on the other side of that breakdown. Others without white body privilege may feel hopeful, witnessing the shredding of the story that's never empowered them and in fact has done just the opposite. Any of us might well feel overwhelmed and/or paralyzed when we turn toward the now-irrefutable evidence of climate change, the extinction of species, and environmental collapse.

This book and my work respond to my own sense of urgency. *We need to be in action.* And we need to do so from a new level of maturity, from true adulthood, from our Feminine Sovereignty. We're becoming the change, growing ourselves into the people who can respond to this urgency with creativity, optimism, vigor, and, I hope, *some humor.*

What This Book Asks of You

This book invites you on a many-layered journey to develop your own personal sovereignty and to grow yourself into a compassionate sovereign steward of our planet in your own unique way.

Taking in the information and perspectives shared is necessary yet insufficient. My hope is that you'll move beyond the 8 Pillars as "mind candy" – interesting, even inspiring ideas you simply consume (i.e., read) – to transforming and growing yourself into your potential and in the direction of regenerating yourself and our world. This only happens when you take what you're learning and experiencing and bring it home into your heart and body and let it question you, stimulate you, provoke and work you, change, grow, and evolve you.

Step One: Your Learning Question

This works best when you're in charge. I invite you to create a *Learning Question* for yourself that will guide you through the various themes presented by the pillars. According to Zahra Davidson, founder of Huddlecraft, a Learning Question grounds and fosters lifelong learning. She says: "A Learning Question is your own unique course title. It frames your goals, challenges, or curiosities as a site for active exploration and response. It's an itch you have to scratch."

A Learning Question is open-ended and designed to foster inquiry rather than focusing on coming up with answers. In fact a good Learning Question will keep generating more questions to take you deeper into the topic. Your question will help you be purposeful, creative, and accountable to your growth. Plus it'll help you expand out of your normal sphere into new possibilities and potentials. If you'd like to know more about Learning Questions and how to create one for yourself, check out Davidson's article in the bibliography.

Here are a few examples of potential Learning Questions relevant to this book:

- How can I build the strength I need to engage with life fully even during challenging times?
- What do I need to learn and understand so that I can free myself from the past and stand strong in the present and future?
- What does sovereignty mean to me, and how can it help me live my best life?
- What's my role in regenerating myself and our world?
- What do I need to let go of and create to become fully my best self?
- What makes me feel enthusiastic and on purpose?
- How can I improve my communication skills so my voice is heard and I can fully hear others?
- How can I make peace with the past experiences of my ancestors so I can be fully present in the here and now?
- How can I learn to live in the world with greater compassion and care?

You want your question to be personal and specific to you, your life experience, and what you're longing to heal, experience, and/or create. Also you may choose to revise it as you spiral through the pillars. I've provided a sample Learning Question or two at the beginning of each pillar that I invite you to adopt or modify as you choose. Having one or two for each pillar may help you better integrate and make relevant what you're receiving as information on that theme. It's when you take information and apply it to your life that it becomes useful and beneficial. As Abraham-Hicks astutely once said: "Information does not teach. Only life experience does that."

My Learning Question in writing this book is: *How can we grow ourselves into the people who can meet the big challenges in the world today with resilience, creativity, intuition, camaraderie, and optimism?*

Let's pause and breathe for a few moments. Maybe close your eyes so it's easier to turn your attention inward. Ponder why you picked up this book in the first place. What intrigues or attracts you? What are you hoping you'll discover, learn, shift, or create through reading it? What do you hope opens up for you? What do you long for? What's the best possible outcome you can imagine? What are you willing to do in order to help bring this desired outcome into reality? Play around with a few possible Learning Questions to get started.

I invite you to have a special journal and your favorite pen – and colored markers if you like! – on hand as you're reading. I'll invite you to pause and ponder and make notes in your journal on a regular basis. In addition at the end of each pillar you'll find questions to stimulate your reflections and support your integration of the material. And of course you'll want to visit your Learning Question(s) often to keep you focused and on track.

Step Two: Taking Your Turn

At the end of each pillar you'll find a section called *Your Turn*. This section includes four subsections: *Self-Assessment*, *Spectrum of Expression*, *New Desired Capacities*, *Reflection Questions*, and Learning Question reminders. To take full advantage of what's being offered, *it's vital that you engage* with this section. Sometimes that may not be easy. But we already know that we grow and evolve by the way we respond to challenge. These sections direct your attention to different ways in which the theme of that pillar may be experienced and expressed in relation to power and to your daily life.

Self-Assessment

The *Self-Assessment* includes examples of awakened or empowered traits, shadow traits, and disempowered traits in relation to that chapter's theme. It supports you to reflect upon your current relationship with this theme and to learn more about what being empowered vs disempowered in this area looks and feels like in everyday life. You of course will be the one to discern if and how this assessment resonates with you – or not – and you're invited to come up with your own examples that speak directly to your experience. You'll collect the results of your assessments and review them in the final chapter, *What Now; What's Next.*

Spectrum of Expression

The section *Spectrum of Expression* divides into three aspects: awakened or empowered, shadow, and disempowered. *Awakened* is a term I take from the yogic wisdom tradition.[4] We *awaken* our power within through practices that release the energy of limiting beliefs and harmful

---

4 The term "awakened" has come to be used by many different people with different emphases. I choose to refer to the yogic wisdom traditions both because of my training in this field and also because of its ancient, time-tested philosophy practiced by millions of people over millennia. This isn't a "New Age" idea. Rather this is the outcome of devotion and practice of yogic science.

conditioning and also build our life force. As we *awaken*, we become increasingly aware of ourselves as energetic and spiritual beings and as part of the Great Web of Life. Becoming *awakened* in this tradition empowers us not through asserting our power over others but rather through building our power within so we can engage with the world with a clearer mind, an open heart, a stronger body, a regulated nervous system, and a compassionate, caring attitude toward all of life. ***This is a key purpose of Feminine Sovereignty.***

Shadow as I use the term means the ways in which we use the power of this pillar to manipulate or control other people or situations. The descriptions illuminate ways that power-over dynamics continue to haunt our consciousness in ways we may not even realize. Western culture teaches us that these shadow expressions are the appropriate way to create safety, security, and success in a dangerous world. This conditioning is so much a part of the air that we breathe that it feels *normal.* Yet it stems from fear and scarcity, and it doesn't support our thriving or healthy, satisfying relationships. The purpose of this shadow aspect in the Spectrum is to raise your awareness about unconscious (and conscious) ways you may be engaging with life and with others that inhibit your awakening and keep you stuck in the power-over paradigm.

The *Disempowered* expression can take the form of either subordinating yourself to someone or something you deem to be more powerful than you, such as a partner, a boss, a family member, or an institution. Or it could be that you've rejected the power of the pillar because you've seen or experienced it being misused in a power-over way. Often in my work in Human Design, I witness the ways clients disempower themselves in relation to a certain kind of energy because they've experienced its shadow expression being used against them. You may reject the power of emotions, for example, if you were subjected to anger or abuse when you were young. Or you may feel wary about collaborating with others because you experienced someone(s) else in the collaboration aiming to manipulate and control the direction or outcome of the project for their personal gain or for the benefit of their organization over that of their partners.

You'll be invited to reflect on the Spectrum of Expression in each pillar so you can gain more awareness of where you're at in this moment. It's vital that you do this without making yourself bad or wrong for how you've behaved until now. Judging yourself is a wily way in which you assert shadow on yourself, seeking to control or manipulate yourself into an approved behavior. *That's definitely not the point.* Instead this awareness opens an opportunity for you to consider what may need tending, healing, or forgiving or what new desired capacities you'd like to develop.

New Desired Capacities

The third section on *New Desired Capacities* offers suggestions for how to shift your expression in areas where you've been disempowered or exhibiting the shadow aspect. Or it could be about growing yourself in areas and ways that haven't received your attention or that maybe you didn't even know about. In this way you'll be guided to digest, integrate, and then act upon what you learn as you read. This process will facilitate you making real in your life the potential of what the pillars offer you on your evolutionary journey of awakening and becoming sovereign. In all of this I offer suggestions and recommendations, but it's vital that you make the journey your own.

Reflection Questions

The fourth section, *Reflection Questions*, invites you to review your Learning Question and the pillar-specific Learning Questions that head each pillar. You'll also find different kinds of questions that direct your attention to key themes raised within the pillar so that you can deepen your awareness of them by applying them to your life. Feel free to respond to those that resonate with you and leave the rest. I suggest that you write about them in your special journal, so you have a record of your journey. It's so easy to forget where you've been once you've moved on.

Step Three: Your Temple of Sovereignty

As you move through the book, you'll be invited to imagine and create your own *Temple of Sovereignty* based on your own version of the pillars. As you exit the matrix of modernity, having your own sacred temple space gives you a place to explore your potential, heal your wounding, and grow your capacities. This temple is a portal into a new life inhabited by an evolving *you*. You're in charge of what this looks and feels like, and how it supports you as you grow day to day.

I'll offer suggestions along the way, yet this creative process is all your own. You can draw and paint, collage, sing songs, tell stories about your Temple and its pillars, or simply let it inspire your imagination. Play with color, form, structure, resonance. Let it evolve along with you. Whatever you choose, never underestimate the power and significance of your co-creative abilities, activating your intuition and creativity in the service of living as a whole person with all your intelligences active and alive.

I've created a beautiful gift for you, an online program that guides you through creating your own Temple of Sovereignty. You can access it on the Resources Page. Enjoy!

Primary Evolutionary Tools

Throughout I'll be offering you a wide, eclectic array of tools and practices. Each of the pillars calls forth specifics as suits its theme. Running through all of them are two primary wisdom traditions I rely on every day: Human Design and Kundalini Yoga. While each of these is a complex and beautiful system, you don't need to have prior experience with them to receive the primary benefits I'll be offering you. Please resist giving in to overwhelm and confusion, and instead engage with this material with curiosity and willingness. I'll be inviting you to pause, breathe, and reflect often. If you want to know more about these wisdom traditions, you can begin with what I've included on the book's website, FeminineSovereigntyBook.com.

Human Design and Quantum Human Design

Through the pillars I'll be referring to aspects of the Human Design system. Many people are attracted to Human Design to better understand what's true and authentic for them. It's *uncannily accurate* and can be affirming and liberating, which is one of the many reasons I've chosen it as a primary evolutionary tool. In this book I won't be teaching you how to interpret your specific Human Design chart, although you may well come to understand yourself better from what I share. I'll focus on specific aspects of the system that are beneficial for all of us. Human Design presents a template for an evolving humanity, as well as for each of us individually. As such it provides profound guidance for us collectively on our evolutionary path.

I draw on Human Design because it's incredibly helpful in moving from disempowered and shadow expressions of ourselves into more awakened and empowered ones. I've been exposed to *many systems* over the years, and Human Design is the first one that's reached all the way into my innermost being and said: *Hello love, I know you. I know the deepest, most profound, most disruptive truths about you.* And you know what? It was right. That's why I bring tidbits to you. You can decide if you want more or not.

If you're new to Human Design, I encourage you to take in the essence of what I share and consider how this relates to your life. *You don't need to be a student of or expert in Human Design to do this.* If you're intrigued, I encourage you to get your own Human Design chart here: YourFreeHumanDesignChart.com. When you register for it, you'll also receive my e-book series *Getting Started with Human Design* and the *Reflection Journal* as a gift. These e-books walk you through the elements of the Human Design chart and guide you in applying what you discover to your own life.

Whether you're familiar with Human Design or not, what matters is for you to receive the fundamental teachings offered that apply to all of us, regardless of your specific design.

While each Human Design is unique, you, like all of us, have access to and have experienced in some way all aspects of the Human Design chart. The differences among us have to do with what I call your *core energies* or "definition" (what's colored in on your chart), which you experience all the time, and your *variable energies* or "open" (what's white on your chart), which come and go. For our purposes here, *that specificity isn't so important*. Please resist the tendency to think you need to know all the details to get the most out of what I'm sharing. That way leads to overwhelm, confusion, and frustration with your eyes rolled up in the back of your head, and that's not necessary. *Please trust me on that.*

If you're familiar with Human Design, I encourage you to come to what I offer with fresh eyes and beginner's mind. I may interpret the system differently than you've come to understand. *Human Design has its own life force* and is evolving just as is everything. My approach is informed by the leading-edge work of Karen Curry Parker, creator of *Quantum Human Design* (QHD) and my mentor. Parker created QHD to help us understand what she calls the "higher expression" of the elements of the Human Design system. She says that Ra Uru Hu, the founder of Human Design with whom she worked for a number of years, focused mostly on helping us understand what he called the "not self," or the conditioned self that's disconnected from the more authentic self revealed by Human Design. Apparently he intended to develop language for this more authentic self, but never did. Her contribution in creating QHD has greatly expanded what this system has to offer.[5]

I learned both traditional Human Design (THD) and QHD from Parker, along with programs from Jovian Archive (the founder's school). I chose Parker because I align with her quantum, metaphysical perspective that informs her coaching approach to Human Design. She and I agree that everything is changeable and Human Design guides us toward expressing our fullest, most empowered potential. I've extended what I've learned from her based on my own life experience and decades of working with clients and students. She and I are still aligned even as we each explore and expand the horizons of possibility Human Design offers us.

Traditional Human Design is often taught as a deterministic system that in my view isn't in the best interests of the client or student. Teachers and readers claim to tell you who you are, what your destiny is, what kind of work you should do, what kind of person you should be in relationship with, and how you should live. I don't ascribe to that point of view. In

---

5　Ra Uru Hu himself evolved the Human Design system considerably over the years. In addition a number of different branches have grown out of traditional Human Design, including the popular Gene Keys.

fact I think it's harmful, as it strips you of agency and choice and positions the teacher or reader as an expert who knows better than you do what's true and right for you. *I deeply disagree with that.* My perspective is that your life experience – the family and the community you grew up in, your education, your culture, your choices, and so much more – profoundly influence your sense of self and how you'll understand your Human Design. I often say: *I'm the expert on Human Design. You're the expert on you.* I would *never* inhibit your personal sovereignty by asserting I know better than you what's best for you. That's not my role here (or anywhere). You'll discover just how committed I am to your personal growth, spiritual healing, evolutionary process, and sovereignty as you read through this book.

Deconditioning

While Human Design serves as an incredible tool for mapping our intuition and other aspects of our potential, it doesn't provide us with a way to clear the programming that's in the way of our fullest expression. In the Human Design community we commonly talk about the need to "decondition," recognizing that the overculture has programmed us away from much of what's possible and valuable for us. By the time I came to Human Design, I'd already spent years in the personal growth and spiritual healing realm exploring and facilitating many ways of healing and deprogramming ourselves. In my work with clients I combine my expertise in Human Design with awareness and energy practices that liberate us from the limiting and inhibiting beliefs, stuck emotions, and stagnant energy that keep us tied to the past or in fear of the future. Principle among these practices are Kundalini Yoga, breathwork, and conscious movement.

Kundalini Yoga

Throughout the first half of this book, I share with you about Kundalini Yoga's ability to help you clear your mind, cleanse your energy field, build your physical vitality and resilience, and fuel your radiance. I hope to inspire you to explore new practices you may not have tried before, as I've found these practices to be the most potent yet gentle ways of moving and building energy I've ever experienced. We'll draw on yoga's deep teachings about our connection with Spirit, the rich complexity of our energy fields, and how we can strengthen our nervous systems and boost our physical vitality.

You don't need a pretzel body to explore the yoga I share with you (I don't have one).

In fact most of what I share focuses on philosophy, breathwork, and simple movements that can be done by most people and even in a chair. You're invited to do whatever you can, at the pace and frequency that's right for you. In the chapter *Your Daily Date with the Divine*, I'll give you options for designing your own spiritual practice that includes Kundalini Yoga if you choose. I'm not going to take you on a deep dive into the yoga traditions. Plenty of resources exist for that, and I'll include some at FeminineSovereigntyBook.com. As with Human Design, I aim to make what I share accessible, meaningful, and actionable for you even if these technologies are new to you. As always, you're in charge of what's useful to you.

Onward!

You'll have many options on this spiraling journey of becoming the change, empowering and expressing yourself, and growing yourself into someone capable of meeting the challenges of today not just in your own life but in relation to our world. In this we'll be developing our sovereign self in the first four pillars, and our sovereign steward self in the last four pillars.

You may want to read the book all the way through, then go back and dig into the Reflection Questions, practices, and dive into your Learning Question. Or you may want to read a pillar at a time and pause at the end of each to do the assessments, read the Spectrum of Expression, create New Desired Capacities, and ponder the Reflection Questions. Whatever order you decide to go in, I implore you to make this commitment to yourself: that you'll make the time for and devote your attention to working with these elements in the Your Turn sections. This is what'll make the difference between reading this book as an intellectual and perhaps emotional exercise or as a transformational journey to a new you. Of course it's always your choice.

Whatever path you take, I'm going to be walking shoulder to shoulder with you, your hand in mine, on every step of this journey. I invite you to allow me to lead you so you can relax and receive what's being offered. If you're accustomed to being in charge yourself (sure you are), letting me lead the way can be particularly rejuvenating even if you find it a bit difficult to let go at first. I've walked many times every path I'll be taking you on, and I've already taken many seekers with me before now. I know where the tree roots are that might trip you, and the bog that looks like solid ground but isn't, and the likely places your mind has laid traps to keep you from moving forward. I've got my headlamp and a backpack with water and band aids and a sunhat just in case we need them. Your terrain is uniquely your own, so you'll have to decide for yourself where you need to stop for rest and where you want to forge forward to get to a quiet place next to the creek to camp for the night. *Whatever your pacing, I'll be there to rest alongside you and help make coffee in the morning. You won't be alone.*

Co-Creating with the Flow of Life

*Having faith in one's primary and indivisible relationship
with the generative force of the Universe
and intentionally acting in concert with it.*

"The only constant that exists is the interwoven flow of consciousness that animates all life. It is the movement of that flow that carries us along and ties us all together. We are all moving as one stream of consciousness in a flowing river."

—Sherri Mitchell, Weh'na Ha'mu' Kwasset
(She Who Brings the Light)

Do I feel connected to Spirit?

Do I embrace my intuition and my creativity?

Exploring the Web of Life

As your eyes close, soft spaciousness beckons you in. Darkness dances with light. Turn away from the world outside, and an inner realm emerges. Your inner felt sense traces your form, noting where your skin border meets the space around you. An unfriendly opinion about your shape flits across your inner expanse, careening off the cliff of your awareness. You'd banished it, but its shadow has been persistent. Your belly, then chest, expand as your diaphragm descends, and you settle more comfortably in your seat. Your spine seeks a new height as your breath reshapes it from the inside. You call the parts of you that have scattered to come home to you now.

Released from the overpowering nature of the visual world, your other intelligences line up for your attention. Your breath takes on sound as you breathe and slightly constrict your throat. Your ears open and drink in the *clump clump* of footsteps upstairs and the hum of the refrigerator. Images parade across your inner reading screen, recycled from dreams, aspirations, affirmations, and the television you watched last night. You make a note to yourself to change the flowers on your altar; their scent tells you they're past their prime. Frustration from yesterday's exchange with your brother lingers as you watch part of you gnaw on what you didn't say quite the way you wish you had.

You begin to breathe deeply, counting 1 2 3 4 5 6 7 8 on the inhale and 1 2 3 4 5 6 7 8 on the exhale. You focus on counting and the way your torso and belly expand and contract with each breath. Your thoughts soften and slow down, barely a murmur. A quiet stillness descends. The darkness behind your closed lids begins to hum with potential, drips and blazes of light punctuating its rhythm. Your perception moves outward in all directions, past the edges of your physical body. Shimmering all around you, your energy field embraces your physical form. You begin to float inside a spaciousness that stretches beyond your ability to see or feel it. An ancient primary part of you has always known this place, and it returns here whenever it can wrest your attention away from your analytical mind and a busy life.

Your awareness toggles between a sense of your inner landscape filling out your inner form and an infinite space inside of which your form dissolves. Space stretches out in all directions, in front, behind, left, right, above, and below you. You're floating inside a sphere of light 360 degrees around you. You touch a dimension of *no-time no-space just expanse* – for a moment. You drop into that space, your gratitude and delight at your future calling you forward. You giggle as you experience the emotions of already having in your life what you've been desiring. The expanse between desire and manifest reality collapses here in space, where all things are possible. You breathe deep, memorizing the feeling of this new reality and knowing that as you do so, at some point it will drop into form. A few more deep breaths, then you slowly open your eyes, stretch your spine, and bow to the mystery. You're excited for your day and what's to come.

We Humans Are Spiritual Beings

We begin here, dear Reader, at the beginning. Ancient yogis call this space the *Hiranyagarbha* (हरिण्यगर्भ), the *Great Cosmic Womb*. Quantum physicists call this the unified field. This vastness infinitely pulses with waves of potential. Out of this field crystallizes all that we know as physical, material reality – including you! Our sovereignty connects us with, rather than separates us from, the Flow of Life (my preferred word for the divine). Our sovereignty recognizes, bows to, and expresses the Flow of Life.

Indeed you already breathe inside of, as part of, along with, the Great Web of Life, the name many indigenous peoples give to the mystery that animates and connects us all. The creative intelligence of the Universe expresses itself through you, seeing through your eyes, feeling through your skin, creating with and through you. You could never be alone; you're always and forever part of, an expression of, the All That Is.

You may have felt it when you spent the day hiking, soaked in the muttering of the forest, or washed by the spray of the sea, or suffused with the fragrance of springtime's rioting blossoms. You may recognize it gazing into the eyes of an infant or just before an elder makes her transition into the next life. You may feel it in the embrace of your bonded lover, or while dancing as if no one's watching, or when singing, your voice ecstatically raised in chorus with others. So many portals open into this vastness, always present, always waiting, always beckoning to and welcoming you.

You live simultaneously as an aspect of this source energy, vast beyond your imagining, and also as an individuated being with your own physical body, life experience, ancestry, and personality. The yogis even have a saying that expresses this: *Humme Hum Brahm Hum* (we are one; we are many). When chanted with devotion, it inspires and instills in us a felt sense of this paradoxical aspect of our nature.

Was that just a dream? you wonder as you drop back into everyday reality. *Was I just imagining that?*

Interesting how we tend to act as if what we imagine *isn't true*. As if imagining is somehow unreal, not trustworthy, not to be valued, and that what we imagine should be discarded. I like what the bard Gwilym Morus-Baird says: "Stories and myths are rarely real but always true."

What are your creativity, imagination, and intuition but your interface with the All That Is?

The Universe, the Flow of Life, the god-force, the All That Is, Source energy, all name the vast intelligence that has created and continues to create the universe – the multiverse – as we know it. It creates by nature, and you, as one of its expressions, also create by nature. You can't not create, as this process is intrinsic to you. Creativity isn't just about what we call *the arts*; creativity infuses every one of us in our own unique ways. You receive a spark of divine inspiration and channel it through your own consciousness so that that spark becomes intelligible to you. You translate the spark into an image or words or a felt sense, and something new emerges. Every time you have an insight, an epiphany, a *download*, an AHA moment, you're co-creating with the Flow of Life.

What an incredible gift to have such a potent relationship with Spirit!

Sometimes we name experiences like these *imagination* or *intuition*. Intuition, according to the Random House College Dictionary, is "any way of knowing that is not logical, rational, or reasonable." That's not a very helpful definition because intuition is defined by *what it's not* rather than by *what it is*. We don't have very nuanced or comprehensive language for intuition, and because of that its diversity hasn't been well understood. Fortunately this is changing, as a few extraordinarily intuitive individuals have created schools and academies both to give language and understanding to many kinds of intuitive or psychic gifts and to train people to understand and develop them (e.g., Desda Zuckerman, Academy of Intuition Medicine, Aesclepion Healing Center, California Institute of Integral Studies).

I define intuition as the way in which the *you* of everyday, three-dimensional reality receives guidance from your inner being, your higher self, or your soul (depending on how you want to name your inner guidance). *Intuition* describes many ways in which you tune in to and receive information, guidance, cautions, epiphanies, insights, out-of-the-box ideas, and urgings from sources that are nonphysical or at least noncognitive. Hunches. Gut feelings. Dreams. Images. Inner knowing. Inner guidance. Sounds, songs, movements, music. Body sensations. So, so much becomes available to you when you expand your view of what's possible and beneficial.

As it turns out we have many nonlogical or intuitive ways of knowing. Human Design maps many different forms of intuition and inner guidance to which we all have access. Some of us have more of it than others readily available (or "defined") in our Human Design, while others may pick it up more from others than from within, at least initially. Yet we all have access to these forms of intuition, and we can all develop them if we choose. It's just that you might not have developed your abilities if no one ever talked about it when you were growing up, and you never saw it modeled by the adults around you.

My experience, having worked with hundreds of clients and thousands of students over the years, is that *everyone is intuitive* in some way. This isn't just the realm of *special people*. We're all far more intuitive than we've been led to believe. Yet very few of us have had our intuition honored by the people around us. For example, when I was a kid my intuition made the adults around me uncomfortable, so I learned to distrust and then suppress it. I've heard similar stories from many people for whom I've done Human Design readings. So many of us have learned to ignore our inner guidance, or simply not take it seriously. *Does that sound familiar?*

Over the course of this book, I introduce you to several kinds of knowing and forms of intuition as they're mapped and illuminated by the Human Design system. For more than twenty years I've been reclaiming and cultivating different aspects of my own intuition. Yet during most of that time I sometimes felt unclear and uncertain about what I was doing, what I could trust, what was genuine guidance, and what was wishful or fearful thinking. I know these questions haunt many people, as they've often expressed them to me.

When I discovered Human Design I realized the power of this system to help us understand and cultivate our intuition in myriad ways. My inner guidance is very clear that we – all of us – would benefit from developing this aspect of our being. My sense is that we'll come to know, understand, and create strategies for addressing our big collective challenges not through logic and reason but through guidance we receive from the Flow of Life. *Frankly we need all the help we can get.*

Fortunately the Flow of Life courses through the cosmos, through our solar system, and through each of our lives, animating and enlivening all that it touches. The Flow of Life moves along the Web of Life, energy rising and falling in wave patterns full of potential. The creative intelligence of the Universe rides upon and directs these waves, creating synchronicities in your life in response to your thoughts, emotions, and the clarity and quality of your energy. Quantum physicists are beginning to explain what the ancient yogis knew thousands of years ago: we're energetic as well as physical beings, and when we change our energy our outer reality begins to change. As we discover and develop our ability to attune to this Flow of Life, to create and act in concert with it, we receive its guidance and benefit from its power. This means we don't need to work so hard, figure things out, or make things happen – *and life becomes much, much easier.*

What Gets in the Way:
Isolation, Separation, and an Angry God

Yet the norms of the *overculture* teach us separation and isolation. Too often the overculture is mired in a limited and limiting version of western science, which herbalist and visionary Stephen Buhner calls the "statistical mentality." It rejects our intuitive gifts as irrational and illogical, which they are! We've been taught that we need to see something to believe it, that we have to be able to count and categorize something for it to be real, and that we have to be able to prove and replicate something in order for it to be true. This way of understanding reality has enabled us to map and manipulate the physical world with power and precision. And yet it's only one of many ways of understanding reality.

During the Enlightenment, European men birthed western science (there are other forms of science, as we'll see) based in a love for rationality and reason. In doing so they began to differentiate themselves from what they called "nature," etymologically defined in the 1660s by John Locke in his *Two Treatises of Government* as "the material world beyond human civilization or society; an original, wild, undomesticated condition." In separating themselves from the living world, they authorized themselves to study "nature" as an object that's *out there* and definitely not *in here*. In this way they made themselves superior to not only the living world but all the people they categorized as part of nature, and therefore different and inferior to themselves, including women and non-Europeans.[6] (For this

---

6　See Carolyn Merchant, *Reinventing Eden*. We'll revisit the construction of nature in western culture and its consequences in Pillars Seven and Eight as we explore indigenous world views.

reason I use the term *living world* rather than natural world as it's more accurate and less freighted with history.)

This inaccurate assertion of European male superiority justified the march of colonialism and capitalism across the globe, subordinating or eliminating indigenous people, the creatures of the wild, the green ones, and the mountains, rivers, forests, and oceans. Unfortunately much of what we call *science* today is funded and shaped by profit-driven forces that have no concern for the well-being of land and people. These forces have supplanted royalty as the power-over version of sovereignty, hidden behind the droning imperative to *buy, buy, buy* and *consume, consume, consume*. The momentum of *this kind* of western scientific way of knowing, unchecked by an awareness of a commitment to what's best for land and people, has contributed greatly to the biggest challenges we're collectively facing today.

And so sometimes you may feel alone. You may feel separate from other people, from the forests and the rivers, from the god-force. You look around you, eyes open, the world full of objects that you've learned to name and categorize and evaluate. You look down at your body and see its outline and feel where your physical form meets the form of the chair you're sitting in. Your eyes, skin, and flesh telegraph to you where *you* begin and end and where the book or tablet or Kindle you're holding begins and ends. You knock on the table next to you, and it feels solid to your touch. You look out the window and see trees, houses, and cars, and you perceive them as *not you*. The distinctions feel so basic, so obvious now, that you can't quite remember what the oneness felt like.

Many people who grew up in organized religions were taught that they are separate from as well as subordinate to God. Organized religions often insist that an intermediary must interpret God's will and facilitate one's relationship with the divine. Many times, rules and requirements structure access to the divine, and if you don't follow them, then you're *not part of the flock*. Power accrues to the organization and its intermediaries as they hold the keys to your salvation. Maybe an angry God, depicted as an old white man with flowing hair and beard sitting on a cloud, looks down upon humanity, doling out judgments. Maybe you feel judged under this God's watchful eye. Fear, abandonment, and a sense of isolation undermine your ability to connect with others and with the living world. This may in turn foster divisive, conflicted, and even violent behavior.

When religious perspectives and practices feel confining and punishing, many push away the organization altogether as not in their highest good. They become agnostic, or atheist, or turn to a different way of understanding Spirit altogether. Even so, religious programming can run impressively deep, orchestrating one's perceptions of reality. Both this programming and the rejection of it can inhibit your willingness and your ability to consciously connect and co-create with the Flow of Life. This sense of isolation and separation undergird the belief that life is happening *to you* and you're *at the mercy of* outside circumstances. This in turn fosters *victim consciousness*, a sense that your life is out of your control and it's all you can do to try to manage what's coming at you. It's so ingrained in our ways of perceiving the world that it can be very subtle yet no less undermining to our agency and personal power.

And it's true that some aspects – even many aspects – of life are out of your control. As powerful as you are as a co-creator with the Flow of Life, you can't control everything that happens in the world or even what happens to you or the ones you love. When life circumstances challenge you – from difficulties with your partner or children or someone you love dying to a global pandemic and the economic impacts of that – it can be easy to fall into that victim stance. At times like this you may find it difficult to believe in a friendly and supportive Universe and feel connected to the Flow of Life.

I've had periods in my life – during my divorce for example – when it was very difficult to feel and believe in the support of Spirit. Victim-y thoughts pounded through my mind, and it was all I could do not to be taken over by them. At times I lost that battle and fell into a deep, dark hole. My mind felt colonized by my justifications and rationalizations, and my emotions stimulated the pain of my unhealed parts. I was *in it*, lost without perspective, looping and chewing over conversations, situations, agreements broken. I was lost inside my mind and my pain, and I couldn't feel my inner guidance or intuition. I felt isolated, alone, and if not abandoned, certainly not in touch with or supported by Spirit.

Maybe you've had a loved one die, or you've lost an important relationship, or you've been attacked or abused physically or emotionally, or your house has burned down, or your child has been ill. Even more, you may witness other people's circumstances, and you begin to wonder: How can we truly live in a compassionate, loving universe if so many children are being killed by gun violence or dying of starvation? *How indeed?* So many situations can challenge your faith and make you wonder what's true.

Life challenges all of us, although the types and severity of the challenges vary greatly. None of us is immune. While you can't avoid challenge, you do have choice about how you respond to it. At first you take the hit of it. You feel shock, surprise, anger, pain, frustration, shame, confusion, disappointment. *The big question is: Then what?*

We'll dive into this more in *Pillar Two: Emotional Wisdom*, where we'll unpack why we become triggered emotionally and how we can best respond. Here let me underscore that you always have choice about how you *respond* to challenges. Suffering is an option, but it's not required. Suffering arises when you hang on and give your energy to painful emotions stimulated in response to a situation or circumstance. The Buddhists and Byron Katie say that suffering arises when you fight "what is," whatever is happening or has happened. Suffering arises from our interpretations and judgments and conclusions.

- He shouldn't have done that.
- They should've promoted me, not him.
- He shouldn't have lied to me.
- She shouldn't have left me.
- He shouldn't have died.
- She shouldn't have gotten sick.

None of this is to say that abuse is okay, or losing someone isn't painful, or it's easy dealing with illness. *Not at all.* Part of developing your personal sovereignty involves meeting challenging situations with as much equanimity, inner power, and authority as you can muster so that you can change what needs to be changed – to the degree that that's possible – and accept that which you cannot change. At the same time you may have the tendency to fight something that you can't change. When someone dies, you can't bring them back. When someone lies to you, you can't turn that person into a truthteller. If you or someone becomes ill, yes, you can do everything you can to help yourself or the other person heal. Yet their illness is also a present reality that, if you fight it and make either it or the person bad and wrong, will create unnecessary suffering.

When you fight the things that have already happened (stuck in the past) or you imagine will happen (worry about the future), you energetically and emotionally chain yourself to that situation. You cannot be free – or be sovereign.

During the course of my relationship with my child's father, I had several periods during which, as I said above, I was *in it*. I struggled against how things had unfolded; I suffered as I mulled over how things could have, *should* have been different. I gave myself migraines as I made him wrong for things he did. And who suffered when I did that? *I did.* Possibly my child did, too, intuitive as they are, picking up on my distress as much as I tried to hide it. (My kid is nonbinary and uses them/they pronouns.) Of course I didn't want that!

I surrendered to the Flow of Life the part of me who wanted to be right, who wanted retribution, who wanted things to be different. I stepped out of feeling isolated and alone and stepped into my inner knowing that I'm part of a vastness much larger than I can imagine, and remembered that much of what occurs in my life isn't up to me and that I'm not going to understand it all. I can't control everything that happens, and I can't control other people. I can show up, aim to be kind, and do the best I can every day. That's what I can do. Over time and with intention and practice, I was able to shift my perspective, not to agree with or condone, but to accept what had happened and then let it go. Remembering that *I'm not actually in charge* really helped me do this.

I've discovered that the more I'm aligned with Spirit, and the clearer my energy, the easier my life becomes. I learned that the ancient yogis had developed sciences of their own many millennia before western science even sparkled in Isaac Newton's eye. Through these yogic energy practices, I've come to develop a higher degree of command and influence in my life. I can't do this when I'm lost in the maze of my wounded mind. I reclaimed my sovereignty and set myself free by handing over my judgments and pain to Spirit – and then practiced letting it all go.

My version of personal sovereignty isn't about being able to control everything that happens to me, as some proponents of the Law of Attraction would suggest. This isn't an absolute power like that supposedly endowed in the royal sovereigns of old. This sovereignty instead builds *power within* rather than power over others or over many circumstances. We can honor our agency and ability to choose and also recognize that each of us is but one being inside a dynamically shifting universe of interconnected beings.

This sovereignty bows to the creative intelligence of the Universe, seeks support and guidance from it, and purposefully co-creates with it.

The spirituality I embrace and offer to you understands each of us to be a center of consciousness, of life force energy, within the All That Is. You can have no more direct connection with Spirit than to recognize that Spirit is always expressing itself through you, that indeed *you are Spirit*. You may not feel it when you're in the midst of a crisis, or when your faith has been challenged, or when you witness what human beings are capable of doing to one another. Yet that primary relationship with the Flow of Life can never be truly broken, only fogged over with pain or anger, rejected out of frustration and confusion, or hidden by cultural conditioning.

Many people who've turned away from organized religion are drawn toward less structured, less rule-oriented, and less dogmatic forms of spirituality. You can find your way to a new relationship with the divine as you recognize that each and every one of us expresses an aspect of that totality; *each of us is divine* in our own right. As you embrace your wholeness, cultivate your intuition and inner knowing, and build your inner strength and power, you'll come to realize just how much you are the creator of your own experience. You simply need to remember that you co-create your life with the Flow of Life, not alone in your individual, separate psyche. As you let go of victim consciousness and build your capacity to feel Spirit always loving you, guiding you, and supporting you, your experience of life will shift dramatically. As you practice this, you'll discover that you're more in command of your life than you may have realized, and also have more support than you've imagined.

Accessing Your Intuition and Cultivating Your Creative Power

Creating Your Own Reality

Being introduced to metaphysics twenty-five years ago by Bob Proctor changed my life. Up until then I'd focused largely on social justice, and legal, political, and social structures that created and perpetuated racism, misogyny, and other forms of inequality and oppression. The idea that you "create your own reality" was new to me; it took me a while to digest the idea given my background. I mean how do you reconcile slavery, genocide, and traffic in women and children with the idea that *you create your own reality?*

The short version of what I've come to understand is that we've been living through what the yogis consider to be a "dark age" in which colonialism, exploitation of people and Earth, and rule by violence have been the norm for thousands of years. Similarly indigenous peoples in North America have multiple prophecies that speak of this time when the birds forget where to go, the land is ravaged, and the waters and air are no longer safe to drink and breathe. Inside this dark age, we've forgotten that we're all part of the same Web of Life, and that what's done to one is done to all. We see ourselves as separate, isolated beings doing the best we can to survive and succeed in a harsh world. The *Story of Progress*, which I mentioned in the *Introduction*, justifies this worldview and ascribes different roles to different peoples and beings inside this hegemonic hierarchy of domination. *Oh that's a mouthful, isn't it?*

Growing up inside of this Story of Progress has programmed us into believing that this story is natural and inevitable; it's *just the way things are.* When we buy into this, our creative power gets co-opted into reproducing this mindset and system, albeit unconsciously, even though that's not what we consciously believe or what's in our best interests. We need to liberate ourselves from this insidious story so that we can retake command of our co-creative power and direct it where we will.

When introduced to metaphysics, I embraced the prospect of consciously, purposefully working with Spirit and energy to create the life I wanted. Until then I'd been agnostic, having stepped away from the Christianity I was raised with and not yet replacing it with anything else. Contrary to some popular opinions metaphysics isn't a *New Age phenomenon* but a rekindling of ancient wisdom traditions out of Asia that include Buddhism, the Vedas, and the Upanishads. This way of understanding reality was a breath of fresh air in what otherwise felt to me like an increasingly confining and bankrupt way of being and perceiving.

As I mentioned in the *Introduction*, I was *ready for a change.* Although I'd accomplished a lot by that time, I'd done it at great personal cost to myself in cycles of burnout. I knew there had to be a better way, and I was eager to explore it. During those first years I created vision boards, wrote and recited affirmations, and trained my mind to focus on what I wanted rather than on what I didn't want. *Maybe you can relate?* Initially I created a lot of success with Nikken, the company I was partnering with. I doubled my income from my teaching job at Columbia in fifteen months and awakened an entrepreneurial spirit in me I didn't fully realize I had.

Yet I also felt baffled by the way I could easily create in certain areas of my life and not so much in others. I celebrated when I reached my intended goals, and I felt confused when other aspirations went sideways. I knew that my connection to Spirit and my understanding of how to work with Spirit wasn't as consistent and reliable as it could be. I suspected that something inside me was in the way, but I *didn't know what it was.*

How do you heal the wounding that keeps you tied to the past and inhibits your ability to move forward? How do you then free yourself from insidious programming from the overculture? How do you create the expanded states of consciousness that enable you to feel yourself as part of the Web of Life and to consciously co-create with the Flow of Life? Indeed how do you grow yourself into your true potential, which is far more, I believe, than you or any of us currently imagine? How do you become empowered enough to face humanity's big challenges and create the world you'd be happy to leave to future generations, the Thrutopian Imperative?

Big questions, right? The rest of this chapter and book responds to these questions. Key components include:

- Embracing your many intelligences so that you have all of your faculties available to you
- Discovering how to take command of your energy so that you're at choice in engaging with life
- Consciously and purposefully cultivating your relationship with Spirit so that you (re)establish your conscious connection with the Flow of Life and receive guidance from your own inner wisdom, the teacher or *guru* within

Together we'll explore perspectives, tools, and practices from a variety of sources to support your evolution, primary among them being Human Design and the yogic traditions.

Human Design and Intuitive Ways of Knowing

When I discovered Human Design I knew I'd found something that was entirely different than anything I'd studied or practiced before. While my nerdy self was fascinated by the elegance and complexity of the system, it was my heart and inner knowing that drove me to become an expert. Human Design revealed to me ways of working with Spirit and understanding my intuition and creativity that were entirely new to me (this is common in my experience). By providing us with practical ways to approach our relationship with the creative intelligence of the Universe,

Human Design helps us heal feelings of isolation and separation, empowering our sovereignty in many ways.

I'll introduce you to several ways this elegant and sophisticated system illuminates and values intuitive intelligences not well known and certainly not appreciated by the overculture. As I've done hundreds of readings, clients often list at the top of their take-aways discovering and coming to understand and honor their intuitive abilities. So many of us suspect that we're intuitive or have evidence of our abilities, yet we don't understand it, trust it, or know what's genuine intuition as opposed to what's fear or something we just *made up*.

Human Design is an energy system (not a personality system) that reveals specific, tangible, and reliable forms of intuition to which we all have access. ***We're all intuitive; we're all imaginative; we're all creative.***

Yes, what comes most easily to you probably will relate to your specific Human Design. Yet it's also the case that Human Design includes *innate intelligences* that are potential in all of us. You just may never have learned about them or developed your capacity in these areas. As we saw earlier, most of us have been overly developed in our left-brained capacities to the exclusion of our other faculties, leaving us *impoverished*.

Human Design helps you bring more balance into your life by mapping three distinct ways of knowing, two of which we could call intuitive, and only one of which is logical. Logic and reason enable you to calculate, analyze, strategize, and plan, all important qualities from your left-brained intelligence that runs through the "Logic Circuit." The overculture, steeped in the mindset of western science, privileges this logical way of knowing, and we've all been programmed into believing its veracity. Part of developing your sovereignty involves liberating your logical mind (as well as your intuition) from the ways in which it's been co-opted by profit-drive forces masquerading as truth behind the banner of science they've paid for.

Ironically logic stands perplexed when faced with forms of knowing that can't be counted, tracked, tested, analyzed, and reproduced. In fact logic and reason as they're often invoked can't see outside their view of reality as solid objects that can be touched, counted, and manipulated.

This way of perceiving gained authority during the seventeenth century. Often it was used to judge and dismiss, for example, Earth-based spirituality and traditional forms of healing as *superstition:* unreliable, unscientific, and possibly even *wicked* or *evil.* Logic and the left brain are innocent here; they were colonized as powerful forces to support the self-serving attitudes and actions of a few.

In stark contrast, Human Design helps correct and balance this lopsided view of reality by inviting us to embrace our right-brained as well as our left-brained ways of knowing. It maps specific qualities of right-brained energy in what's called the "Sensing Circuit," as it moves through the human energy field. We'll explore this more in *Pillar Three: Vitality, Embodiment, and Connection to the Living World.*

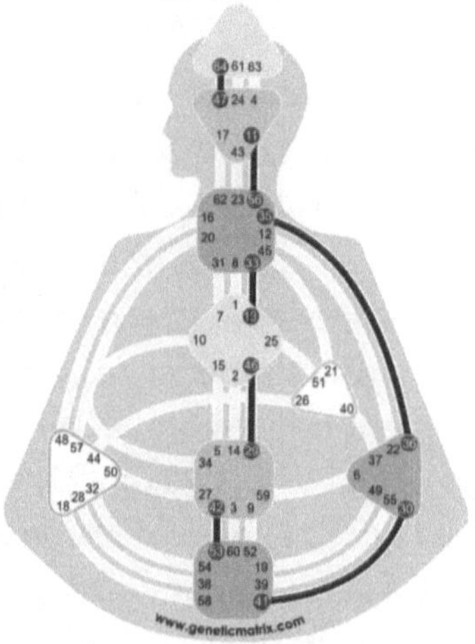

This right-brained energy is creative, expansive, sensual, experiential, and embodied. This way of knowing expresses through our body wisdom, our lived experience, and epiphanies we receive. It emerges directly from our *felt sense* of our connection with the All That Is, experienced as sensations, emotional energy, imagination, passion, devotion, creativity, storytelling, or a desire for new experiences and adventure.

We co-create with the Flow of Life through the Sensing Circuit as we access and express the right-brained thinking and emotional centers of the brain. Neuroanatomist Jill Bolte Taylor has identified the right-brain emotional center as the source of our ability to experience the oneness of the Web of Life. According to her research our experience of reality from this aspect of our being differs dramatically from that understood by our left-brain thinking center. Through the Sensing Circuit we receive big breakthrough ideas, and our task is to honor and hold them until the time and conditions are right to bring them into form.

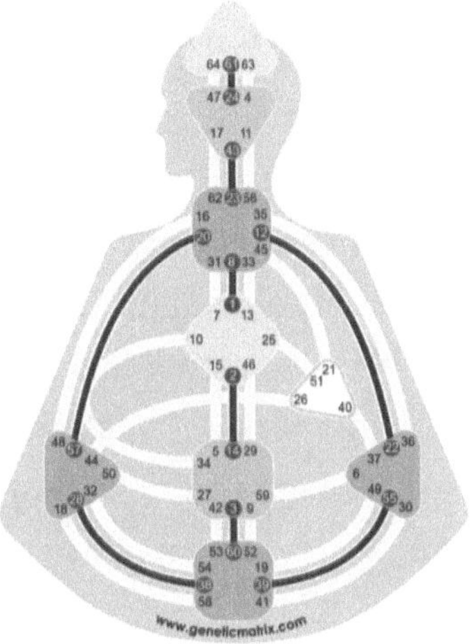

Human Design also introduces us to a unique form of intuition in what's called the "Knowing Circuit" that I haven't seen represented anywhere else. The Knowing Circuit intuits based on insights, images, understandings, and knowings that you *download* from the Flow of Life. Mystics throughout time have received experiences, inspirations, and ecstatic states through this aspect of our being. Psychics and intuitives of all persuasions similarly access this energetic highway.

With this *direct access to spiritual information* you know things you didn't learn from a person, book, video, or class. *You simply know.* You can't prove it. You can't trace where you learned it. You can't repeat it, and it isn't logical or rational at all. This could be information about a person, or insight about what to do in a certain situation, or inner guidance about a direction to take or not take. This is a large circuit in the Human Design system and virtually everyone has some of this defined (colored in) on their chart, though they may or may not be aware of it. *Maybe you?*

Fortunately you can reclaim and cultivate your intuitive capacities, expanding your repertoire of faculties and becoming *more whole.* Your intuitive abilities may not have received your attention, or you may even have suppressed them because they don't fit into your family's or the overculture's view of what's valid and valuable. As such they may be undeveloped or atrophied. You can't lose them, however; they're just lounging or napping, waiting for you to notice them again.

Human Design Types, Strategy, and Authority

Every system has its types, and Human Design is no exception. The five Human Design Types are the first and most fundamental aspect of the system everyone learns. It's like knowing your sun sign in astrology. The Types help us understand our role in life, how we're designed to work with Spirit, and how we access and process energy. (Human Design Types aren't personality types, like you'd find in Myers-Briggs.) Every Type has its intuitive and creative way of working with Spirit called its "Strategy."

The five Human Design Types are Generators, Manifesting Generators, Projectors, Manifestors, and Reflectors. The Human Design Types are based on your *core energies*, which are "defined" (colored in) on your chart. Recall that everyone has access to the entire Human Design chart in their energy field. What differs from person to person and chart to chart is what's colored in and what's white. Your definition or core energies are where you have ongoing, ready, reliable access to specific qualities of energy, and a consistent, even fixed, way of experiencing them. The parts that are white we call "open," and you'll experience these qualities of energy differently depending on your life experience and who you're around. In the open parts of your chart you will temporarily pick up and amplify the defined energies of those you're physically close to. This can feel great or not so much, depending on how the people around you are expressing that energy. (More on this in the section called Spectrum of Expression toward the end of the chapter.)

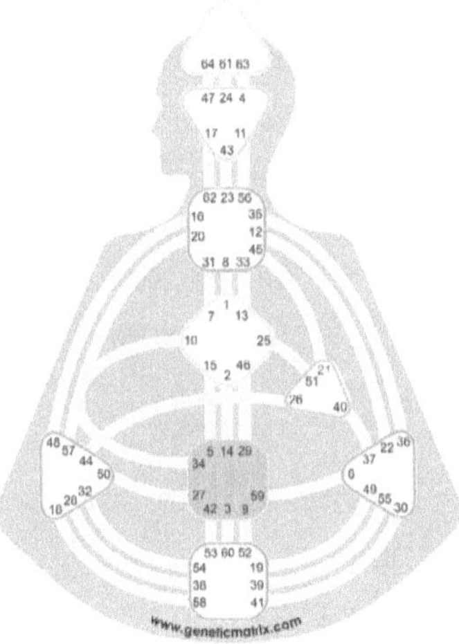

For brevity's sake I'm going to focus solely on Generator Types here, as we make up seventy percent of the population. Pure Generators and Manifesting Generators have the "Sacral Center" defined (colored in) on our charts, making this energy consistently available to me. This is the center for life force energy (e.g., prana, shakti, chi, or ki) and is the most powerful *engine* in the chart. Engines or motors in Human Design give you energy to engage with life. If you have this colored in on your chart, you should have access to abundant, reliable, and sustainable energy. This is what makes us the builders, often the workers, of the world. Even so, Generators and Manifesting Generators can burn out if they're not living in alignment with their design. *I'm living proof of that!*

How do you avoid burnout and enjoy this abundant energy? By using your *Strategy* – and *I can pretty much guarantee it's not what you think!* Generator Types are designed to "wait to respond" and not to initiate. I know, what does that even mean? When I first discovered Human Design

I found this idea extremely disruptive. *What?!* I thought. *That can't be right. I've been initiating my entire life. I'm an Aries Sun. Aren't I supposed to get things going?*[7] This was so challenging to my self-concept that I turned my back and walked away. In my pigheadedness I wasn't yet ready to take in what the system had to offer me. (Please don't let that happen to you.)

When I picked up Human Design five years later, after *I'd burned out again*, this was the question to which I circled back. What does it mean to "respond"? How do you do that? I was perplexed and curious. I knew my main mode had been initiating and making things happen. I'd accomplished a lot, but that success came at a high personal cost. I learned that only Manifestors, who are eight to nine percent of the population, are designed to initiate directly out of their own creative impulses. Yep, that means ninety-one to ninety-two percent of us *are not*.

My goodness, who knew, right? I was certainly trained to initiate and act like a Manifestor. *How about you?*

According to Human Design, we Generators are designed to respond to clues, keys, and signs that show up in our outer reality. "Waiting" as I came to understand it,[8] mostly means to *not initiate*, especially from one's mind, but instead to be receptive, to pay attention to what comes my way and then respond to it. The premise is that the Flow of Life will bring you things to respond to based on your intentions, desires, and aspirations, and also on right timing and what's in your highest good. Having a positive spiritual orientation to life makes it easier to tap into and trust this way of living. Believing in a punishing God or that there's no divine force at all will make it difficult for you to trust your Strategy and access the true power of your design.

I decided to explore what it meant to "respond" for a couple of months

---

7 This is one of a number of important examples of how Human Design differs from astrology. Best to take these systems with their own logic, which overlap but are definitely *not the same*.

8 "Waiting" for Generator Types can also mean our need to be patient as our lives unfold. Generator Types learn and grow through work, and it takes time for this to happen. Patience really helps – and faith fuels patience.

and see what happened. I stopped initiating, pausing everything I was doing, and started waiting for something to respond to. Very soon I realized that I had many things to respond to all the time! It could be something in an email, on social media, in a book I was reading, in a conversation with a friend or colleague, or in a program I was participating in. Opportunities abounded. *Ok, step one, check.* But ... how was I to know *what to respond to* and *how to respond?* How could I determine which elements in my reality really came to me from Spirit and which were simply in my sphere? This is where my best way of making decisions according to my Human Design came into play, what's called my *Authority.*

Intuitive Decision-Making

Human Design teaches that you have an inner "Authority" (in some cases more than one) that's your own guiding light, your North Star if you will.[9] Your Authority expresses your best way of knowing what's right for you and when it's the right time to engage with something or someone – or not. There are several kinds of inner Authority, and every one of them is highly intuitive; none of them is logical, rational, reasonable, or analytical. None can be tested or proven. *See how disruptive and counter-cultural this is?*

Human Design understands that while your analytical mind may be filled with great ideas and powerful strategies, it doesn't know *what's yours to do, when to do it, and if you have energy for it or not.*

In fact in Human Design we say: "Never make decisions with your mind." *Crazy, right?* I'm not sure about you, but I was taught to think things through, analyze the possibilities, and strategize the desired outcome. And it's not that none of this has a place, as they certainly do. They just don't have the *final* word. My experience is that the analytical mind literally *doesn't have the capacity* to make final decisions. Consider

---

9   Reflectors, the rarest of Human Design Types (one percent of the population) according to Human Design, have "no inner Authority." This can be misleading as *everyone* has *inner guidance.*

for a moment your own experience. That aspect of yourself has trouble settling on anything. It tends to come up with caveats, what ifs, and *did you consider?* statements. It can fall prey to FOMO (fear of missing out) too. As soon as it makes a decision it comes up with reasons that counter it! That's exhausting as well as crazy-making.

I have "Sacral Authority." All Generators and Manifesting Generators have Sacral Authority because we all have defined Sacral Centers (the colored-in square in the illustration above).[10] For us the Sacral operates as an intuitive and vital interface with our inner being, the wise one within. This center not only gives us potent, reliable energy, it also *responds* to yes/no questions with an *uh-huh* or *unh-unh.* The Sacral doesn't use words because *it's primal.* Although we say "gut knowing" or "trust your gut," ironically you may or may not feel this in your gut at all. At this point I feel the response in my head nodding or shaking and sometimes in my whole body. I've seen many variations of how Generator Types experience Sacral responses, including different sounds, body movements, and sensations. Everyone needs to experiment and practice to develop their awareness of this potent inner ally.

I've discovered that when I use my Authority to determine right timing a clear *uh-huh* (yes) means my actions are aligned with the Flow of Life. As I move forward with that *yes*, I ride a wave of cosmic energy, and I don't need to use so much of my own personal energy in creating what I want. This has made everything easier, less draining and stressful, and it's *protected me from burnout.*

When first learning you may find it difficult to access this inner guidance because most likely you're highly accustomed to making decisions with your analytical mind. Of course you are! Pretty much all of us were taught to do this: make lists of pros and cons; crunch the numbers; analyze the data; be rational and logical; and of course be able to explain and defend your position. This programming runs so deep! And yet when I

---

10 The printout of your Human Design chart may say that you have Emotional Authority or even Splenic Authority (mine says that). If that's true for you, please don't get confused. Instead go to my YouTube channel and watch my videos about Sacral Authority and Emotional Authority so you can get the details!

ask people how they feel about making decisions, they often share how overwhelmed, confused, and frustrated they are. Those lists of pros and cons and all that data can be overwhelming. Like I said – exhausting and crazy-making!

There's an art to asking your Sacral questions so you get the kind of information you're looking for. After all, yes/no questions can be inherently limited. Making this shift from mind-centered decision-making to intuitive-based decision-making takes intention, focus, and practice. And it's OH so worth it! I have several videos on my YouTube channel that show you how this works with actual clients. If you're a Generator Type, your Sacral can become your best friend who's always with you and eager to help. *You really are never alone.*

What I love most about having developed this intuitive aspect is that now I only do what I have energy for and only at the right time. Doing this protects me from burnout and makes my life *so much easier and simpler.* Rather than agonizing over whether I should do something or not, I simply ask my Sacral. And if I get an *uh-huh* I do it, and if I get an *unh-unh* I don't.

> *"Wow, Maggie, I cannot believe how free I feel now*
> *being able to feel my Sacral and know that I can make*
> *clear decisions for myself. My mind gets so confused and*
> *overwhelmed. What a relief! This is life changing."*
> —GM

This method is surprisingly simple yet not always so easy given our deep conditioning.

Clearing Our Minds, Taking Command: Kundalini Yoga

While Human Design enables us to map our intuition and points to places where we need to decondition, it doesn't *show us how* to do that. For that we need to look elsewhere. I've found Kundalini Yoga and breathwork more generally to be highly effective at moving energy, opening awareness, and thereby helping us decondition.

When you think of yoga you most likely think of the physical *asana* practice that's become popular in the west. I want to honor the master yoga teachers who traveled to the west beginning in the 1960s as part of the awakening of humanity that was happening at that time. Their teachings from many lineages have blessed us, helped us raise awareness of our bodies as energy, taught us the value of meditation, and promoted the physical, mental, emotional, and spiritual benefits we can receive from the physical practice of asana (the postures).

Much of what we know of the energetic sciences of Asia has been *watered down* to be more accessible to and palatable for western audiences. For example you can now find yoga classes in many towns large and small throughout the United States (and online since Covid), and most people have heard of yoga even if they've never practiced it. Most westerners choose the aspect of yoga that best matches our programmed preferences for intensity, material reality, and the belief that for any physical practice to be valuable it must involve discomfort and even pain. Unfortunately many haven't been interested in (or were never exposed to) the richness of its spiritual philosophy and its technologies for awakening and enlightenment.

I remember being in class one morning during the opening chant when the woman next to me muttered, "I hate this. I came here to work out, not for religion." While I consider yoga more spiritual and philosophical than religious, I knew what she meant. For her and many others, yoga has been reduced to a fitness practice. This attitude has impoverished us and prohibited us from learning the even deeper, more profound potential inherent in the system. Asana, for example, is but one of eight "limbs" of yoga, as explained in *The Yoga Sutras of Patanjali*, the foundational text of yoga practice and philosophy.

I've done many different forms of yoga – most of them focused on asana, the physical practice – for over twenty-five years. Yet when I was introduced to Kundalini Yoga I met something entirely new. The physical practice alone can bring about significant changes on multiple levels – emotional, energetic, and spiritual as well as physical. Opening the body and stretching connective tissue releases energy trapped in the muscles, joints, and tissues. But the practices in Kundalini Yoga focus on affecting our subtle energy bodies (did you know you have more than one?) in specific ways for different outcomes. *This is yogic science at one of its heights.*

Kundalini Yoga teaches that you can uplift your state of consciousness, opening up lines of communication that otherwise may be clogged with too much mental activity or undigested emotions. When your mind is cluttered with too many thoughts and programs, or your heart is walled off from too much pain, it's hard to access your intuition. This means it may be difficult for you to feel your Sacral response if you're a Generator Type, for example, or tap into the creativity of your Sensing circuit. In this case you'll need to change your state of consciousness in order to access your intuitive abilities. The breath, movement, mantra, and meditation practices based in Kundalini Yoga are the fastest, most efficient way I've discovered to do just that.

Did you know that *the breath* is the only physiological function that's both automatic and can be intentionally manipulated? I learned a lot about the power of the breath and what inhibits it during my training and years of practice and teaching as a Clarity Breathworker long before I discovered Kundalini Yoga. Like your heart beating, your lungs must continually breathe for you to live, so your smart body does it without you having to think about it. Yet due to unhealed trauma most people breathe shallowly, as they are still imprinted by an earlier shocking experience. Over time this greatly inhibits your aliveness. Even after you've gained awareness about your trauma, triggers, and patterns, you probably still have constellations of energy stuck in your physical and energy bodies. Conscious breathing enables you to release imprints of shock, associated emotions, and limiting beliefs from the cells of the body. Breathwork addresses the *energetic rather than the psychological component* of what holds you back and gets in the way of your full expression and power. My trainings in both these fields, my lived experience, and my experience supporting clients have shown me the purifying, enlivening, uplifting, and even magical qualities of the breath.

"Pranayama," another one of the eight limbs of yoga, involves working with the breath in different ways to create specific effects. While all conscious breathing techniques liberate stuck energy and clear the body, pranayama enables you to build, harness, and direct your energy. Kundalini Yoga often combines breath practices with dynamic movement or holds to direct the energy you're building to specific places in your energy bodies, especially the "ajna chakra." The ajna chakra (not to be confused with the Ajna Center in Human Design), also known as the *third eye* or *command center*, sits in the center of the head. Sending energy to this area of the body influences the pineal and pituitary glands, stimulating your internal pharmacy. Not only does this feel great – endorphins, anyone? – it also helps open your inner knowing by activating and fueling your *intuitive mind* as opposed to your analytical mind. (We'll dig into this more in *Pillar Four: Radiance and Energetic Adeptness*.)

Kundalini Yoga gives you the tools you need to effectively decondition yourself, as Human Design recommends.

These practices also enable you to take command of your energy, building a radiant body of light that nourishes and enlivens you. As you become adept at this, you become *less susceptible* to the influences of outside forces, including other people's energy, opinions, and actions. This helps you become more sovereign of your energy field, your thoughts and emotions, and the actions you take in the world. You'll find aspects of yogic philosophy informing the pillars in many ways. Together we'll explore key themes such as:

- understanding ourselves as an expression of (not separate from) the divine
- a compassionate and grateful approach to all of life
- practicing equanimity in the face of adversity
- devoting oneself to spiritual/energetic practices as a path to empowerment
- taking responsibility for one's experience
- acting with kindness even when fierce

We've been blessed to receive teachings and practices from this ancient wisdom tradition that for many centuries were held close and not publicly shared. As my teacher says, *we are following in the footsteps of the ancients.* While you don't need to ascribe to Hinduism or Buddhism to practice yoga, do honor this gift with the respect it deserves.

In our Feminine Sovereignty online community you'll find specific practices you can try and see how they support, enliven, and influence you. Let's close this portion of Pillar One with a story that illustrates what we've been exploring.

Sarah's Story

I worked over a period of months with a woman in her late sixties; we'll call her Sarah. She came to me because despite having done well in her life in terms of her profession and material gain, she felt stuck inside. She was exploring what to do next and considering becoming more politically active, but that didn't feel quite right. When I read her chart, I asked her if she realized how intuitive she was.

She looked at me with a puzzled expression and said, "Well, not really."

I asked her if she received downloads, fully formed ideas seemingly dropping out of nowhere.

She said, "Yeah, sure, doesn't everyone?"

And I replied, "Well no, not to the degree I imagine you do."

Sarah didn't have a lot of the Logic Circuit defined in her chart, but even so, like most people, she'd highly developed her left-brained intelligence and used it to guide her. Ironically she had a lot of the Knowing Circuit, mentioned above, defined (colored in) in her chart. As we worked together over the next few months I guided her to get more in touch with this superpower of hers that she'd had all along but didn't appreciate or know how to use. I helped her value the guidance and insights she was receiving from the Flow of Life and practice purposefully co-creating with this benevolent force. We expanded her morning routine practice, called "Sadhana" in Sanskrit, from mostly ballet to include specific energy practices from Kundalini Yoga and focused meditation. Her intention was to intentionally tap into and then journal about her inner messages.

As she began to record and honor the divine guidance she was receiving, her outlook on life shifted dramatically.

Rather than analyzing and evaluating herself and her world using her logical, linear way of thinking, she became receptive to insights and inspirations that then opened up whole new pathways and possibilities for her. She became adept at feeling and understanding the world as energy, not just as material reality. Synchronicities arose as new people and opportunities showed up her in her life unexpectedly. Her relationships improved as she stepped out of taking other people's behavior personally, realizing they were simply expressing their Human Design.

In fact she became so enamored with Human Design through taking my *Activate Your Superpowers* program that she began doing mini-readings for her friends and family. Not only did she no longer feel stuck but she came to perceive herself, other people, and the world around her in an entirely new way. She became hopeful where she'd felt despondent. She became curious where she'd felt blocked. She became excited and motivated where she'd felt like she was trudging through life. By the time we'd completed our time together she was pursuing new interests and a way of being in her life that hadn't even been visible to her before.

"It's just so huge, Maggie," she told me. "I can't even say how different my life is now."

Take Time to Assess, Integrate, and Apply What You've Learned

Wow! Thank you for reading through this pillar. I know I've shared a lot of information, ideas, and perspectives with you, some of which I imagine are new to you. Let's both take a couple of big breaths – ahhhhh. Now it's your turn.

I've designed this section to guide you to absorb, digest, and integrate the themes of each pillar. As mentioned in the *Introduction*, my hope and intention are that you'll not just consume what I've offered here but also *bring it into your life* in meaningful ways. Because when you do, if you're open to it, this material will grow and transform you. If you feel the need to skip over this section, please make sure to spiral back later so you can make real in your life what you're receiving from this book. You know best how you take in and integrate new information so you can grow.

You'll find this same structure at the end of each pillar customized with the themes specific to that chapter. Below you'll find:

- **Self-Assessment**
- **Spectrum of Expression**
- **Pause, Reflect, and Review**
- **New Desired Capacities**
- **Reflection Questions**

Self-Assessment

Now that you've had a chance to explore the potentials and pitfalls associated with Pillar One, it's your turn to check out where you are currently with all of this.

Through this assessment process you'll identify strengths and capacities you've already developed through your life experience. You'll also assess areas in which you may have been wounded or simply have yet to build capacity. This assessment is just for you and is meant to be illuminating rather than judgmental. Please be kind rather than judging yourself!

At the end of the book you'll have a chance to pull together your responses to give you a holistic view of where you are now and your desires, intentions, and plans for how to move forward.

Instructions

Give yourself a number 1–5 for each statement. Five means it's totally true for you, one means it's true occasionally. Leave it blank if it doesn't speak to you at all. Add up the numbers from A and B and subtract B from A. This gives you your *Sovereignty Score* for this pillar.

(A) Strengths and Capacities Developed

[   ] I have a daily or regular spiritual practice that keeps me suffi-
    ciently grounded, resilient, buoyant, and able to meet my life's
    challenges with equanimity (most of the time).
[   ] I feel confident in my ability to deliberately create with Spirit
    and do this on a regular basis.
[   ] I trust that Spirit has my back even when things don't go the
    way I want them to.
[   ] When I feel stressed or challenged, I know how to ask for
    guidance, and I'm open to receiving and acting upon it.
[   ] I trust my intuition and act upon it when the time is right,
    even when my mind doesn't like or understand it.

(B) Wounded / Lacks Capacity

[   ] I don't believe in anything beyond the physical, material world.
[   ] I trust only what I can see, count, test, and prove.
[   ] I know that if I want something, I have to make it happen.
    I rely on my own abilities and power.
[   ] I feel alone and abandoned by Spirit much of the time.
[   ] I am at the mercy of what life throws at me.

A = _____   B = _____   A - B = _____

This is your Sovereignty score for Pillar One.

If you have a positive score, this means that you've developed capacity in this area. The higher your score, the greater your strengths.

If you have a negative score — more checked from (B) than (A) — then this is a pillar where you'd benefit from building more capacity. The lower the score, the less in touch you are with the beneficial attributes of this pillar.

Spectrum of Expression

The Spectrum of Expression outlines three ways of expressing the themes, energy, and power of the pillars. Collectively we're evolving out of the power-over/disempowered paradigm that characterizes western civilization. Nevertheless we're still subject to expressing power in these ways, often without even realizing it. The three aspects of the spectrum will help you identify your tendencies and, I hope, reveal to you unconscious patterns, beliefs, or behaviors so you can become at choice about whether to continue or change them. Consider this an exploration in understanding power in the service of building your *power within*, the foundation of your personal sovereignty, and the inner support for your sovereign self.

As you read through this part, consider what feels most accurate or true for you. It's possible to resonate with all three expressions, although typically one will be stronger than the others. Reviewing this will affirm strengths you've already developed and will reveal perspectives that may be in your way as well as capacities you may want to develop.

Awakened/Empowered Expression

In the awakened or empowered expression of co-creating with the Flow of Life, you realize that you're an aspect of Spirit in human form even if you don't always know what that means. Your intuition is keen. You know how to tap into your inner wisdom, and you're comfortable relying on and following your inner guidance. You understand how you're designed to dance with the Flow of Life, each day practicing your Strategy and Authority according to Human Design. You honor your creativity as a pathway between your everyday self and your inner being and/or the Flow of Life. You understand yourself as an innately creative being who continually designs your experience by what you choose to focus on. You express your creativity in ways that inspire, uplift, inform, and guide you.

You take responsibility for what comes into your life without blaming or making yourself (or others) wrong when challenges arise. You meet challenges with curiosity and seek out the opportunities for growth that lie within. You know that as you understand yourself as the locus of creative power in your life you become more at choice regardless of the situation. Even though you're not in command of all that happens in life, you realize you're in command of how you respond to what arises. You tap your inner guidance for creative ways of responding to challenges that arise in your outer world.

As an antidote to our logically oriented and entertainment-saturated world, you have a daily spiritual practice during which you cultivate your relationship with the divine. You embrace this as a self-love practice and make it your priority. You clear and uplift your energy, reflect upon your life experience, set intentions for how you'd like your life to unfold, and turn over to Spirit the job of *making things happen.*

(I call this daily practice *Your Daily Date with the Divine.* It's so important that I devoted an entire chapter to exploring what this is and offering you several options for how you can create this for yourself if you haven't already or if you want to update what you've been doing.)

Shadow Expression

Shadow expressions always have to do with exerting power over another person or persons, a situation, an organization, or even oneself.

Organized religions express shadow when they seek to control devotees, for example, by asserting that an intermediary is needed to access the divine. In this case elaborate rules may be created that dictate approved and disapproved behavior with enforcement falling to the representatives of the institution. "Fire and brimstone" preachers assert power and authority over the parishioners, for example, by claiming to know God's will. Women may be relegated to subservient status, while people with different beliefs may be considered heathen. Unfortunately our world history teems with examples of this power-over dynamic over many millennia, many lands, and many peoples. Individuals may exert this shadow expression in their families and communities, using the threat of God's wrath to control people's behavior.

You might also exert this against yourself. The character Silas in the book and film *The DaVinci Code*, for example, routinely flagellates himself as part of his spiritual practice of surrender to God and his spiritual mentor. Ironically this behavior toward himself makes Silas feel powerful in carrying out the actions he's been directed to do.

Profit-driven forces may invoke scientific studies they've funded to direct and even dominate conversations, policies, and actions. Similarly individuals may do this to either gain power or profit for themselves or to calm their fears of the unknown or what they don't understand.

Disempowered Expression

Our world fosters distraction and even addiction to outside stimuli such as social media, television, movies, news, etc. More than ever before it's possible to be unaware of one's inner reality and completely focused on the external world. It's so easy to farm out your imagination to the entertainment industry and give up your ability to consciously co-create your life.

A disempowered expression of this pillar would be being unaware of rejecting your connection to the divine.

- You might not believe in a higher intelligence. You might feel alone, an isolated, only-physical being in a solely material world.
- Or you could feel strong in your independence and self-determination. Yet you'd be in the habit of using your mind to make decisions and likely exhaust yourself trying to make things happen.
- Or you might identify with, or have been programmed by, an organized religion that teaches subjugation, and you might feel disempowered in the face of that.
- You might adhere to what some people say is science and research without digging deeper to see what the actual studies are saying, or considering how the research might have been designed to benefit profit-driven forces more than genuine scientific inquiry.

Pause, Reflect, and Review

Take a few moments, as you read through the *Spectrum of Experience*, to feel into what's true for you. You might want to write about your current understanding, how your relationship to these possibilities has changed over time for you (if it has), and if so what your journey has been like.

Now go back and review your Self-Assessment.

- Do you think or feel any differently now that you've dug in a bit deeper?
- Do you want to change any of your answers?
- Or do you want to add to the lists offered, noting what's been especially true for you?
- At this point are you aware of wanting to develop new capacities in this area? If so start a list of your own or continue reading for my suggestions that might help you get started.

New Desired Capacities

Below is a list of potential capacities you may feel drawn to and want to develop. This list is suggestive and far from exhaustive. Some may appeal to you while others may not. (Feel free to add your own!)

Rank this list (or your own list) in the order of significance to you, one meaning this is a high priority for you, and five being "not relevant to me, at least not now."

- [   ] I'd like to be able to trust that I'm not alone and that I live in a compassionate Universe.
- [   ] I haven't been able to create a regular spiritual practice, but I'd like to, as I sense that would benefit me.
- [   ] I want to feel more resilient and be able to face and navigate life's challenges with more ease and acceptance.
- [   ] I'd like to be able to access and trust my intuition more. Right now this feels hit or miss, and I don't know why.
- [   ] I want to be clear about what's divine guidance and what's my fear or my personality.

[   ] I'd like to know more about my Human Design and how
       it can help me open up and trust my intuition.
[   ] Practices to help me clear and uplift my energy sound
       really beneficial. I'm going to check out the breathing
       and yoga practices in the Feminine Sovereignty online
       community.

Once you've ranked these possibilities, record your top two priorities in your journal. Ask yourself what you can do this week to begin to develop this valuable skill. Remember that *beginning is often the most difficult part*, so plan to meet your resistance and *overcome it*.

Reflection Questions

I invite you to review and ponder these questions in any way that works for you. Feel free to respond to the ones that resonate for you and leave the rest. You may write about them in your journal (highly recommended), take them into meditation or on a walk with you, make a sketch or painting about how they make you feel, or some other way that works for you. Writing down your reflections provides you with a record of your experiences, which can be very helpful later. As we evolve we tend to forget where we were, and that makes it difficult to appreciate how much we've grown.

> What did you discover about yourself through the Self-Assessment and Spectrum of Expression? Did you feel affirmed in some way? Did anything surprise or disturb you? Are you inspired to develop any new capacities?

> What can you do this week to begin to develop this valuable new capacity? What resources do you need? What do you need to prepare? Is there any resistance you need to face and overcome? Who in your life can support you and help hold you accountable?

> Apply what you learned or realized in Pillar One to your primary Learning Question. What does this teaching add to your inquiry? What was your Learning Question(s) for this

specific pillar? Make a few notes about what's arising for you including how this feels in your body.

> What would become possible if you were to truly know that Spirit has your back? That you're supported at all times? And that you'll always have what you need *when you need to have it*?

> Do you have a regular daily or spiritual practice? If so what benefits do you receive from it? If not has something been in your way or has it just not been important to you or what you've thought about? What might open for you if you created and dedicated time and energy for this? (See the chapter *Your Daily Date with the Divine* for ideas if you need them.)

> Do you deliberately create with the Flow of Life? If so how has that been for you? What methods have you used? How effective has this been?

> Pull out your Human Design chart and review your Type, Strategy, and Authority. (If you don't have it yet, go to YourFreeHumanDesignchart.com, and get it.) Have you been practicing using your Strategy and Authority, or is this entirely new to you? How might your life change if you knew and purposefully worked with the Flow of Life in this way?

> Are you curious to explore Kundalini Yoga practices? If so you'll find videos of practices to try on the *Resources* webpage. If this is new to you I recommend you start at the beginning and work your way through, as the exercises are progressive. If you're already familiar, enjoy!

> If you were to imagine, sketch, or dance this pillar into your Temple of Sovereignty, what would it look, feel, and/or move like? As Pillar One, does it have a special foundational place in the whole? If so how would you characterize it? Under what circumstances and for what purposes will you visit your temple? What will help you build this sacred inner sanctuary?

Emotional Wisdom

The ability to experience your emotions in ways that uplift, heal, and integrate and do no harm. The ability to harness creative emotional power and direct it toward the outcome desired.

"Be open to new ways to heal and regulate
– both by yourself and with others –
and it will foster greater connection
and promote transformational intimacy."

—Diane Poole Heller, PhD

Am I in command, not control, of my emotions?

**How do I build, harness, and direct
my emotional energy?**

Navigating Emotional Life

"I know. I know. I hear you," you say into the phone. On the other end your friend is panicking. "Tell me exactly what happened," you say. You listen attentively, tuning in to her trembling voice, sorting through the details to get as complete a picture as you can.

"Okay, so there's standing water everywhere. Did you get everything off the floor that you could? *Great.* Is the water still rising? It's supposed to hit peak soon if it hasn't already."

You breathe deep as you listen, willing yourself to calm. She needs you to be calm and clear because she can't be for herself. You reach down into the ground and up into the sky for support.

"Sweetheart, *I know this is scary.* You don't know what's going to happen, what the extent of the damage is, or what you're going to do after this. Yeah, I got it. And I got you. You're going to be okay. I know it's a mess, but *it's going to be okay.*"

You wish you were as certain of that as you're projecting to her. But you know that sense of stability and certainty is what she needs to hear right now.

"Look, I'm going to get in my car, go grab my brother – he's always good in situations like this – and we'll be over in about an hour. In the meantime I want you to get everything off the floor that you can, and then go upstairs and do your best to relax. There's not much else you can do in a flood."

She's crying loudly, you're crying softly. "Tears are good," you remember your Mama saying.

After you hang up the phone you sit for a moment, placing one hand on your heart and the other on your belly. Closing your eyes you breathe down into your belly, expanding your chest and slowly releasing tension on the exhale. You reach for gravity to hold you. *This, too, will pass,* you repeat inside, *this, too, will pass.*

And it will. You know that disasters – large and small – really suck! They come when you don't expect them, they throw you off course. They demand your attention, and give nothing in return.

But you can do this. She can do this. Your brother can do this. All of you together can do this.

Your heart slows down. Your breathing regulates. Your shoulders relax.

We're all going to have a big rant and cry when this is over, you say to yourself, *but right now we've got some shit to deal with*. That gets a little smile out of you, not because this is a happy situation but because this isn't the first time you've had to deal with, well, *life*.

I got this! you think as you pull out of your driveway. *We got this. It sucks, but we got this*. And off you go to help your friend because that's what friends do.

We Humans Are Emotional Beings

Our hearts feel touched. Our spirits uplift. We feel bonded with others. We feel distress and fear, joy and delight, worry and concern, confidence and strength. Our innate emotional range is deep and wide. Emotional energy is extremely powerful and when honored and understood can be used to fuel our creations as well as enhance our lived experience. Emotional wisdom honors this primary somatic and energetic intelligence, encouraging us to develop deeper understanding of ourselves and each other. Emotional wisdom supports our personal sovereignty by giving us command of this potent, creative force.

We're also communal beings. Our emotions can connect us or break us apart.

We're physiologically designed to be connected to other people. Babies who don't receive touch and attention don't thrive and can even die. When we're securely bonded (e.g., partners, parent and child, close friends) we help each other regulate our emotions and our nervous systems through a process called "co-regulation." In the presence of another person we trust, we release the hormone oxytocin, and this helps us relax and feel safe, fostering feelings of joy, connection, possibility, and aliveness.

According to therapist and author Diane Poole Heller thousands of studies have shown the effects of a bonded partner or parent on helping to regulate the heartbeat, brainwaves, breath, and other physiological features of their beloved in a stressful situation. In fact when we spend a lot of time with someone we trust, our nervous systems intertwine into a combined field sometimes called a "social nervous system." A well-regulated social nervous system feels nourishing and supportive and fosters a deep sense of togetherness and belonging. When my child was small and had trouble winding down, for example, I'd lay them on my body, where they'd fully relax and in short order fall sleep.

For many years I practiced conscious dance as part of a small, intimate community that gathered every Tuesday night. Our closeness created a communal nervous system that was pleasurable, bonding, and enlivening. Even though one or more of us might have had a difficult day or be struggling with an issue, when we came together our connection enabled us to co-regulate so that everyone felt held, loved, and uplifted – all without words! It also enabled us to dance quickly and in proximity without running into each other because we could *feel* where each of us was inside that shared nervous system.

Can you think of a situation in which you co-regulated your emotional energy with others? What did it feel like? How did it change you? Did you realize how valuable this was at the time?

Emotional wisdom includes knowing how to regulate your emotional energy on your own or with others so that you can enjoy a rich emotional life, yet not be taken over by your emotions without your conscious agreement. You want to be able to feel your emotions and have that energy run through you without overwhelming you. You don't want to be at the mercy of your emotions either: anyone who's been overwhelmed by fear or anger knows the danger of that. When emotions overwhelm you, it's hard to clearly hear or feel or see your intuition. The communication pathways are distorted by this powerful energy.

Yet you don't want to reject and suppress them either. Suppressed emotions don't disappear; instead they drill down deeper into the body and, if left unattended, can create physical discomfort and even illness. As Carl Jung once said, "What you resist persists." And I like to add: "And goes deeper." Of course anyone can temporarily be overtaken by emotion; the question then is: how much, for how long, and what to do next? Instead of *suppressing* them, you need to learn to *sequester* potentially harmful emotions like fear or anger, containing them until you have the time and energy to attend to them in healthy ways. Ideally you feel and honor your emotions even as you learn how to manage and contain them.

We'll dive deeper into the complexities of feeling, honoring, and managing our emotions a little later in this chapter. But first let's explore an aspect of emotional energy that's not talked about as much: *its creative power*.

Creative Power of Emotions

Abraham-Hicks, perhaps the best-known teachers of the Law of Attraction, talk about the "astonishing power of emotions" to help you attract more of what you want into your life. From their point of view, the kind of emotions you're experiencing indicate how you feel about what you're wanting more of: uplifting, inspiring emotions indicate your positive anticipation, while depressive and resentful feelings indicate your lack of faith that you'll be able to create and receive what you desire. They call this your "vibrational alignment" with whatever it is you're focusing on – a romantic relationship, meaningful employment, or thriving health, for example.

In their foundational book *Ask and It Is Given* they've gone so far as to offer an "Emotional Guidance Scale" that lists twenty-two emotions in order of their vibrational frequency (higher to lower). They instruct us to gradually raise our vibration from frustration, for example, to pessimism and then to boredom, contentment, and finally hopefulness rather than trying to jump directly from despair to delight. The point here is that the higher your vibration, the more positive your emotion and the more attractive and receptive you become to whatever you're focusing on. *Plus, hey, you feel good too.*

David Hawkins, author of the groundbreaking *Power vs Force*, also offers an emotional scale that moves from shame, which is the "lowest" and least powerful emotion, to love and compassion – the "highest" and most powerful. Hawkins argues that the power of the love of great avatars such as Buddha and Christ was so great that it was able to balance out the lower frequency of emotions of millions of people who were alive when they were. The higher the frequency of your emotional tone, the closer you are to the frequency of the All That Is, or the Flow of Life, which is pure agape love.

In the Kundalini Yoga traditions, we use *kriyas* (specific combinations of postures, movement, breathwork, and mantra) to build high-frequency energy.

This is why people flock to opportunities to sing and dance to Sanskrit words: it raises your vibration, and *it feels really good!*[11] Similarly at concerts the power of music stimulates bodily and energetic movement and opens our hearts – you may even burst into an ecstatic state! The quality of your emotions may shift with the tone and frequency of sound and words, even as you're held and moved, your body/mind/spirit becoming an instrument played by the artist(s). I remember being at vocalist k. d. lang's concert (many years ago) when she moved the audience so deeply that we spontaneously and as one rose to give her a standing ovation. She had us, as they say, in *the palm of her hand.*

Sporting events may similarly stimulate emotions, though the type of energy created can be adversarial rather than uplifting. The highest expressions of this kind of experience emerge when the audience admires and appreciates the talent and skill of the players and the thrill of competition and how that stimulates greatness, rather than focusing so much on who wins. I get choked up when I witness an extraordinary ice skater or gymnast, my heart touched by the beauty, athleticism, commitment, and joy of the athlete.

What might become possible if we were able to harness the power of emotions expressed at a concert or sporting event and direct it toward creating the "more beautiful world our hearts know is possible"?

I first learned about the creative power of emotions during my years with Nikken and studying with Bob Proctor. He exposed me to myriad books older and more recent that detailed the power of the mind to create your own reality. Proctor stressed the importance of the quality of the emotions with which you said your affirmations. He instructed, for example, to always begin with: "I am so happy and grateful now that …" It wasn't enough to say the words; you had to cultivate the genuine feeling

---

11   Sanskrit is a celestial language (not one for everyday life) that works more through sound than through meaning. The frequencies of the sound current produced by Sanskrit words create an altered state of elevated consciousness – bliss.

as well for the affirmation to become magnetic. Like the yogis, he deeply believed in the power of gratitude to attract what you want into your life, drawing on this emotional energy to *create your own reality.*

I found this practice both uplifting and effective. As I said in the *Introduction,* I was able to draw on his teachings to make my way out of academia and into a new life. Not long after I left Columbia I became a devoted student of Abraham-Hicks, using their methods to shape a life I'd never imagined before. While I found this practical as well as provocative, I also had mixed results, and I didn't know why. It was as if my intentions and affirmations slid off certain areas of my life like they were Teflon. At the time I suspected that this had to do with unconscious agreements I wasn't aware of. Now I'd say that I needed to decondition or deprogram myself. Unfortunately neither Proctor nor Abraham-Hicks were helpful to me in understanding what to do about this. I had to look elsewhere, and we'll do that together in just a little bit.

We're going to dive more deeply into the magnetic quality of your vibrational frequency and your emotional tone more in *Pillar Four: Radiance and Energetic Adeptness.* For now, I'm bringing in the *attractive nature of emotional energy* to expand and balance our impressions of emotions as just feelings – sometimes pleasant, sometimes annoying. Emotions often get a bad rap in the overculture, being seen as immature, inconvenient, irrelevant, distracting, disruptive, and even dangerous. (This is an aspect of the legacy of the rise of rationality mentioned earlier.) And yes, if not well regulated, energetically strong emotions like anger, fear, and especially hate can become dangerous. Yet this pervasively negative view of emotions impoverishes our life experience, as having a rich emotional life is part of our birthright as human beings. This negative attitude also cuts us off from some of our most creative energy as well as our deepest pleasures with one another.

Understanding Emotions

We don't understand emotions all that well. The Scientific Revolution asserted the validity of left-brained logic, reason, and analysis in contrast to intuitive and spiritual ways of knowing. As Carolyn Merchant points out, and we noted briefly in Pillar One, logic was gendered as masculine and superior, and intuition, emotions, and Earth-based spirituality were gendered as feminine and inferior, unreliable, and even *superstitious or wicked*. This legacy continues to run deep in the psyche of westerners, organizing our perception and perspectives often without us even realizing it. The Scientific Revolution fueled the Story of Progress, and we've been very attached to the benefits we've received from both.

Unfortunately this has led to us judging and rejecting so many aspects of our being, including our emotions. At one point when I was coming to terms with the influence of my emotions I tried talking with my father about our family dynamics. When I asked him how he felt about it, he responded with exasperation: "I don't know. We never talked about emotions when I was growing up. This isn't something I understand."

My mother, on the other hand, was frustrated with herself because she cried easily and she didn't like it. For her emotions were distracting and inconvenient because *they got in the way* of her being able to express herself *rationally*. Growing up inside this environment I, like many of us, have had to seek out my own emotional education.

I've done Human Design readings for many women who give me a puzzled look when I tell them how emotional they are. (I'll explain what I mean by this in the last section of this pillar.) Often they're in a high-powered job, and I ask: "Would you be taken seriously at work if you were to be emotional?" Every one of them has said more or less: "Oh God, no, I wouldn't." And so they suppress their emotional energy in order to be seen as capable, reasonable, reliable, and *definitely not influenced by their hormones*.

In some ways the cultural call to suppress one's emotions is worse for men, as their approved range of emotions is *exceptionally small*. They get taught from an early age not to cry, not to be angry, not to be emotional at all really, and to prioritize their analytical minds instead. As we saw in Pillar One, our analytical minds, while valuable, are but a small portion of our wholeness. Men get to be excited at sporting events, for example, or maybe at a rock concert or even playing video games. This great diminishment of men's emotional lives – we're talking *big blinders* and a *tight bridle* – often leads men to get their emotional needs met through sex alone. Sex also is seen as manly, a mark of manhood in fact. Imagine the intensity of energy that must build up for men behind sex and anger. *That's a lot to manage.*

I think that's one of the reasons the Mankind Project (MKP) has been so successful. According to Bill Kauth, one of the project's founders, participants in their signature workshop, The New Warrior Training Adventure, receive the opportunity to tap into deep emotions with the support of a circle of men. In this facilitated and well-held container, men get to express themselves and become vulnerable in ways they may never have before. According to their website, they "believe that emotionally mature, powerful, compassionate, and purpose-driven men will help heal some of our society's deepest wounds ... we are willing to look at and take full responsibility for the pain we are also capable of creating – and suffering."

I agree, yes, that many of our society's deepest wounds may be healed as men – and all of us – cultivate our emotional wisdom inside the richness of our emotional, creative lives. Let's dig deeper into what this is all about and what's at stake.

Emotion

"Emotion" literally means *energy in motion*. According to Bolte Taylor, the neuroanatomist we saw earlier, emotional energy will rise and fall in the span of ninety seconds if you don't keep feeding the thought or belief that stimulated it in the first place.

Ninety seconds. Interesting, right?

Watch small children as their emotions continually rise and fall; often they're laughing or crying and can go from one to the other in a matter of seconds. They don't get stuck or fixated in one emotional expression. We can learn about emotional flow from young children if we can tolerate how we feel in the presence of their strong emotions. Many times the emotional flow of children (and other adults) can be triggering for adults who've been trained to suppress their own emotions. Without even realizing it, you might move to quiet or silence a child because that's the way you were treated when you were young. In these moments we teach them which emotions are okay for them to express and which are not.

For example, a favorite game with babies is making faces at them, giggling or tickling them, or holding up things for them to look at in an effort to get them to smile. And I get it; there's nothing quite so endearing and heartwarming as a baby's smile! Yet this is also how babies learn that smiling is a desired and acceptable behavior while crying and screaming are not. In this way, even from the earliest age, we begin to receive messages about and be conditioned by what the adults around us prefer and deem appropriate.

Estuck

I created the term *estuck* to describe what happens when we don't allow emotional energy to flow as it's designed to do. In the case of a challenging or confronting situation you may freeze, hold your breath, and do your best to meet or get away from what's happening. This triggers the autonomic nervous system and stimulates the amygdala, releasing adrenaline and cortisol, slowing digestion, breathing, and even conscious thinking. All bodily resources rush to your aid so that you can deal with the apparent danger in your midst.

The question is: Are you actually in real and present danger or are you simply reacting to something as if you were? To support yourself, you may grasp hold of your interpretation or your judgment and you hang on. This can go on for days, months, or even years depending on the magnitude of the experience and your interpretation of it. This happens most with the stickier energies of anger, grief, shame, bitterness, disappointment, or frustration – much to our detriment, as these energies will eat away at you from the inside.

Usually these *estucks* are rooted in either judgments we have about something that did or didn't happen, or unresolved trauma.

In both cases a constellation made up of thoughts, emotions, and energy is formed and *sticks* somewhere inside. These constellations create blockages in the mental, emotional, and energy bodies called *samskaras* in yogic philosophy. If not attended to, these blockages create emotional discomfort. Eventually they can affect the physical body as well, creating discomfort, pain, and even illness. In their earlier stages, these constellations of stagnant emotions, stuck energy, and judgmental thoughts create "triggers," flash points that when touched flare into emotional reactions that typically exceed what's happening in the present moment. Such triggers can be very confusing both for the person experiencing them and for anyone else who's around.

As a kid I experienced this because my father had a habit of suddenly (it felt to me) becoming angry when moments before nothing seemed amiss. To me as a young person this was scary and confusing. I couldn't tell if I'd done something to make him act that way. Ironically I don't think he knew what had happened either; he seemed oblivious of what was going on inside. Since none of us understood what was going on at the time, we did our best to simply calm down and move on. We never talked about it later, and I don't have the sense that he looked deeper inside afterward. Such a "triggered" reaction was just part of normal life when I was growing up.

Pause for a moment and take a deep breath. Have you witnessed someone else having a strong emotional reaction to something that felt out of proportion to the situation? Maybe it disturbed or scared you. Have you experienced something mysterious popping out of your subconscious only to seemingly disappear as the energy settles? Make a few notes or a drawing about how this was for you.

Fortunately we've become much more aware of what's happening inside of a triggered response like this since I was a little girl. The ever-growing and evolving field of psychology has provided us with ways of understanding the links between current reactions and past experiences, and how to unpack a more accurate sense of what's going on. I've benefited tremendously from my experiences with psychotherapy, and I often recommend that people begin their self-development journey by exploring the ways in which their early, typically familial, experiences continue to influence them today.

In this pillar and the chapter devoted to it, however, we're focusing more on the *perceptual, patterned, and energetic aspects of emotional wisdom* than on the psychological. We've developed a relatively psychologically sophisticated society. People can often tell you things like: *Oh, I tend to feel anxious because my mother wasn't very available when I was a child.* Ideally this awareness would lead you to realize there's no real and present danger to feel anxious about and to do a practice to move that energy. Unfortunately some people remain attached to that experience of neglect – it's become part of their identity – and use it as an excuse to continue their dysfunction.

This means that rather than focusing on the specific memory or experience, and the stories and interpretation you have about it, it's better to focus more on *how you've been conditioned to act (or not act)* in certain ways and the energetic mechanics of how this works more than the specific content. When you know how to become aware of and work with these mechanics, then you can apply this approach to triggers whatever their specific content. As you do so, you foster your command of your energy, cultivating your sovereignty of your inner landscape.

Association

Have you ever found yourself wandering down a path of thoughts or images that only link up in your mind because of your personal experiences? One moment you're driving along and you pass that store where you bought the strawberries that were already bad at the bottom, then you're remembering how embarrassed you were when you brought them to a party and the person you were hoping to start dating got a bite of one of the moldy ones, then you're thinking of the mold under your kitchen sink that isn't horrible, but you can smell it, and you've been meaning to call your friend who knows about such things, but you remember she's out of town, and you're longing to get away for a while, maybe that place you stayed with your other girlfriend and ... the next thing you know you're pulling into your driveway.

Your subconscious makes sense of your experience by associating seemingly disparate situations in spiraling rather than linear ways.

Just consider all the different people, places, and situations that show up in your dreams! Emotional triggers arise through association. Associations happen so quickly that most of the time you're not even aware of what's happening. Next thing you know you're pondering a memory that seemingly has *nothing to do with* what you were focusing on just a moment before. Yet if you're able to backtrack and then follow your mind's journey, you'd discover a string of associations threaded together by the associative workings of your subconscious mind. An unhealed trauma will continue to influence your awareness by associating something in present time with the earlier traumatic experience. It will do this over and over again until you've attended to the unhealed, tender part inside. This is why we have repetitive dreams and experiences until we do the inner healing work they're calling us to do.

Many associations contain emotional content and potent energetic charge. These associations propel you through your selective memory, connecting experiences together that to some part of you feel similar, even the same. Your mind-journey emerges from your experience and is unique to you. Mine necessarily differs from yours because my life experience and how I've interpreted it are mine alone. This is one reason siblings may recall childhood memories very differently and grow into quite different people over time. *Our associations differentiate and often define us.*

That's why you can be having an intimate dinner with a new friend you're romantically interested in, and a song begins to play, and then next thing you know your heart is trembling because that was the favorite song of yours and the past love who left the relationship without an explanation. If the hurt still stings (or worse) you may find it difficult to hear what your new friend is saying, barely noticing that their mouth is moving as you hold your breath and try not to cry.

Of course this can work in the opposite direction as well. One night while dancing with a new love, I put on Miles Davis's *Kind of Blue,* one of my favorite collections at the time. He stopped and stared at me. A moment later, after some cascade of memory had poured through his awareness, he said: "I listen to this album every morning." We both took this as a *good sign,* as our paralleled associations with this music were positive. It took me over a decade to be able to listen to it again after our relationship ended because from that moment on I associated that album with him.

Associations occur all the time and at lightning speed. The subconscious mind outsizes the conscious mind like the universe outsizes the stars you can see in our sky. According to one of the founders of the new biology, cell biologist and best-selling author of the *Biology of Belief*, Bruce Lipton, "When it comes to sheer neurological processing abilities, the subconscious mind is millions of times more powerful than the conscious mind." Many, many associations benefit us moment to moment.

- Oh, that feeling means I need to go to the bathroom.
- Oh, it's that time so I'll wake up now.
- Oh, I'm at a friend's house, and I get in my car and drive home – all without consciously thinking about how to turn on the car, drive, or what the route is. This becomes so automatic that sometimes you might find yourself driving home when you really meant to stop at another store first.

Associations create patterned experiences, many of which are helpful. I mean who wants to think about how to walk or brush your teeth every day? You learn how to do these things through focus and repetition until you master them. When that happens you've imbedded that process in your subconscious memory, so you no longer have to use your focus and conscious mind to carry out the actions. It's great that you don't have to learn or even practice your primary language each day. Yet not so great when you keep avoiding that one street, even though it's a faster route, because one time you saw a dead deer there, and it scared you. Even so, while that's annoying, it's far from harmful, right?

What can be harmful is when your throat clenches up at a meeting and you struggle to get words out because you associate speaking up to authority figures with being reprimanded as a child whenever you tried to speak your mind. Or maybe you have trouble imagining what you want because you associate doing so with being told to "stop daydreaming and pay attention" when you were in school. Or maybe you long to share your wisdom yet somewhere in the recesses of your subconscious your epigenes (ancestral imprints) associate being visible and noticed with being burned alive or having your head cut off.

I know that might sound dramatic, but I've witnessed this in many clients and have experienced it myself – once we became aware of the deeper layers of what was going on. All these patterns operate in the subconscious below the level of your conscious awareness. At least they do until you become aware of them, until you foster the ability to gain perspective on your thoughts, emotions, and behavior, and then ask, "Hmmm, why is this so?"

> Why do I act this way in these situations?
> Why do I feel this way when this happens?
> Why do I shut down or act out when so and so does X or even when I think about it?
> What's going on inside of me that I experience my life this way?

These vital questions open portals into your inner landscape that help you wrench yourself free from unconsciously acting out programs you set in place years and even lifetimes ago. With intention, awareness, and practice, anyone can develop perspective on and even shift these programs rather than simply living them out as if they're your destiny. To do that, you need to become aware of your default lens.

Your Default Lens

You'll find it very helpful to identify what your *default lens* is. This is the interpretive lens through which you automatically come to understand what's happening outside of you as well as inside of you.

For example:

· Do you tend to receive comments from other people as criticism?
· Do you assume that other people mean well?
· Do you become offended when someone has a different opinion or point of view? Do you perceive this as degrading or an insult?

- Do you take things personally, as in other people's actions and opinions are about you specifically?
- Do you evaluate or judge intense energy as anger or attacking in some way?
- Do you perceive other people to be dangerous and untrustworthy?
- Do you feel the Universe to be friendly, antagonistic, or disinterested?
- Do you believe in the innate goodness of most people?
- Do you believe that other people are out for themselves, so you need to protect yourself and/or be aggressive in order to be safe and to thrive?

These are all default lenses through which you may be automatically interpreting what's going on around you without consciously thinking about it. This kind of interpretive lens, which we all have, colors and often distorts your experience and your understanding of what's going on. The more each of us can become aware of our default interpretive lens and how it's influencing us, the easier it will be for us to be able to understand ourselves and each other.

For example, I've been in relationship with two different men who interpreted any kind of intensity that wasn't joy as anger. (They both grew up in environments in which anger was commonplace.) Intense energy rises up in me when I'm experiencing all kinds of different emotions, such as distress, confusion, disappointment, dismay, shock, and overwhelm. I didn't enjoy having the richness of my experience *reduced to anger*. Their default lens led them to react to my intensity in patterned ways, creating automatic, subconscious interpretations that weren't helpful and made communication and connection difficult.

You can get into real trouble when you believe that you're seeing things clearly and yet you've been triggered by an undigested bundle of traumatic energy. Unfortunately this is so commonplace that most people think of it as *normal*. At the same time more and more of us are becoming aware of how this works and developing our emotional wisdom in relation to it.

Observation and Empathy

When you feel triggered you lose perspective. Old associations and your default lens take over. Then you interpret the situation in relation to these and create stories that explain why you're right (and usually why the other person is wrong). This is why the great Indian philosopher and yogic teacher Krishnamurti said that "the ability to observe without judgment is one of the highest faculties you can develop." True observation, as opposed to interpretation, requires that you step outside your self-centered way of perceiving.

Similarly Marshall Rosenberg, the brilliant creator of Nonviolent Communication (NVC), quips that we're all so conditioned to believe that we're not good enough that we'll translate almost anything into criticism. Maybe you've had the experience of sharing with someone and suddenly realizing that they're translating what you think is a neutral or innocent comment into a criticism of them or something they did. Or maybe you recognize this in yourself? We usually call this *taking things personally*.

Understanding this tendency, Rosenberg developed a system of communication that emphasizes slowing down, differentiating between observation and interpretation, and developing empathy for yourself and others. This approach helps you pause, first of all, then disentangle your awareness from the rapid response that jets out of your subconscious based on a past experience. During this pause you practice sorting out an objective observation of what happened – as if it was being recorded by a video camera – from your interpretation (usually your judgment) of what occurred.

Rosenberg and Krishnamurti both point to the liberating and healing power of being able to step outside of your own perspective and (at least attempt) to see the situation more objectively. NVC also teaches the significance and healing power of being able to take in another's point of view. Sometimes we call this *walking in someone else's shoes*. Doing so can be a real eye – and heart – opener. In fact you may find it astonishing and disruptive to truly take in that other people have a different, sometimes a very different, perspective on the same event or situation. Like turning the lens on a kaleidoscope, what you once saw so clearly may suddenly appear very differently. Learning this opens the path to empathy, the ability to understand and appreciate another person's point of view even when – especially when – you don't agree with it. This is a core skill in NVC.

Observation and empathy often create a *pattern-interrupt* that disrupts your default lens, liberates stuck energy into motion, and opens new possibilities. Most of the time you live inside your programmed thinking, recycling similar thoughts and emotions day after day. You have to *purposefully choose* to think differently and practice working with your emotional energy to liberate yourself from this conditioning. This is the first step in building your emotional wisdom.

Building Your Emotional Wisdom

What if something distinct from anything you've learned about emotions is happening energetically? What if much of what's happening has very little to do with your psyche and more to do with your energetic makeup?

Human Design shows us exactly that. This system provides insight into how we experience and process emotional energy that's entirely different than any other teaching or model I've ever encountered. In contrast to psychology, *Human Design helps us understand our emotions energetically.* What I'm about to share may disrupt your self-concept, I hope in a beneficial way. When I first learned about this aspect of my Human Design, my whole life appeared in a different light. I felt a lot more compassion for myself. This was illuminating and confirming and ultimately liberating as well. *Let's see how this is for you.*

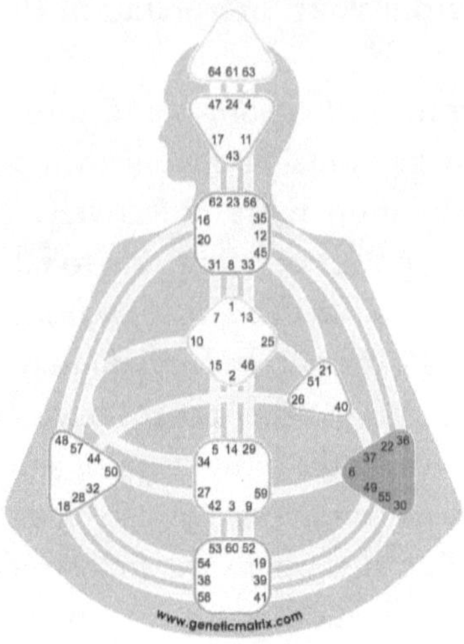

Human Design emphasizes the power of emotional energy by dedicating an entire energy center to it, the *Emotional Solar Plexus (ESP) (see illustration)*. The ESP isn't the only place in the Human Design chart where emotions appear. Rather it's more about the *creative power* of emotional energy. Like the Sacral Center we explored in Pillar One, the ESP is one of four *engines* or *motors* in the Human Design system, which means it's a locus of energetic power.

Understanding the ESP will help you in two primary ways: first, this brings you a new perspective on the Law of Creation, which we'll dive into in detail in *Pillar Four: Radiance and Energetic Adeptness*. And second, you can discover so much about why you (or someone you love) may be "moody" without really knowing why and why we may be strongly influenced by each other's emotions. To understand this we need to explore what happens when you have the ESP defined (colored in) or open (white) in your Human Design chart.[12]

---

12 Remember that definition is what's colored in on your Human Design chart. Whatever is defined on your chart is a form of energy to which you have ongoing, ready, reliable access and a consistent way of experiencing it. What's white in your chart you still will have experienced many times in your life, but your experience of it will vary depending on who you're around.

Emotional Definition

Fifty percent of the population is emotionally defined. If your ESP is colored in, chances are you'll experience some kind of emotional tone most of the time, which is known as your "emotional wave." If this is you, at times you'll feel more "up": extroverted, buoyant, filled with possibility, energized, and excited. Other times you'll feel more "down": introverted, tired, sensitive, melancholic, uncertain, and introspective. The magnitude of your emotional wave will be influenced by the specifics of your Human Design chart, by how you've been conditioned to respond to your emotions, and by how you hold and care for yourself when you're "down on your wave." The intensity and quality of how this feels can vary a lot from person to person.

Understanding your emotional wave can give you a new perspective on any negative self-talk that might arise from having fluctuations in the quality of your emotional energy.

I've spoken with many clients who thought something was wrong with them because of their "moodiness." They couldn't attribute how they were feeling to anything in particular, like something that happened or something someone said, so they couldn't find a *reason* for what they were feeling.

Many people make themselves wrong for being on the low part of their wave, for feeling more introverted, tired, tender. This is unfortunate because this part of the wave can be remarkably creative and poignant, as it's *emotionally sensitive.* I remind my clients who are emotionally defined that much great art has been made out of melancholy: novels, poems, songs, stories, plays, dances, etc. I did a reading for an emotionally defined man who already knew about his wave before he came to Human Design. He said that he tends to write a song when he's feeling melancholy (he's a musician). I said YES! when I heard this, and acknowledged him for having developed his own functional, soothing, and creative way of being with his wave.

Having compassion for yourself will help shift you out of self-judgment and into understanding, acceptance, and caring for yourself when you're feeling low on your wave. I always recommend naps, baths, walks in nature, writing in your journal, painting, singing, or doing something either restful, nurturing, or creative. The more you care for yourself without fueling any negative self-talk or judging other people, the easier time you're going to have. And it will be easier to tap into your own inner being to receive whatever guidance or insights might be waiting for you even when you're low on your wave.

I've done readings for people who are emotionally defined, yet they say they're not emotional. If this is true for you then you may have learned to suppress or reject your emotions. Most men and many women have, too, so you're not alone if this is you. This is understandable given our lack of education about and acceptance of emotions. Yet your emotions are your birthright, and they enrich your experience. I encourage you to open to your emotional energy as you learn more about how to manage and direct it.

Emotional Openness

The other half of the population is emotionally open, meaning that the ESP will be white on their chart. Being emotionally open doesn't mean open-minded or open-hearted, and it also doesn't mean you don't have emotions! *Everyone has emotions.* I'm emotionally open, and I definitely have my own emotions. It's just that when you're emotionally open you'll experience emotions differently than those who are defined. *Let's unpack this a little.*

People who are emotionally open are known in THD as "true empaths" because we can feel other people's emotions. Conversely you may feel emotionally neutral much of the time, especially when you're not around other people. Being open, remember, means that you don't have *consistent* energy in that part of your Human Design, but you still have an ESP just like everyone has the entire Human Design chart, and you've experienced its energy many times in your life.

For example, when you're with other people, you may pick up their emotional energy and amplify it. When you're with people who are feeling excited, enthusiastic, ecstatic, loving, or otherwise "up," picking up and amplifying their emotional energy can feel great. After all, you'll experience even stronger sensations than they do. However the opposite is also true. When you're around someone feeling angry, sad, fearful, disappointed, or frustrated, potentially you'll feel that even more strongly.

This can be particularly difficult for children who are emotionally open. When I was a kid, I picked up a lot of emotions that my parents were suppressing because for their generation it was inappropriate for them to express them. Yet suppressing emotions doesn't mean that energy goes away. Rather it simmers below the surface and sometimes bursts out at the most inopportune times, as I mentioned with my father's outburst above. The sensitive, emotionally open child (or adult) will pick up that suppressed emotional energy of other people and amplify it. This can lead to the child being made wrong for the emotional energy that they're expressing even though *it's not theirs*.

If you're emotionally open, feeling and amplifying other people's emotions can be either delightful or quite uncomfortable and confusing. It can lead you to avoid emotionally challenging situations and becoming conflict-avoidant and possibly passive-aggressive. This is because you may not like being around other people with strong emotional energy, suppressed or expressed, particularly if it's anger or grief or shame or something else that doesn't feel good to you. You may not even realize that the emotions are someone else's; I certainly didn't know what was happening when I was a kid. It wasn't until many years later when I learned my Human Design that I had the *face-palm* moment – of course!

Challenging relationship dynamics can emerge between emotionally defined and emotionally open people. For example an emotionally open person may *disappear* either physically or psychically in an effort to protect themself from feeling and amplifying another's emotions. Or they might become the peacemaker in the family, seeking to placate others so that at least on the surface emotions feel calm. *Classic co-dependent behavior.* At other times this person might become extremely expressive – dramatic even – because they've been conditioned by having so much emotional energy amplified in them that emotional intensity becomes their norm. In this case they learn to generate and express emotions habitually even though in the past so much of this emotional energy wasn't even their own. (I think some of my emotional intensity comes from that kind of conditioning – although I've got plenty of intensity in my chart too.)

Learning who around you is emotionally defined or open can be eye-popping for relationships.

The way your energy interacts with another can be quite confusing if you don't know what's going on. One of the great benefits of understanding your own and other people's Human Design is that you can de-personalize the ways your energy fields interact with each other. You may also be able to stay neutral even in the midst of other people's emotional expression.

Even if your ESP is open, you can learn to take command of your energy and your emotions through energy work. This is one of the huge benefits of combining Kundalini Yoga with Human Design. In Pillars Three and Four we'll explore ways to work with your physical and energy bodies so that you can be in command of your emotional energy. My experience is that when you clear out stagnant emotions and also build your own auric field, you empower yourself whether you're emotionally defined or open according to Human Design. You don't need to simply be at the mercy of other people's energies, including their emotions.

In fact you can learn how to work with emotional energy to your advantage. For example when you're triggered you can recognize that state, pause, and move energy through movement or breath to diminish the intensity. This will enable you to gain perspective and be present with yourself, witnessing compassionately. At that point you'll be more at choice about how to respond rather than reacting automatically. You can unpack and identify the underlying stimulus for the trigger, the past experience that's activated by what's happening in present time. You can come to know yourself well enough to know what tends to trigger you and why and what to do when that happens.

Becoming aware of and responsible for your emotional energy, your triggers and unhealed wounds, and your conditioned as well as your chosen behavior fosters your personal sovereignty and is a hallmark of the sovereign self. You become more clear, stable, compassionate, and in command when you interact with others even in very challenging situations. If you don't do this inner work, your life may well be orchestrated from deep inside the subconscious (where the unhealed parts are) without you desiring or even being aware of it. This can lead to being reactive, afraid, aggressive, or offended in your relations with others. You may unconsciously perceive the world through your default lens, making unconscious associations and wondering why certain situations keep repeating themselves. On the other hand when you do the inner work to discover the source of your triggers and attend to this with loving compassion, *everything in your life changes.*

Jean's Story

A vibrant and vivacious woman in her thirties came to me for support with her relationships and her career path. Let's call her Jean. She grew up in a tight-knit family and community with deep ties to their ethnic heritage. With an open ESP she was especially attuned to the moods of her parents. Her father, in particular, trained her from a young age to cater to his wishes and desires, so much so that she found it difficult to know what she wanted for herself. She'd pursued and excelled at the career path her father laid out for her. But she was increasingly disillusioned with the work and headed toward burnout.

As we worked together she came to see that she didn't have clear or firm boundaries or a strong sense of what was and wasn't right for her. She overworked because her organization was under-funded and under-staffed and she believed in the significance of the work itself. She habitually catered to other people's needs and lacked awareness of her own. Everyone loved her because of her ability to tune in to and anticipate their needs. She received satisfaction from being able to support people in this way, but it was wearing thin. She knew her relationships and her job were draining her, but she didn't exactly know why or what to do about it.

Together we designed a morning Sadhana practice that included dance, breathwork, meditation, and writing. She decided to put herself first in the order of her day. This way she could focus on tuning in to her own thoughts, feelings, and needs before getting caught up in the intensity of her work or the demands of other people.

As she came to understand the potential dynamics of her open ESP, she began to see how entangled she was with her family and her work.

A big piece of her identity was built on her ability to support others, so unpacking this disrupted her sense of self. She started setting boundaries at work, not beginning early or working past a certain time. She unraveled the way she was personally invested in the success of actions at work, realizing that forces much larger than she were influencing these outcomes.

She also reflected on her choices to accommodate her father's desires for her. In the culture he grew up in, children, especially girl children, followed the path laid out for them by their parents, from career choices to arranged marriages. He hadn't tried to arrange a marriage for her, but he'd let it be known that it was her job to do as he said and he emotionally manipulated her to get what he wanted.

Her father wasn't a bad man, and the tactics he employed are quite common. Most of us have been conditioned into some form of co-dependence in which the emotional well-being of different individuals are tangled up together. Some people overtly and purposefully manipulate others emotionally to get what they want, using the shadow aspect of emotional power. Others do this unconsciously, simply carrying out the ways in which they were taught that families and relationships work.

As Jean gained perspective on her upbringing she became more aware of her habits of unconsciously accommodating others and was able to start shifting them. She also grew increasingly aware of how she expected other people to act and the way she judged them if they didn't live up to her (unspoken) expectations. She became able to draw back from both her tendency to cater to others and projecting her expectations onto them. Slowly she disentangled herself and focused on building her power within.

A Pure Generator, she learned how to use her Strategy and inner Authority to dance with the Flow of Life and to gain access to her inner guidance. By the time we completed our time together, she knew how to get clarity for herself about what she wanted and how to go about creating that. She'd trained in a new field and was preparing a portfolio for her transition. She'd made peace on the inside with how she'd been raised and had a much clearer understanding of how to create meaningful relationships that could foster both sovereignty and intimacy.

Working with Your Inner Child, One of Your "Parts"

Relationship expert, marriage and family therapist, and *New York Times* best-selling author Katherine Woodward Thomas offers this helpful analogy: We all have many "parts" of our personality, each with her own perspective, story, needs, and desires.[13] Sometimes one of the wounded parts inside vies for control, jumping into the driver's seat of your life without you agreeing to or even realizing it! You may find yourself acting out compulsively to get attention, for example, or hiding out to escape notice, or lashing out to get revenge. No inner child belongs in the driver's seat because, well, they're a child and they're not mature enough to drive on the road of life; *they can't even see over the dashboard.*

In response to the dangers of the inner child in the driver's seat, sometimes you might try to lock them in the trunk where they won't be a bother. Yet that creates unwanted consequences such as dullness or deadness inside as the little one locked away curls into a fetal position, feeling herself rejected and abandoned. Or maybe you'll start to experience stomach- or backaches as she screams and kicks trying to get out.

Whichever the case, the best place for this inner child, according to Woodward Thomas, is inside the car, in the back seat, safely strapped into her car seat. From that position she can see where you're going on the road of life; she can observe and contribute without the responsibility of being in charge. She's accepted, included, and cared for. And she even has a voice.

Most people I've worked with are aware of different aspects or "parts" of themselves. One client who was particularly theatrical talked about her

---

13 Founder of Internal Family Systems Richard Schwartz popularized the idea that we have different "parts" of our personality that play different roles stemming from different motivations. I was first introduced to the notion of "subpersonalities" by Sanaya Roman, channel for Orin. They created a guided journey to work with your subpersonalities called "Overcoming the Self-Destruct," a title that aptly names the potential consequences of one's subpersonalities being in charge of one's life. Of course the great psychotherapist Carl Jung spoke of subpersonalities as well as archetypes that arise in the collective unconscious. Literature abounds on working with the inner child. I've also heard from many people over the years about their "committee," "roundtable," and "wisdom counsel," all populated by inner aspects of self.

"committee," different faces of self with whom she'd talk. Others have a council, circle, or coven that includes aspects of self and sometimes supportive, nonphysical guides and ancestors.

The Power of the Pause

If what Bolte Taylor says is true about emotions, what might happen if you were to pause for at least ninety seconds when you feel triggered before you do or say anything? This takes attention and practice! When an unconscious program gets triggered, that response happens so fast because of the processing power of the subconscious. We call this a knee-jerk reaction, right?

What if you were able to press the pause button, not to reinforce freeze but to give yourself time so that the intensity of energy can fall, and give your cerebral cortex a chance to chime in?

If you can pause long enough to take command of the situation during those ninety seconds when the little one has jumped into the driver's seat (or tried to), you'll be able guide her back into her car seat. You can gain awareness that what's happening inside you has antecedents from long ago, and associations have been activated. You need a little time to differentiate between past and present. (This would be moving from the left-brain emotional center to the right-brain emotional center in Bolte Taylor's work.) Later, when you're in a quiet space, you can ask the little one within how she's feeling and what she needs, core tenets of NVC, and then listen as she lets you know what's happening for her. I've created a *Self-Connecting Practice* based in NVC that guides you through this. You can find it in the Resources Section of our Feminine Sovereignty online community.

Slowing down and pausing serves other purposes as well. I had the good fortune to participate in a healing workshop, led by the great pioneer in pre- and peri-natal somatic psychology Ray Castellino, called *Womb Surround*. He shared the principles of his work, one of which is "the power of the pause." In that context calling for a pause gives everyone a chance to take in and digest what's just happened. We all benefit from slowing down our communications, using fewer words, and listening and feeling more. (We'll dive into this more in *Pillar Six: Communication that Connects*.) I learned also that the pause provides your nervous system with a chance to recover from a shock or a trigger and then relax and receive what's happening.

I emphasized the value of the pause during my work with a lovely couple who'd been married for thirty years and were deeply entrenched in an unhealthy dynamic. When we started, they habitually responded to each other with lightning speed in ways that harmed each other. They knew this, but the pattern was so fast and familiar they couldn't find their way out on their own. As they learned to slow down, explain less, and listen more, they were also able to feel more. As they did this, we all could feel the energy shifting and the social nervous system of the three of us softening and opening in response. I knew at this moment that we were really getting traction with unraveling their patterns.

Human Design also teaches, as mentioned above, the benefits of pausing and taking time to get clear about what's true for you, especially when emotions and/or the ESP are involved. Pausing helps you discern if now is the right time, if others are receptive to what you want to share, and if you're in command of your expression or in the throes of an unconscious program. Yes, you have to practice becoming aware of your conditioning, *and it's oh so worth the effort!*

Power of the Breath

Breathwork practices create energetic flow in the fastest, most effective way I've ever experienced. The word for breath and spirit are the same in many languages. *Inspiration*, according to online etymology dictionary Etymonline, literally means the act of inhaling, "to put life or spirit into the human body." How you breathe is how you live; when you change the way you breathe, you change the way you experience life. When you're shocked, you stop breathing, and this imbeds the experience in the cells of your body. No amount of talking will release that energy, but conscious breathing will.

During my years as a certified Clarity Breathwork Practitioner and Trainer, I worked with hundreds of clients and students using the power of the breath to unlock stuck places inside that couldn't be cognitively resolved or even known. I witnessed imprints from birth trauma, other lives, and early life rise to the surface on the crest of the breath to be recognized, reviewed, unraveled, and released. The cells of the body energetically hold memories from our whole lives and other lives, and when super oxygenated they tremble, shake, and eventually burst open, releasing a tremendous amount of energy. As this happens the breather often receives insights and new perspectives on familiar situations, and experiences emotional flow from tears to laughter to bliss (not necessarily in that order). I have a free program that introduces you to this practice and guides you through a short session; you can find the website in the bibliography.

As I mentioned earlier, more recently I've developed my expertise in pranayama. Pranayama includes a huge range of practices designed to create specific effects such as reducing anxiety, opening the heart, building prana or life force energy, releasing anger, cleansing the auric field, and so on. Suffice it to say here that working with the breath in time-tested, proven ways will support you enormously in developing your emotional wisdom by helping you get your energy in motion where you've been *estuck*. During retreats I've done with my yoga master, I've experienced myself and witnessed in others emotional energy releasing through tears while doing a Kundalini Yoga practice. Most of the time this energy doesn't have specific content like a memory or story. It's simply energy that's been trapped in the cells of the body making its way up and out through tears. *Miraculous*!

Take Time to Assess, Integrate, and Apply What You've Learned

Phew! Exploring the many facets of emotional energy can bring up a lot! Take a few deep breaths with me and tune in to how you're feeling right now emotionally, energetically, physically, and spiritually. Pausing to tune in supports your inner awareness and your ability to absorb and integrate what you've been learning.

I've designed this section to guide you to absorb, digest, and integrate the themes of each pillar. As mentioned in the *Introduction*, my hope and intention is that you'll not just consume what I've offered here but also bring it into your life in meaningful ways. Because when you do, if you're open to it, this material will grow and transform you. If you feel the need to skip over this section, please make sure to spiral back later so you can make real in your life what you're receiving from this book. You know best how you take in and integrate new information so you can grow.

You'll find this same structure at the end of each pillar customized with the themes specific to that chapter. Below you'll find:

- **Self-Assessment**
- **Spectrum of Expression**
- **Pause, Reflect, and Review**
- **New Desired Capacities**
- **Questions for Reflection**

Self-Assessment

Now that you've had a chance to explore the potentials and pitfalls associated with emotional wisdom, it's your turn to check out where you are currently with all of this.

This section includes two parts. This first is an assessment process through which you'll be able to identify strengths and capacities you've already developed in relation to this topic, and also areas in which you may have been wounded or simply have yet to build capacity. This assessment is meant to be illuminating rather than judgmental. Please be kind rather than punitive with yourself!

The next part outlines the Spectrum of Expression for Pillar Two in terms of its three aspects: awakened/empowered, shadow, and disempowered. As you read through this part, consider what feels most accurate or most right in relation to yourself. It's possible to resonate with all three expressions, although typically one will predominate over the others. Reviewing this will give you further clues about strengths you've already developed, perspectives that may be in your way, and the capacities you may want to focus on developing.

At the end of this section, you'll have the opportunity to explore what new capacities you'd like to develop for yourself so you can gain more finesse in emotional wisdom.

Instructions

Give yourself a number 1–5 for each statement. Five means it's totally true for you, one means it's true occasionally. Leave it blank if it doesn't speak to you at all. Add up the numbers from A and B and subtract B from A. This gives you your Sovereignty Score for this pillar.

(A) Strengths and Capacities Developed

[　] I feel my emotions deeply without having them control me, at least most of the time.

[　] I purposefully use my emotional energy to create more of what I want in my life.

[　] I'm able to enjoy and appreciate my uplifting emotions without attaching to them.

[　] When I feel triggered I pause and reflect rather than react. When I've gained some insight I'm able to express how I feel without blaming or shaming others.

[　] When I experience powerful "negative" emotions, I look inside to discern what previous experience(s) might be influencing me. This gives me perspective on what's happening in the now so I can avoid projecting my default lens onto others.

(B) Wounds or Lack of Capacity

[　] Most of the time my mind is really busy, and I don't feel much of anything.

[　] I wish I could get my emotions to go away, as they just get in my way.

[　] I hate it when other people make me angry or hurt me. This makes me want to get back at them.

[ ] I often find myself in situations that challenge me emotionally, where I either want to run away or lash out.

[ ] My emotions undermine my ability to be powerful and respected in my work. It's better not to feel anything.

A = _____   B = _____   A - B = _____

This is your Sovereignty Score for Pillar Two.

If you have a positive score, this means that you've developed capacity in this area. The higher your score, the greater your strengths.

If you have a negative score – more checked from (B) than (A) – then this is a pillar where you'd benefit from building more capacity. The lower the score, the less in touch you are with the beneficial attributes of this pillar.

Spectrum of Expression

The Spectrum of Expression outlines three ways of expressing the themes, energy, and power of the pillars. Collectively we're evolving out of the power-over/disempowered paradigm that characterizes western civilization. Nevertheless we're still subject to expressing power in these ways, often without even realizing it. The three aspects of the spectrum will help you identify your tendencies and, I hope, reveal to you unconscious patterns, beliefs, or behaviors so you can become at choice about whether to continue or change them. Consider this an exploration in understanding power in the service of building your *power within*, the foundation of your personal sovereignty, and the inner support for your sovereign self.

Awakened/Empowered Expression

The awakened or empowered aspect of our emotions has two aspects. First is when you can feel your emotions without being completely overwhelmed by them unless you consciously make the choice to allow them to do so. For example during a joyous moment of receiving a gift from someone you love, or seeing your child walk for the first time, or accomplishing something you've been working on for a long time, you may choose to give in completely to that feeling of exaltation, celebration, or delight. Or when someone you love passes away, grief may rise up strongly, and you may make a deliberate choice to let it take you over. In each case these emotions will move through you until you settle back into a more neutral place.

Alternatively you may choose to sequester feelings of anger, fear, disappointment, or dismay until you have the time and space to dig into the deeper reasons you're feeling this way. This way you can keep yourself from reacting in ways you'll later regret. Yet sequestering calls for also circling back to how you were feeling, or allowing the feelings to rise again, with the intention of processing what's happening at a deeper level. In this way you build your self-awareness, self-understanding, self-knowledge, and self-compassion. When you do, you build your emotional wisdom, lift the frequency of your emotional energy, and become more in command of this potent force inside of you.

Sequestering as opposed to *suppressing* emotional energy can be very effective and respectful. Sequestering means containing your emotional energy for the time being with the inner commitment to attend to your emotions when you have the time and space to do so. You can do this on your own or with others.

Secondly, emotional energy is creative. The second awakened expression of emotional wisdom is when you intentionally and purposefully build and direct your emotional energy in relation to the *positive outcome or future* you envision. This involves elevating the frequency of your emotional energy so that it resonates with that which you desire and activates the attractive force of the heart. We'll dive deeper into this topic in *Pillar Four: Radiance and Energetic Adeptness* when we explore the radiance, magnetism, and power of the heart.

Shadow Expression

The shadow aspect of emotional energy is when we use this power – either consciously or unconsciously – to gain power, authority, or a specific outcome by manipulating or seeking to control or direct others or a situation with our emotions. *Shaming and blaming* is an obvious example that's far too common and accepted as okay behavior. Anger, frustration, and disappointment can all be used to try to control a situation, an outcome, or a person. Often we think of this as coming from people who are bullying, but this can also come from someone who's operating out of victim consciousness whether they realize it or not.

Acting from anywhere in the victim-perpetrator-rescuer paradigm can express the shadow aspect of emotional energy because each position operates inside of a power-over/disempowered dynamic. Ironically people coming from victim consciousness can be just as powerfully controlling of other people and their environment as the more obvious perpetrator type.

Disempowered Expression

The disempowered aspect of emotional energy comes in several guises. Not feeling your emotions and claiming not to have emotions tops the list. Just because you don't feel your emotions doesn't mean you don't have them. It just means you've gotten so good at ignoring or suppressing your emotions that they're locked away deep inside, layered over with *energetic body armor*. Unfortunately that can lead to ulcers or worse. My grandmother was a great example of this. I remember her drinking a glass of milk every night to calm her ulcers. She was a highly intelligent and intellectual woman who very rarely expressed emotions of any kind.

Being at the mercy of your emotions also disempowers you. This happens when unhealed traumas and hurts from the past go unresolved and then surface as a trigger. You may find yourself either shrinking and slinking away from a challenging situation or yelling and acting out only to wonder later why you did that. Emotional energy is very powerful, and if you don't learn how to be with it and ultimately command it, it will control and direct you without your conscious agreement. Either that or it will begin to eat away at you from the inside, causing emotional and eventually physical pain and even illness.

Pause, Reflect, and Review

Take a few moments as you read through the Spectrum of Expression to feel into what's true for you. You might want to write about your current understanding, how your relationship to these possibilities has changed over time for you (if it has), and if so what your journey has been like.

Now go back and review your self-assessment.

[   ] Do you think or feel any differently now that you've dug
    in a bit deeper?
[   ] Do you want to change any of your answers?
[   ] Or do you want to add to the lists offered noting what's
    been especially true for you?
[   ] At this point are you aware of wanting to develop new
    capacities in this area? If so start a list of your own or
    continue reading for my suggestions that might help you
    get started.

New Desired Capacities

To help you think and feel your way through this, I've created a list of
potential capacities you may feel drawn to. This list is suggestive and far
from exhaustive. Some may appeal to you while others may not. (Feel free
to add your own!)

Now rank this list in the order of significance to you, one meaning
this is a high priority for you, and five being "not relevant to me, at least
not now."

[   ] I'd like to be able to feel my emotions, but not be over-
    whelmed or ruled by them.
[   ] I want to learn how to harness my emotional power to
    create more of what I want in my life and less of what I
    don't want.
[   ] I'd like to be able to find peace and calm even when my
    life feels really challenging.
[   ] Developing better boundaries with other people would
    really benefit me.
[   ] I want more clarity about what's mine and what's some-
    one else's. Sometimes I get very confused about whose
    emotions are whose.

Once you've ranked these possibilities, name your top two priorities.
What can you do this week to begin to develop this valuable skill?

Reflection Questions

I invite you to review and ponder these questions in any way that works for you. Feel free to respond to the ones that speak to you and leave the rest. You may write about them in your journal (highly recommended), take them into meditation or on a walk with you, make a sketch or painting about how they make you feel, or some other way that works for you. Writing down your reflections provides you with a record of your experiences, which can be very helpful later. As we evolve we tend to forget where we were, and that makes it difficult to appreciate how much we've grown.

> What did you discover about yourself through the self-assessment and Spectrum of Expression? Did you feel affirmed in some way? Did anything surprise or disturb you? Are you inspired to develop any new capacities?

> What can you do this week to begin to develop this valuable new capacity? What resources do you need? What do you need to prepare? Is there any resistance you need to face and overcome? Who in your life can support you and help hold you accountable?

> Apply what you learned or realized in Pillar Two to your Learning Question. What does this teaching add to your inquiry? What was your Learning Question(s) for this specific pillar? Make a few notes about what's arising for you including how this feels in your body.

> What were you taught about emotions as a child? Was this helpful or difficult for you – or both? How do you think this may still be influencing you? How can you make peace with your past so you can be freer in your present?

> How do you relate to and feel about your emotions? Are you able to express them in ways that feel appropriate and good to you?

> Can you think of a situation(s) in which you've co-regulated your emotional energy with others? Who were you with and what was that like?

> What are a few characteristics of your default lens? Do you have different lenses in different situations and with different kinds of people? What do you tend to assume? Which characteristics of your default lens support you and which do not? Is there anything you'd like to shift in your perspective?

> On a scale of 1–10, how would you rate your ability to respond rather than react to a challenging situation in which you might feel triggered? Do you feel able to express your emotions in ways that support your well-being and are beneficial to you and others?

> Pull out your Human Design chart. Is your ESP colored in or not? Review the discussion above about being emotionally defined or open. Does this resonate for you? What have you learned about yourself and your past experiences? What will you do or understand differently as a result of knowing this?

> What would your interactions with others be like if you were consistently able to respond rather than react in a situation that challenges you?

> What do you do to uplift your emotional energy? Have your tried breathwork or other forms of energy work to do this? What's your experience been like?

> What might open up for you if you were to uplift and master your emotional energy and then harness and direct it here as you will?

> If you were to imagine, sketch, or dance this pillar into your Temple of Sovereignty, what would it look, feel, and/or move like? Under what circumstances and for what purposes will you visit your temple? What will help you build this sacred inner sanctuary? Take out your journal and explore.

Vitality, Embodiment, and Connection with the Living World

Being physically vital, fully embodied, and aware of oneself as part of our planetary ecosystem and a member of the living world.

"You are cooling stardust from the birthing
of our planet out of our own star."

—Sue Hoya Sellers, master painter, futurist

"The body is not an object or machine.
It's thousands of processes in motion
– continually."

—Susan Harper, founder of Continuum Montage

How do I feel about my body?

How do I treat her?

Your Body: Your Most Intimate, Longest-Term Relationship

You stretch as you open your eyes, squeezing and relaxing your muscles. Rubbing your hands up and down over your arms and legs, you gently slap your face and neck, screwing up your face and sticking out your tongue. "Ahhhhh," you sigh as sleep falls away and aliveness begins to grow. You rub that spot just under your right ear where your neck has tightened up recently, slowly moving your head around on top of your spine. "Yes, I'll be careful," you murmur to your neck. "I'll pay attention and listen to you."

A long, deep drink of water quenches thirst after a long, deep night of sleep. Welcoming your body, you circle your hips widely to the right, then to the left. Your joints loosen and warm as your circling lubricates and opens them. You spiral your right foot and hip outward, then inward, then the other side. Next come wrists, elbows, and shoulders, then twisting your torso side to side, lengthening your spine. You reach up, grab one wrist with the opposite hand, and pull up and over, lengthening that whole side of the body. After you do the other side, you interlace your fingers and turn your palms upward to the sky, breathing in and out as you reach your arms up out and down. As the yogis say, *you're only as old as your spine.*

You put the top on your tea and pull on your boots as you head out into the mist. The Sun peeps through the fog but not yet with much warmth. Your neighbor walks her dogs, and kids run by on their way to school. You feel the sidewalk give way to the softer path as you move into the trees. As you wander you tune in to the Earth pushing up against you, embracing you, gently holding you to her body. You know yourself made from her minerals, filled with her waters, animated by her wind, fueled by her fires deep within. You pause and stand for a moment, reaching down into the Earth like a mountain, your head its peak.

Yet you're also always continually in motion: shifting, growing, dissolving, gurgling, consuming, integrating, and excreting. Your fluids resonate with and respond to oceans and rivers and waters *everywhere.* Life force energy courses through you, pumping your blood, beating your heart, expanding and contracting your lungs. Purposefully you breathe in the breath of the trees even as they breathe in yours.

Your body warms as you move over hills, joints loosening, muscles spiraling as they reach and pull. Your breath comes quicker, your heart beats faster, your aliveness and vitality grow as you dissolve lingering drowsiness. Your spirit aspect, your soul, looks out into the world through your eyes, feels with your skin the drips from the trees, and smells with your nose the sweetness of narcissus that wafts up to you as you pass by. You close your eyes and drink in the warmth on your cheeks from the sun just unveiled.

You nod to the squirrel running across your path and smile at the raven signaling her mate nearby. Dew steams from the meadow even as you turn back onto the sidewalk and toward home. Embodied and connected, you move forward vibrant, vital, awake, aware, *and ready*.

We Humans Are Physical Beings

You've been gifted with an extraordinarily profound and complex form, at once so fragile and so adaptable and resilient. Your consciousness continually manifesting in human form, magnificent and utterly unique.

These bodies make us capable of immense pleasure – when we're embodied and can feel through our senses and our energy bodies.

Often we equate pleasure with sexuality, and certainly healthy sexuality creates profound sensations and experiences of pleasure, especially when linked with heartfelt intimacy. Yet opportunities for pleasure surround you when you pay attention: the smell of lilacs, ocean spray, and freshly baked bread. Tiny iris and bold orange poppies along the trail in springtime. Moss underfoot near that spring you like to visit. The velvety fur of a kitten and that blue cashmere sweater. The brush of your lover's fingers across your cheek and the soft sound of their sigh. Mango bursting across your tongue and that hazelnut and brussels sprout dish you love so much. The river running softly in summertime, roaring in the spring. A heron balances on one leg, blue against gray granite.

Susan Harper, master teacher of *Continuum Montage*, helps us understand our interrelatedness with what she calls "context." You're "an expression of the planet in a human configuration," she says, including the minerals in your body, breathing in the vapors of "the green ones," breathing out food for them, drinking in water that hydrates and purifies even as it resonates with all the waters everywhere on the planet (and even in the cosmos). You gain awareness and support as you're able to feel yourself and what's "outside" of you simultaneously and more deeply. She calls this a "gifting process" inside of which you become more sensitive, letting yourself be touched by sounds and smells even as you also give back with your attention and your actions. This bigger, wider, richer range of sensations enables you to metabolize your experiences with greater ease, pleasure, and delight. *Ah, what a blessing!*

Harper invites us to perceive "the body" as "processes in motion" – thousands of them, in fact! – rather than as a solid physical form. For example, yes, your skin defines the edges of your physical form. Yet even on your skin your microbiome busily interacts with your environment, taking in what's useful and keeping out what could be harmful. Your largest organ, your skin exhales toxins, sloughs off dead matter, and thankfully receives your exfoliating and oiling with nourishing nutrients. Seventy trillion cells or more, always humming with profound intelligence: lungs breathing, organs digesting, cleaning, repairing, creating, heart beating, blood flowing. Even during sleep, you're never truly still.

As much as western science has come to know about the body, it has nevertheless been inhibited by its default lens of Newtonian physics, which perceives the body as a machine of pulleys and levers more than as the biological marvel it actually is. This default lens influences, even determines, our perception of the body as a chemistry lab that can be manipulated with pharmaceuticals and *repaired* by removing or replacing *faulty* parts. Developing your personal sovereignty includes liberating yourself from this mechanistic view of your body (remember Buhner's "statistical mentality" in Pillar One) and coming to appreciate the ways in which you're always co-creating with Spirit through the miracle of your physical form.

Pillar Three invites you to build your capacity to love, appreciate, care for, and enjoy your body. Even though your body is your birthright, this is not a small or easy task, largely because of your conditioning but also because of your lifestyle. Your ancestors gifted you with the opportunity for life, often through great challenge, hardship, and peril themselves. As you begin to embrace your body and foster this most intimate relationship, you help heal not just your own experience, but that of others like you and your forebearers. This is big and important work – and it's also satisfying and pleasurable.

Pause here and consciously breathe. Close your eyes, put your hands on your heart, and feel its beating. Have a moment of gratitude and appreciation for this miraculous creation. The you of everyday life, what's her relationship with her body like? If she's your most intimate, longest-term relationship, how have you been nurturing or neglecting that relationship? What can you do today to nurture her?

Being Disembodied

Mindfulness teacher and author Jon Kabat-Zinn once said, "Wherever you go, there you are." While he was inviting us to be aware of where we are in our minds (e.g., what are we thinking, attending to, avoiding?), the very same could be said of our bodies: *wherever you go, your body is there too.* Yet because of your conditioning and habits you may forget that.

In fact you may live *as if you don't have a body at all.*

Especially now. Maybe you sit and focus, gazing at a computer screen (I'm doing that right now as I write this), sometimes for many hours without moving much. Our bodies help us get from place to place and they enable us to see what we need to focus on. Our hands enable us to manipulate a keyboard and touchpad, eat food, brush our teeth, get dressed, drive a car. We privilege the cognitive and cerebral, which of course goes along with our statistical mindset and the overculture's emphasis on disembodied infotainment technology. Given this, *dissociating becomes the norm.*

We're designed to move, yet often we spend most of our time sitting; our energy settles, our muscles and connective tissue tighten to support our sedentary lifestyle. And then you wonder why your neck hurts, or your back aches, or you can't sleep well. You get annoyed because you're tired and grumpy and don't have as much energy as you'd like, not fully appreciating these as consequences of your behavior.

But you may not think about your body a whole lot, like you don't think about your car. You just head out of the house, almost late, throw your stuff in the backseat, plug in the GPS and the audiobook, and off you go. You're still thinking about the conversation that turned uncomfortable and you're afraid you offended your boss. Or why you don't have as much in the bank as you thought you had. Or what if it rains the day you've planned to go for a walk with Natalia, who you haven't seen in ages? And it's only when your whole shoulder begins to ache, like when the low tire pressure light appears on your dash, that you're pulled out of your mental revelry to notice this body you're in. *Oh huh, yeah, I guess I need to pay more attention here*, you think.

Maybe you start to feel pain or you get sick. Then you're just as likely to feel irritated and even angry as you are to feel compassion. At its worst, the body feels like an enemy. Like it's attacking you. I mean why else would you feel pain? Or feel bloated and gassy? Or have some weird autoimmune condition no one can figure out? Or have cancer and your body is literally eating itself? You just want someone or something to fix it. Make the pain go away. Go to a doctor. You're busy. *Can't I just take something for this?* you wonder.

Years ago we bought a house in Oakland that was infested with powder-post beetles. These little buggers are much more damaging to a house than termites, and the only fix was to tent the property and use a lot of pesticides to kill them. The man we bought the house from had been renting it out for a number of years and had even moved away to another county. He'd had renters come and go, and no one had really loved or fully occupied that house for a long time. On top of that the house had been empty for over six months while it was on the market. *No wonder*, I thought, *that it's been infested. No one has been here to care for it, to watch over it and make sure it gets what it needs.* So by the time we received it, the treatment had to be extreme.

Something similar happens with our bodies. When no one's home, no one's caring and watching over her, no one's listening or, worse, someone's judging and criticizing her, then the doors swing open to unfriendly visitors. Harmful bacteria and unfriendly viruses can take root. You feed those microbes their favorite sugary foods and then you wonder why they set up whole colonies inside you. *Abandoned housing (bodies) makes a happy home for the weary traveler.*

Why have we abandoned our bodies? Why do we ignore our bodies until they hurt? Why do we criticize our bodies as if they are inadequate and not showing up for their jobs? Why do we perceive our conscious awareness as separate from our physical form, as if they are two entities? When you're not *in your body*, you're vulnerable to things outside yourself in a way that you're not if you're more physically embodied, *just like my house in Oakland.*

Criticizing the Body

I don't think I personally know a single woman whom I haven't heard criticize her body at some point. It doesn't matter what shape, size, color, age, or kind of features she has: something always seems to be at issue. The size of her belly, the texture of her skin, the quality of her hair, the shape of her hips or breasts. Almost any body part can come under attack. Women can even compete with each other about whose body has more imperfections: who has the bigger belly or hips, better or worse skin, who has more weight to lose or more wrinkles to worry about. I think perhaps this is particularly rampant in the United States. I hope that women elsewhere haven't been so heavily conditioned to hate their bodies.

I can criticize my own body. I'm more aware of it now, and I don't feed that kind of self-harming when I catch it. I'm embracing my wrinkles and accepting changes in my skin. Still, I color my hair and I like being a certain size. On a difficult day when I haven't had enough sleep, I can find plenty I don't like so much. Mostly I watch this inner dialogue now, a movie playing itself out *with barely an audience in attendance.*

But it's so insidious, so deeply programmed in us. We're surrounded by air-brushed, media-generated images of women who don't exist in nature. Unnaturally long legs, hair that can't possibly belong to a human being, smoother-than-baby-bottom skin. It takes energy to constantly push away the presentation of *beautiful* women that streams out of social media and television and movies. Even when we know so much of this imaging is fake, it can be difficult and exhausting to draw the psychic boundaries we need to be unaffected by it.

Of course for those of us who are gender nonconforming, who have been assigned a racial categorization other than "white," or who are differently abled, the dissonance can be deafening. The continual barrage of messaging that says: *you need this product, and this product, oh and this one, too, in order to just be okay.*

Makeup and Beauty

I've been shooting a lot of video as I've been building my YouTube channel, so I decided to watch a few videos about makeup application. I'm pretty ignorant in this department. My mother only wore red lipstick while I was growing up and even then not often. I didn't wear makeup much until I started speaking on stages and shooting video. That's when I discovered that without makeup in those situations I would have what I call *pancake face*, meaning a flat face with no visible features.

I knew watching makeover videos was entering into what could be considered *dangerous territory*, but I thought if I walked away with even an idea or two that would help it would be worth it. I couldn't believe the number of products used in these videos. For what was called a simple, "natural-looking" makeover — we're not talking going out on the town or even a romantic evening — these Youtubers used anywhere from fifteen to thirty products. *Seriously.*

What an enormous industry offering solutions to problems generated by the culture at large. According to Statista.com, revenue in the cosmetic industry in 2022 was *$534 billion*, with the United States the largest share at twenty percent. *Wow.* How much money have you spent on your bag of makeup? Mine is somewhere over $500, and I know I'm on the low end.

Why do we think we need to paint ourselves? If the urge arises from a genuine appreciation for an aesthetic you love, that's one thing. A friend shared with me once that she felt she was adorning the Goddess when she put on her makeup; she was devotional. That feels lovely to me. But if the urge arises from a *not-good-enough* place, an *I-have-to-fit-in* place, an I-*won't-be-acceptable-if-I-don't* place, then that's another story altogether. Sometimes we've embraced the cultural norms of beauty and tried to fit in with clothing or makeup or body gestures or weight or size. At other times we've rejected all that and gone in the opposite direction. We put on weight. We refuse to preen. We wear sack clothing. All a big f-u to mainstream photoshopped fictions of what a woman should look like and who she should be.

Where does this drive to control and manipulate our appearance come from? Although men have this to some degree, it's nowhere near as extreme for them *on the whole*. Let's take a breath and dig into the past to find out.

The Body Remembers

Historically *as women, our bodies haven't been our own. Literally*. Fathers basically owned their daughters and traded them to men who would become their husbands. And then those husbands could do pretty much what they wanted with their wives, including raping and beating them and forcing them to work in whatever ways they wanted, including prostituting them or working them to death.

Under patriarchy we had no legal sovereignty, no ability to direct our own lives if our desires ran counter to what had been dictated for us.

And we had no recourse in the face of violence and coercion other than appealing to other powerful men in our lives to protect us. We barely existed under the law. One definition of the saying "rule of thumb" is the diameter of a stick with which a man was allowed to *beat his wife*. Our reproductive capacities, in particular, have been controlled, even legislated. After fifty years of acknowledging and protecting women's command of our own bodies, we're seeing a resurgence of draconian measures giving control of our bodies to the state and in some cases to other citizens.

All of this has been more extreme, far more extreme, for women whose racial and ethnic groups have been colonized in the last few hundred years. Raping the women, after all, is a time-tested tactic to subordinate a population, and if that doesn't suffice, slaughtering the women and children might. While we don't experience this *very much* in the west today, this still happens in communities around the world. The tribal rights of men over women go deep.[14]

Despite law and culture, many women didn't simply submit to being victimized. We learned that beauty and catching the attention of powerful men could help us gain some modicum of authority over our own lives. We competed with, manipulated, and back-stabbed each other, doing whatever we thought we needed to do in order to gain power over each other. In this way we embraced the *shadow aspect of beauty*.

Violence among women was particularly vexed between Euro-American and African and African American women under slavery. Slaveholding men legally could coerce enslaved women to be their sexual partners, raping them if necessary or desired. Slaveholding women resented the attention given to enslaved women even if the enslaved women didn't desire it or fought it off. Slaveholding women could be particularly cruel to the enslaved women they suspected or knew were the recipients of their husband's attention, taking out their frustration and anger on the women — or their children — since they couldn't or didn't want to do that to their men.

Indeed racially charged hierarchies among women have been the norm in westernized countries, a legacy we continue to grapple with today.

Some white women use their race and often their economic privilege to exploit and subordinate women of color. Indigenous women, Middle Eastern women, Latin American women, Asian women, as well as African American women have all been exploited by white women as their

---

14 A notable and vital exception to this is the ongoing abuse and disappearance of indigenous women from many nations inside the United States. Law enforcement is notoriously lax in investigating these crimes.

nannies and housekeepers. This poorly paid labor force has enabled their employers to join the white-collar workforce and build their own financial independence. Even more, a plethora of white women are rising into leadership among the radical Christian right. They seek to reestablish and fortify white supremacy, as was the norm in the southern United States for eighty-plus years during segregation (and of course before that under slavery). *No wonder many women of color are suspicious of white women's call for solidarity among women.*

To help us heal these violent histories of hierarchy and separation that are stored in our bodies, therapist, author, and thought leader Resmaa Menakam offers his groundbreaking book *My Grandmother's Hands. Menakam teaches "Somatic Abolitionism," practices enabling us to grapple with and heal the trauma from racism and white supremacy that is lodged in our bodies whatever the color of our skin and ethnic heritage.* He's researched the ways in which our trauma bodies continue to operate inside us so deeply and insidiously that *we think it's who we are.* He even suggests that what we believe to be cultural differences may more accurately be understood as *our trauma bodies interacting with each other.* While much important work on understanding and healing trauma has been done in recent years, Menakam's focus on Somatic Abolitionism brings our attention to the effects of trauma easily overlooked because they're so imbedded in our psyches. Most white people are unaware, for example, of the generational trauma we experience as colonizers or the descendants of colonizers because it's so ingrained in us. George Floyd's murder in 2020 helped many white people become aware of their own ingrained trauma as well as develop an increasing awareness of and sensitivity to that kind of trauma in people of color, especially Black people.

As we seek to gain command of our inner landscape, we're served by coming to terms with the ways in which our bodies have been written upon, some would say socially constructed, by profit-driven forces for at least five centuries. As Yoga 12 Step Recovery teacher Nikki Meyers once said, "Your race was assigned to you: it's not something you were born with."

Body Awareness

Simply naming this history can activate stored energy that then begins to ache or throb. Our bodies store memories and intelligently direct our focus to places inside that need our attention. Undigested trauma lives on deep within. In addition to our own lived experience, we also often carry ancestral trauma and imprints from our assaults on the Earth. Recently I shared with a friend that her experiences of injuries to her body aren't simply personal; as a sensitive and empathetic woman she may well be mirroring what's happening in the living world around her. *Maybe you've felt this way at times?*

Physical or emotional abuse, sexual assault, bullying, so many experiences can make you feel unsafe in your body. I've worked with many clients who were abused as kids and oftentimes they learned to *leave their bodies* because they couldn't physically leave the room or the home. Caught in a situation they couldn't change, retreating into their mind and imagination enabled them to endure something frightening or abusive (or that they experienced as such). Steven Kessler, therapist and author of *The 5 Personality Patterns*, calls this the "leaving pattern," one of five energetic responses to feeling overwhelmed that we create when young. (This work updates and simplifies Wilhelm Reich's character structures, if you're familiar with them.) If you have the leaving pattern, then when you feel overwhelmed you tend to dissociate. It could be that you physically leave if you can, but often you just retreat inside to a place where you feel you have more control. You might start to daydream, or energetically travel to another place in nonphysical, or simply focus on your thoughts to forget about your body.

We all experience at least one and usually two of the five patterns that Kessler outlines in his work. (The five patterns are leaving, merging, enduring, being aggressive, or rigid.) While Kessler calls these *personality* patterns, I find *energy* patterns to be more accurate, as these name what we do *energetically* when we feel overwhelmed. Learning more about this work is well worth the effort, as it illuminates the automatic way you energetically respond when feeling overwhelmed. Becoming sovereign includes becoming aware of such unconscious patterns and responses to outer circumstances so you can unravel, heal, and evolve them.

Typically these survival patterns outlive their usefulness when you become an adult with more command over your choices, experiences, and outer circumstances. For example with the leaving pattern, learning to leave your body probably was a smart and effective survival strategy in a situation you couldn't leave or change, which is often the case for children. Yet when this pattern continues into adulthood, when you are able to choose your environment and the people you surround yourself with, your tendency to "leave" will undermine your full functioning and experience of life.

If you don't become aware of and loosen the hold these patterns have over you, then you'll continue to see the world through the default lens they create and act in accordance with it. This inhibits your clear perception and binds your energy into certain specific ways of responding, limiting your options. When you're able to break out of these patterns, you'll liberate your consciousness along with a lot of energy that's been locked up inside of them.

When you feel disassociated or disconnected from your body, it can be very difficult to feel like you belong here on Earth.

Bodies are complex, and your relationship to your body is complex. As you develop your body awareness and become willing to contact and heal your trauma, you become more able to heal and grow. You then become more alive and vital, more embodied, more at home in the body and at home here on planet Earth: the two are inextricably intertwined.

The "aggressive pattern" is my main pattern, and "leaving" is my secondary one. When I feel upset or overwhelmed, my body quickly fills with energy that wants to move up and outward. As I mentioned in Pillar Two, people around me often have interpreted this as anger coming at them. And honestly sometimes it has been. Yet many more times it wasn't – but the intensity of this *energy pattern* made it feel that way to other people. Learning this has helped me realize how I can influence others, and this encouraged me to develop greater command of my energy so that when it rises up it doesn't go out toward others. I've had to build my capacity to notice when this pattern gets activated and then use my tools – such as pausing, breathing, or doing something physically intense – to contain or dissipate the energy so I can become clear-minded again. It hasn't been easy, but it's been very worth the effort.

What do you know about what you do energetically when you feel overwhelmed? Take a few breaths and tune in. Without even looking up Kessler's work, do you resonate with any of the patterns (leaving, merging, enduring, aggressive, rigid)? You may consider them tendencies and not understand their function. Does this serve or undermine you? What could you do differently now that you know? Explore in your journal.

Building Your Vitality, Embodiment, and Connection with the Living World

In Pillar Two we looked at how Enlightenment philosophers promoted the value of logic, reason, rationality, analysis, and strategy, all left-brained characteristics. The overculture, fuel by western science, has positioned these characteristics as the *only valid path* to knowledge and truth ever since. Yet we're so much more than that, and life is so much richer than can be accounted for by this way of being.

Fortunately, as we first saw in Pillar One, Human Design helps right this imbalance by mapping and validating both the Knowing Circuit and the Sensing Circuit, which is right-brained energy.

Bolte Taylor, as we saw in Pillar One, also helps us understand, *anatomically*, the role and attributes of the right brain, further emphasizing their significance. Let's take a closer look at the Sensing Circuit.

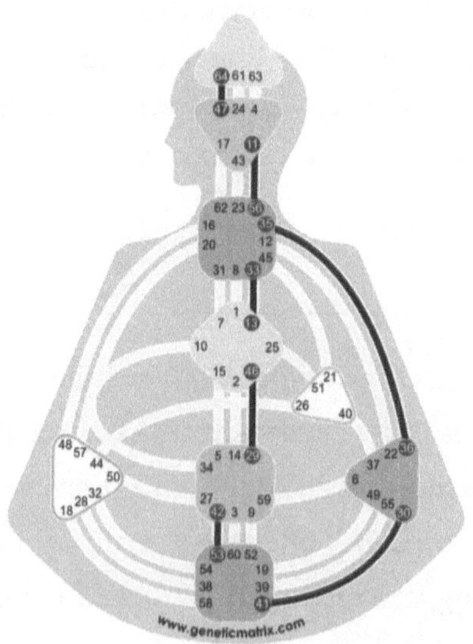

The Sensing Circuit begins in the right brain, crosses to the left in the Ajna Center, runs down the left side of the body, then back up the central channel in front of the spine to the Throat Center.

As we saw earlier, this energy is creative, experiential, spatial, embodied, emotional, imaginative, expansive, and spiritual, and includes the quality of storytelling. We revere these qualities in artists, musicians, dancers, athletes, and writers, yet often think we don't have them ourselves. *I'm not creative* and *I'm not artistic* are common attitudes. Our conditioning tells us creative works are *nice*, but *not truly significant* and not all that *valuable.* That's one reason it's difficult for artists to make a living, right?

Yet Human Design shows us that right-brained energy, mapped in the Sensing Circuit, is just as significant as left-brained energy, mapped in the Logic Circuit. Ironically these circuits mirror each other. When I meet with someone who has a lot of the Sensing Circuit in their chart, I spend significant time exploring with them what is their relationship to this energy, explaining that it's one of their superpowers and they'll benefit from owning and expressing it.

One man who came to me for a reading had more definition in the Sensing Circuit than any other circuit in his chart. I asked him if he did creative work or was aware of his right-brain power.

He tilted his head and said, "No, mostly I work with doctors, and we're science-based in what we do."

I went deeper. "Were you ever more creative or musical, maybe as a kid?"

His face lit up as he said, "Yes! I played the piano and the violin. I also liked to act things out, like from a TV show or movie. I was also a star athlete. I've always been physically active."

"What happened?" I asked.

"Well," he replied, "there came a point when none of that mattered as much as other things in school. I also got picked on a bit for playing the violin. The other guys didn't think it was something guys do. So I quit."

"Hmm, okay, I can understand that," I replied, even as my heart hurt for him a bit. "This is a superpower in your chart. It sounds like you haven't used it in a long time, but that doesn't mean it's gone. You can't really lose it. You told me that your wife has been telling you she'd like you to be more sensitive, less driven all the time. Would you consider picking up an instrument again or doing something creative? It just might help you break out of that left-brained dominance and open up new possibilities for you."

He had a little smile on his face as if this had never occurred to him. "Yeah," he said wistfully, "I really did like playing that violin."

Playing an instrument is experiential, embodied, expressive, and creative. It requires concentration, practice, commitment, and even devotion if you want to get good at it. Even though I have just one gate (out of fourteen) defined in my Sensing Circuit, I feel very embodied due to my years studying dance and many forms of movement and somatic practice. I love to express myself creatively through movement, including Kundalini Yoga. I've developed my capacity in these areas so that they've become a welcome and supportive part of me, and you can, too, if you want. So much becomes possible when you do.

> *"We can attune to the fact that in one sense it's my breath. But in another way, we could say we're part of a breathing planetary body that breathes us all night long. When we're sleeping, we don't have to be aware of it. Breathing is happening. I can attune to the larger planetary breathing body that is breathing each one of us. Breath is life."*
> —Susan Harper

An Embodiment Practice

Take a moment now, dear one, and place your left hand on your heart and your right hand on top of the left. Close your eyes and deepen your breath. Can you feel your heart beating? Amazing, right? Your heart beats your entire life, never taking a break! Notice how your belly and chest fill and empty with every breath, air flowing in through your nostrils and carbon dioxide flowing out as you exhale. You welcomed breath into your body as you made your way out of your mother's body at birth. You will bid breath goodbye as your heart stops, your spirit drops this form, and you walk into your future. Heart beating, lungs breathing, on and on without you needing to *make anything happen.*

Now, with your eyes still closed, see if you can feel your body from the inside. See if you can tune into:

- your body's shape from the inside
- your hands on your chest as it rises and falls
- your chest with your hands by shifting your perspective
- your right hand on top of your left
- your left hand lightly pressing up against your right
- where your body touches the chair or sofa you're sitting on
- the Earth under you, under the building you're in
- the Earth pushing up against you, inviting you to soften and receive her support
- the embrace of gravity

How do you feel now after tuning in?

As Harper notes, "gravity is a force of belonging." The planet holds us here even as she spins at an unfathomable rate around both her own axis and around our own star. *You belong here,* Gaia whispers silently, *you are made of me just as I was made from our Sun, our own star.* Indeed gravity keeps us in relation to our planet and each other, and gravity holds our planet and all of us in the fiery embrace of our star. "You are cooling stardust," as Sue Hoya Sellers, visionary painter and futurist, once noted.

As you expand your awareness to include your body and the ways in which your body resides inside a complex web of relationships, you can become aware of resources available to you that otherwise may be opaque to you. Susan Harper suggests that much of our suffering arises from living inside a *too narrow version of our body* and its and our relationship to the world around us. If you live inside a self-concept that understands you primarily as *a mind,* you cut yourself off from your body. If you perceive yourself as an autonomous body, you cut yourself off from the breathing of the trees; the dance of Moon and fluids that creates tides inside of you as well as in the ocean; the profound sense of being held by the planet. *How lonely is that?*

Honoring the Cycles of the Living World

Before western science especially and still today, indigenous people all over the world orient themselves to the cycles of the Sun and Earth that create days, seasons, and years. The Celtic peoples of what is now the

United Kingdom and Old Europe, my forebearers, organized their lives in relation to the Celtic Wheel with four major touchstones at the apex of winter and summer (Solstice) and the balance points of Spring and Fall (Equinox). Samhain (commonly known as Halloween) marked the beginning of winter and time for preparing for hibernation; and Beltane (May Day) marked the beginning of summer and the time for planting and celebrating fecundity. Many of us currently honor these cycles and orient ourselves to these Earth-based holy days rather than to Christian ones (which often were placed on top of the more ancient ones).

Indigenous peoples of the Americas created monuments to mark the changes of season. For example the Incas created Machu Pichu, the Maya created Chichen Itza, and the ancient pueblo people of what is now New Mexico created Chaco Canyon, all of which mark changes of season in some way. The pyramids and Sphinx of ancient Egypt, too, mark changes in season. These monuments speak to us from ancient times, giving us a glimpse into these cultures' worldviews and relationship to the cycles of time. The ancient Mayan calendar, for example, tracks centuries of astronomical movements with accuracy astonishing to modern western people.

As electrical and internet technology have grown, our relationship with these cycles has deteriorated. Those of us in the global north now live in a 24/7/365 culture. You literally can, and some people do, work around the clock every day of the year. Some thirty-five percent of the US population doesn't get the minimum recommended amount of sleep (seven hours per night), and eight out of ten teenagers don't get the recommended eight hours of sleep on school nights. Too little sleep results in chronic sleep deprivation, depression, and a plethora of health issues.

How much sleep do you get? How rested do you feel?

Before electricity and central heating became the norm, people often slept or were in bed for twelve to fourteen hours a night during the winter months. Long periods of rest fostered deep dream states and connection with the imaginal realm. Storytelling, crafting practical objects infused with meaning and symbol, and creating and mending clothing and coverings for sleep occupied the cold and shorter days. People emerged from this semi-hibernation hungry, yes, and also deeply rested and prepared for the expanding and demanding days of spring and summer. Then they slept less, worked physically harder, and reveled in the rooting, sprouting, blossoming, and fruiting of their harvests and the world around them. *It was a very different life.*

It's time we recognize that we've traded *vitality* for *comfort* and *convenience*. Ouch, right?

Our physiology has been more or less the same for the last 150,000 years or more.[15] Yet in the last 150 years, and especially in the last 50, our lifestyles have changed dramatically and our bodies and nervous systems are suffering. You don't have to be victimized by these changes; you have agency and choice about how to live even if some things are out of your control. Becoming sovereign includes reestablishing or establishing more deeply your relationship with your body and her needs and desires. It's vital you give yourself what you truly need, not what profit-driven forces want you to consume.

We all need to gain understanding about what harms us individually and collectively and do what we can to avoid, mitigate, and eliminate those factors. *Healing and evolving ourselves and regenerating our world are intricately connected.*

Nurturing Your Physical Vitality

Your physical body is made of the elements of the Earth plus animating life force energy and your own soul force. Your physical body suffers when you disregard the fundamentals: nutritious food, clean air and water, plentiful sleep, and fluid, nonregimented movement. Our ancestors had most of these in abundance, though at certain times of year or in some years they went hungry. Inside of what Riane Eisler calls "dominator societies," sometimes people were deprived of food, water, or sleep, but that was because of human intervention, not because of lack in the living world.

In today's living world, in places most affected by the Story of Progress, ironically many, even most, people suffer from a lack of all of these things.

---

15   The most recent estimate I heard from Ursula Goodenough, Professor of Biology Emeritus, is homo sapiens emerged 300,000 ago. *Wow!*

People in poorer, especially urban, communities suffer more in terms of air and water pollution and lack of access to nutritious food. Ron Finley, known as the "Guerrilla Gardener," notes that asthma rates are much higher among children in his neighborhood of East Los Angeles (a lower-income community of color), for example, than in the more affluent community of Beverly Hills, which is nearby. Yet even those with more resources experience poisons in commercially grown food, air polluted by cars and industry, pain and dysfunction from sedentary lifestyles, and, as I said above, not enough sleep.

You really have to be intentional and focused – devoted even – to provide your body with what she needs. Some of this requires investing money, others time, and all of them your attention. The predominance of commercial farming, the junk and fake food industry, the oil and gas industry, and big pharma – all profit-driven forces – make it difficult to find nutritious food, and clean air and water. Finley got tired, he said, of having to drive twenty minutes in order to buy a tomato that hadn't been poisoned by pesticides. He took matters into his own hands, turning the parking strip in front of his house into a vegetable garden. He's now started a movement of urban gardeners in his community that grow and provide fresh, nutritious food in what's otherwise a food desert.

In my research for this book virtually every advocate for regenerative civilization that I've heard from says the first thing any of us can do is to begin to *grow our own food*.

When you do, you have command of what goes into the soil and how you treat the plants. Plus you also begin to build your relationship with the living world and with your own body. You can start with herbs on a windowsill or a few pots on a patio or porch if you don't have access to a yard. Many resources are now being developed for people in cities to grow food in the most unexpected places and ways. (More about this in Pillars Seven and Eight.)

You have command over what you put into your body. You decide what to eat, what to drink, what medications and supplements to take. You can begin by taking another look at what you do habitually and being honest with yourself if it's serving you. It's so easy to be habituated if not addicted to sugar, caffeine, gluten, fried foods, dairy products, alcohol, and pharmaceutical as well as recreational drugs. Market forces thrive on us consuming these things; marketing and media normalize this behavior. Taking off the blinders created by these forces can reveal the surprisingly dysfunctional habits many of us share.

I could, and in the future I may, write a whole book about food culture, as I've been a student and advocate for food as medicine for decades. I've upgraded my physiology and remade my body more than once with the power of food. I invite you to bring more consciousness into this area of your life. My experience is that many people feel very attached to their food and find making changes difficult. Part of this is cultural, part habitual or addictive, part ignorance, and honestly part is simply laziness! As you take a deeper look, see what's true for you.

Some things are common to all of us. Some are very idiosyncratic. For example some people swear by tomatoes, and for others they are poison. Some can eat gluten with no ill effects, while some can do so in Europe and not in the United States (*interesting, right?*), others feel much better if they avoid it most or all of the time, and still others are truly allergic. As I make suggestions about what to choose, you'll need to decide what works and is the right timing for you. I just invite you to notice if you feel triggered, dismissive, or otherwise resistant. If so *why is that?*

- **Nourish your body**: Eat more vegetables, especially green ones. You can't overdo it. Juice them if you'd like or put them in a smoothie. Fruit is great, too, in moderation, as it does have a fair bit of sugar (fructose). Juicing fruit concentrates the sugar, so it's best consumed in small amounts.
- **Care for your blood sugar**: Eat less sugar and simple carbohydrates (flour products); drink less alcohol. Spiking and crashing your blood sugar makes you feel horrible. This may add you to the diabetes epidemic we're experiencing in the US these days.
- **Avoid poison**: Select organic and non-GMO food. This standard is far from perfect, but it's the only thing we've got right now. Yep, it's more expensive. It's also more nutritious, and it won't make you or the Earth sick. Check out "The Dirty Dozen" in the bibliography for the foods you most need to buy organic.

- **Choose fresh, unprocessed food**: If it comes in a box or a can and is shelf-stable, it's been processed and probably contains preservatives. Read the label. Can you pronounce all the ingredients? If not don't eat it or eat sparingly.

- **Eat *real* food**: Has it been around for at least a hundred years? Some items, like olives and olive oil, have been around for millennia and have stood the test of time. (Make sure it's real, cold-pressed virgin olive oil though.) Others are *food-shaped objects* made out of human-made ingredients.

- **Local and seasonal**: Shop at farmers' markets, either organic or regenerative if possible. The food will be fresher than what you get in the grocery store and guaranteed to be in season. You'll also be supporting cleaner, healthier farming practices. If you don't have a farmers' market nearby, then shop at the nearest natural food store and seek out what's locally grown and in season. Request it if they don't already have it.

- **Try something new:** Diversity supports your microbiome and overall health. There are 7500 varieties of apples, yet you see maybe ten in the grocery store if you're lucky. Seek out new varieties of familiar foods and food new to you. Ask at your farmers' markets and request more varieties at your local natural foods store.

- **Filter your water:** Virtually all water now has been contaminated either with glyphosate (a main ingredient in Roundup®), heavy metals, plastics, pharmaceuticals, and other poisons. Buying water from springs high in the mountains requires burning fossil fuels and plastic bottles, so that's not your best choice. Filtering your water is less expensive too. Use filtered water for cooking and ice as well as for drinking.

- **Filter your air:** If you live in an urban area or in wildfires areas like I do, filtering your air really supports your lungs. Particulate matter that you can't see can be very damaging. Not only that, common products inside the home – like paint and carpets – can outgas *for years*.

- **Use nontoxic everything:** Dish soap, body wash, toothpaste, laundry soap, bathroom cleaner, makeup – anything you clean with or put on or in your body. Even fragrances can disrupt your hormone levels and neurotransmitters. *Is it really worth it?*

And then also, in the service of your vitality:

· **Get at least seven to eight hours of sleep every night:** Get off electronics a couple of hours before your turn out your light (no TVs in the bedroom!). Read a book. Have a restful conversation. Do a restorative yoga practice. Write in your journal. Have sensual/ sexual play with yourself or others. Take a salt bath.
· **Grow something:** Especially herbs, vegetables, and flowers for bees, butterflies, or hummingbirds. Discover the cycle of the seasons by tracking when to seed, plant, tend and water, and harvest. Eat your own food and share your bounty with others. Sequester carbon in the soil with perennials and trees native to your area.
· **Move often throughout your day:** Stretch when you get up and throughout your day. Get up, move around, wiggle your pelvis, ribcage, and shoulders. Go for a walk. Go to the gym. Ride a bike. Do some yoga or Pilates. Dance! So many ways to move.
· **Regularly practice some form of conscious breathing:** Take a few long, deep breaths when you wake up and before you go to bed. Explore how different breathing techniques influence your body and your perception. (More on all of this in the chapter *Your Daily Date with the Divine.*)

Pick one or two suggestions from this list – or from new ones that occur to you – and explore bringing this into your life this week. You might pick one that feels easier and one that feels more difficult so you stretch yourself but don't try to take on too much at once.

Track in your journal how this experiment works for you – how do you feel (physically, emotionally, energetically), what do you welcome, what do you resist? What needs to shift inside of you and in your outer reality to integrate this change? Make sure to acknowledge your efforts and celebrate change.

Take Time to Assess, Integrate, and Apply What You've Learned

Terrific! How are you feeling now that you've dug deep and wide into the themes of vitality, embodiment, and the living world in Pillar Three? This material can be activating. Give yourself a break to pause and reflect on these themes as they appear in your life.

I've designed this section to guide you to absorb, digest, and integrate the themes of each pillar. As mentioned in the *Introduction*, my hope and intention is that you'll not just consume what I've offered here but also bring it into your life in meaningful ways. Because when you do, if you're open to it, this material will grow and transform you. If you feel the need to skip over this section, please make sure to spiral back later so that you can make real in your life what you're receiving from this book. You know best how you take in and integrate new information so you can grow.

You'll find this same structure at the end of each pillar customized with the themes specific to that chapter. Below you'll find:

- **Self-Assessment**
- **Spectrum of Expression**
- **Pause, Reflect, and Review**
- **New Desired Capacities**
- **Questions for Reflection**

Self-Assessment

Now to identify strengths and capacities you've already developed in relation to this topic, as well as areas in which you may have been wounded or simply haven't yet built capacity. Let's see what you discover.

Instructions

Give yourself a number 1–5 for each statement. Five means it's totally true for you, one means it's true occasionally. Leave it blank if it doesn't speak to you at all. Add up the numbers from A and B and subtract B from A. This gives you your Sovereignty score for this pillar.

(A) Strengths and Capacities Developed

[　] I love, enjoy, and appreciate my body despite its "imperfections."

[　] I feel physically vital and have the stamina I need to do what I want in life (most of the time).

[   ] I know what my body needs to be well and I provide
that regularly (high-quality food, fresh air, clean water,
movement, time in nature, rejuvenating rest).

[   ] Even though I may be mentally active much of the time, I
also know how to and practice being *in my body* every day.

[   ] I recognize that I'm part of the larger living world, that
my body is related to the body of the Earth, and that the
health and vitality of both are intricately and inextricably
connected.

(B) Wounds or Lack of Capacity

[   ] I spend most of my time in my head. It's where I feel most
comfortable.

[   ] I have to drink coffee (or another caffeinated drink) in
order to get going and keep going through my day.

[   ] I dislike, even hate my body at times. I criticize it often. I
don't like the way it looks or how clothes fit me.

[   ] Sometimes I go outside, but mostly I prefer doing things
on my computer and my phone.

[   ] I don't have the time or money to spend on organic
designer food. I get what's convenient and what I can
afford.

A = _____   B = _____   A − B = _____

This is your Sovereignty Score for Pillar Three.

If you have a positive score, this means that you've developed capacity
in this area. The higher your score, the greater your strengths.

If you have a negative score – more checked from (B) than (A) – then
this is a pillar where you'd benefit from building more capacity. The
lower the score, the less in touch you are with the beneficial attributes
of this pillar.

Spectrum of Expression

The Spectrum of Expression outlines three ways of expressing the themes, energy, and power of the pillars. Collectively we're evolving out of the power-over/disempowered paradigm that characterizes western civilization. Nevertheless we're still subject to expressing power in these ways, often without even realizing it. The three aspects of the spectrum will help you identify your tendencies and, I hope, reveal to you unconscious patterns, beliefs, or behaviors so you can become at choice about whether to continue or change them. Consider this an exploration in understanding power in the service of building your *power within*, the foundation of your personal sovereignty, and the inner support for your sovereign self.

Awakened/Empowered Expression

In the awakened or empowered expression of Pillar Three, you give attention to your physical body every day. You know that how you feel emotionally and mentally are intricately tied to the health, vitality, and well-being of your physical body. You move in ways that feel good to you, as you recognize that humans are designed to move. You feel sensual and connected to yourself as a sexual being. You enjoy experiencing life through your senses: smelling roses, tasting chocolate, feeling your kitty's fur, hearing your favorite music, appreciating the beauty of a permaculture food forest. You feel at home in your body and play with your relationship to gravity.

You honor the seventy trillion cells that work together to create your physical home. You recognize that these cells have consciousness, too, and that they're busy breathing, digesting, and moving blood and lymph, all so you can live your life. You speak to your body with love and respect and feel gratitude for her even when you're not feeling great. In that case, you turn inward and ask your body what she needs. You may take in the advice of experts, but you also know that you're the one in charge of your health and well-being and that when you listen to your body, she'll guide you.

Shadow Expression

You're expressing the shadow aspect if you use your looks and sexual appeal to manipulate and control others, even subtly or unconsciously. This might include, for example, seeking to gain attention and favors from others, pitting yourself against others for the attention and approval of men, or tearing down others based on their looks. You might use sex to gain power. Alternately you may use physical strength to get your way or to force others to do your will. You might also have this attitude toward your own body, seeking to manipulate and control it, or criticize or punish it.

Another dimension of this is when you dominate the natural environment, particularly in ways that harm the ecosystem and living world. In terms of the collective, you can see this in the ways we've been extracting as much power (coal, oil, gas, trees) and other "resources" (e.g., precious earth metals especially for electronics) as we can and leaving dead and toxic places in our wake. Yet you can also find this closer to home in how you treat the land you're living on, for example using pesticides, herbicides, chemical fertilizers, cutting down trees, disturbing natural waterways, or even building a house.

Disempowered Expression

Chronic illness, body dysphoria, and eating disorders are all disempowered expressions of this pillar. You feel disconnected from your body. You may even see it as an enemy that's turned against you. Maybe you live in your head and lose track of even having a body. You may have mastered not feeling your body, probably to mask discomfort, pain, or trauma. Alternately you often criticize and beat up on your body. You may do this emotionally or mentally, or you may even do this physically.

In terms of our world, you believe there's nothing you can do to support the healing of our planet. You have given up hope for regeneration and do your best not to think about what's happening to our ecosystems on a larger scale. You express or experience denial of climate change, species extinction, and environmental collapse.

Pause, Reflect, and Review

Take a few moments as you read through the Spectrum of Expression to feel into what's true for you. You might want to write about your current understanding, how your relationship to these possibilities has changed over time for you (if it has), and if so what your journey has been like.

Now go back and review your self-assessment.

- Do you think or feel any differently now that you've dug in a bit deeper?
- Do you want to change any of your answers?
- Or do you want to add to the lists offered, noting what's been especially true for you?
- At this point are you aware of wanting to develop new capacities in this area? If so start a list of your own or continue reading for suggestions that might help you get started.

New Desired Capacities

To help you think and feel your way through this, I've created a list of potential capacities you may feel drawn to. This list is suggestive and far from exhaustive. Some may appeal to you while others may not. (Feel free to add your own!)

Now rank this list in the order of significance to you, one meaning this is a high priority for you, and five being "not relevant to me, at least not now."

- [　] I'd like to cook more. I think it would be fun and less expensive to eat good food that way.
- [　] Even though exercising has been hard for me, I'd like to find something I enjoy and stick with it. I think I'll feel better and have more energy if I do.
- [　] I don't want to keep being so critical of my body. I know I've been conditioned by what I see in the media and I know it's not even real bodies that we see with all the airbrushing that's routine now. I'd like to begin liking, even loving my body. It's the only one I've got!

[   ] I'd like to create a garden this year, even just a small one,
       so I can be in touch more with what's growing when and
       weather patterns. I'd love to have some flowers I can cut
       for the house, herbs, and a few of my favorite veggies. I
       can even start in pots first.
[   ] I'm going to make sleep more of a priority for me. I have a
       tendency to stay up late and I don't even know why exactly.
[   ] Okay, I'm inspired! I'm going to tear up my lawn and
       plant food.

Once you've ranked these possibilities, name your top two priorities. You'll find many more suggestions in Pillars Seven and Eight for what you can do to build your capacity in these areas. What can you do this week to begin to develop this valuable skill? You'll find helpful suggestions to support you with this in the next section.

Reflection Questions

I invite you to review and ponder these questions in any way that works for you. Feel free to respond to the ones that speak to you and leave the rest. You may write about them in your journal (highly recommended), take them into meditation or on a walk with you, make a sketch or painting about how they make you feel, or some other way that works for you. Writing down your reflections provides you with a record of your experiences, which can be very helpful later. As we evolve, we tend to forget where we were and that makes it difficult to appreciate how much we've grown.

> What did you discover about yourself through the self-
  assessment and Spectrum of Expression? Do you feel affirmed
  in some ways? Does anything surprise or disturb you? Are you
  inspired to grow your capacity in any particular area?

> What can you do this week to begin to develop this valuable
  new capacity? What resources do you need? What support
  do you need? What do you need to prepare? Is there any
  resistance you need to face and overcome? Who in your life
  can partner with you and help hold you accountable?

> Apply what you learned or realized in Pillar Three to your primary Learning Question. What does this teaching add to your inquiry? What was your Learning Question(s) for this specific pillar? Make a few notes about what's arising for you including how this feels in your body.

> Do you feel physically vital and have the stamina you need to meet your life? On a scale of 1–10, how much energy do you have most days? What do you do to nurture and care for your physical body? What else could you do that would be supportive and feel good to you?

> Do you know what your body needs in terms of food, rest, exercise, massage, sex, healing modalities, or movement? Do you have a practice of asking your body what she needs and listening or tuning inward for a response? Do you give her what she asks for?

> How embodied are you? Are you able to engage with life through body awareness and experience that is nonverbal and movement-oriented? Can you sense through your body? When you close your eyes, can you trace the outline of your physical form with your mind's eye? Can you tell where your body is in space from the inside? What helps you develop your *felt sense*?

> What's your relationship with the living world, such as the ecosystem of the place where you live? Do you know what trees and plants are growing around you? What kind of birds live nearby? What's your relationship with the animals in your area?

> Do you spend time with your feet directly on the earth and drinking in the warmth of the sun or the replenishment of rain? Do you tune in to the embrace of gravity? Does it help you feel that you belong here on planet Earth?

> What would become possible for you if you were to practice *being in your body*, listening to your body wisdom and that of the living world?

> If you were to imagine, sketch, or dance this pillar into your Temple of Sovereignty, what would it look, feel, and/ or move like? How is it similar to the first two pillars? How is it different? How do the pillars relate to each other? What different strengths do each of them bring?

Radiance and Energetic Adeptness

Having the energetic power and resilience to effectively meet life's challenges with confidence and clarity. Knowing how to build and harness your energy and direct it when and where you will.

"Yoga is not an ancient myth buried in oblivion.
It is the most valuable inheritance of the present.
It is the essential need of today
and the culture of tomorrow."

—Swami Satyananda Saraswati

"We are only as strong and vital as is our energy.
The more we dissolve conflict and harmonize,
the more our radiance shines through."

—Kia Miller, founder of Radiant Body Yoga

How do I care for and nourish my *energy* body?

**What do I need to become more resilient
and in command of my energy?**

Understanding Our Personal Energy

Sitting tall, you close your eyes and begin to turn away from the outer world and inward to your inner world. The ritual form of your body stabilizes you in the physical world. With this foundation set, you're free to bring your attention to your spine. Beginning at the base, your root and pelvic floor, you trace with your awareness a column of light just in front of your physical spine, *the central channel.* You travel the channel from your pelvic floor to the sacrum, lower back, center back and hanging ribs, shoulder blades and sternum, back and throat, occiput, and skull resting on the top. As you trace this pathway, your spine lengthens and expands. Where your attention goes, energy flows.

Deepening your breath, you lengthen the inhale and the exhale, expanding your ribs, lungs, and capacity for life force energy. As you do, your nervous system begins to relax and soften. The inner tide of your breath captures your focus as your eyes roll upward to settle their focus in the middle of your head. Your *felt sense* awakens as your inner awareness traces the outline of your form, the place where skin meets your auric field. A gentle wave of awareness moves across your shoulders, chest, belly, and lower back as each aspect is felt, *seen*, touched, and appreciated.

You begin a sequence of movements and specific breaths that you've been practicing each day for the last thirty-five days. Soon you'll choose a new one, but for now you're enraptured with how this sequence – this *kriya* – has captured and lifted you in ways you haven't experienced before. The memory of its effect calls you each day to practice again; you're committed to creating the particular frequency this kriya provides. No words can fully express how this moves you, and at this point you rarely even try. As you practice, you enter a realm where words don't dominate or often even apply, freeing you to focus on other, also proficient intelligences. Deep in your being you trust the journey into other realms.

Through physical practice you jump start energy that's stagnated while you've been sleeping. Flexing and extending your spine, you awaken your nervous system and stimulate cerebral spinal fluid. Connective tissue opens as you vigorously move your arms. The fire grows within as you pump your belly with your breath. At the end of each movement, you gather the energy at the base of the spine and pelvic floor, and squeeze it inward and upward along the central channel to the center of the brain, stimulating the pineal and pituitary glands and the hypothalamus. Each round builds on the one before, a specific yogic technology designed to open and focus your creative mind.

At the end of the sequence, you sit quietly and very still. The energy you've generated settles and integrates even as your awareness of your energy body, your auric field, expands. Uplifted, calm, centered, grounded, and energized, you memorize the quality of energy you're experiencing. You feel into the space inside your head, one of your *inner thrones*, and then into the space around your head. Space leads into vastness in front of you, behind, above, below, left, and right. You reach your consciousness into the unified field, imagining waves collapsing into particles in response to your intentions. Your mouth curves into a smile as excitement grows inside as you imagine experiencing what you long for. You linger for a moment, adding detail and nuance to your inner yet cosmic experience.

Eventually you spiral back inside your physical form. Before you open your eyes you shine a golden light of protection around the edge of your auric field. It's rich and vibrant now, full of your own soul essence. You've cleared any energy that's not yours, mended the rip in your field that happened during an argument the day before, and stoked your inner fire. Now you're ready to greet a new day.

We Humans Are Energy Beings

I'm lying on a massage table, and the doctor of Chinese medicine is placing needles all over my body. I feel like a pin cushion. This is the first time I've experienced acupuncture, and I don't really know what to expect. As she's about to stick a needle into my wrist, she turns her face to look at me and says: "Zing!"

I feel a rush of energy all the way from the top of my shoulder to the needle now poked into the underside of my wrist. The sensational feels electric though not painful, as when shocked by electricity running through a wire. I muse: *ahhh, so that's what they mean by energy!* This is how I came to experientially, not just conceptually, understand acupuncture and Chinese medicine as working with the electric-like energy animating the body.

Over the last fifty years here in the west, we've been the fortunate, though sometimes reluctant, recipients of this energetic wisdom developed in Asia over millennia. When I was living in New York City in the 1990s, I knew that something wasn't right with me, but I didn't know what. I went to my western medical doctor several times and underwent a number of tests. *She assured me that I was fine.*

But I wasn't. I knew I wasn't, but I didn't know what the issue was either. *Have you ever felt that way?*

I asked around, and a friend in my feminist writers group recommended someone she'd been to who offered Chinese and Tibetan medicine. So off I went to Greenwich Village and into a brownstone where my life would change forever. After my sessions with Dr. Marsha, I felt the most exquisite sense of ease, calm, curiosity, and compassion. I'd float out of her office and wander around the city, enjoying the bustling people and passing shops and art galleries until I landed in Washington Square Park. I'd watch the old men playing chess, the dog walkers, and the children running past, all with my heart wide open. Sun on the trees felt brighter. The grass seemed greener. Even the bench I sat on felt more comfortable than I'd remembered. My experience of life and even my sense of what was real had shifted. Eventually that shift became my new reality.

This doctor introduced me to an entirely different way of understanding what creates and what destroys health. This knowledge eventually empowered me not only to change my physiology but it also supported me to leave my job teaching at Columbia University and move into the healing arts. My education about human energy had begun.

My ignorance wasn't unusual. My experience is that most of us know very little about our own energy. As is true regarding emotions, we have a very limited vocabulary when it comes to human energy. Where I live in Northern California people say things like *that person has great energy* or *the energy in that place was funky,* yet neither of these statements really tells us very much other than something felt "great" or "funky." *We're not very energy literate.*

Our Personal Energy Crisis

I speak with people every week who tell me how burned out they are or have been, and often they don't really know why. We're facing an energy crisis on a personal level, with so many people suffering from sleep deprivation and adrenal fatigue. We've been expending our energy faster than we can generate it, which mimics what we're doing collectively as well. Our 24/7/365, technologically driven society has something to do with it, but that's far from the whole story. To gain a deeper understanding we have to develop a broader and longer perspective.

More and more of us are realizing the limits of healing systems that treat the body as a chemical experiment that can be manipulated with pharmaceuticals or a machine with replaceable parts.

Increasingly these medications soothe or mask symptoms, but they don't resolve or heal the underlying condition. People take pills to wake up, pills to go to sleep, pills to calm their anxiety and their digestion, pills to balance their hormones, pills to increase their libido and fertility, and pills to block their fertility. Yet do any of these approaches understand, much less address, what's *actually causing* the issues?

During my first appointment with Dr. Marsha, I listed my complaints, all of which seemed separate to me. She'd been taking notes, and when I was done she turned the paper toward me so I could see it and said, "This is what you're eating."

I was astonished. "How did you know that?" I asked.

She answered, "Because of your pulses and your symptoms." She had a diagnostic system that accurately told both of us what was aggravating my body, and that led to a treatment protocol that changed my physiology – forever. What a far cry from my medical doctor's exclamation: *You're fine!*

Maybe you've had an experience like this when suddenly the world shifts as your perspective changes, and you realize things aren't what you thought they were just a moment before. You may not be sure (yet) what's true, but your assumptions and expectations no longer feel accurate. This happens often when you shift from a default lens into a broader perspective. In this case my perspective went from being focused on the physical world to one that includes the nonphysical, energetic world.

Since those days with Dr. Marsha I've benefited from investing in many energetic practices, forms, and ways of being. My experience with the highly effective and noninvasive healing I received from Chinese medicine stimulated me to seek out and explore dimensions and experiences beyond the physical world. At first what I learned challenged some of my most basic assumptions about reality. Having grown up in the United States, I was taught to *see it to believe it* and only trust something you can touch – meaning *when it's in form*. I was conditioned to believe that energy was what we used to warm our house, cook our food, and run our cars, not something that had anything to do *with me*.

This isn't surprising given that here in the west, our science has focused on understanding and manipulating the physical world. The physical world has been presented as what's real, in contrast, for example, to *superstition*, which western science aimed to debunk. What a huge change it was, after all, to discover and accept that the world is round and revolves around the Sun! But unfortunately many other ways of perceiving reality, like Earth-based spirituality, were demonized, and other forms of healing, so-called *old wives' tales*, were thrown out because they couldn't be proven.

Western science's expertise in manipulating the physical world has led to enormous technological developments in the realms of building and construction, transportation, manufacturing, and more recently in computer-based information technology. One result has been a high standard of living in western countries in terms of ease and comfort, and also sanitation and hygiene. We've had a fairly simplistic understanding of energy as something we harness and usually burn to fuel our technology.

At the same time, these advances have depended upon utilizing energy lodged in the living world, such as oil, coal, forests, rivers, and soil, and extracting the power from them. Another result then, one often not talked about and even hidden from view, has been increasingly *degraded ecosystems*. As noted in Pillar Three, we've traded our vitality and the vitality of our living world *for our comfort*. It's no coincidence that chronic, sometimes mysterious, illnesses have grown exponentially alongside the degradation of our environment.

What are we to do?

Facing Deeper Truths

First of all when we recognize and take in the primary relationship of our own bodies and the planetary body, as we explored in Pillar Three, we begin to break through our (purposeful) denial to face deeper truths. I've observed that often the degree of one's denial correlates to the amount of privilege one has. After all, having resources and race and/or gender privilege can protect you from the worst of the consequences of our collective actions – at least for now. As *White Fragility* author Robin DiAngelo notes, privilege can make us fragile and deeply uncomfortable when that default lens is seen for what it is.

Take a big breath and reflect on what's true for you –
in this moment – in this regard. Notice what's happening
in your body and with your breath. Do you feel any
resistance or sense of being unjustly blamed?
Or are you nodding, perhaps grimly, with recognition?
Take a moment to write in your journal if that would be
helpful. Be honest with yourself – and kind.

Coming out of denial can be distressing and disruptive. We don't stay willingly ignorant for no reason. Oftentimes we prefer denial over truth because we feel afraid, disappointed, and depressed in the face of the truth. Facing this situation can stir up shame, blame, grief, horror, and dismay, and often our first impulse is to look for a way out. Emotional energy rises and we want relief.

This is exactly why you need to foster your emotional wisdom – being wise about what's going on inside – and also your energy adeptness, so you can release anxiety and build stamina, resilience, hope, and the ability to act effectively. As you build your inner power, your *mettle*, and your nervous system, you'll be stable and resourced even when witnessing the big challenges in our world today.

In later pillars we'll explore how you can, and what you need, to participate in regenerating our communities, cultures, ecosystems, and institutions so that you can live in right relationship with others and the living world. These will be the steps needed to grow yourself into one of the sovereign stewards our Earth desperately needs us to become.

Here in Pillar Four we'll bring together and expand your understanding of what's needed to build your inner power, to become sovereign of yourself and in command of your inner landscape. You need this foundation so that you're strong, clear, capable, and compassionate in your communications and collaborations. Feeling weak, tired, triggered, or alone and cut off inhibits your ability to truly listen and work through challenges with others. Feeling entitled or like a victim distorts your perception like mirrors in a fun house; unfortunately these conditioned ways of being are more common and run deeper than most of us typically realize. If you don't take responsibility and deprogram yourself in this regard, then your distorted perceptions will arise in and potentially derail even your best efforts to work toward positive change.

As you face the deeper truths of what's going on in the world and inside yourself, you become increasingly able to be the *change-agent* you have the potential and desire to become.

To do this you need command of your energy as well as of your emotions and form. In this pillar we'll explore how Kundalini Yoga practices enable you to clear and build your life force energy, and how Human Design reveals how you can gain command of your core energies and turn what may feel like character flaws into superpowers. We'll also explore the energetic power of the heart from several perspectives, and how you can learn to activate and harmonize with it. In this you gain more command of what comes into your life, co-creating with the Flow of Life by uplifting and working with your energy. But first let's pause to consider the ancient wisdom traditions from which our current understanding of the human energy field arises.

Different Kinds of Science

As I discussed above, western science has focused on understanding and manipulating the physical world. Its view of energy is that which we extract from the living world to use as fuel for our technology or for our bodies in the case of food (calories). On the other side of the world, different forms of science have focused on understanding and manipulating energetic forces that animate the world, including our human form.

Throughout many parts of Asia, sages, yogis, practitioners, spiritual teachers, and doctors have explored and experimented with energy in myriad ways for many different purposes *for thousands of years*. Those of us in the west are fortunate to now be receiving perspectives, teachings, and practices from these wisdom traditions that until just a few decades ago typically had to be studied in specific circumstances under the guidance of a master of the form or practice. We do well to recognize the significance and longevity of these forms of science, so different from that created in the west.

Taoism, for example, explains the nature of the world by investigating the continually shifting dynamic between two primary forces called yin and yang. When I was working with Dr. Marsha I learned much about yin and yang through studying and practicing *macrobiotics*, an approach to understanding food as energy and medicine that originated in Japan and is based in Taoism. Yin and yang each have many characteristics, the simplest to understand being an expanding force and a contracting force, respectively.

As this classic symbol shows, these forces are always morphing into one another to create balance. An underlying premise is that the living world and the Universe are always seeking balance, though balance is never fully achieved but rather is *an ideal around which we swing*. For example on the Equinox, which happens twice a year, the length of day and night are the same – a moment of balance. Yet it literally lasts a moment as the inexorable march of the change of seasons moves on, days or nights lengthening depending on the time of year. In this view any extreme always calls for its opposite, just as a pendulum swings from one side to the other. In this all things are connected and influence one another; nothing is truly separate or without consequence.

"But to find the balance is the purpose of this time
To restore the balance of the Universal Mind."
—Shimshai

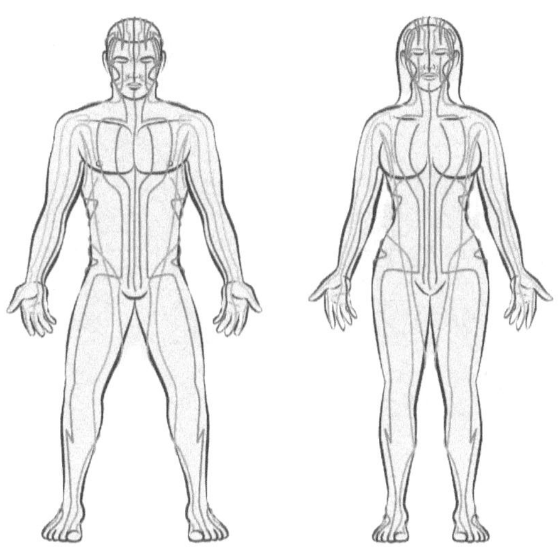

The march of western civilization and science across the world has created deep imbalances in many places. Such is one result of only seeing the world as material reality that can be captured and exploited while being blind to the consequences that an energetic perspective might provide.

Different branches of energetic science map the human energy field in different ways. Chinese, Tibetan, Korean, and Japanese medicine, for example, work with the "meridians," energy highways that run throughout the body. Needles, hands, and other devices are used to stimulate and clear energy at specific points along the meridians to create intended effects. Doctors trained in this system focus on understanding and manipulating the life force energy of human beings to create healing and balance.

"Stagnation = illness. Circulation = health" reads a fortune taped to the file cabinet of one of my Chinese medicine doctors.

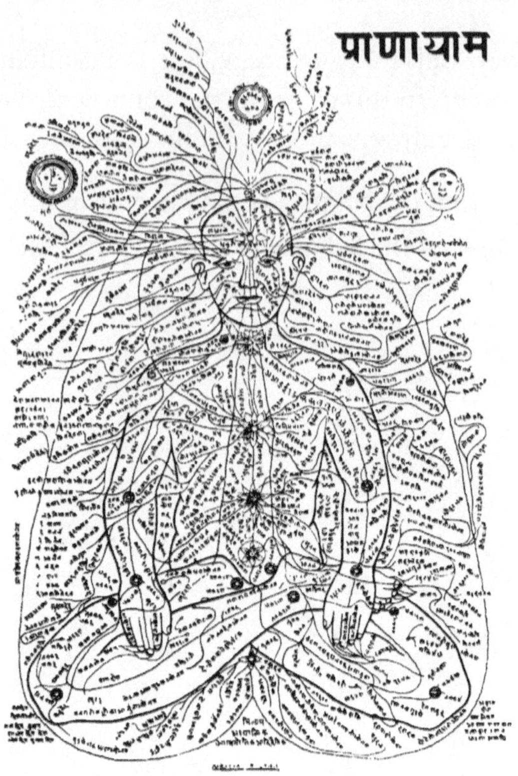

Ayurvedic medicine out of India also works with the 72,000 *nadis*, rivers of energy that run through the human form, similar to the meridians (see image). Ayurveda relates to the yogic tradition, overlapping disciplines emerging from a shared perspective and knowledge of the complexity of the human energy field. In the Radiant Body Yoga teacher trainings I've done, I learned about the ten (!) bodies, only one of which is the physical body, called "the meat body."

Yogic science offers multiple maps of our energy bodies, the most well-known of which is of the seven primary chakras (energy centers) just in front of the spine, shown in the picture that opens this chapter. In Kundalini Yoga we focus on stimulating the navel to clear, activate, and fuel the power center there. Indeed many systems recognize the significance of this area of the body, called the *hara* or the *lower dantian*, and practice building, harnessing, and directing this energy in forms such as tai chi, qi gong, judo, aikido, karate, and other martial arts. (More about Kundalini Yoga in the next section.)

In applying yogic science to my understanding of Human Design, I've discovered ways to work with your Human Design that are highly effective, empowering, and enlightening (pun intended) whatever your specific design. Unfortunately I've seen many people who feel at the mercy of forces outside themselves and don't think they can do anything about it. I've supported clients who are very open in their charts (a lot of white), for example, to better manage the ways in which they're influenced by other people's energy so they remain in or regain command of their own experience. This gives them choices about how to feel and strategies for how to care for themselves. We'll explore this in detail later in this pillar; but first let's take a closer look at what some of these outside forces are and where they come from.

Signs of a Compromised Energy Field

Do you ever feel drained, overwhelmed, confused, overly sensitive, overly reactive, or fearful? These can all be signs of having a compromised energy field. Virtually every week when I do Human Design readings for clients, I hear stories of fatigue and burnout. Now many factors contribute to this epidemic, some of which we discussed in Pillar Three, and others we'll explore in *Pillar Five: Know Your Purpose and Your Contribution*.

Here I want to call your attention to the *energetic aspects* of burnout. In more electricity-based, technologically developed parts of the world, we first learned about the energetic danger from living in proximity to electrical substations. These stations gather, transform, and distribute massive amounts of electricity. You can hear the crackle and feel the buzz if you're nearby. Added to this, Wi-Fi, Bluetooth, and cellular constantly bombard us with frequencies with which our physiology is not designed to interact. Certain people are more clearly depleted by these energies than others, yet all of us are impacted to some degree. People in large cities are particularly at risk because of the density and interactions of so many different Wi-Fi and cellular energies. I moved to a small town outside the San Francisco East Bay Area in part to live in an energetically quieter place.

Your auric field, the field of energy that extends outward from your physical body from a few inches to several feet, requires attention and care just as your physical body does.

I don't know about you, but this isn't something I grew up with! I was intuitive and energetically sensitive as a kid, but I didn't have words or understanding about this back then. No one in my family or my community talked about such things. Anything like that was considered esoteric at best or even "kooky." The first time I saw a Kirlian photograph of an aura I thought, *interesting*, but I didn't really believe it was real. My conditioning led me away from many of my gifts because *they didn't fit in* with what my family and culture valued. It's taken me many years to grow my capacity for understanding myself and the world as energy, so if this is new to you, you're not alone!

Dr. Marsha was the first one to alert me to the fact that I had a *depleted energy field*. I knew I was tired and a bit depressed, but I thought that was simply from having a demanding job and a challenging relationship. While those were contributing factors, the deeper reasons stemmed from years of eating food that wasn't right for me, taking medications including long-term antibiotics, being on the computer for many hours and days at a time, and living in New York City. This on top of a few years of drug use in my teen years added up to a depleted energy field.

Many factors may contribute to a depleted or damaged energy field. Physical or emotional trauma, undigested emotions, chewing on past experiences, nursing grudges, obsessing over betrayals, and even clinging to outdated beliefs and fighting change can negatively impact your energy. Many people have tears and holes in their auric field, and they feel vulnerable and fragmented as a result. A busy mind, negative thinking, confusion, and overwhelm are a few common symptoms of a compromised field, as they indicate an inability to have clear and grounded thinking (which is a form of energy). As it turns out, living in opposition to your Human Design will drain your energy, as you strain to make the world bend to your will rather than living aligned with how you process energy and moving aligned with the Flow of Life. In this case you must use so much of your own energy to engage with life that without proper rest and care you're likely to end up on the couch, exhausted, maybe wondering what happened.

Energetic Sensitivity

Even more, Human Design reveals why some of us are more energetically sensitive, why we're more influenced by other people's energy, and some of what we need to maximize the benefits of our design while minimizing the potential pitfalls. Let's remember that Human Design is an *energy system* rather than a *personality system* (although it has implications for character and personality traits). It maps the human energy field in certain specific ways and shows us how we process energy. When you align with the most awakened expressions of your design, you live, work, and play in the most effective, empowered, and efficient ways possible. In the next section, we'll explore an example of what I mean by this.

One of the biggest benefits I've gained from Human Design, and that I teach my clients, is how to name, understand, and take command of specific Types and qualities of our own energy.

Its map of our human energy field relates to yet differs from the chakra system from the yogic traditions. (If you're a student of the chakra system don't confuse yourself by assuming the Human Design energy centers are the same as the chakras. They're not.) As you can see from the images at the beginning of this pillar, Human Design has nine energy centers while most representations of the chakra system have seven. The two systems both represent the central channel, called the *sushumna* in Sanskrit, which runs just in front of the spine from the tailbone and pelvic floor to the top of the head and beyond.

In the following section, we'll explore how we work with this central channel in Kundalini Yoga and why this is so significant. Let's recall that Human Design doesn't show you what you need *to do* to mend, heal, purify, and grow your energy field. It can help you discern areas of life *where you need to decondition*, but it can't guide you as to *how to decondition* exactly. For that you need practices designed to stimulate, build, harness, and direct your life force energy, opening the path to becoming *energetically adept.*

Harnessing Energy, Radiating Light, Becoming Magnetic

Why is it that some people experience synchronicities and seem to attract into their life whatever it is they want? Why is that some people feel so good to be around? Why is that some people can uplift the energy of an entire room simply by their presence? *Why indeed?*

Building Your Inner Fire and Power

One beautiful August I stumbled into a workshop at the Esalen Institute with Kia Miller, founder of Radiant Body Yoga (RBY). I assumed we'd mostly practice the familiar asanas, as I had in other yoga retreats. I was excited to be away from home in a stunningly beautiful location for five days and to reinvigorate my love and practice of yoga. Little did I know that RBY is based in *Kundalini Yoga* and what I was about to experience would open up possibilities I didn't know existed.

Early on the first morning Kia led us through a series of simple movements while seated to unkink our hips and spines from traveling – and from life. Even though I'm not a morning person, my resistance began to melt as my body warmed up, and the power of the group took over. In the practice that followed I experienced the ancient technology of *kriyas* found in Kundalini Yoga. Although I'd practiced asana-based yoga for twenty years or more and was surprised we weren't doing that, I was immediately drawn to the more explicitly *energetic* focus of this practice.

On the last day of the retreat, we did a particularly challenging and extended kriya practice. We'd been building up to it all week and we were ready. During the meditation at the end, I sat in a field of light so bright I'd have closed my eyes – only my eyes were already closed! I felt buoyant, radiant, calm, alert, grounded, and illuminated at the same time. I was a radiant beacon of light shining out into the room and beyond. My mind was quiet and clear, my body humming with the life force energy we'd cultivated the last couple of hours and days. This was a state of consciousness that I wanted to be able to access at any time, and now I knew how to do it.

Throughout the week I'd had tears run down my cheeks as emotional energy released from deep inside my energy body. Most often this happened as I was practicing *Breath of Fire*, one of two primary breaths in Kundalini Yoga (it sounds really intense but isn't really). Many other people were having similar experiences as the vigorous practice and the energy of the community and teacher created a powerful container for healing. Interestingly I had no story or content attached to these moments of emotional release, and others reported the same. I'd discovered and was experiencing processes through which emotional healing *occurred without having to psychologically process* prior experiences.

My experience with Clarity Breathwork earlier had taught me that many times even after someone has come to psychologically understand their triggers, they wouldn't necessarily be able to prevent them from occurring or lessen their severity. That's because *the energy of the trigger* was still active in their energy body. That's why we need practices that go beyond psychological healing and focus on *moving energy*. Clarity Breathwork facilitates emotional release and healing, yet oftentimes it requires a significant amount of emotional processing as well. It also doesn't have the *precision* of this ancient yogic science to create specific effects with specific formulas of breath, movement, *mudra* (hand and arm positions), and *mantra* (Sanskrit words set to music).

In Kundalini kriyas I discovered *specific instructions* for releasing past karma, for example, opening up the throat or heart chakras, clearing stuck emotional energy (like anger or grief), activating my creative mind, or connecting with the creative intelligence of the Universe. This science of the human energy field includes proven, time-tested practices for cleansing, purifying, activating, building, and directing our energy in ways that heal, uplift, and enlighten. Indeed all yogic practices have this as their aim; yet for those accustomed to vinyasa flow classes that focus on the physical postures, kriyas can seem strange. Indeed Kia called it "the weird yoga" in that first retreat, although I'm sure westerners thought that asana practice was pretty weird when they first encountered it too.

Typically in our kriya practice we stimulate prana – life force energy – in the lower body, harness it with the breath and energy locks called *bandas*, then direct that energy upward through the central channel into the heart and the center of the head, the *ajna* or *third eye*.

Kriyas include either vigorous movements (especially of the arms) or holding specific positions (mudras of arms and hands) while engaging in different kinds of breathwork (pranayama). Sometimes *mantras* add a sound current either sung out loud, listened to, or repeated internally. As mentioned above, words in the ancient, celestial language of Sanskrit each have particular resonances that *transmit spiritual information through frequency* as much as through meaning. As each part of the sequence completes, you sit very still so that you can observe and memorize the quality of energy you've built. Kriyas vary tremendously in length and level of difficulty, from very simple, short actions to elaborate series that go on for an hour or more. Whatever your level of familiarity with yoga or energy practices, or how physically fit you are, there's always a place to begin that you can build upon as you become stronger and more resilient and adept.

Through these practices you're able to clear energy you picked up from other people, repair tears and holes in your auric field, release residue from past hurts and trauma, and build your field into a *dense ball of light* that *protects* and *nourishes* you. In this way you can disrupt and cleanse yourself of conditioning that inhibits and distorts your perception, and open to new potential. It's like you've created your own energetic environment over which you have command. This makes you much less susceptible to the influence of other people's energy, outside influences, and even human-made energies like Wi-Fi, Bluetooth, and cellular. I invite you to practice kriyas along with me in our Feminine Sovereignty community (the QR Code is on the Resources Page).

Yoga and Human Design

Kundalini Yoga partners exceptionally well with Human Design. It gives you purchase on what Ra Uru Hu, the original founder and developer of Human Design, called the "not self." The "not self" names the conditioning that leads you away from empowered and awakened expressions of your design. Human Design can reveal this outdated or unhelpful conditioning to you; Kundalini Yoga can help you release that conditioning from your auric field and the cells of your body. Together they offer a potent and effective system for understanding and appreciating yourself, uplifting your energy, building new capacities, and actualizing your full potential.

I've found that Kundalini yoga practices increase my vitality, clear my mind, and help me have more command of my energy, even the particularly challenging energies I have in my Human Design. (In the next section, we'll explore a specific example of what I mean by this.) I'm particularly open (white) in my Human Design, which means that much of my design can pick up energy from other people and temporarily amplify it. This can be great or not so great depending on the quality of that energy, as we saw in Jean's story in Pillar Two. I benefit a lot from having regular *energy hygiene* practices that cleanse the parts of my design that are open and tend to taste other people's energies. Building my auric field makes me much more stable around other people, stronger and more resilient, sensitive yet with good boundaries, even though so much of my design is open.

During a reading I did for a woman who had seven of the nine centers in her Human Design chart open, she shared with me that sometimes she "loses herself" when she's with other people. That's not necessarily a bad thing, as we discussed, if the situation and the people are right. But she wanted to have more choice. I knew she led retreats, so I asked her if this happened to her when she was leading a retreat. And she replied: "No, not at all."

Curious, I asked, "What do you do differently when you're leading a group?"

She closed her eyes and pondered for a moment, then her eyes sprung open and she said: "Oh! I know exactly what I do. I always prepare by building energy in my core, my central channel, and I feel great. By the end of the day I need to be alone, I've learned that much over time, so I can let go of everyone else's thoughts and needs and come back into myself."

I replied: "Great! You already know what to do, you just need to practice this now before you gather with anyone."

Her eyes lit up and I could feel her excitement building as she realized she had far more command over her experience – in all situations – than she'd realized.

Just as each pillar has a Spectrum of Expression from awakened and empowered to shadow to disempowered expressions, our Human Design has one as well. Our evolutionary process, our soul curriculum if you will, invites us to discover and learn to express and embody the highest, most uplifted possibilities of our design. My work with power relations in Feminine Sovereignty has influenced my interpretations of Human Design energies. What's considered "lower" by most Human Design experts I've differentiated into two different aspects: shadow and disempowered. This distinction vitally informs how we invoke, express, and embody *power* in very different ways. Let's dive into a specific example to see how this works.

For the places where you're "defined" (colored in) in your design, practices like this support you to uplift yourself into the empowered and awakened (rather than the shadow or disempowered) qualities of your definition, and to keep your energy moving where it may get stagnant. Remember that defined aspects of your chart are where you have a consistent, even fixed, way of experiencing that energy. Depending on your life experience, you may be expressing any aspect of the Spectrum of Expression in your definition. It's possible to change how you're experiencing your definition, but it takes focus and practice to do so. Energy practices give you the tools to uplift and evolve those expressions as needed.

Reminder: You don't need to understand the Human Design system to receive value from what I share with you here. Focus on the essence of what I'm sharing rather than being concerned about the specifics of Human Design. Also remember that everyone has the whole chart in their energy field. What differs from person to person is whether or not we have a reliable and consistent experience of that energy or if it varies depending on who we're around. Even if an aspect is open (white) in your chart, you've still experienced that energy many, many times throughout your life.

Character Flaws or Superpowers?

Have you ever had the experience of saying something and wondering why you said it? Like it just popped out of your mouth without your conscious intent? Or have you ever found yourself busy, busy, busy yet not really getting much done? Or maybe you love to learn, and you dive deep into whatever you get engaged with, yet you always feel like you don't know enough so don't put into action what you've learned. Or you typically have a to-do list, and no matter how much you accomplish, your list keeps getting longer and you can't relax and have fun because your list is always hanging over you.

If any of these ring true for you, I can assure you *you're not alone*! These are among the many common challenges that I witness in myself and in my clients. When any of these are happening, this means that powerful energies in your Human Design chart are more in control of you than you are of them. I often tell my people that *if you don't learn how to manage that energy, it will manage you.* The good news is that Human Design provides you with the keys you need to gain command of the energies active in you so they serve rather than undermine you.

When I first began to truly study Human Design, I was surprised to recognize aspects of myself that I'd considered *character flaws* to be, inside this system, either shadow or disempowered expressions of parts of my chart. Knowing this, I was then able to create a new relationship with these aspects of myself and to practice shifting to the empowered and awakened expression. I also grew more compassionate and accepting of myself where before I'd been more judgmental. Seeing these challenges in my chart and knowing I shared them with others helped me see that *nothing's wrong with me*, and I wasn't even doing anything wrong. I simply didn't understand how I tend to process energy or how to change it when I wanted to. Once I had that knowledge, I knew the path I needed to take command of my experience.

This is one of the things I love most about Human Design: its way of giving you new perspectives on your own ways of being that have been confusing or disturbing and casting them in a new light.

In addition learning the empowered and awakened expression gives you *precise guidance* about what to do instead. As you make that shift you become in charge of your energy and able to direct it when and where you will. In this way you can turn apparent character flaws into superpowers.

Let's look at a specific example.

The Gate 51

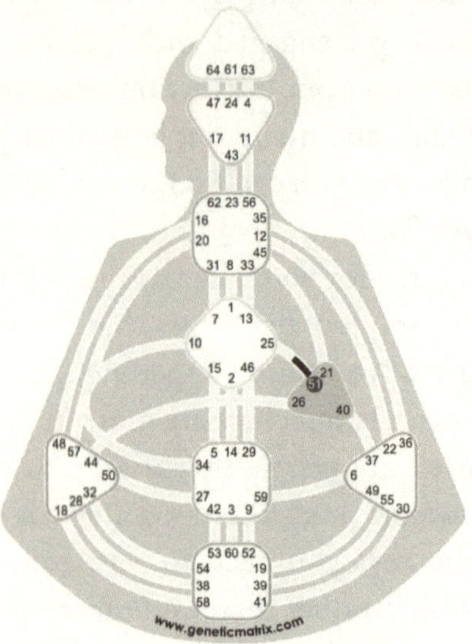

I have the Gate 51 "defined" (colored in) in my Human Design chart. This means that I have a ready and reliable access to this energy and a consistent, even fixed way of experiencing it. This is the "Gate of Shock" in traditional Human Design and the "Gate of Initiation" in Quantum Human Design.

This gate is considered one of the "gnarly gates" because it's very powerful and when not well managed can wreak havoc without your conscious intent. It's called the "Gate of *Shock*" for good reason. This gate gains power because of the energy center and circuit in which it's located. We're going to take a closer look to give you context; if you get overwhelmed with the specifics, *it's fine to skip them.*

The Gate 51 is on the Will Center, which, according to Human Design, is half of the energetic heart center. It's one of four motors or engines in the Human Design chart, which means that it and its gates all have energy that acts as fuel to engage with life. In addition, this gate is in the "Centering Circuit," which is known to have an *especially penetrating quality.* This kind of circuitry can be very influential simply by its nature. A person with this defined in their chart will be energetically felt by other people when they walk into a room without them having to say or do anything. (I have most of it defined in my chart.)

Are you starting to get a sense of how potent the energy of this gate is?

This energy can take you over if you don't know what it is or how to use it. This happened a lot to me before I came to Human Design. I'd find myself saying things that shocked others and I also attracted shocking experiences into my life. I didn't have the language for or understanding of what was happening. I felt at the mercy of both situations, ones that came at me from the outside, and ways of behaving that I didn't consciously choose. As you might imagine, this was painful and confusing for both me and other people. *Maybe you can relate?*

"Shock" is best understood as either the shadow or the disempowered expression of this energy. Remember that a shadow expression is when you attempt to manipulate or otherwise gain control of a person or situation through letting loose this energy toward others. I did this unconsciously before I understood what was happening *as energy.* I did this especially in situations in which I felt offended or distressed or wanted to prove or protect myself. Very often shadow expressions are unconscious (though not always). I have known of people who shock others purposefully because they think it's amusing (it's not) or they enjoy the sense of control over others it gives them.

The disempowered aspect of the Gate of Shock would be *when you attract shocking experiences.* I definitely had this happen to me, and it wasn't fun. I'd think I had things handled or knew what was going on, or even that I was just minding my own business, and *boom,* something would seemingly come out of nowhere to shock and disrupt me. *Ouch.*

When I learned about this gate in my Human Design many things in my life began to make sense. I was able to forgive myself for the ways I'd behaved in the past, for things I'd attracted into my life because I didn't know any better. And I committed myself to consciously, purposefully cultivating the awakened and empowered expression of this gate: "Initiation into Higher Consciousness."

I realized that in some situations I'd already been doing this in my work with clients both in my teaching and in my mentoring, but I wasn't consciously in command of it yet. When I was grounded, resourced, and feeling on purpose, I was able to access the more awakened expression and use it to initiate myself and others into expanded states of awareness and consciousness. But if I was tired, distracted, or in any way out of sorts, my insights could be delivered with more heat and force than I intended, sometimes hurting or offending others. I was excited when I learned about this gate because I could feel that understanding this aspect of myself better would give me purchase on this potent energy. To better understand it, I looked at the *mate* of this gate – meaning the gate on the opposite side of its channel.

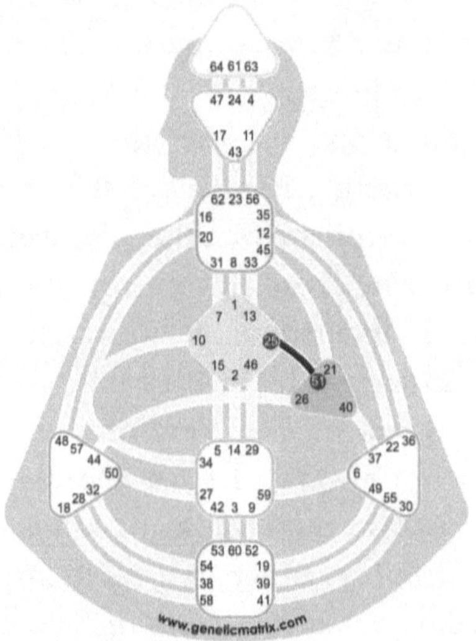

The Gate 51 connects with the Gate 25, the "Love of Spirit," and is half of the Channel of the Shaman/Priest/Priestess. Although I don't have the Gate 25 defined in my chart, I've experienced its energy many times in my life (as we all do with our open parts). I love knowing that this potentially shocking energy can be uplifted by its connection with the Love of Spirit. As part of my mentoring work I've intentionally developed a *felt sense* of this channel so that it resonates at the highest frequency possible.

Initiating energy is often *disruptive*, but it needn't be *shocking*. When being initiated, what's outdated needs to break apart and fall away so that something new can have space to emerge. Initiating involves shifting into a higher frequency and sometimes into a different form, leaving behind an outgrown identity perhaps, limited ways of moving through the world and interacting with others, or stunted perceptions or stuck emotions. Any of these can feel quite unsettling and disruptive as the ground you once stood so squarely upon crumbles and makes way for who you're now becoming.

"Thank you for being so confronting
and benevolent at the same time."
—a client's email to me

Taking command of this energy gives you enormous power to interrupt patterns, stimulate breakthroughs and epiphanies, and make visible and possible new potentials. It's a vital tool for shamans and mentors in the personal and spiritual growth realms. Yet you can use this energy to initiate yourself over and over again as you grow and evolve.

Are you beginning to get a sense of what can be revealed for you when you dig into the specifics of Human Design? Interesting, right?

So many problematic aspects of our lives can be illuminated and transformed when seen through the lens of Human Design (traditional and Quantum). Employing potent energy practices, such as those in Kundalini Yoga, supports you in cleansing, uplifting, and reformulating difficult parts of your design. You can heal trauma and energetic wounds with practices that open stuck places, release stagnation and hurt, and fill you up with the compassion, love, and light of your own soul essence. Together these two wisdom traditions provide you with effective tools for building your energy adeptness.

Power of the Heart Center

"Our spiritual heart is a most beneficial,
yet under-used aspect of our true nature and potential."
—from *Heart Intelligence* by Doc Childre,
founder of the HeartMath Institute

As we've been exploring, the quality of your energy highly influences how you experience your life. *The more you gain command of your energy, the more command you'll have in your life.* In Human Design, yogic traditions, and recent science, the energy of the heart plays an especially influential role. Many kriyas, for example, focus on healing, opening, and expanding the energy of the heart chakra. Yogic traditions understand the heart to be the source of our love energy, which is naturally radiant and magnetic. HeartMath Institute (HMI), a (western) science-based research organization, has mapped, calculated, and analyzed the magnetic field of the human heart. According to their studies, the heart's electrical field, commonly called the aura, is *sixty times stronger* than that of the brain. And Human Design has its own unique way of understanding the heart with powerful implications. In this section, we'll look at how these knowledge systems interface and inform each other to create a rich understanding of the energetic potency of the heart.

Consider how you feel when you're around somebody who's radiant or charismatic. You just want to be around them, right, maybe do what they do. "Charisma" is a "spiritual gift from God," according to etymonline. com, a sense of being *filled with light*. Radiance makes you magnetic as its high frequency attracts, uplifts, and influences. My very radiant yoga master, who we heard about earlier, created *Radiant Body Yoga* to name explicitly the purpose of what she teaches. Many of our practices focus on the heart center in different ways, freeing, healing, and cultivating the powerful energy there. The quality of your heart energy impacts your ability to attract into your life what you really want even as it also determines how your radiance influences other people.

Entrainment

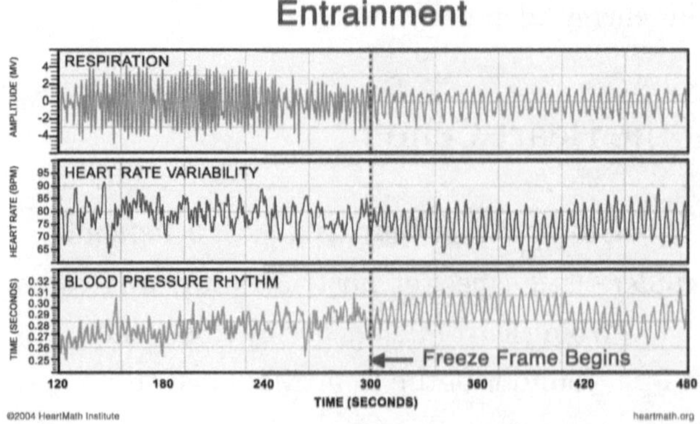

The HMI has created many practices that include breathing, stillness, and meditation to create what they call "heart coherence." Their studies show that when you engage in their practices, your heart rate, pulse, and respiration all settle into a beautiful sine wave and also entrain with one another (see illustration).

Two profound outcomes arise out of coming into coherence like this. First, according to their studies, all bodily systems when in coherence function optimally, and spontaneous healings may occur. Many leading transformation teachers, like Dr. Joe Dispenza and Gregg Bradon, draw on HMI's research in their healing work. (Dispenza also teaches a breath-work practice right out of Kundalini Yoga.)

HMI has shown the positive impact of groups of people practicing heart coherence at the same time with the same focus, and how this can be directed toward supporting greater coherence *across the globe*.

They've also studied the positive impacts of bringing into coherence your own heart with the magnetic field of the Earth. As we saw in Pillar Three, we humans are a part of the living world, and HMI is showing just how true that is. They've created opportunities and technology to enable regular people like you and me to contribute to raising and harmonizing the frequency of our world. *Exciting!*

The Law of Creation and the Human Design "G-Center"

In Pillar Two we looked briefly at how emotional energy influences what we attract into our lives. What we focus on expands, and especially that with which we become emotionally engaged. Since this can happen with what we're afraid of just as much as with what we desire, by using our emotional energy wisely we can super-charge our conscious intentions, making them more attractive. Human Design helps us see this process of creation in a new light. In addition to the role of the ESP, Human Design also has its own understanding of the magnetic field of the heart.

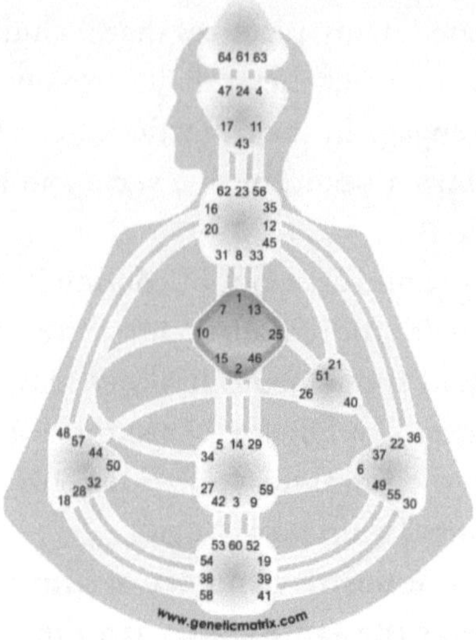

In Human Design the qualities we typically associate with the heart reside primarily in the "G-Center."[16] As you might expect, this is the center for love, lovability, identity, and direction. According to the lore of Human Design, an attractive force called the "magnetic monopole" resides in one of the gates of the G-Center. The magnetic monopole is a magnet that *only attracts*, and it's the compelling force that brings people, resources, opportunities, and experiences into your life.

Similarly, in the yogic traditions we also understand the heart to be magnetic, and HMI has now proven this in a western scientific way. All three perspectives agree on both the sheer power of the heart – in yoga it's considered *a sun* – and also its attractive, magnetic force. It's exciting and confirming when different systems address the same topic in different yet compatible ways, revealing different facets of the subject.

Human Design has its own version of the Law of Attraction we looked at in Pillar Two. According to Karen Curry Parker, my Human Design mentor and creator of Quantum Human Design, the quality

---

16 According to the lore of Human Design, the heart chakra split into two energy centers during a transmutation of the human energy field at the end of the eighteenth century.

of your emotional energy "calibrates" the vibrational frequency of the magnetic monopole. Your positive anticipation about the future you desire then sets the frequency of the magnetic monopole. The higher the frequency, the more magnetic you become. Parker also helps us understand that you can influence what the Flow of Life brings you by asking open-ended questions about what you want in your life. These are questions that share with the Flow of Life what you're mulling over, imagining, and wanting to receive guidance about. You don't try to answer these questions; you're musing and open to what the Flow of Life will bring you and that you then get to respond to, or to invitations that come your way. Here are a few examples:

- I wonder what's going to be the best possible work for me to be doing between now and the end of the year.
- I wonder what resources I'm going to need to do that work.
- I wonder who the people are that I'm going to want to connect with in order for that to come together.

Or:

- I wonder what's going to be best for my body to be healthiest.
- I wonder what's going to make me feel the most vital and embodied and alive.
- I wonder if there are changes I need to make with what's going on with my lifestyle for me to feel that way.

Or:

- I wonder where my next love relationship is going to come from.
- I wonder where I'm going to meet that person.
- I wonder if there's anywhere I need to be online or in person to meet that person.
- I wonder if there's any way I need to grow myself to align with the person I want to be with.

The next step is to pay attention to the inspirations and the potentials you receive intuitively, and also what shows up in your outer reality. Seventy percent of us (Generators and Manifesting Generators) are designed to respond to things outside of ourselves, while twenty percent of us (Projectors) are designed to be recognized and invited to participate in opportunities. That means that ninety percent of us are designed to enter into things by being *expectant* and *receptive* rather than by trying to *make things happen.* (Only Manifestors are designed to do that.) For the vast majority of us, working with our energy, intentions, and focus enable us to influence the invitations we receive and what comes into our outer reality that we then get to respond to.

No need to passively sit around waiting for the phone to ring when you can get clear about what you want, get excited about how it will manifest, and practice uplifting your vibration so that you become a radiant, magnetic force to bring it into your life.

A Simple Practice to Foster Your Radiance

Sit up tall in a chair or on a cushion. Have your feet flat on the floor if you're in a chair. Set your intention for your practice: *what would you like to feel, let go of, gain insight about, attract, or create?*

With your awareness reach down into the Earth and up into the sky, following the column of light that connects you to the creative force of the Universe. Trace this column of light as it runs just in front of your spine from tail to crown. Breathe into your heart, feeling the center of your chest expand under the influence of your attention. Reach your arms out to the side, filling your lungs, growing your width. Take a few deep breaths down into your belly, into your lungs, all the way up to the top of your head. Relax your arms, pause, and be very still. Notice how your energy has changed.

Reach your hands above your head on a sixty-degree diagonal, spreading your fingers wide and pointing them to the place where the wall meets the ceiling. Relax your shoulders, letting your arms rest on your shoulder blades. Imagine that your arms are an extension of your heart. Sense your beating heart and the power in the center of your chest.

Now grab light from above with your hands, and quickly yet gently strike your elbows into the sides of your body. Reach up again with an inhale, then as you exhale pull the arms in again rapidly and with enthusiasm. Imagine moving just the bones of your arms so that you don't overuse your muscles. Do this 108 times.

When you're done, finish by inhaling and reaching upward once more while holding your breath. Reach upward as you squeeze the muscles of your pelvic floor inward and upward, directing the energy up the spine and into the heart. Feel the energy of your heart grow and your chest widen. Now bring your hands toward one another overhead, turning them so that your fingertips touch. Hold for thirty seconds if you can (or exhale when you need to). As you exhale, reach your arms out wide to the sides, clearing your auric field, then rest your hands in your lap, palms up.

Sit very still, letting the energy settle. Breathe gently. Use your awareness to track what's happening in your auric field as best you can. Don't worry if you don't know how to do this – *because part of you already does*; you just may need practice. Compare how you feel now to how you felt when you began. Sit for at least five minutes or lie down to fully integrate your experience.

NOTE: *Don't do anything that feels painful.* If you have a shoulder injury, imagine doing the movement with a rapid inhale and exhale. You'll still receive the benefit. If you can't do the full 108 repetitions, do as many as you can, rest, and begin again. It's normal to feel challenged when first doing one of these exercises, and it will get easier with practice. Also some burning sensation in your shoulders is to be expected. This isn't a negative sign. It means that you're teaching your nervous system to be resilient. Be discerning between an uncomfortable sensation and true pain that's your body's signal to stop. Be wise and caring with yourself. It's not worth it to hurt yourself. And the benefits of building your stamina are immense.

Lena's Experience

Inside my online community I teach a new kriya practice each month. One of the participants in my *Activate Your Superpowers: Understanding Human Design* program had this to say about her experience:

> "Since I found your videos on YouTube, only three months ago, much has changed for the better. I was at a low point and living in survival mode then. Now I'm doing the kriyas every day and discovering the empowered/awakened expressions of my design. It really makes a difference, and I thank you from my heart for all the encouragement and empowering perspectives you share, teach, and embody."

Take Time to Assess, Integrate, and Apply What You've Learned

I'm so glad you're here! Before diving in, take a moment to place your left hand on your heart and your right hand on top of that. Breathe and feel the rise and fall of your chest. Give thanks for the miracle of your body, your beating heart, your breathing lungs, and the trillions of cells humming along doing their vital and precious work, fueled by life force energy and your soul's light. Wow.

I've designed this section to guide you to absorb, digest, and integrate the themes of each pillar. As mentioned in the *Introduction*, my hope and intention is that you'll not just consume what I've offered here but also bring it into your life in meaningful ways. Because when you do, if you're open to it, this material will grow and transform you. If you feel the need to skip over this section, please make sure to spiral back later so that you can make real in your life what you're receiving from this book. You know best how you take in and integrate new information so you can grow.

Below you'll find:

- **Self-Assessment**
- **Spectrum of Expression**
- **Pause, Reflect, and Review**
- **New Desired Capacities**
- **Questions for Reflection**

Self-Assessment

Now that you've had a chance to explore the potentials and pitfalls associated with developing your energetic mastery and becoming radiant and magnetic, it's your turn to check out where you are currently with all of this.

Instructions

Give yourself a number 1–5 for each statement. Five means it's totally true for you, one means it's true occasionally. Leave it blank if it doesn't speak to you at all. Add up the numbers from A and B and subtract B from A. This gives you your Sovereignty Score for this pillar.

(A) Strengths and Capacities Developed

[   ] I recognize that I'm an energetic as well as a physical or material being.

[   ] I like to practice creating what I want in my life as energy
     first to pave the way for what happens in the physical
     world. This makes my life much easier.
[   ] I love to do practices that help me build my life force
     energy. I not only have more energy to do things when
     I do, I also find that people and things I want are more
     attracted to me.
[   ] When I feel off, stressed, or out of sorts, I practice breath-
     work that helps me release tension, uplift my energy, and
     shift my perspective.
[   ] I appreciate and avail myself of energy-based medicine,
     like Chinese and ayurvedic medicine, that helps prevent
     disease before it starts.

(B) Wounds or Lack of Capacity

[   ] I feel foggy, confused, and overwhelmed a lot of the time.
[   ] I often don't have the energy I want and need for what I
     want to do. I find myself dragging a lot.
[   ] Sometimes I react to things that happen or what people
     say and it's like I'm taken over; I say and do things later
     that I wish I hadn't.
[   ] I like to work out. Physical effort feels good to me. That's
     what matters.
[   ] Meditation has never worked for me. My mind is too
     busy, and I can't sit still like that.

A = _____   B = _____   A - B = _____

This is your Sovereignty Score for Pillar Four.

If you have a positive score, this means that you've developed capacity
in this area. The higher your score, the greater your strengths.

If you have a negative score – more checked from (B) than (A) – then
this is a pillar where you'd benefit from building more capacity. The
lower the score, the less in touch you are with the beneficial attributes
of this pillar.

Spectrum of Expression

The Spectrum of Expression outlines three ways of expressing the themes, energy, and power of the pillars. Collectively we're evolving out of the power-over/disempowered paradigm that characterizes western civilization. Nevertheless we're still subject to expressing power in these ways, often without even realizing it. The three aspects of the spectrum will help you identify your tendencies and, I hope, reveal to you unconscious patterns, beliefs, or behaviors so you can become at choice about whether to continue or change them. Consider this an exploration in understanding power in the service of building your *power within*, the foundation of your personal sovereignty, and the inner support for your sovereign self.

Awakened Expression

In the awakened or empowered expression of your energetic adeptness you build your power within to become radiant and magnetic. As you become illuminated with your own soul essence and life force energy, you raise your vibrational frequency, calming the analytical mind, uplifting your spirit, and cultivating your conscious connection with Spirit and the All That Is.

With practice you may become a beacon of light that serves to uplift others simply by your presence. You model what's possible and create an energetic pathway for others to follow to develop their own radiance. You express your power to serve others from the overflow of your own energy.

You command your own energy so that you may be strong, resilient, stable, and grounded even as you're also connected to the cosmos. You offer and serve but don't seek to control others. You provide what you're offering without any energetic strings attached, feeling confident that Spirit rather than you is in charge of the outcome. You trust that showing up fully and providing your offering is sufficient. You honor other people's sovereignty by energetically respecting their ability to choose what's right for them.

Shadow Expression

Shadow expressions always have to do with exerting power over another person or persons, a situation, an organization, or even oneself. The human electromagnetic field is very powerful and can be used in a variety of ways to control or manipulate others. Martial artists who've learned how to control and throw their Qi can be extremely powerful – and dangerous. Of course martial arts may be practiced with the intention of avoiding conflict rather than seeking control over others.

A more subtle example is when we use our electromagnetic field to capture other people's attention. One of my teachers calls this "throwing a glamour" over others, a kind of *energetic seduction.* She admitted that she and her husband did this routinely when they were in a band without even realizing they were doing it. This isn't necessarily done with malintent, such as in this case. This behavior stemmed from a performer's desire to *capture* the audience, to enthrall as well as entertain.

I've also experienced – as perhaps you have – particularly charismatic public speakers who use their energy power to enroll their audience in whatever it is they're offering, whether it's their book, their program, a retreat, or whatever. The distinction between this and someone who expresses the awakened aspect is that this person has a specific desired outcome *to which they're attached* in some way. You can tell the difference when someone's trying to manipulate you into a sale and when the offer is given cleanly and with your highest good in mind.

Disempowered Expression

As I said at the beginning of this chapter, here in the west we're not well versed in the realm of energy, and most often we try to go at something on the physical level. So many people have low energy even though they exercise and try to eat the right food. Yes, these things do affect your energy for sure as we discussed in Pillar Three. However this isn't directly working with your energy, clearing, and building your life force and power in the ways that are most beneficial. We can be disempowered by our ignorance.

Victim consciousness, negative thinking, participating in gossip, or being judgmental will drag down your vibration, making you less magnetic yet ironically more likely to attract difficult situations and relationships. Suppressing your enthusiasm and vitality trying to fit in, or suppressing yourself out of fear because you don't want to be noticed, will lower your energy.

Pause, Reflect, and Review

Take a few moments as you read through the Spectrum of Expression to feel into what's true for you. You might want to write about your current understanding, how your relationship to these possibilities has changed over time for you (if it has), and if so what your journey has been like.

Now go back and review your self-assessment.

- Do you think or feel any differently now that you've dug in a bit deeper?
- Do you want to change any of your answers?
- Or do you want to add to the lists offered, noting what's been especially true for you?
- At this point are you aware of wanting to develop new capacities in this area? If so start a list of your own or continue reading for my suggestions that might help you get started.

New Desired Capacities

To help you think and feel your way through this, I've created a list of potential capacities you may feel drawn to. This list is suggestive and far from exhaustive. Some may appeal to you while others may not. (Feel free to add your own!)

Now rank this list in the order of significance to you, one meaning this is a high priority for you, and five being "not relevant to me, at least not now."

[   ] They say everything is energy, and I'd like to understand more of what that means in my day-to-day life.

[   ] I'm interested in learning how to create a calm and quiet
      yet alert state. That sounds so good!
[   ] I want to know how to become radiant and magnetic so
      I can attract more of what I want in my life.
[   ] I'd like to be able to stay more neutral when things are
      challenging. I feel like I squander my energy by getting
      too amped up about things.
[   ] Even though yoga is a bit strange, I'm open to trying new
      things. I understand that the ancient yogis knew some things
      we don't have so much of here in western culture, and I'd
      like to learn more. I'm going to try a few of the practices
      available in the Feminine Sovereignty online community.

Once you've ranked these possibilities, name your top two priorities. What can you do this week to begin to develop this valuable skill? You'll find helpful suggestions to support you with this in the next section.

Reflection Questions

I invite you to review and ponder these questions in any way that works for you. Feel free to respond to the ones that speak to you and leave the rest. You may write about them in your journal (highly recommended), take them into meditation or on a walk with you, make a sketch or painting about how they make you feel, or some other way that works for you. Writing down your reflections provides you with a record of your experiences, which can be very helpful later. As we evolve, we tend to forget where we were, and that makes it difficult to appreciate how much we've grown.

> What did you discover about yourself through the self-as-
  sessment and Spectrum of Expression? Did you feel affirmed
  in some ways? Did anything surprise or disturb you? Are you
  inspired to develop any new capacities?
> What can you do this week to begin to develop this valuable
  new capacity? What resources do you need? What support
  do you need? What do you need to prepare? Is there any

resistance you need to face and overcome? Who in your life can partner with you and help hold you accountable?

> Apply what you learned or realized in Pillar Four to your primary Learning Question. What does this teaching add to your inquiry? What was your Learning Question(s) for this specific pillar? Make a few notes about what's arising for you including how this feels in your body.

> How aware are you of your own energy field and how energy runs through your system? Would you benefit from discovering more about this aspect of yourself?

> What do you do to regulate, strengthen, and care for your nervous system? Did you know that this is one of the keys to being healthy and vital in intense and challenging times?

> Have you ever experienced one (or more) of the healing systems developed in Asia that focus on the strength and flow of your vital energy, your life force energy or prana? If not do you feel you'd benefit from it? Is there a reason you haven't? If you feel resistant, write in your journal about what's coming up for you.

> Do you feel at the mercy of other people's energies? Or of human-made energies like Wi-Fi, Bluetooth, and cellular? What can you do to clear and build the strength of your auric field so that you're more protected?

> How "open" is your Human Design? Pull out your chart and see how many of the nine centers (the geometric shapes) are white in your chart. If you have five or more of them that are open, you have quite a bit of openness. After reading this pillar, do you have new insights about how this might be influencing your life experience? Explore this in your journal.

> Are you curious about Kundalini Yoga and how it might benefit you? Have you done this practice or another that also works to clear and build your energy? How has that been for you? Are you willing to make this a priority in your life knowing what it can do for it?

> What might open up if you were to become adept at nurturing this critical part of your electrical system?
> As you're building your Temple of Sovereignty, how does this pillar show up for you? What color is it? What texture does it have? How does it fit with the others? What unique contribution does it make to the whole?

Your Daily Date with the Divine

*Each day giving focused attention to clearing
and building your energy and your connection
with the Flow of Life for the purposes of healing,
awareness, and receiving inner guidance.*

"Sadhana ... is the ritual of centering ourselves
within our SELF that enables us to walk through
life with an open heart and with grace."

—Kia Miller, founder of Radiant Body Yoga

"We make things holy
by the quality of our attention."

—Martin Shaw, writer and traditional storyteller

What is my daily spiritual practice?

**How do I devote time, energy,
and attention to my divine connection?**

Sadhana is a Sanskrit word (साधन) meaning personal or daily spiritual practice (pronounced sa-da-na.) Sadhana is the heart of any yogi's devotion. I do some form of yoga every day, usually a kriya I've learned or created from elements I love. I encourage you to include energy practices, but you may design your daily date with the divine any way that suits you; the key is to begin – and keep going!

Pillars One through Four explore the primary components you need for taking command of your inner landscape and building your power within, foundations for your personal sovereignty. All these components may be attended to and cultivated during your Sadhana practice. Although this word and the specifics may arise out of India, the notion of a daily spiritual practice is and has been shared by many different people and cultures all over the world. As the world becomes more intense and uncertain, you vitally need *stronger practices* to prepare you to meet your personal challenges and those, collectively, with others.

We Humans Are Habitual Beings

We tend to do the same things most days if not every day. The way we make coffee or tea in the morning. The way we wash and brush our teeth. The way we check the news, our email, our social media. The way we think about our day, our partner or kids, our work, and about who we believe ourselves to be.

We recycle and reinforce our self-concept with our habits, mostly thinking the same thoughts we thought yesterday, and doing similar things today to what we did yesterday.

Our habits both support and limit us. They keep us from having to rethink and plan every element of our days and our experience. Habits organize our perceptions, choices, and behavior. This makes us more efficient and can be comforting by providing us with structure we can rely on. At the same time, this structure pushes to the side other possibilities by directing us into sameness. When I habitually drink a large glass of water before I have my coffee, I'm supported by this habit. When I habitually ignore my body's many cries for water, I'm not supported by this habit.

The question then is which of your habits support you and which do not? And even more, what habits can you develop that will enable you to develop your life in the direction you desire?

Sadhana is definitely a habit worth cultivating.

We live in highly stimulating environments, overly saturated with images, sounds, and, as previously mentioned, electricity, Wi-Fi, and cellular frequencies. Yet we've had the same physiology for the last 150,000+ years, while these stimuli have been with us for only a few decades. Our nervous systems aren't designed for this kind of environment, and the stress of it contributes to increased rates of anxiety and depression, chronic illness, suicide, murder, and more. In addition our technology seduces us to focus outward onto mass-produced entertainment, information, and "content" from millions of content creators. The dopamine hits we receive from electronic devices can more than habituate us to focusing on them. More than ever, then, we need to *proactively* clear our energy, build our inner mettle, connect with Spirit and the living world, and give ourselves time to *self-connect* and *self-correct*.

The one thing you have command over in life is your relationship with yourself and the thoughts, emotions, energy, decisions, and behavior that arise out of that. During Sadhana you turn away from the outer world and tune in to your inner world. You break the trance of outer obligations and responsibilities, your *cravings* and *aversions* (as the yogis would say), and your ongoing, often negative mind chatter. When you allow your mind to habitually chew over the past and project into the future, you dissipate your energy, as it travels off in various directions often without much purpose. Yogis call this "spending your prana." Most of the time we're not even aware that we're doing this because we're so habituated to it and busy focused forward and outward.

During Sadhana, you give a hundred percent of your attention to yourself in the here and now. You'll notice when your mind wants to take you elsewhere and you'll have the opportunity to practice coming back to yourself again and again. Where attention goes, energy flows. And, I would add, *you experience what you practice,* whether you're conscious of it or not. Just as an athlete gains command of their body or a musician develops their skill with an instrument, you'll become increasingly adept the more you practice.

Turning inward makes it easier to connect with your *inner being* or your soul-self, the source of your intuition and inner guidance. Yet to receive that guidance you need to transition out of your habitual, everyday state of being, where you're managing barrages of information, stimuli, and demands. You need to give yourself an *off ramp* from ordinary reality and an *on ramp* to your connection with yourself and with Spirit.

In this chapter I share with you what I've learned and practiced to prepare for and then connect with my inner wisdom and harmonize with the frequency and wisdom of the Flow of Life. Much of this arises from yogic wisdom traditions. I encourage you to try my suggestions and see how they influence and support you. You may already have practices that work for you, and I'm not suggesting that you stop or reject them if you do. Think of this as expanding your repertoire with new possibilities. As always run my suggestions through your own system to determine what works best for you.

If you don't already have a regular practice in place, I highly encourage you to create one. You'd be amazed at how your experience of life changes when you prioritize your own well-being and your relationship with Spirit. I'd always thought this was a *good idea*, but I had a lot of resistance for all kinds of reasons. So if you feel resistant or hesitant, I get it! Unless you live in a spiritual community in which the routine and power of the group supports your practice, you'll need to develop your devotion and make this a priority. Creating new habits isn't all that easy; yet once they're in place they can greatly support your well-being.

> "We need to be willing to set aside time and to attend to
> the inner experience with the same enthusiasm we
> may attend visiting a new country for the first time."
>
> —Kia Miller

How It Began for Me

It took me months to create a habit that stuck. I'm not a morning person and I've never liked exercising early in the day. My old morning habits kept getting in the way. I'd be consistent for a while and then drop off. Yet over time I discovered that the more I practiced the longer the effects of the kriyas stayed with me. I became calmer, more centered and grounded, more uplifted and in a state of possibility *almost all the time*. When I did react to something I had ways of moving that energy quickly, safely, and effectively. And I noticed I didn't feel as capable or resourced when I didn't practice. As life became even more uncertain and intense during the pandemic, I finally committed to my daily practice. And now that I have, I experience a greater steadiness to my emotions, energy, and sense of purpose and possibility than ever before.

The specific sequencing of exercises I'll share with you is particularly effective for releasing stuck energy, opening up the physical body, resetting your energy system, dispersing overstimulation, building strength and prana (life force energy), calming and quieting the analytical or chattering mind, cultivating awareness of your energy, and nurturing your relationship with the divine. In this way, you shift out of your habitual state of being in ordinary reality and harmonize instead with the frequency and wisdom of the divine. Inside the Feminine Sovereignty community I've included different kriyas you can practice with me. I encourage you to explore and experiment with them based on what you feel you'd most benefit from now.

Sadhana may not be the cure for all your ills, but it helps you become someone who's equipped to face and address the challenges of our times, the purpose of Feminine Sovereignty.

I had to experience the effects of regular Sadhana before making it a non-negotiable. Maybe this will be true for you?

My Sadhana Practice Based in Kundalini Yoga

My practice includes three main elements: *self-connection, self-correction,* and *self-creation.* We need to prepare ourselves, as I mentioned above, to connect with ourselves and with Spirit. The first part outlines the fundamentals of sequences that foster self-connection. The second part offers avenues for self-correction during which you *course correct* on your journey of life. The third part offers ways of (re)creating yourself and your life in alignment with the more empowered and awakened expressions you sense are possible.

There are literally hundreds of possible combinations for Sadhana practice inside the Kundalini Yoga tradition. During my teacher training I experienced over fifty sequences specifically for early morning practice, and that's just a taste of what's available. The sequences are designed to create specific effects, and everyone finds their favorites. Even so the practices tend to follow a similar sequence, which I share with you here.

Typical Kundalini Yoga Sequence[17]

Tune In

Tuning in marks the moment of leaving ordinary reality to dive into your inner landscape. Have a simple ritual that you do each day that facilitates moving your awareness inside. Light a candle. Ring a bell or chimes. Burn a little herb or incense. Sing a specific song or mantra. Ritually doing this at the beginning of each practice signals your transition from ordinary reality into a spiritual and intentional space and state of mind.

Traditionally in Kundalini Yoga we use the mantra *Ong Namo Guru Dev Namo*, which means (loosely) *I bow to the creative consciousness in all things, I bow to the teacher within*. Many people simply use *om*, believed by the yogis to be the primordial sound of the Universe.

Set Your Intention

Since energy flows where your attention goes, purposefully direct your life force so the Flow of Life knows what you're focusing on and where to

---

17 I've created a several kriya sequences that you can do with me. These are available in our exclusive space inside our Becoming Sovereign Quantum Retreat Center here: BecomingSovereign.mn.co. Join us!

support you. Choose a focus that matters, simple or more complex. Say it silently or out loud. This can be as simple as *I'm here to clear and uplift my energy* or as specific as *I'm preparing myself for my big meeting today so that I'm grounded, clear, articulate, receptive, and well-resourced.*

Move to Open Up Your Body

Personally, I like to move first before I do anything else. I begin with a *circle every joint warm-up*, a series of simple movements that opens up my body and lubricates the joints. I learned this from another of my favorite yoga teachers; she said, in speaking about a daily practice, that if all you do is this sequence, that's enough.

Additional Movement Practice or Exercise

I typically follow this sequence with a few asanas (postures) such as cat-cow, downward dog, plank, cobra, and warrior poses. Many people like to do sun salutations or their own sequence of postures that help them loosen up, warm up, stretch connective tissue, and build muscle tone. I don't like exercising in the morning so my sequence is fairly brief. Some people love to exercise in the morning and may do a full asana class, ride a bike, go for a run, or otherwise work out. Working out isn't necessary at this stage though. Mostly we move so that we're then able to sit with the body comfortable and relaxed. Do whatever you need to do to get to that state of physical readiness.

I also do "navel work" to activate energy in the power centers of the lower body. Yes, this will help flatten your belly! But even more this will awaken and enliven your core energy. In yoga we call this the *navel center* or *third chakra*. As I mentioned in Pillar Four, the navel has 72,000 *nadis*, which is the Sanskrit word for the channels of energy that run through the physical and energy bodies similar to the meridians in Chinese medicine. Working the muscles in this area activates the flow of energy in the nadis, bringing us great vitality and resilience.

Kriya Practice

Now that you've prepared the body, *let's move some energy*! As I said above, there are literally thousands of kriyas designed to create specific effects. As an introduction I'm sharing a few suggestions you can get started with right away. The skills build upon each other, so I encourage you to start at the beginning and work your way through.

NOTE: Virtually all of the kriyas can be done in a chair as well as sitting on the floor or on a cushion.

Conscious Breathing

Long Deep Breaths (LDB) and Breath of Fire (BOF) are two of the foundational breath practices for Kundalini Yoga. Many of the kriyas call for these breaths, so getting familiar with them and practicing them is your first step.

LDB invite you to focus your attention on your breath and consciously slow it down and deepen it. Try breathing in for four counts and out for four counts. You can expand to longer as you become more relaxed. You could pause for one or two counts at the top of the inhale and bottom of the exhale. There are many variations of this breath. Just doing any of them for five minutes will affect your energy and influence your state. This is a particularly good one to do if you need to calm down, release anxiety or stress, slough off other people's ideas and energy, and reconnect with yourself.

Breath of Fire sounds intense but it isn't when done correctly. In fact practicing more gently makes it possible for you to do this breath for long periods of time (thirty minutes or longer). The easiest way to learn it is to stick out your tongue and pant like a dog, pushing your belly in on the exhale and inhaling on the release. The emphasis is on the exhale, but it's vital that you also inhale or you won't feel good in short order. Once you've got the hang of it, close your mouth and breathe through the nose, out and in like a bellows.

In terms of a sequence, if this is all new to you, you might try three minutes of BOF followed by five minutes of LDB. After each round, pause and notice how you feel. Make sure to give time to tuning in to the changes in your energy because it's this new state you're after. Try to *drop in* to the experience, meaning shifting your consciousness from the busy mind of ordinary reality to a settled awareness that's calm, centered, and bright. Your energy will have shifted and expanded. See if you can sense your body from the inside, tracing its inner outline and shape. Move your awareness up the inside of your spine, which is where your *central channel* of energy runs vertically through your energy field. The more you do this, the more you'll notice.

The main point is to shift your energy into a more expanded and elevated state. You're creating an altered state of consciousness that's attuned more to your *frequency* than to your *form*. Breathwork and kriyas are potent tools for working with the energy body upon which the physical body is formed. When you uplift and invigorate your energy body, you also nourish and enliven your physical body. Try it!

Key Elements to Include

However you design your practice, make sure to include these elements:

- At the end of each action, inhale and hold your breath. Gather energy in your pelvic floor and push it up your spine from the perineum to the center of the brain (third eye). This is how you harness and direct the energy you've just built and stabilize it in the higher energy centers. This will help open your intuition and access your inner guidance. Exhale when you need to and relax completely so that the energy can expand.

- After each action or round, sit quietly and allow the energy to settle. Pay close attention to the new frequency you've just created and see if you can memorize how it feels. Give yourself anywhere from thirty seconds to several minutes to familiarize yourself with and integrate the new frequency. In this way you'll raise your baseline frequency over time and with practice. You may choose to lie down and rest at this point to fully settle and integrate.

- Once you've completed the breathing practice or kriya and rested for a few minutes, sit and meditate for at least five minutes. Keep your mind very focused so that you don't allow all this energy you've built to dissipate through habitual thinking. Here are two of my favorite ways to stay focused and give my mind something to do even as I'm meditating:

  - Follow energy moving up the central channel just in front of your spine on the inhale and down the central channel on the exhale. You can note each chakra or each Human Design energy center. This helps develop inner awareness and energetic sensitivity.

  - With your eyes closed, tap into the dimension of space all around you. Access this through the right-brained portal into the unified field or the Great Womb. To begin, imagine the space in front of you expanding outward five feet, ten feet, a hundred feet, or more. Once you have a sense of that, tune into the space behind you as it reaches backward (into infinity!). See if you can feel the space in front and behind simultaneously. Then do the same to the right, giving yourself enough time for the felt sense to attune to this direction, and to the left. See if you can sense front, back, right, and left simultaneously so that you can sense the entire horizontal plane. Advanced: Do the same with above and below you and see if you can access a sensation of floating in midair.

· You may choose to continue sitting in meditation for as long as you like. My recommendation is that you only do this as long as you can stay focused inside your body or in the energy around you. If you find that your mind is becoming active and energy is dissipating into thoughts of what you're going to do later (or the equivalent), it's best to stop. You've done what you can for today and that's enough. It's better not to practice "spending your prana" in casual thinking because, remember, *you experience what you practice.*

Self-Correction and Self-Creation

Now that you've opened up and moved the body; built, harnessed, and directed your energy; settled and integrated; and practiced feeling yourself and the world around you as energy, you're in a receptive state during which you can receive guidance from your inner being and the Flow of Life, and also effectively review your life with loving kindness.

Of course not everything goes well, and sometimes we do things or don't do things that upon reflection we wish we hadn't or had. That's okay. Better than okay, in fact, because when this happens we get more information about and potentially better understanding of ourselves. And when we understand better, we can do better, right?

For example:

· Maybe you spoke harshly to someone and you didn't even realize it until later.
· Or maybe you didn't speak up about something that bothered you and now it's festering inside.
· Or maybe you ate or drank something and you didn't feel very good the next day.

- Or maybe you didn't thank someone when you might have and now you feel bad that you didn't express your appreciation to that person.

I'm sure you can find a few examples from your own life.

Course-Correcting

Course-correcting means observing yourself with a clear, not a critical eye, and asking what you could have done or could now do differently.

- Maybe you realize you could have paused before something harsh came out of your mouth, and then taken a few breaths before you responded. You could even dig a little to get to what you feel may have stimulated you to react in that way. Usually a strong reaction stems from an experience you had earlier (that morning or as a child), and identifying the earlier cause can bring you great awareness and freedom.
- Or maybe you could have asked for some kind of support that would have made it easier for you to speak up. Or now that you realize you didn't speak up, is it possible to circle back around to that person(s) and share what's on your mind and heart? Can you do this from a compassionate place that helps you connect with rather than control the other person(s)?
- Or maybe you could reflect upon why you ate or drank that thing. Was it social, just doing what others were doing so why not? Was it emotional and a way to avoid feeling something you didn't want to feel? Was it habitual and just something you do even though your body doesn't like it? Was it a way to be unkind to yourself, even subconsciously? When you uncover the deeper reason(s) you can make new choices from a wiser, kinder, more informed place.

***Have you ever wanted a "do-over"?* To take back what you said or did, or do something when you didn't before? That's what *correcting* really is.**

Once you have an idea of why you did what you did and what you could have done differently, imagine yourself taking the new actions.

See yourself speaking up or not. See yourself saying thank you with true appreciation. See yourself choosing to eat or drink something you know your body would like.

Doing this gives yourself a new energetic experience. And when you fuel your vision with high-frequency emotional energy, you help imbed this experience in your subconscious. Your subconscious can't tell the difference between something you experience in physical reality and something you imagine. So when you imagine and emotionally charge your new vision of what could have happened instead, you begin to rewrite the past and create the foundation for a future in which you are more at choice and less reactive or unconscious.

Pretty cool, huh?

So correcting isn't about flagellating yourself!

Please don't do that. If you do that you'll just create more of the same, and *that's not what we're up to here.*

Instead, *correcting* taps your imaginative, creative power, which runs through the Sensing Circuit and the Emotional Solar Plexus, and energetically transforms *what was* into *what could have been.* When you do that you pave the way for a different future in which you're more conscious, aware, and at choice because you're wiser now.

Practicing Forgiveness for Yourself and Others

Practicing forgiveness during your Sadhana can free you to be more alert and aware in the present moment. Doing this in the morning sets a new tone and acts as a potent reminder if you find yourself at some point in your day falling into the abyss of resentment or guilt.

When you feel resentment, anger, or pain toward another person, you remain energetically tied to them. Have you ever found yourself stewing over something that happened days, weeks, months, even years ago, the thoughts and emotions breaking into your experience and taking over your perception? The next thing you know you're in the midst of a conversation either attacking and blaming someone else or trying to explain and defend yourself. This has happened to all of us, and when it does it's a clear sign that forgiveness is needed.

Forgiveness practice is a particularly good addition if you've been feeling stuck rehashing a situation and blaming yourself or someone else for *whatever*. That could be the way someone acted or didn't act toward you. It could be a way that you acted or didn't act toward someone else – or toward yourself. Very often people assume that forgiveness is about the other person and for the other person. But it's not – *it's for you.*

A Personal Example

It took me over two years of regular practice to break the energetic and emotional ties I'd had to my child's father. We'd divorced some years before and after a difficult transition period we'd created what for a time was a well-functioning and supportive co-parenting relationship. Then one day he sent me a letter saying he'd no longer speak to me and that, no, he wouldn't talk with me about it.

This news came at a time when our teenager was very ill with a chronic disease and I was so busy caring for them that I'd not really worked for almost a year. I had spent most of my savings and was continuing to invest in naturopathic doctors and treatments. He didn't provide financial support or help with determining how to support our child. Mostly I had asked him for emotional support, and mostly he'd done what he could to provide it. And for that I was and am grateful.

After I got over the surprise, I felt resentful for a long time. I did my best to talk myself out of it, to spiritually bypass the betrayal I felt because I knew it was eating me up inside. But then I realized I needed to be more proactive so that I could truly free myself. I began to practice forgiveness – for me, not for him.

I tried to justify his behavior based on what I knew about him, telling myself he was doing what felt right to him based on his personality and perceptions. But none of that really worked. Beneath the anger and resentment was a lot of pain and hurt. And I came to see that this is what I needed to address: *my feelings, not his behavior.*

As painful as it can be, the truth is that people can and do exit families when they feel the need to do so. Clearly he felt the need to do so. What I realized is that I'd still been committed to a version of family that he didn't share. I had to forgive *myself* for being attached to the idea of him being a support to me and our child because it was that attachment that was causing me pain.

I began to talk to the part of me who really wanted things to turn out differently, to let her know that I understood how stressed out and alone she felt with the burden of it all. I started writing out forgiveness statements:

- I forgive myself for believing that he should show up for me and for our child in a certain way.
- I forgive myself for believing that the world should go the way I think it should.
- I forgive myself for investing my life force energy into a relationship that drains rather than nourishes me.
- I forgive myself for ignoring what might have been obvious had I been willing to be more honest with myself about the person my child's father had already shown himself to be.
- I forgive myself for the attitudes about family I've created that have been detrimental to me in this situation.
- I forgive myself for co-creating a situation with him that he felt he needed to exit and couldn't talk about.
- I forgive myself for judging him because he's different than the way I want him to be.
- I forgive myself for being tied to the past.
- I forgive myself for my need to be right. (Ouch.)

I did this day after day, writing out my forgiveness statements, breathing into them, allowing my emotions to rise and fall. I could feel the bonds I'd still been holding onto but that he'd released long ago dissolving. And I started to feel more and more free.

Until one day, I began to feel – not just angrily imagine – that instead I'm better off without him around. And that at this point, he's irrelevant to me. I no longer wish him harm (I did wish that for a while). I simply have no space in my consciousness for him anymore, and we're all better off that way.

Self-Forgiveness

In the end, *forgiving yourself is what sets you free.* You have the ability to do this, although it can be difficult to turn your attention away from the person, persons, or situation that you feel hurt, betrayed, abandoned, or controlled you, and turn toward yourself instead. You can feel a kind of distorted satisfaction in blaming someone else for how you're feeling, and that can become *quite addictive.*

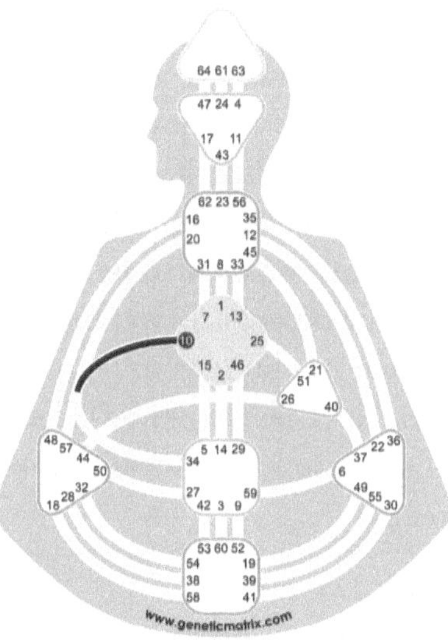

In Human Design the Gate 10, known as the Gate of Self-Love, is also known as "the blame gate." Because we live in a society that typically teaches us to critique if not hate ourselves, we tend to blame ourselves for, well, *just about anything.* That becomes so painful that we direct the energy outward toward others as judgment (blame). And then we attract blame from others because that's the frequency we're in. *Ugh.* The antidote: be more loving to yourself whenever blame and judgment rear their harmful heads. You really can change this — but if you keep fueling the blame, anger, and resentment *you'll never be free.*

Turning inside can be painful as you acknowledge your part in something that was difficult. But as long as you focus on someone or something outside yourself, you can't see or feel your own part in the dynamic or the situation. And you don't have command over other people and the outer world; your inner world is your domain. Taking a hundred percent responsibility for your part in any situation – and no more! – will build your emotional wisdom and inner power and free you from co-dependence.

Celebrating

Often we forget to acknowledge and celebrate, so focused we are on either what didn't work out the way we wanted or what we want next. One of my spiritual teachers pointed out that it's the nature of consciousness to expand and desire more consciousness. Because of this we tend to keep focusing forward on what's next and not give ourselves credit for where we've been, what we've accomplished, and the growth we've experienced.

You create a positive feedback loop when you begin to appreciate and celebrate even what you consider to be small things in your life.

When you celebrate your experience, you fuel your worthiness, deservedness, and self-love. When you build your worthiness, deservedness, and self-love, you'll find it much easier to acknowledge and celebrate yourself.

Please notice if you begin to have clichés running through your mind when you read this, such as:

· Stop tooting your own horn.
· Who am I to think I'm so great?
· Watch your head or you won't be able to fit through the door.
· Don't be such a *narcissist*.

And then the list begins of things you didn't do, or you wish you hadn't done, or the things you did poorly, or ways you felt embarrassed … and on and on it goes. But if and when this happens you have the opportunity to separate your conscious mind from these clichés and see them for what they are: **programmed responses handed down by the overculture, not *truth*.**

Sigh. Now isn't that a relief?

Even the most "enlightened" people I know have their own versions of this kind of self-criticism, so be assured there's nothing special about you in this regard. ;) Catching this kind of negative self-talk is yet another cause for celebration! Every time you celebrate, you underscore what matters to you. You send a message to the Flow of Life that says: *More of this, please.* You shift your energy into the frequency of appreciation and gratitude, and that makes you very magnetic.

Set a timer for three minutes and make a list of everything you have to celebrate from your last day (or last week if you need to stretch a bit). Here's one of mine for the last couple of days:

· Woke up early on my own this morning to do my Sadhana practice (didn't need my alarm).
· Slept better than I have been lately.
· Got some advice from a friend about what's wrong with my cat, and now I feel better equipped to get the right help for her.
· Cooked the tri-tip perfectly last night (yes, I eat meat).
· Took the whole weekend off and read, rested, took walks, spent time with friends.
· Am feeling more ease coming into my writing …

Nothing terribly momentous and yet just writing and acknowledging this puts a smile on my face and creates warmth in my heart.

Thanks and Gratitude

"Abundance can be experienced by having gratitude for
what you've already received and experienced."
—Sufi saying

I love the *pattern-interrupt* this saying creates in the mind of scarcity. Consumer culture feeds scarcity consciousness and relies on us feeling empty, unhappy, and disappointed so that we'll buy something to feel better. Cultivating gratitude for what you've already received and experienced disrupts habits of retail therapy and false longing and replaces it with appreciation, plenty, and thankfulness.

Like celebration, gratitude invites you to pause, reflect, and acknowledge what's already here, already present, already received. So much, so much, so much, right. You already have and have experienced so much.

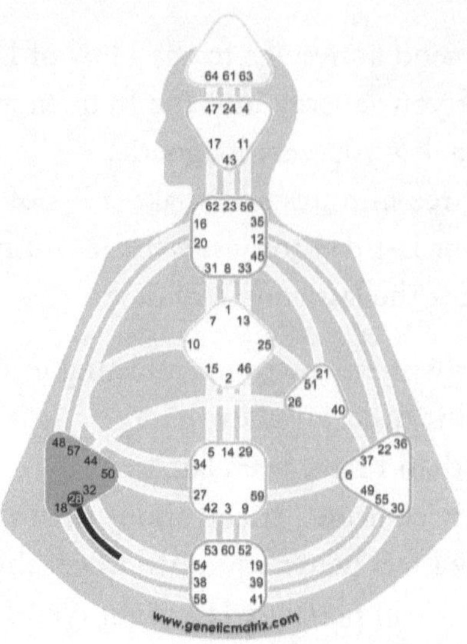

With this perspective, we can shift our attitude from suffering and struggling to experiencing situations as challenges that invite our innovation and creativity. The Gate 28 in Human Design is known as the "Gate of Struggle," and it's been renamed in Quantum Human Design as "Challenge." I have this gate defined in my chart and I know this energy very well indeed. Earlier in my life a sense of struggle felt common to me; I also understood struggle to be a positive force in movements for civil rights for all. Now I really like the way Dr. Joe Dispenza talks about challenge as our opportunity to grow: "We are all presented with brilliant opportunities disguised as impossible situations."

When you learn how to tap into the quantum field, you realize that the challenges life brings your way are providing you with an opportunity to practice your ability to create your future. As I've come to accept myself more and more because I know my Human Design, I recognize that struggles I've felt in the past often arose from trying to be something or someone I'm not. *Struggle is an attitude*; it's a choice. *Challenge is inevitable*. While not evenly distributed, life brings all of us challenges. So then what? Rooted in a sense of gratitude and a belief that the Flow of Life has your back, challenge becomes the opportunity to innovate, to walk on the leading-edge step into the unknown, and to create something new.

Your Gift to You

Whatever you choose to include, aim to build a consistent practice.

This is a time just for you to connect with your body, your feelings and emotions, your soul-self, and the Universe. Sadhana is an act of self-love as well as self-care. You matter. The quality of your energy and mental/emotion state influence everything in your life – and everyone in your life.

You can resolve emotional triggers, heal and strengthen your body, build your radiance, and become sovereign of your inner experience. You can change patterns you've had your entire life. *You can turn what you thought were character flaws into superpowers.* You can step out of the power-over/disempowered paradigm by building your *power within*. You can become an influential force for positive change as together we create the world we'd be proud to leave to future generations. You've just been building the foundation. Next we'll turn to how we engage with others as sovereign beings becoming compassionate sovereign stewards of our planet.

Spiraling Outward

Having spiraled inward through your inner landscape as you begin to build your sovereign self, now you begin spiraling outward into the world with other people. Having discovered – and practiced – the keys to developing your power within, now you'll discover more about the *right use of power* and *sharing and rotating power and leadership*. Having created new strengths and capacities in your inner world, now you'll begin to focus on becoming the sovereign steward you have the potential to become and that our world needs you to be.

As you were shown in Pillar One, you're a center of consciousness, yes, a focal point of energy that expresses through the processes we call *the body*. In Pillar Two, you saw yourself as subconscious patterns expressing through programs you inherited from your ancestors and developed during early life, and discovered ways to evolve beyond those patterned ways of being. Through a different lens in Pillar Three, you explored the paradox of being a distinct physical form, with skin as your boundary, moving through a dense, material, solid world and also as a community of seventy trillion cells humming in concert to create your experience. And in Pillar Four, you came to feel and know yourself as a body of energy that exceeds your physical form, blending indistinctly out into the quantum field where you create your desired life as energy first. You're now appreciating yourself as a *multidimensional being*, complexly moving through layers of time and space, myriad processes constantly in motion.

> "I am large, I contain multitudes."
> —Walt Whitman

So far we've focused on these four aspects of the inner landscape, mostly in isolation. This has enabled us to go deep with each topic, like a portrait lens that brings your face into focus and blurs the background. In this next section, we'll pull the camera back, revealing layers of context and ways in which we live inside our cultures and environments. In truth we don't live as isolated, autonomous individuals, as the proponents of masculine individualism would claim. We live in the world with eight billion other people who have vastly different experiences, assumptions, expectations, and aspirations arising from myriad cultures, languages, and historical experiences.

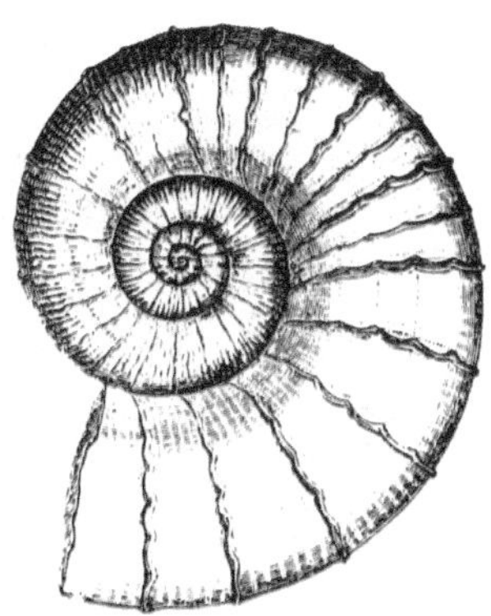

As we move into Part Two, you'll begin to spiral out of your interiority to engage in the outer world in different ways. Your journey in Part Two rests on your development in Part One, for in truth you're always already experiencing your interiority in the context of the outer world and other people. Your degree of understanding and skill in co-creating with the Flow of Life; being emotionally wise; feeling vital, embodied, and connected with the living world; and building your energetic adeptness and radiance will influence your experience of the second four pillars. We aren't leaving behind the first four – in fact quite the opposite.

Developing your sovereign self based in the first four pillars forms the foundation of your Feminine Sovereignty in your relationships with others. Most certainly you'll spiral back inside to one or more of the first four pillars as you engage with the possibilities and challenges presented by the later four. *This is by design.* Although the Gregorian calendar has programmed us to believe that we live in linear time, long before this concept arose we understood our lives in terms of cycles of seasons, as we saw in Pillar Three. We knew that as the days come and go, temperatures rise and fall, and flowers blossom and die so that fruit can emerge. When we come around the wheel again beaches may have shifted, a grandmother oak may have fallen, and children too small to ride a horse are now tall enough to do so.

As the spiral of life turns, you come back around to a similar place, yet you're not the same, and the landscape isn't the same, and the reprise sounds different somehow.

Of course in a book we have words to read and pages to turn, and so we feel we're moving forward along a more or less linear trajectory. Please remember that clean lines don't exist in nature and instead have been constructed by human beings, and books are one such example! I'll refer to earlier pillars as we go forward; I invite and entreat you to spiral back to the topics raised earlier as much as you like and feel are needed.

Processes of development are often presented as a linear progression, yet that isn't accurate either. If you find that a familiar theme arises – a patterned response you thought you'd handled, for example – don't believe for a moment that you've *fallen back there*. You haven't lost all the growth you've accomplished. Instead please understand that you're different, your life and landscape are different, and now you are able to meet something maybe you didn't have the knowledge, experience, or capacity to meet before. It's not two steps forward, one step back. More accurately you've entered a new springtime, and yes, the crocus are the first to show their faces again, but this year they sing of possibility rather than of sameness.

The Purpose of Feminine Sovereignty

Recalling the larger purpose of Feminine Sovereignty, this book provides you with a framework for stepping into your role as a *wayshower*, *change-maker*, and *leader of some kind*. You'll discover and create your own way to midwife yourself into a more healthy, vibrant, equitable, regenerative, and creative New World you'd be proud to leave to future generations – the *Thrutopian imperative*. Feminine Sovereignty evolves individualistic notions of sovereignty into becoming compassionate sovereign stewards of our planet who make the well-being of all beings, including the living world, our priority. As such, yes, we need to grow ourselves along the lines laid out in Pillars One through Four. While this is necessary, it's also insufficient if our intention is to evolve beyond individualism and the extractive ways that characterize it.

The sovereignty of individualism doesn't value communication (Pillar Six), collaboration (Pillar Seven), or compassion (Pillar Eight). This version of sovereignty, imbedded in the Story of Progress and the American Dream, values autonomy, self-determination, and personal freedom, *but not responsibility*. It leaves aside the matter of how we live in the world with other people, the other beings with whom we share this planet, and the Earth herself.

This sovereignty covers up the power dynamics that undergird its force. Individualism became the philosophy that justified the behavior of Euro-American men in "pioneering," creating industry, and exploiting white women, BIPOC, "natural resources," and the land itself. *I can do whatever I want,* this perspective asserts, *as long as I don't harm others* (meaning others like me). Every man for himself. May the best man win! Every man can make his own fortune, and his situation in life results (only) from *his own efforts.* Nowhere in this philosophy does responsibility for the consequences of his actions figure in. Nor does accountability to the well-being of other people, other species, our ecosystems, or the communal water and air supply. (We're the only species who've agreed it's okay – if tacitly – to poison our communal air and water supply.)

Feminine Sovereignty, in contrast, values and calls for Pillars Six, Seven, and Eight. These pillars evolve sovereignty to include ways of being, acting, and perceiving that acknowledge and honor the radical diversity of our world and our interconnectedness in the Web of Life. I use *Feminine* to name the *relational quality of existence.* Feminine Sovereignty, then, while acknowledging the power and responsibility of each of us to grow ourselves emotionally, physically, energetically, and spiritually, also situates us *in relation to* each other, other beings, and the Earth.

The question arises: How do sovereign beings best communicate and collaborate for the highest good of all? How do we acknowledge and support each other's sovereignty as we work together to create the New World we sense and long for?

We heal and grow ourselves so we can dissolve the false separations that pit us against one another. These separations make it possible for us to traffic in women and children, destroy ecosystems for the short-term gain of a privileged few, subordinate portions of the world population based on their skin color and national origin, and make war that devastates communities and kills tens of thousands of people. These behaviors express an *adolescent humanity* that, when not tied to responsibility and accountability, has led us to the precipice of world disaster. (If you've parented a teenager, you'll know what I'm talking about.) We need to evolve beyond this *immature narcissism*, and quickly, or the next generation(s) will pay the price for our inability to act.

Okay, I know that's a lot to take in, so let's take a couple of big breaths together. Put your hands on your radiant heart, feel the solidity of the ground underneath you, breathe in the breath of the trees, and know yourself to be on the right track, right here, right now. Tune in to what's arising for you now. Doodle or journal to help you digest your feelings about this material.

Stepping into greater leadership usually surfaces fear. As you expand, you'll hit the edges of what's known and understood. You'll have a choice: Do I continue to move forward through this inner boundary or do I retreat into familiarity? It would be easy to close down and turn away. Notice if that's something you feel like doing or habitually do. If so can you make a different choice?

I'm standing right here next to you, and I, too, breathe deep in moments like this. *That's okay.*

Better than okay, in fact. Breath is one of our most important and powerful allies as we face what's difficult and decide to not turn away. My experience is that most of us live at *a fraction of our potential* and think that's fine as long as we're *successful* by social or familiar standards. You're here because you want to activate, express, and embody more and more of your potential in ways that fulfill and satisfy you and contribute to the larger Thrutopian project. This takes courage! *And you're not alone.*

The Fulcrum Point

Moving on, you step onto the fulcrum point provided by Pillar Five. The notion of *purpose* you might think of as more of an inside experience – *the feeling of being on purpose*, an energetic and emotional *felt sense*. Rather than a treasure box to discover hidden somewhere, purpose unfolds, morphs, grows out of your actions and attitudes, stimulates your longings, and fuels your actions. Being *on purpose* sings your soul song, bringing juicy meaning into your otherwise dry days. Leaning into purpose, you open your arms to its fraternal twin: contribution. Contribution moves you outward to relate with other people and the living world. *What are you here to give?* How do you express your energy, love, compassion, passion, insight, and enthusiasm out into your family, communities, organizations, environments, and ultimately the world?

Birthed from the same human desire, purpose and contribution help you know that who you are and what you do matters.

Feminine Sovereignty calls you to look outward and to become aware of how you influence others and the impact of your choices. Both Human Design and Kundalini Yoga teach you to understand your influence *energetically* as well as by your words and actions. This appreciation for the significance of your energy brings a new layer to your understanding and new tools for how to work with it. Indeed although both these wisdom traditions seem to focus on the self alone, in truth they also provide unusual and vital insights for your relationships and interactions with other people. We will continue to tap their wisdom and guidance as we move into the next four pillars.

Context: Historical, Cultural, Familial

As you spiral outward into the next four pillars, you'll do so as someone who's been deeply influenced and often conditioned by the context in which you grew up and came of age. You've learned much about who you are, what the world is, what's possible (and not possible) for you inside the container of your upbringing. Some people embrace their upbringing, others resist or fight against it. Most of us experience a combination of the two.

The environments, the historical moment, and the social conditions predominant in your experience of your first two decades flavor your relationship to spirit, your emotions, and your physical and energy bodies. It's easier for those of us with more privilege and resources to feel we can transcend our upbringing – this the *allure of individualism* at the heart of the American Dream. This is an *illusion*. I know, for example, that my skin color and educational level have afforded me opportunities not as readily available to people with darker skin and who did not have the advantage of an academic family growing up. To deny that would be, well, *silly*. And yet so much of our conditioning invites us to do that – if you're white, resourced, well-educated, and from the United States.

All of this becomes abundantly clear as soon as we move into the world with other people. We immediately discover how segregated our world is, even though that's no longer legally prescribed. Languages, communication styles, cultural mores and expectations, and even what's called "common sense" differ dramatically among our diverse population here in the US and certainly across our world. It can be easy to repel or offend someone without meaning to if you're not paying attention to this heterogeneity and assume that other people see the world as you do. *Those with more privilege tend to do this.* Privilege often fuels entitlement so that those with more resources and/or social capital assume and assert that their way of seeing and doing things is the *right way* and others are backward (*barbarian*). Often those with less privilege and fewer resources have had to accommodate those with privilege to make their way in the world. Some of this is obvious; much of it can be invisible.

One step we need then is to make visible the different contexts in which people with different backgrounds may understand our themes of purpose, contribution, communication, collaboration, and sovereign stewardship.

In Pillar Five, we'll build your awareness here as the foundation for your outer-world themes to come. As we do so, I invite you to consider the environment in which you grew and came of age, the assumptions and expectations common among your people, and how you understand the influences these have had on your world view, your choices, and your behavior. I anticipate as we go along that you'll also discover new contours to your inner landscape that have been there all along but may have been out of sight. This can be uncomfortable and disturbing as well as illuminating. And so goes the path of evolving ourselves into our full potential as sovereign beings.

Know Your Purpose and Your Contribution

Knowing one's place in and contribution to the larger world in ways that inspire, satisfy, regenerate, and influence.

"Purpose is a stable and generalized intention
to accomplish something that is at once
personally meaningful and at the same time
leads to productive engagement with some
aspect of the world beyond the self."

—Viktor Frankl

When do I feel the most *on purpose*?

What is *mine* to do and give?

Fuel Comes When Feeling on Purpose

It's 4:30 p.m. and the Sun has climbed up and over the top of the sky and is headed toward the edge of the world. You look out the window, nod to Grandmother Oak, and let her know that, yes, soon you'll turn away from the computer and head out into the garden. You hear the collard greens and lettuces and snap peas softly singing of sweetness and butterflies and bees and you know soon it will be time to forage among them for dinner.

Even so you find it difficult to get up and turn away. You still feel fire in your belly from your day creating the model of the project you've been working on. Pieces that felt jumbled and disorderly today began to find their places, and you can feel if not yet see the shape of the whole. You'd started working early as the light had only just started sneaking through Grandmother Oak's arms and peeking in your window. You have a conversation with yourself, gently reminding yourself that tomorrow you can pick this up again. You've learned to tear yourself away before your body begins to talk to you or you start to slump from fatigue. Even though the energy feels endless, you know it's not; you also need the freshness of basil and smiling black-eyed Susans and to stretch your limbs before making dinner.

It wasn't always this way. As you shut down your computer and pull on your rubber boots, you remember how ambition once drove you to ignore your inner voice and keep your light burning late into the night. That ambition nearly killed you, or so it seemed, when your energy collapsed and your passion dried up and it was all you could do to make sure your child had dinner that night. Never again, you'd silently vowed, never again.

Tuning out the droning messages of culture – *do more, produce more, buy more, consume more, more, more, more* – you'd turned inside and looked around differently than you ever had before. So many things you'd loved had atrophied from neglect; they stared back at you from under dusty eyelids with an uncertain sigh. *Will we ever have life again?* they wondered. A crack in your chest let you know you were looking in the right direction even though you could barely see through your own veiled vision. *I didn't even realize you were in here*, you'd said to the dusty eyes. *I'd forgotten all about you.* Dismay and discomfort rise up: *What have I done?* you'd wondered. Your former plans and aspirations lay crumpled at your feet. *What have I done, what have I done? What didn't I do?*

And you'd realized that all those other *things* that the droning of the world told you to want were not what made you feel alive.

The smell of damp soil brings you out of your reverie and into the garden. You're confident that the pieces of the model you've been working on will make themselves into a cohesive community overnight. You can let the mystery work its magic while you harvest, see how much your teenager is willing to share with you over dinner, then make your way under the covers with that novel you've almost finished.

You've spent but not overspent your fuel for the day. You're relaxed knowing that tomorrow, if not the next day, the project will have constructed its form and you'll have what you need to take the next step. You have a vision of how this model will help make your town energy-independent once enough people get on board. You may not be an engineer, but you understand the dynamics of community, and that's far more important than the technology. The technology has existed for years, you smile ruefully. It's more a matter of helping others see how it can be done, and then cultivating the will to make it so.

We Humans Are Purposeful, Contributing Beings

My experience is that most people find it more helpful to seek out what makes them *feel on purpose* rather than *finding their life purpose*. Purpose is intangible, a feeling or state of consciousness rather than a thing to be discovered or uncovered. When *feeling on purpose* you might feel a deep sense of being *used well*, that you're contributing the best of what you have to give, that you're expressing your *best self* in how you're showing up in the world. That feeling of being on purpose arises when your actions and attitude contribute in a positive way to something that matters to you.

If feeling on purpose names an inner state of being, then contribution names that which you provide to something outside yourself: your family, team, community, neighborhood, the ecosystem in which you live, organizations you admire, clients or customers you serve, and so on. You can point to ways you've contributed to a project, or to a person or group of people, or to an organization. Even if it's something like holding space for a couple or a group to work through their differences, contribution still feels more tangible than being on purpose. Purpose and contribution walk hand in hand through your days, providing you with fuel and direction.

The *feeling of being on purpose* reflects your direct connection with your inner being, your soul-self. It's like your little self – the you of everyday life, the you that you know as you – and your infinite self – the great being who animates your body with a portion of her energy – dance harmoniously together through your days. Visionary activist astrologer Caroline Casey once shared with me that the old definition of "enthusiasm" is that "which makes the god within you dance" (the *Oxford English Dictionary* says "inspired or possessed by a god "). What is enthusiasm but your inner fire pumping to the beat of your heart's desire and how that desire and fire express out into the world?

The fire of enthusiasm burns away the dross of doubt, suspicion, and fear, opening the clear path before you into your desired future.
It refuses to be thrown off track by others' opinions and warnings, preferring the direction channeled from deep within. Not even needing words, enthusiasm's fire lights possibilities not visible from inside more compressed and conditioned states of consciousness. When the god within you dances, waves of potential crystallize into particles of form at the focal point of your attention. Your inner divine being is in command, and your human self, relieved, joyfully follows her energetic direction. When aligned and clear, this relationship creates the feeling of being *on purpose* and *making the contribution* you came here to make.

Spiritual practice facilitates this relationship, which is why we began with this in Pillar One and filled out possibilities in *Your Daily Date with the Divine*. It's not necessary to have a spiritual practice to feel on purpose; I certainly felt on purpose when I went to graduate school and became a professor. But when that career disintegrated inside me, I was lost as to what to do next. My whole life had led me to my job at Columbia, and when I left, I wandered into an unknown world. Fortunately I walked into an environment, as I shared earlier, that introduced me to metaphysics and inside of which I began to learn about working with intention, energy, and spiritual power.

My Father's Experience

Some people arrive in this world knowing what they're here to do. My father was one of those people. He knew from an early age that he'd be an English professor and he proceeded along that path, entering college at sixteen, getting his PhD just eight years later, and teaching his first classes at Amherst College within days of his twenty-fourth birthday. His father was an English professor at Cornell University, and both of my father's siblings became professional intellectuals, one as a classics professor and the other as a prolific political thought leader and writer. Yes, this feels a bit like the baker's son becoming a baker, but for my father it was also true that teaching was his true calling.

One afternoon he returned home from the university, cheeks flushed and stride full of confidence, saying how fulfilled he felt doing "what he was born to do." Even though his trajectory was clear early on, his experience was anything but static or routine. He wasn't one of those profs who appears with notes crumbling from age at the edges. He'd arrive at class with a place to start, a passage from whatever it was the class was reading, and he'd instigate and facilitate a dynamic dialogue, demanding that students think deeply and participate fully. The challenge of getting his students to contribute made the god within him dance! I was fortunate enough to take three classes with him when I went back to college in my early twenties.

His love of teaching stayed with him until the end of his life. After retirement he continued to lead several book groups populated by former students of all ages, and twice a week he drove an hour north to the correctional facility in Everett, Washington, to teach English courses for credit to men incarcerated there. His sense of purpose in teaching and spreading his love of literature exceeded his job and infused his entire way of being.

I'd say my father was the exception rather than the rule. Most people I've worked with and known haven't been clear from a young age and instead have had their paths unfold as they've grown. Oftentimes they've had to outgrow their conditioning as their first step. My mother's journey provides a case in point.

My Mother's Experience

My mother, an intelligent and highly educated woman like her mother, began her adult life in traditional ways as a wife and mother, as did so many women of her kind in the 1950s. She'd taken in the post-World War II dictate that women leave the labor force and focus their energies on homemaking, leaving work to men who would support them. She was conditioned to believe that her best contribution was to her family – and no farther. For fifteen years she cooked and cleaned, made Halloween costumes and Christmas cookies, and engineered homemade ice cream cakes for our birthdays long before 31 Flavors existed. Although she enjoyed much of what she did, and certainly she loved all of us, she was following the path laid out for a woman of her race, class, and educational level.

The trance of the perfect '50s family life broke apart during the 1970s when my mother discovered feminism. She'd already been growing out of her white, middle-class mindset by participating in the Civil Rights Movement in the largely African American neighborhood I grew up in. Feminism blew apart so much of what she – and all of us – took for granted and that, to us, was "just the way things are." She discovered perspectives and language that helped her understand both her own submerged discomfort and many of the ills she'd experienced and witnessed but for which she had no context.

That awakening was so profound that she became a devoted political feminist the rest of her life. Though the specifics changed over the years, she felt that fire of enthusiasm when advocating for the radical notion that women are people, too, and are equally deserving of opportunity, respect, recognition, protection under the law, and self-determination. She modeled for me what it meant to engage with and disrupt cultural programming at its most fundamental: how we understand who we are, who we can be, and what's possible. She lived the feminist truism that *the personal is the political.* She was so on fire that she spent months at a time in North Dakota and Wyoming supporting the local National Organization for Women (NOW) offices in their bid to pass the Equal Rights Amendment (it didn't pass). She spent months as an "outside agitator," as she called herself, far from home, for a cause that gave her purpose out in the world beyond what she'd experienced as a homemaker.

I witnessed my parents grapple with the implications of feminist thought and unraveling their assumptions and expectations about gender and gender roles. To his credit, my father took this on with characteristic zeal, becoming one of the first professors to teach women's literature and to call himself a feminist at his university. I got to watch him support her work in the world as she'd done for him for so many years. Feminist purpose came to them later in life and in embracing this new worldview together, they grew closer rather than farther apart, as happened to so many other couples during that time. In different ways they took command of their lives, harnessing their energy and intellect, to pursue a life of purpose in which they both grew themselves into their potential and contributed to the world in myriad ways.

My mother modeled for me what a life could be like in which purpose unfolds rather than being felt and understood from early on. From my current vantage point, her experience feels much more common than that of my father. She didn't know what her greater life's work would be because what became her purpose as well as her profession *wasn't yet available* when she was young. Also she had to confront and grow out of cultural programming about who she was supposed be and what was supposed to be her purpose – homemaker, wife, and mother – far more than my father. He felt authorized, as an educated white man, to pursue the career of his choice, whereas she did not even see this as an option.

As I came of age and stepped into my future, I organically conjoined influences from both of my parents, becoming a literature PhD with an emphasis in African American and Women's and Gender Studies, and the Director of Undergraduate Women's and Gender Studies at Columbia University. My sense of purpose emerged out of and was structured by the environment in which I grew up, familial and communal. Although I didn't continue in that profession, I've never regretted my choice to grow myself in that direction, as all that experience continues to inform and influence my experience and my choices to this day. Today my inner direction guides me in ways not logical, rational, or cognitive. This direction and sense of being on purpose emerges from my connection to the Flow of Life, as we explored together in Pillar One.

The Purpose of the Story of Progress

Historically as a species our purpose has been to survive and ensure that our children and grandchildren survive. (Ironically that does not seem to be our number one priority at this point.) I remember my grandmother (the same one who drank milk for her ulcer) saying: "Until recently we've mostly been occupied with populating the planet." As a privileged woman of her generation, I don't think she ever questioned the fundamental assumptions and expectations of the culture she grew up in as far as the Story of Progress goes. Undergirding her statement lies this sentiment:

"Go forth and multiply. Subdue and take dominion over the beasts and the planet."

Whether or not that's what God *actually* said, or what ancient followers of the Torah or the Old Testament believed, this is certainly the way that western culture has operated for millennia. My grandmother was not alone in believing that "humanity" had been fulfilling its purpose as we went forth and multiplied, subduing the animals and Earth in the process.

The Story of *Progress* is a story of *civilization*, the story of *empire*. This story lays out our collective purpose along similar lines but with a twist: do so in ways that privilege increasingly sophisticated building and weapons technology. This empowers those who own and wield those technologies to manipulate the physical world and dominate people. The ancient Romans were so good at this, and although they weren't the first to build empires, they were particularly adept at spreading their version of it. Their purpose was to bring wealth to Rome to fund their art and architecture and standard of living for their citizens. But of course they did this by *civilizing the barbarians* who lived in the lands they'd invaded and occupied and by extracting and exploiting as many *resources* from the land and people as possible. This theme of exploiting people whose technology is less ferocious and extracting from their lands has continued ever since.

Though this was millennia ago, we're haunted to this day by this worldview.

The world's elites purposefully embrace and express it to their financial advantage. Even for those of us who want to think differently, this Story of Progress is buried so deep in the psyche of western culture that it takes a lot of effort on our part to excavate and eradicate its roots inside us.

The purpose promoted by the Story of Progress is: work hard, work harder so you can consume more, get a bigger house, a fancier car, send your kids to elite schools, and take vacations in exotic locations. Yet inside, confusion arises as we bring into view the devastating consequences caused by this purpose. For generations so many of us wore blinders against these consequences and steered our reins and bridle down the path the story laid out for us. As we take off the blinders and our view expands, the path becomes less appealing even as it still tugs at us.

I mean, who doesn't want a new pair of beautiful shoes? Or a faster computer? Or a phone with a better camera? Or …?

One place our addiction to growth shows up is in our ongoing desire for growth in the stock market and retirement accounts. In conversation with a close friend, she said: "Ugh, how can I unhook myself from wanting my money to grow?"

How indeed?

Take a moment to pause, tune in, and reflect on your attitude toward economic growth, which in our world today continues to depend on exploitation and extraction. This might be one of those moments when the energy of the Gate 51 (Shock/Initiation) helps you initiate yourself into a more awakened state of consciousness – and that can be disruptive and uncomfortable. That's okay. Now you have the tools of emotional wisdom and energetic adeptness to support you to meet moments like this with greater aplomb. Make a few notes or doodles in your journal before moving on.

Unhooking yourself from the vestiges of empire that lurk inside isn't a small or easy task.

And it's critical if we're going to become sovereign of ourselves and also sovereign stewards of our planet. One of the reasons *life purpose* has become such an important topic for so many is that as we disentangle and detox from millennia of colonialism, we may face an echoing chasm inside where the story of progress once blared at such high volume it was near impossible to hear anything else.

Who would we be, who are you now, without that drive to accumulate and consume?

The Purpose of Peoples

The story of empire is not a simple one of good guys and bad guys. So many peoples have been afflicted by its march across the world, often revisiting upon others what was done to them once they get the chance.

Although this is a global phenomenon, let's zero in on the example I know best: the United States. A kind of dread and distress may rise up inside you as you confront the fact that the land you live on was invaded and colonized by Europeans and their descendants and once was part of the native lands of indigenous communities. I'm sure you know this already, cognitively, and yet most of us do our best to keep this awareness out of the forefront of our minds. After all, what do you do with that awareness? This book says: *develop your Feminine Sovereignty so that you can look this fact squarely in the eye and then make new choices.*

For those of us who are white, the purpose of our forebearers was to create a new life here in *America* after leaving – escaping really – the plague, religious or political persecution, economic hardship or collapse, starvation, genocide, and other devastating experiences. In the eighteenth and nineteenth centuries, aristocratic forces had "enclosed" for their own benefit huge swaths of land that had formerly been owned in common or traditionally used by people of the villages. The common people lost their traditional food ways and were forced into cities that didn't have the infrastructure or will to accommodate them. Famine, political unrest, and industrialization continued to spur Europeans to flee their homelands. Their purpose was to survive, hoping to create a better life for themselves and their children.

Yet they brought with them traumatized mentalities, and as Resmaa Menakem has pointed out, they unwittingly sought relief from their own distress by traumatizing whoever they could, especially the darker skinned, non-European people they encountered. They even used the diseases that had plagued Europe as biological warfare against the indigenous populations. This is an ugly example of how attitudes, behaviors, and trauma get passed down from one generation to the next. Fortunately we're capable – with intention, awareness and perseverance – of breaking this ancestral lineage. And *it's our responsibility to do so.*

Many others from Asia, the Middle East, and Latin America have emigrated here with similar purpose – to find financial opportunity, religious and political freedom, and escape from environments devastated by war, famine, climate change, and multinational capitalism. Generations of Africans were transported here against their will. Their purpose on one level was to survive the journey here and the brutalities of slavery, and to forge avenues for community, relationships, joy, and dignity in whatever way they could. Of course the myriad efforts of African Americans built large sectors of the US economy, industrial as well as agricultural.

Indigenous Americans have done their best to survive the onslaught of peoples from all over the world over many generations who came here, took their land, cut down the forests, slaughtered the animals, and mined the mountains and rivers, creating wealth for themselves and their own communities. Indigenous Americans have had to contend with centuries of encroachment on lands they've lived on for millennia, forcibly being removed, exterminated, and/or having their food ways and cultures obliterated. Despite this many indigenous peoples preserve, teach, and practice their ancestral languages, ceremonies, perspectives, and ways of being, even when they were *outlawed by the United States.* Some seek sovereignty of their ancestral lands and over their food ways, their purpose being to carve out a place for themselves where they can be in command of their environment and ecosystems, where they can (re)build their cultures.

Most of us living in the United States have been uprooted from our ancestral lands, either by our own choice or by having it forced upon us. Indigenous Americans have been forcibly relocated, African Americans' ancestors were brought here against their will, other peoples of the world left their homelands behind. All of us who came from elsewhere live on ancestral lands of indigenous peoples, and we no longer have contact with the land and environment of our forebearers. Such *unrootedness*, while different in so many important ways for different peoples, still similarly feeds a lack of belonging and raises questions as to our purpose.

Author and *sacred gardener* Steven Martyn notes that *so many of us feel shame and uncertainty about belonging* because of what we've done to the Earth. Even though western culture has done its best to program us into believing that we're separate from the Earth and the living world and therefore we can dominate it, somewhere deep inside we know this to be untrue and that actually what we've done to the Earth we've done to ourselves and to each other. As we saw in Pillar Three, we're made of the Earth, we're dependent upon the Earth, we're inextricably intertwined with her and the living world.

Make a few notes in your journal reflecting on your own upbringing. How was your experience influenced by the cultural, ethnic, economic, educational, religious, racial, sexual, and gendered context in which you grew up? How have the identity characteristics you've been assigned, and that you may or may not identify with, play a role in shaping your perceived opportunities? What kind of assumptions and expectations were common? How did you relate to them? What kind of social, educational, and/ or economic privilege did you grow up with? What have you acquired since then? How have you used – or how can you use – your privilege to be of service? Being able to step outside your own inner landscape to understand the environments in which you've grown and operate may prove helpful in sorting through why purpose and contribution feel complex and perhaps confusing to you.

Cultural Imperative: Conform and Consume

Get an education. Get a good job. Marry someone you adore. Have some kids. Buy a house. Get promoted. Enjoy your family (if you're lucky). Save for retirement. Hope for the best.

That was a common version of life purpose not so long ago. My parents lived this out during my formative years. Some version of this story continues to haunt much younger generations. During a podcast interview, a young man shared how, by age twenty-six, he'd accomplished what he set out to do, what he's been taught was the path to success and happiness. He had a well-paying job with potential for growth, a wife, and an apartment in San Francisco. But he felt hollow inside and at the time he didn't really know why. He lacked *a sense of purpose*, he said. Because of that he began to reflect on the assumptions and expectations that had guided his journey, and to seek inside himself for meaning.

Generation by generation the Story of Progress crumbles as the consequences of its foundational premise become increasingly difficult to ignore. My Gen Z, nonbinary twenty-something shared with me a few years ago, speaking with the authority of youth, that their generation has already accepted that they will *die at a young age* because of environmental collapse. Even as teenagers, they saw the writing on the wall in ways older generations have been refusing to acknowledge. Of course climate activist Greta Thunberg, age twenty at the time of this writing, is the best-known voice for her generation, one who refuses to remain silent.

While options proliferate in our complex environment, real opportunities for satisfying and meaningful work can feel surprisingly rare. During the *Great Resignation* of 2021 and 2022, countless droves of employees walked away from long-held jobs, silently shouting: *there must be more than this!*

I suspect one reason so many people seek guidance about their purpose is that they know somewhere inside that the tracks we've been on lead directly off the cliff of climate change and ecological collapse, and support the ongoing inequities created by systemic racism, misogyny, xenophobia, and the extractive, exploitative practices of multinational capitalism. Somewhere inside *we know this*, yet that awareness lies buried under our fear and despair. We long to feel *on purpose*, to make a meaningful contribution, yet in this midst of this context doing so may feel distant or near impossible. *How can what I do matter*, you might wonder? *What ground do I have to stand on?*

Let's both take a few deep breaths. Phew! This can be a lot to take in and digest. Our practice now is to look and contemplate rather than turn away. To breathe and notice without having to do anything else right at this moment. How are you feeling right now? How does your body feel and what emotions are moving through you? Take a moment and be with what's arising. Let yourself just observe and feel. Oftentimes we don't allow ourselves to feel because we'd rather do something to relieve the sensations. Right now you're building your capacity to be with perspectives that may be painful without immediately trying to change or fix something.

Exploring Your Purpose and Building Your Contribution

What's My Purpose? The Role of Human Design

Clients arrive at my virtual door with the hope I can answer this question for them. This is one of the most frequent questions I receive when someone comes to me for a Human Design reading. The people I work with feel a deep need for their lives to be meaningful and satisfying. They want to know that who they are and what they do matters. Finding a *good-paying job* and having a family are not enough. In fact often when I first meet someone they have (or have had) a good-paying job with benefits, yet they feel unsatisfied inside, wondering, *is this all?*

At root we want to be part of something greater.

Even though the world is now full of people, and technology has sped up our communications, many people feel *more isolated* than ever. Mobility, uprootedness, endless entertainment consumed alone, and the desperate pursuit of a dream that no longer feels compelling eat away at many of the things that once made life meaningful. It's surprisingly easy to feel lost and uncertain about one's place, path, and purpose. Our family's experiences can no longer guide and direct us as they once did. Inside our global society, inside this immense whole, the question arises: *what's my place, my role, inside of this totality?* If I really am a unique being – and you are! – then *what is truly mine to do?*

My experience is that Human Design can create a starting point for you to explore what makes you feel *on purpose*. When I work with a client, I facilitate their process of discovery and possibility rather than dictating to them who they are and what their purpose is. I don't agree that anyone can do that for you because, as I've said, I may be an expert on Human Design, but *you're the expert on you*. You can have an area of your Human Design chart colored in (defined), yet not feel a kinship to it. Would it be my job to tell you that you must embrace this part of your design? Or if you do feel drawn to part of your design that's white (open), is it my job to say that's not part of your design so it's not part of your purpose?

No, none of that. Not in my world.

At the same time I relish the opportunity to share with clients how intuitive and creative they are, for example, or how much power they have access to, or how they can turn something they've felt was a character flaw into a superpower. Generators and Manifesting Generators, as we saw in Pillar One, are designed to dance with the Flow of Life in specific ways that are part of our role as *builders of the world*. According to Human Design that's our purpose, and what we create is our contribution. Many times your Human Design chart will reveal and explain aspects of yourself that you may have suspected but rejected or not understood. Or maybe you simply did not see how this part of who you are would play a role in your life.

When I discovered that I have a lot of "individual circuitry" defined in my chart, so many aspects of my character and my life fell into place.

Individual circuity is here to be different, it's here to bring change. It does not fit in. It sees and understands the world differently and may seem *freakish* at times. It's also where the *evolutionary impulse of humanity* runs through the chart and where *genius* lives. Discovering this enabled me to release so much confusion and judgment about why I am the way I am and why my life has unfolded as it has. I've come to embrace how I think, feel, and am different from others with open arms and a deep sense of appreciation for this *purpose*.

Having grown up as a white kid from an academic family in a working-class, primarily Black community, I felt different in many ways. I had friends, but I didn't fit in. When I was older and I found myself in predominantly white environments, I felt different. Often I didn't fit in there either; I just saw the world differently. I thought something was wrong with me that I just seemed to see, connect, and feel things in ways that didn't align with most of the people around me. This is one of the reasons I left Columbia and the academy, only I didn't know it at the time. I just knew that the environment felt claustrophobic and I had to get out. My life experience fostered my sense of being different, as well as this being in my chart. Turns out I'm not designed to work in an institution, organization, or company. I'm much better on my own so that I can follow where my differences lead me. I'd already figured this out based on my experience and I still felt validated and uplifted when I learned this is a key aspect of my Human Design.

So yeah, Human Design can reveal ways of understanding yourself that can help you feel on purpose. Still your *sense of purpose* is always in *a dynamic relationship* between what's defined in your chart, your life experience, and what you feel to be true for you. For example I've been drawn to and have practiced dance, movement, and many forms of somatic expression and healing for more than four decades. I've built expertise in embodiment and I now offer to my clients and followers physical and energetic practices (Pillars Three and Four) to support their healing and evolution. Yet I only have one gate defined in the Sensing Circuit, which is where embodiment and somatic awareness live in the chart. And the gate I have defined is a storytelling gate rather than one focused on embodiment. I've become wise in this area because I've focused my energy here so much. But just looking at my chart, you'd never say *you're here to master embodiment and share that with others.* In fact my Human Design mentor was taken aback when I pointed out that I have just one gate defined in the Sensing Circuit, saying: "you've always seemed sensual and embodied to me." *And I am.*

Your Human Design doesn't dictate who you should be or how you should feel. It's a much better tool for opening possibilities, releasing you from conditioning, and confirming what you suspect than it is for telling you what to do. It's not a *formula*.

I find it interesting how much people want someone else to tell them who they are and what they should do. I see my role as *facilitating* my client's self-discovery and self-development with new information that can clarify what's been confusing and give voice to and name what they already suspect to be true. My experience is that people with even very similar charts can have wildly different interests and desires and experiences in life. Yes, when you connect with someone who has your same Type or profile, you may be amazed at some of your similarities; this happens for people in my programs who work in focus groups based on aspects of their design. At the same time, my students also recognize their diversity alongside their similarities.

When people use Human Design to *dictate to you* who you are and what you should and shouldn't do, always run it through your own system to discern if what they say *feels right* to you. Sometimes you may be resisting something that's true for you because it doesn't fit your current self-concept, so it's always good to check for that. But other times it may just not be accurate *for you*. Unfortunately some interpreters fall into the shadow expression of Human Design, using it as a tool to gain power, authority, and a modicum of control over other people, often unconsciously. That's one version of becoming an expert in today's world. Don't fall for that.

Discovering my individual circuitry did not, for example, tell me what kind of profession to have. It confirmed for me the conditions and environment in which I would thrive, which is as a solopreneur. In contrast, two women I've done readings for have both *individual circuitry* and *collective circuitry.* Collective circuitry relates to global issues, institutions, infrastructure, organizations, government, and big companies. These women thrived inside of an institution of higher learning and a multi-national corporation respectively *so long as* they also had autonomy to be in charge of their own teams. They were able to bring their breakthrough ideas to the table and have them appreciated, and didn't have anyone telling them what to do. Under those conditions they thrived. But when one of them had a new micro-managing supervisor come in, the job became intolerable, and she left, feeling forced out.

Another woman I know tried for years to have her own business. She trained as a life coach and in multiple healing modalities. She was very successful working in a global tech company and she thought it would be great to have her own healing and coaching practice where she could explore and express a different side of herself. While she had a few clients here and there, she'd never been able to get traction on doing her own thing. When I read her chart, I saw that she has primarily collective circuitry, so it makes sense to me that she'd thrive inside a big organization and wither on her own. Learning this about herself gave her a lot of *relief* from the ways she'd been judging herself for being too or not enough *whatever* to create her own business.

Yoga and Purpose

The purpose of yoga is to elevate the quality of one's energy, to expand one's consciousness, and *to become an example of an evolved being shining light and love into the world.* Our physical and energy practices influence us on many levels simultaneously, as we've seen, clearing, building, and uplifting our life force or prana. This wisdom tradition provides us with the foundational qualities of being that empower us whatever we choose to do in life. It does not direct us as to *what* we should do, other than *practice*, so much as *how* we do it.

Yogic practice allies with us in stripping away layers of conditioning, healing our trauma, and building our power within. Yogic philosophy invites us to explore the "yoke of spirit and form" in our human experience and to extend that understanding to all of life. *Humme Hum Brahm Hum,* as we noted in Pillar One, loosely translates to *we are we, we are one,* the paradox of individuality and oneness inside the totality. Embracing this paradox, really relating it to your everyday life, influences your choices as to lifestyle, profession, and relationships. Working for a company that pollutes the air and the oceans, for example, may cease to be an option, while taking a job or starting a business that pays less and contributes to regenerative culture may become more appealing. Yogic philosophy invites you to review your priorities and give greater attention to where your heart and inner guidance lead you.

Having said this, many yoga practitioners and teachers are also social activists, seeking to bring the values and perspective of yogic philosophy to bear on key issues of everyday life. The purpose of such actions is to transform our lives and our world based in the principles of *ahimsa*, for example, which means *nonharming*. (More about ahimsa in Pillar Eight.) Two projects in particular call to be included here, both founded by women yogis.

Yoga Gives Back

Kayoko Mitsumatsu began studying yoga in Los Angeles in 2006. She writes: "It hit me very hard that I needed to use all my capacity to help others, especially the underserved women and children in India, mother-land of YOGA. I was benefiting so much from the daily practice of Yoga, I had to give back." Mitsumatsu had a background in filmmaking but not in organizing and philanthropy. But she *felt the call* so strongly that she created *Yoga Gives Back* with the support of her yoga teacher and the manager of the studio where she practiced.

Her passion led her to create a nonprofit organization with the mission: "first, to mobilize the global yoga community with gratitude and second, to empower women and children in India to build sustainable livelihood." Mitsumatsu has mobilized yoga instructors and yogis in thirty countries with its mantra: "For the cost of one yoga class, you can change a life." Yoga Gives Back now provides more than 2400 underserved mothers and children with microloans and educational funds. These loans support young girls to get an education rather than having to marry, often before the age of *fifteen*. They support mothers who, although they earn one-fifth of what men earn, make the best poverty fighters. Women use their earnings not only to feed their families but to improve their families' quality of life as well as fund their children's education, giving the next generation a much better chance to live out of poverty.

Mitsumatsu has turned an inner calling that came to her in a yoga class into an international support system for under-resourced women and girls, leveraging her privilege and resources as a Japanese woman living in the United States. She tapped first into her local yoga community, then engaged yogis in the US, Europe, and Asia, all with the purpose of giving back to India, which had given her – and so many of us – so much. Her contribution is making an enormous difference in the day-to-day lives of those who need it most.

Off the Mat, Into the World

Seane Corn, Hala Khouri, and Suzanne Sterling knew that yogic practice on the mat is necessary yet insufficient to bring about a world aligned with yogic principles. They founded *Off the Mat, Into the World* (OTM) as a global, community-focused leadership training organization for yogis to become activists. "Yoga tends to wake things up," notes Leslie Booker, OTM faculty member. "How do I take all this energy and use it to make this world a better place?"

Co-founder Suzanne Sterling acknowledges what we've already been exploring – "the underlying philosophy of yoga is *we are all one*" – and follows through to the next obvious step: "If that's actually true, how does that change our values? How does that change our actions in the world?" The purpose of OTM has been to break down what this means and create a safe space inside of which practitioners can explore difficult issues such as the institutionalized racism, homophobia, and class privilege that haunt the yoga community as much as anywhere else.

And founder of the *Embody Love Movement* and OTM faculty member Dr. Melody Moore admitted, "I never saw myself as an activist. I saw myself as a therapist and maybe an educator, but in no way someone capable of starting a movement … It was because of *Off the Mat* that I learned the skills to understand my positionality [her privilege], my capacity, and to get the tools and resources to understand I did have an ability to create shift in some way." Moore well expresses the trajectory of what's possible for you, *in your own way*, to become aware of the privilege and resources you already have, to build your capacity and skills, and to step off the mat and into the world, fueled by a sense of purpose to make your own unique contribution.

Mitsumatsu, global members of *Yoga Gives Back*, and the founders and faculty of OTM are responding to an inner call and inner imperative to bring the values of their spiritual practice to bear on the world outside of yoga studios with the intention to live the mantra *We are all one, Brahm Hum.* Similar to the principles of Feminine Sovereignty, their vision is that personal and spiritual growth are necessary – and insufficient – and that focusing on connecting inner growth with engagement in the outer world benefits all.

Being on Purpose

Let's take a look at two more examples of women living on purpose and making positive contributions to creating a world they'd be proud to leave to future generations. While the specific characteristics of that New World vary from person to person, a consensus also brews on the fire in the kitchen where the wise women vision together. Let's gather 'round that fire and soak in the purpose and contribution of these soul-inspired women creators.

Shiloh Sophia McCloud, Co-Creator of Intentional Creativity + Curator of Musea

I've known Shiloh for twenty years, and she's one of my Intentional Creativity mentors. I've enjoyed and appreciated watching her develop her work into a global business with participants and teachers trained in her methods now in thirty countries. Shiloh had the great good fortune to have two mothers who, in different ways, were highly creative, entrepreneurial, and supportive of her individuality and development. She felt frustrated when young with the dictates of art school that demanded she learn to represent what she saw outside herself. Instead she worked with her co-parent Sue Hoya Sellers to create a new method that would work for her from the inside. From that came *Intentional Creativity*, a thirteen-step method for healing, evolving, and receiving your own spiritual information *from the inside.*

Shiloh's stated deepest purpose has always been to end violence against women and girls. Her mission is to teach women how to empower ourselves by learning how to paint our own image, thereby wresting away from the media the image we have of ourselves. As we learn to access and own our image and our inner information, we take command of our awareness and consciousness in new ways that help us build our power within. This in turn helps us to heal our trauma, to open new potentials, and to (re)create our lives more on our own terms.

While Shiloh's purpose to end violence against women and girls remains consistent, the specific methods she employs and the forms she creates have evolved over the years. She understands that artists often have been at the forefront of cultural transformation, leading the way in new perspectives and possibilities as well as providing critiques of the overculture. She encourages everyone to engage with art, regardless of their experience and perceived talent, as a way to foster intuition, creativity, healing, and new ways of engaging with life.

Samantha "Foxx" Winship, creator of Mother's Finest Urban Farms

Winship created Mother's Finest because she wanted personally to have more command over her own food, and also to preserve Black and indigenous plant and nature wisdom. She has a two-and-a-half-acre farm in North Carolina where she grows food and creates medicinal products for her family and her community, demonstrating that this can be done by anyone with the desire and will to do so. (Her background is in fashion and makeup, not agriculture!) She notes that backyard farms have always been a mainstay of BIPOC and rural communities, and she provides representation and education for how to do this whatever the size of your land. "Begin small," she says, "with a pot or two on your porch. Just begin somewhere."

She activates her purpose of preserving and spreading Black and indigenous plant and nature wisdom by encouraging kids of color to learn about medicinal plants, beekeeping, chickens, and regenerative farming. Her educational programs bring kids onto the farm (and off of devices) to learn about water reclamation and effects of climate change as well as farming and arts in ways that support "character building, nature immersion, homesteading, trade skills, arts/crafts, awareness, managing tasks, and confidence."

As one of the few Black women in beekeeping and regenerative agriculture, she sees her role as inspiring and opening doors for other BIWOC to reconnect with nature, grow their own food, take command of their health and healing, and free themselves from the food deserts of poisoned, commercial food that have taken over much of the United States. Her kids are homeschooling on the farm, growing up with their feet in the soil, and spending less time with devices in their hands.

What makes you feel on purpose?
What's yours to contribute?

All the women highlighted in the preceding section started out not knowing what they would do or where it would go. They did their own inner work, and out of that grew visions and possibilities that were new to them. They understood they needed to grow their skills and capacity in the outer world as well, and explored and experimented, feeling into what called to them. They listened and persisted, gathered others who felt similarly, and built influential projects, businesses, and movements that positively impact the world.

My mother had no idea she would become a political feminist at the national level. She followed her awakening to the confining nature of gender roles by seeking out others who were also questioning as she was. Out of this she felt called to change policy first locally, then at the state level, then nationally.

Mitsumatsu, Corn, Khouri, and Sterling began with their love for and devotion to yoga. They followed the inclinations that arose for them when they considered how to put yogic philosophy into practice in their everyday lives *off the mat*. Mitsumatsu went in the direction of giving back to "Mother India," while Corn, Khouri, and Sterling took on the task of training yogis to be leaders and activists.

Shiloh Sophia began with her desire to end violence against women and girls and married that with the creative process she developed with her co-parent. Out of this sprang a global phenomenon of women painting their own image and reclaiming their own spiritual information.

Winship realized one day that she didn't know where her food was coming from, what had been done to it, and how it was affecting her body and health. Out of that grew a desire to take command of her food for herself and her family, and then also for her whole community. She reclaimed food ways from indigenous peoples and her African American heritage, and now shares this knowledge through her educational programs.

All of these projects began with a seed of personal interest, took root inside a local community, grew into educational and transformational programs, and blossomed into evolutionary impacts on women around the world. None of these women began as superstars; they followed their internal guidance and kept taking the next steps as they unfolded before them.

And you can, too, in your own way, with your own topic of interest, and at the scale that works for you.

I hope you're not internally listing reasons why these women can do these things while saying to yourself: *But that's not me. I can't do that.* Maybe you haven't been a woman who could do what these women have done. Yet you still have the potential to grow yourself into the woman who can live on purpose and make her contribution to creating the New World in ways that align with your values, aspirations, desires, inclinations, and passions. Or maybe you've felt on purpose and made meaningful contributions and also know you're ready for an upgrade. This has been a common experience for me and the clients with whom I've worked.

Were you hoping I'd give you more of a formula or at least more direction about your purpose?

If you come to me for a Human Design reading, I'll be able to provide you with more specifics that might help you in this inquiry. Since I don't have your Human Design chart in front of me, and I'm not here to write a book solely about Human Design, I'm going to provide you with some guidelines I hope you'll find beneficial. In the next section I provide you with questions and entry points for inquiry that I hope will be evocative and stimulating.

- **What makes *the god within you dance?*** Tracking what gives you energy and what diminishes it will provide clues to your purpose and contribution. *Your inner guidance system communicates through your energy levels.* Enthusiasm and abundant energy signal you're on track, whereas lassitude and exhaustion suggest the opposite. If you're a Generator or Manifesting Generator, your Sacral authority will protect you from going in a wrong or unhelpful direction by saying *unh-unh*, which means you don't have energy for it. It will also affirm with an *uh-huh* when a direction you're considering aligns with what you have energy for.

- **Purpose can claim you**. When appreciating my ayurvedic bodyworker for her thoroughness and skill — *she really is quite gifted* — she shared that another one of her clients asked her recently if she really liked doing her treatments. Her whole face lit up and she said, "Well yeah! Of course I do or I wouldn't do it." She continued that when she first discovered ayurveda she got a full body *YES!* and *felt claimed* by this wisdom tradition. She knew that she needed to explore no further because she'd discovered her match.

- **What do you currently love?** What could you do all day and not get tired or bored? What do you feel devoted to or what would you like to devote yourself to? Is there something you'd love to have be a bigger part of your life, but you've told yourself *it's not practical, I don't have time, I don't see how this will get me anywhere?* If so check it out for yourself and see if your conditioning is clouding your view and undermining your sense of possibility. What might be claiming you but you're resisting it? See if you can lift the veil and create a new reality for yourself.

- **How you express your purpose may change and grow over time.** I've always been a writer and a teacher. I can't help it. These are things I do automatically and I can't not do them. But how I've done them, the topics, the people, the environments, and yes, even the purposes of these activities have changed dramatically over time as my life has unfolded and I've grown and developed. These are activities through which I express myself, and when I'm engaged in them I feel I'm doing what I came here to do. Release yourself from static notions of purpose and contribution and allow them to unfold and shift over time and be dynamic in relation to your life experience.

- **One version of purpose is to become the most fully developed version of your best self that's possible for you in this lifetime.** Human Design guides us as to how to do this in the soul curriculum it reveals through our Human Design chart. The most fundamental aspect of this is to grow yourself into embodying the most awakened and empowered aspects of your design, beginning with your definition (what's colored in) and, as it feels right and relevant, where you're open (white). This mirrors and reinforces what we're doing together as we go through the 8 Pillars and their Spectrums of Expression.

- **You're not your conditioning.** One of your most important steps is to disentangle what you've been conditioned to believe about yourself, about what's possible, and about life from what you may know or feel genuinely inside yourself. This is vital for your liberation and empowerment. When you can identify your conditioning, you're then at choice as to whether or not it's serving you. *Some of it will, some won't.* This takes intention and focus, and it continues throughout one's lifetime as far as I can tell.

- **What might you be resisting?** It's possible that if you're resisting looking at the big challenges we're experiencing in the world today, you've put your own blinders on so you don't have to look that way. My view is that the spiritual/energetic/ environmental call to participate – in some way – in regenerating our culture, our social and political structures, and our world is now broadcasting to everyone willing to hear. *Could it be that you're standing with your back turned and your hands over your ears?* If so what's that about for you? Are you willing to put your hands down, turn around, and listen for what's calling you?

- **Your purpose isn't what you do for a living,** although you may express your purpose or feel on purpose through what you do for a living. If you think your purpose is what you do for a living, then if you lose your job you may feel you've lost your purpose. One friend of mine says she works for Mother Earth, not the specific company that employs her. This has enabled her to feel on purpose when she changes jobs, and it gives her criteria and direction in seeking out where to work and for whom.

- **Purpose isn't the same as contribution.** Purpose is more of a *feeling state,* an inner sense of direction, engagement, satisfaction, and fulfillment. Being used in the best of ways, like the best of you is being brought out and that whatever challenges arise inspire and stimulate you, bring out your creativity, and push you along your growth edge. *Purpose fuels you in the morning and gives you energy throughout the day.* When you feel it even when you're fatigued, you have a pulse of energy inside that feeds you.

· **Your contribution can express through what you do for a living, but it doesn't have to**. Your contribution is what you're doing and how what you're doing benefits the world. So it's more outer-focused, whereas purpose is more inner-focused. My friend who works for Mother Earth makes her contribution to all of us through the work she does helping to bring organic, nutrient-dense, fermented foods out into the world through the vehicle of her company. Doing this work makes her feel on purpose. She may at some point decide to make her contribution through another vehicle, but it will always be focused on honoring Mother Earth and supporting us to be more connected to the vital, living world.

· **You only need to focus on your part of the whole, and in fact that's really all you can do**. Although, yes, so many places might grab your attention that need tending to – e.g., supporting an initiative for urban gardens sponsored by the city where you live, teaching people how to heal from chronic disease through detoxification and healthy food choices tailored to them, working to provide solar power to low-income communities – you simply need to do *your part*. Your part can change and evolve over time. Whatever it is, it needs to be digestible and sustainable in your life. Too often you can become paralyzed in the face of so much that needs our attention and care. Refuse to disempower yourself that way by instead choosing your part, making your contribution, and knowing that's enough. So if you ever find yourself getting overwhelmed by the number and magnitude of the big issues we face, the best thing to do is step back, tune in, and ask: *What is mine to do?* And when you have your answer, and you move forward with what is yours to do, know that it's enough. It's all you can do. And it's enough. Imagine a world in which even fifty percent of the population did that!

Take Time to Assess, Integrate, and Apply What You've Learned

Welcome! I'm so proud of how you've been showing up for these Your Turn sections. Brava! I know the themes of purpose and contribution are just so big for so many people. I hope you found this pillar illuminating and inspiring. Now you get to dig into more specifics for you and your life. Go for it.

As a reminder, this section is designed to guide you to absorb, digest, and integrate the themes of each pillar. If you feel the need to skip over this section, please make sure to spiral back later so that you can make real in your life what you're receiving from this book. You know best how you take in and integrate new information so you can grow.

- **Self-Assessment**
- **Spectrum of Expression**
- **Pause, Reflect, and Review**
- **New Desired Capacities**
- **Questions for Reflection**

Self-Assessment

Now that you've had a chance to explore the potentials and pitfalls associated with feeling on purpose and making the contribution you came here to make, it's your turn to check out where you are currently with all of this.

Instructions

Give yourself a number 1–5 for each statement. Five means it's totally true for you, one means it's true occasionally. Leave it blank if it doesn't speak to you at all. Add up the numbers from A and B and subtract B from A. This gives you your Sovereignty Score for this pillar.

(A) Strengths and Capacities Developed

- [   ] I feel excited about my life and can't wait to get to what I'm working on.
- [   ] Life feels meaningful even when I'm not one hundred percent certain about what I'm doing or my direction in life.
- [   ] I have all the energy I need to do what I want and need to do.
- [   ] I focus on my part, what is mine to do, and know that's enough.

[   ] I follow my inner guidance and I'm fine when the direction changes because I know this is part of my growth and evolution, even if I don't understand it at the time.

(B) Wounds or Lack of Capacity

[   ] I have to stay in this job so that I can provide for my family. It doesn't really matter that I don't like it very much.
[   ] I can't seem to find anything that really draws me in. Is something wrong with me? Am I deficient in some way? Other people seem to know what their purpose is.
[   ] I got good grades. I've got a good job. Why am I so unhappy?
[   ] I feel overwhelmed much of the time with so many options in front of me. I'm afraid of picking the wrong one.
[   ] The issues in the world today are so big that I often feel like nothing I could do would make a difference.

A = _____   B = _____   A - B = _____

This is your Sovereignty Score for Pillar Five.

If you have a positive score, this means that you've developed capacity in this area. The higher your score, the greater your strengths.

If you have a negative score – more checked from (B) than (A) – then this is a pillar where you'd benefit from building more capacity. The lower the score, the less in touch you are with the beneficial attributes of this pillar.

Spectrum of Expression

The Spectrum of Expression outlines three ways of expressing the themes, energy, and power of the pillars. Collectively we're evolving out of the power-over/disempowered paradigm that characterizes western civilization. Nevertheless we're still subject to expressing power in these ways, often without even realizing it. The three aspects of the spectrum will help you identify your tendencies and, I hope, reveal to you unconscious patterns, beliefs, or behaviors so you can become at choice about whether to continue or change them. Consider this an exploration in understanding power in the service of building your *power within*, the foundation of your personal sovereignty, and the inner support for your sovereign self.

Awakened/Empowered Expression

An awakened and empowered expression of Pillar Five would show up as a clear sense of direction about what makes you feel *on purpose*. You'd have plenty of energy for what you're engaging in that would carry you through the inevitable ups and downs of any endeavor. You'd feel hopeful, excited, and committed without needing to know exactly where your efforts will lead you or what impact they'll make. You'd trust in the deeper flow of guidance coming from the Flow of Life and let yourself off the hook for having to *figure everything out*.

You'd feel confident about sharing your enthusiasm and inviting others to join you in some way in making a positive contribution. You'd feel that what you do, and how you do it, contributes to something bigger that you greatly care about and feel connected to. You'd be able to ride the waves of uncertainty with a radiant heart and receptive mind, focusing on where new possibilities may come into view. You'd tumble into bed at night, tired and feeling well used.

Shadow Expression

In the shadow expression of Pillar Five, you'd feel on purpose through actions and attitudes that seek to control and manipulate people and situations to your advantage, or the advantage of your family and/or people. Your contribution would create strategies and structures that bring you power over resources, policies, land and animals, and other people. You'd feel fired up about controlling situations so that they align with your values and aspirations, not taking into account the potential impacts on people and the living world. This way of being is unfortunately very common and a typical way that we've been conditioned to become successful in the terms of the overculture. It's called the *overculture* for a reason, right?

Disempowered Expression

You'll feel disempowered in relation to Pillar Five if you're not in touch with what matters to you or you believe what matters to you is unimportant, insignificant, or even irrelevant. Oy! Possibly you'd fall into the deep, dark pit of despair, believing that nothing you do could make a positive difference, so you don't even try. Or you just might feel jaded about finding meaning in your life. You might focus on what's wrong in the world, either fueling a sense of defeat with your indignation or collapsing on the sofa, paralyzed by the news. You'd allow your mind and body to be colonized by dystopian visions common in movies and media, captured by the intensity and the hormones those visions release. Or you might just be bored and think that's "just the way things are."

Pause, Reflect, and Review

Take a few moments as you read through the Spectrum of Expression to feel into what's true for you. You might want to write about your current understanding, how your relationship to these possibilities has changed over time for you (if it has), and if so what your journey has been like.

Now go back and review your self-assessment.

- Do you think or feel any differently now that you've dug in a bit deeper?
- Do you want to change any of your answers?
- Or do you want to add to the lists offered, noting what's been especially true for you?
- At this point are you aware of wanting to develop new capacities in this area? If so start a list of your own or continue reading for my suggestions that might help you get started.

New Desired Capacities

Now that you've had a chance to familiarize yourself with the Spectrum of Expression for Pillar Five, go back and review what you checked in the self-assessment above. Has your perspective shifted at all? Are you aware of wanting to develop new capacities in this area?

To help you think and feel your way through this, I've created a list of potential capacities you might feel drawn to. This list is suggestive and far from exhaustive. Some may appeal to you while others may not. (Feel free to add your own!)

Now rank this list in the order of significance to you, one meaning this is a high priority for you, and five being "not relevant to me, at least not now."

[   ] I'm willing to explore and experiment, tuning myself to what makes me feel on purpose, even when it goes against what I've imagined for myself in the past.

[   ] I organize my life so that I only do what I have energy for (as much as possible). I focus on what brings me energy and turn away from what drains it.

[   ] I practice trusting that all is unfolding well even when I don't have a clear view of more than the next few steps in front of me.

[   ] I consult my inner guidance to direct me rather than using my thinking brain to try to "figure things out."

[   ] I recognize when my conditioning wants to direct me away from what's true for me and toward what I've been told is safer or more appropriate for me. I have perspective and more choice now about what direction I take and why.

Once you've ranked these possibilities, name your top two priorities. What can you do this week to begin to develop this valuable skill? You'll find helpful suggestions to support you with this in the next section.

Reflection Questions

I invite you to review and ponder these questions in any way that works for you. Feel free to respond to the ones that speak to you and leave the rest. You may write about them in your journal (highly recommended), take them into meditation or on a walk with you, make a sketch or painting about how they make you feel, or some other way that works for you. Writing down your reflections provides you with a record of your experiences, which can be very helpful later. As we evolve, we tend to forget where we were and that makes it difficult to appreciate how much we've grown.

> What did you discover about yourself through the self-assessment and Spectrum of Expression? Did you feel affirmed in some ways? Did anything surprise or disturb you? Are you inspired to develop any new capacities?

> What can you do this week to begin to develop this valuable new capacity? What resources do you need? What do you need to prepare? What kind of support do you need? Is there any resistance you need to face and overcome? Who in your life can partner with you and can help hold you accountable?

> Apply what you learned or realized in Pillar Five to your primary Learning Question. What does this teaching add to your inquiry? What was your Learning Question(s) for this specific pillar? Make a few notes about what's arising for you including how this feels in your body.

> What do you feel enthusiastic about? What draws you in and gives you energy? What could you do all day and not get bored? Why?

> Can you remember a time when you felt *on purpose*? Remember this doesn't have to be what you do for a living! If so how would you characterize it? If not what are your musings about this?

> Do you feel you're making the contribution you came here to make? If so has this changed over time, or has it been consistent for you? If not do you feel something is in the way, or is it more that you haven't focused on this?

> What's your family's experience and place in history? What's your relationship with that history and your feelings about it? How do you think that influences your sense of purpose and contribution?

> If you could change one thing in the world just like that – snap! – what would it be? Could this desire guide you or provoke you into seeing the world and your place in it differently? What action could you take, even a small one, to set this change into motion? Remember the connection

doesn't need to be obvious to anyone but you. (Remember Shiloh's purpose and contributions.)

> How would your life change if you felt on purpose and that you were making your right contribution every day? How would you feel? What would become possible?
> What does your purpose and contribution pillar look and feel like? How does it support your Temple of Sovereignty?

Communication that Connects

The ability to listen deeply, to speak clearly, boldly, and compassionately, and the willingness to be influenced by another's point of view.

"Would you rather be right or would you rather connect? Because usually you can't have both."

—Marshall Rosenberg,
founder of Nonviolent Communication

"Listening as a gift of care."

—Katherine Woodward Thomas

How well do I listen?

How well do I express myself?

The Balm of Attention

It's been a long day, and you just want to curl up and shut out the world. But you can't. You've got too much energy running around inside you to relax, too many thoughts chewing over the conversation you had with your boss. So instead of just heading home, you text one of your besties and see if she's available to have a glass of wine with you. She is, and so you do.

"I'm pretty agitated and kind of confused right now," you let her know. "Can you please just listen for a bit?"

"Of course, sweetheart," she responds. "Go ahead. I'm all ears."

You've been friends for a few years and you've each held space for the other just like this many times in the past. You each hold the other as a sovereign being: whole, capable, intuitive, caring and still human and full of human emotion. You're committed to being available to each other; neither of you really got what you needed emotionally when you were growing up and together you're helping to heal that.

She watches your eyes and face with caring and curiosity, giving you her undivided attention. She reflects back to you key points of what you care about and asks clarifying questions to make sure she completely understands. This helps you deepen your understanding of the situation as well, as her questions draw you out and invite you to consider angles you may not have considered yet. You feel no hurry or pressure to finish up. You bask in the energetic space created by your beloved's attention and as you relax, your distress melts away. Your breathing becomes deeper and calmer. Your heart rate and your thoughts slow down. Your nervous system regulates into a coherent rhythm. Tension drains away, and you fall silent.

You two sit in the pause for a few moments.

"Would it be okay for me to share an observation with you?" she asks.

"Sure," you say because you're ready now.

"I totally get why you're upset and confused. What your boss did doesn't make a lot of sense to me. I would be confused, too, I think." Pause. "At the same time," she goes on, "this feels familiar to me, like when you had that fight with your brother. Remember that?" You nod, assenting. "Does the fight with your boss remind you of anything?"

You pause. "Hmmm," you say. You're tuning in to the feeling in your heart and when you felt it before. "Ahhh. Yeah, I guess it does. It's like that time my brother made that decision without talking to me about it first. Like he didn't care how that decision would impact me. But really … really … it's this feeling I have that … that I don't matter. What I want, what I think we could and should do, that what matters to me matters to them. Ugh, that hurts. I felt that way growing up so much!"

"Yep," she says, "I know exactly how you feel. Sucks, doesn't it? You matter to me and I think you're brilliant." She smiles, tilting her head. "I get that your boss is being a bit of an ass. She could have communicated with you better so you didn't find out from someone else. But I kinda doubt it has anything to do with you specifically. I mean she's always given you good performance reviews, right?" You nod. "Is it possible that she just got careless? Maybe she's overwhelmed with all the changes she has to deal with right now too?"

"Yeah, that's possible. Likely even. She's not a bad person," you respond.

"From what you've told me in the past I would agree; she doesn't seem to be bad or harsh. Sometimes she's just not aware of how what she does impacts other people. Is that right?"

"Yeah, I'd say that's right."

"Do you think you could talk with her about it? Would she be receptive? Or would it be better just to let it go? *If you can.*" She's looking at you intently now.

"I don't know yet. I'm going to have to sit with this for a bit. And do something to move my energy." You shift around in your chair, rolling your shoulders. "I'm still a bit caught in past, but I can move through that."

"Sure you can, honey." She smiles at you. "Why don't you go jump on your trampoline for a while and then sleep on it. I bet you'll be clearer in the morning. You know how to do this."

And you do.

You reach over and give her a hug. "Thanks, babe," you say into her hair.

"Any time," she breathes back.

We Humans Are Communicative Beings

In the regenerating New World I'm imagining, we've developed a much deeper and more complex understanding of the myriad factors influencing our communication. Right now we mostly have a pretty simple understanding of communication: words, tone of voice, facial expressions, and other body language. In this pillar we'll build a broader, more nuanced, and more inclusive understanding of communication that includes aspects from the first five pillars and also the heterogeneity and inequities of our world.

We create meaning from all the different forms of information we give and receive, and if we're not awake, then we'll do so unconsciously through our default lens. When we're awake, we can attune ourselves to our patterned behavior and choose to step outside into new possibilities for ourselves and the perspectives of other people. We're inherently communicative, meaning-making beings, and the more aware and in command of this process we are, the more sovereign we become. Exploring and practicing communication that connects, both with those close to us and those with very different backgrounds and motivations, is a vital component of our *Thrutopian Imperative*.

> "Whether you're aware of it or not, when you interact
> with others you're continuously giving and receiving
> wordless signals. All of your nonverbal behaviors –
> the gestures you make, your posture, your tone of voice,
> how much eye contact you make – send strong messages.
> They can put people at ease, build trust, and draw others
> toward you, or they can offend, confuse, and undermine
> what you're trying to convey. These messages don't stop
> when you stop speaking either. Even when you're
> silent, you're still communicating nonverbally."
> —Jeanne Segal, Ph.D., Melinda Smith, M.A.,
> Lawrence Robinson and Greg Boose for helpguide.org

What you discovered and practiced in Pillars One through Five profoundly influences what you're communicating. Your degree of capacity and command in each of the earlier pillars highly influences how you embody and energetically express yourself. Most of this is *nonverbal*.

In Pillar One, you're communicating with the Flow of Life through your spiritual practice and inner guidance. Human Design shows us the way we're designed to do this through our Strategy and Authority. As Generators and Manifesting Generators, we let Spirit know what we're curious about and desiring through asking generative questions. Then we pay attention to what the Flow of Life brings to us in our outer reality that we then get to respond to with our Sacral Authority. We're in a dynamic relationship based in part on verbal communication: *I wonder* (for example) *how this thing I'm focused on will unfold in my life.* And also through nonverbal communication through synchronicities: *I was just wondering about that and here's an email in my inbox about it!* And also through a somatic, emotional, intuitive, and energetic response from my Sacral saying *uh-huh* and my head nodding in agreement. Doing the inner work of Pillars One through Four especially makes it easier to feel, trust, and follow this inner guidance.

Pillar Two teaches emotional wisdom, which greatly influences your communication. Knowing what your triggers are, for example, (we all have them) can forewarn you about what kind of situations might activate you. Knowing the patterns you tend to fall into when you feel overwhelmed can help you get yourself out of a pattern when you fall into it and maybe even avoid having it activated in the first place. But when you do get triggered, having the capacity to contain your automatic response and not react can avoid a potential blowup and ensure that your communications don't harm other people – or yourself. Emotional wisdom then teaches you to pause, ground, breathe, and move energy through physical activity so you're not at the mercy of your own emotional energy. All these strategies facilitate you either staying in the present moment or getting back into the moment as soon as possible. From this place you become more in charge of your communication – verbal, nonverbal, and energetic.

In Pillar Three, you discovered the significance of *being in your body*, being in loving relationship with your body, and nurturing your physical home. Your posture, facial expressions, clarity of eyes and skin, and ease of movement transmit confidence, a sense of belonging, and being settled. Having rounded or slumped shoulders (very common), a collapsed chest, and a bowed head, for example, transmit a very different message than a head held high, relaxed shoulders, and a fluid spine. A soft, attentive face feels receptive, whereas a tight mouth and clenched jaw feel tense and closed off.

Pillar Four explores the health, vitality, and power of your auric field. When your human electromagnetic field is clear, pure, and strong, it will transmit light and uplift the energy around it, like stepping into the sun on a chilly day. This powerful energy communicates possibility and potentials that other people can sense and feel and invites them to be in your presence, work with you, and receive the blessing of your energy.

Pillar Five reveals that the feeling of being on purpose expresses as enthusiasm. Enthusiasm can be contagious in its ability to attract, open, and uplift other people's energy and sense of possibility. Enthusiasm banishes resistance and doubt with liveliness, nonattachment, and focus on what's being created rather than on what's in the way. By being on purpose and sharing your enthusiasm, you represent and transmit that something new and different, out-of-the-box, visionary, and perhaps even *outrageous* is actually possible.

Developing understanding of and capacity in these different areas enhances your ability to command your communication. Alignment, integrity, wisdom, and ease exude from your sovereign self; purpose and radiance broadcast your power within and fuel your influence in the world. These qualities create a sure foundation upon which to grow yourself into the sovereign steward you have the potential to become.

If you're lacking in any one of these areas, you may create – unconsciously or consciously – dissonant messages that others feel and respond to often without even realizing what's happening. This is why, even as you spiral out into the world with other people, most likely you'll spiral back inward to develop more awareness and capacity in the earlier pillars. Your experiences with other people will signal to you places you need to grow so that you may show up differently and with more command.

One of my Clarity Breathwork mentors used to say: "So you think you're so enlightened? Get into a relationship." Then I would add: "Become a parent!" (He wasn't a parent.)

The Communication Game

Conversation around my family dinner table growing up was lively and loud. Fueled by a bourbon before dinner and a glass of wine at the table, my father pontificated, made jokes with my brother, and set the tone of the evening. My mother threw in her comments, and I blurted trying to get my words in edgewise. Usually no one was listening much except sometimes to my father, who was brilliant, dynamic, and casually domineering. I learned how to be loud, domineering, and maybe brilliant on occasion. But I certainly didn't learn how to listen. That came decades later, and I had to be trained – and then practice. A lot.

Typically we get trained into right/wrong, good/bad ways of thinking and being, which creates a kind of ping pong game between parties. You're on that side, I'm on this side, and we're each focused on volleying back our best shot in hopes of winning the communication game. Have you had a conversation with someone who was determined to have the last word? Maybe you've been that person on occasion? I think that happens because our sense of self-worth gets wrapped up in being right, being more knowledgeable, more informed, more persuasive, getting someone else to either agree with us or otherwise capitulate. Think debate club or even how you probably were taught to write a persuasive paper in high school or college. Get your point across. Address and demolish all objections. And make sure to have the last word.

One of the many reasons I decided to leave academia is that I fundamentally disagreed with the type of debate common among scholars through which they built their careers. I became a professor because I wanted to explore how to recast US American studies with Black people and their experience at the center of it. For me this was an act of regenerative historicism (I didn't have that term then) through which we as a people in the United States could begin to come to terms with the paradox of a democratic republic founded simultaneously on the notion that "all men are created equal" and also relying on enslaving an enormous group of people, genocide of the indigenous nations, and systemic gender inequity.

I expected resistance from scholars who were invested in keeping the United States a white man's country. But I did not anticipate the ways in which scholars who presented themselves as politically progressive did their best to undermine my work (demolish my argument) by asserting that, basically, *resistance has always been futile*. I found this very disheartening; far from having lively conversation among intellectuals that included different points of view and disagreement (which is healthy) that simply felt like a failure of imagination and posturing for tenure. Ugh. *I'd had enough.*

The Challenge: Finite and Infinite Games

Author, speaker, and corporate trainer Simon Sinek sheds light on this subject when he talks about "finite games and infinite games." Finite games are based on specific rules of engagement, clear sides, and timelines, and include familiar games like football, gin rummy, and volleyball. You play these games to win, you keep score, and they end with winners and losers. The level of intensity, seriousness, and ferocity with which these games are played varies tremendously. Until recently these games were largely the terrain of men, both as players and fans. I once had a boyfriend who told me: "Sports is the universal male language. I can walk up to any man and start a conversation by asking about the score of a game."

While another book on gender dynamics lies in wait inside that statement, let's settle here for recognizing the cultural and economic power of professional sports, the *masculine* character of this kind of competition, and its influence on our ways of being in the world. We see this replicated everywhere: video games, spelling bees, cook-offs and country fairs, how grades get configured in school, who gets admitted to what college or university, and even competition among affiliate partners in online launches. Certainly women can be competitive, yet as they participate in finite games they step into a masculine mode and play to win.

Infinite games, on the other hand, operate quite differently. The object of an infinite game isn't to win; it's to keep the game going and to stay in the game. Infinite games have no beginning or end and there are no winners or losers. When you play you need, at least according to Sinek, a "worthy opponent," in his case another company whose work stimulates your company to continue to innovate and to become better at what you do. I'd call this healthy competition because here the point is for each player to continue to grow and evolve and become even better at what they do. The competition spurs excellence rather than determining winners and losers or seeking to dominate.

I found this model very illuminating because, as Sinek points out, we get into trouble when we apply the rules of a finite game to an environment or situation that truly is an infinite game. His examples include politics, business, and education (underscoring what I said above about my disillusionment with the academy); you can't *win* any of these games. You might win an election, for example, but the game of politics continues on and on and on. I would add communication in the realm of relationships as another place we get into trouble when we play to win rather than to keep bettering ourselves and keep the game of connecting going.

Signs that you're playing to win in your communications include:

- Rehearsing what you're going to say to rebut what the other person is saying rather than listening and taking in what they're sharing
- Doing your best to prove that you're right (and the other or others are therefore wrong) and convincing others to agree with you
- Being convinced that your point of view is the better one and not being willing to take someone else's point of view seriously
- Entering into the communication with a specific outcome in mind that you're fully committed to and that inhibits your ability to be open to new possibilities and different points of view
- Energetically "digging in your heels" when someone says something you don't agree with or that makes you uncomfortable
- Talking over someone in an effort to get your point across
- Raising your voice to try to dominate the conversation

Of course there's a spectrum of intensity along which any of these behaviors can be expressed. Some of them might not even be said aloud, yet they structure the way you show up and interact and deeply influence what's possible – or not. Even unconsciously the rules of engagement require that someone wins and someone loses, and my guess is that you tend to fall on one side or the other of that game.

The scene I described above of my family culture around the dinner table definitely feels like a finite game. My father always played to win (he was heavily conditioned by his father to play to win) and he usually did. My mother reluctantly played, but she didn't really like the terms and so was half in and half out most of the time. My brother and I did our best to learn the rules of the game (they were never spelled out) and then to win when we could. This usually amounted to having everyone else's undivided attention for even one to two minutes, and it didn't happen often. The other goal was to receive my father's attention, and often my brother won that game by having a kind of side conversation with him that my mother and I couldn't participate in. It was exciting at times, often chaotic, sometimes confusing, intellectually challenging, and an incredible training ground for future life.

If you receive your first lessons in communication in your family of origin, you also go on receiving lessons in school, in your work environments, organizations and groups you belong to, and your intimate relationships. School typically teaches you to compete rather than cooperate and collaborate with others. A specific class may feel like a finite game: What's the syllabus? What're the assignments? When are the quizzes, papers, and/or exams, and how much are they all worth? *How do I win this game?* you might think. *How do I get an A?* This preoccupation then structures your perception, your motivation, and your behavior. How do I communicate to demonstrate my knowledge and intelligence? If the course is graded on a curve, you know your performance will be judged against that of others: *not everyone can get an A after all.*

This type of scarcity thinking runs deep. It's often carried over into work environments where you work for quotas and performance measures in the pursuit of a raise or a bonus or promotion. This thinking fuels the climb up the corporate ladder, beating out your colleagues for higher positions, more pay, more prestige, more influence, and better benefits. In these school and work situations, being able to assert and argue for your point of view is more highly valued than your ability to listen, reflect, and empathize. This is considered a more masculine form of communication: assertive, authoritative, persuasive, perhaps patronizing, potentially coercive, and typically silencing other points of view. This is the voice of individualism's version of sovereignty discussed in Pillar Four. Connection, understanding, mutuality, and cooperation don't figure in here. *Winning the game* figures prominently in the Story of Progress where empowered men seek to control and manipulate the living world, women, and those with fewer resources and cultural capital.

Yet ironically, as Sinek points out, education – and I would add the game of life – is an infinite, not a finite, game. True education exceeds the bean counting of grades, competitions to prove your intelligence, and being the one to come up with the "right" answer. True education has no end point, provides no accolades, and poses many more questions than it answers.

Are you getting a sense of the damage we can do to each other without meaning to when we try to communicate as if we're playing a finite game? We need a way out of this habitual pattern, which is like a ping pong game. In ping pong you hit the ball across the net with the intention of making it impossible for the other player to return the volley; then you win the point. You can imagine by now how that goes if you engage in conversation that way. Instead imagine paddle ball, a beach game in which the aim is to keep the volley going. All of your effort goes into hitting the ball to the other person with the intention that they can hit it back to you. While this game will end when you get tired, it's much more of an infinite than a finite game.

---

*Pause for a moment and reflect upon the training ground
you had for communication when you were growing up.
What was your family culture like? Did you spend time
together as a family and if so what did you learn about how
to communicate? Did the experience feel like being in a finite
game in which people were playing to win? I think this is
pretty common and very often the experience is gender coded.
Or did you not spend time together and how was that for you?
What meaning did you give to this silent communication?
Make a few notes or doodles in your journal before moving on.*

My Mother and Me

I'm nineteen years old, and I'm sitting in my therapist's office with my mother. I'm sharing about how I felt challenged by the school environment I was in growing up. It wasn't so much that I was a white kid in a predominantly Black neighborhood, although that had its challenges. It was more that this was the inner city, where schools weren't well supported. I'd been bored, distressed, and dissociated by having to spend my days in schools where I learned very little, didn't fit in, and felt afraid much of the time.

When I was younger, I hadn't felt any receptivity on my parents' part to hearing how this was for me (or for my brother). They'd moved us into this neighborhood for two primary reasons: first, because they'd found a house they loved at a price they could afford, and second, because they were inspired by the Civil Rights Movement (it was 1963) and welcomed the opportunity to do something that indicated their solidarity. My brother and I were brought up to have a similar attitude. My parents were convinced that we'd be fine, even though they had no idea what school was like for us. They didn't ask about our experience, and I didn't sense that my experience, if it didn't match their expectations, mattered very much.

Thus the therapist's office. I'd been working with this therapist for a few months and, in her view, I'd benefit from being able to share with my mother my experience in ways I'd never felt I could before. After I'd expressed my first layer (there were many layers), my mother responded with considerable energy, saying: "Well, alright then. When I was a kid …" and she began telling us about how she felt isolated and like an outcast. I became increasingly agitated, and our therapist stopped my mother saying: "You're sharing about your own experience right now. I don't believe you've really heard and taken in what Maggie's saying to you."

My mother was not aware of what she was doing and its impact on me. She'd translated what I'd said into criticism of her (it wasn't), so she countered with her own story to defend herself. In effect she wanted to demonstrate that she'd been a bigger victim than I was. None of this was conscious on her part: through her default lens, she'd felt attacked and so she defended herself. Fortunately she trusted our therapist (and me, too, really) and she was willing to pause, listen, and take in what our therapist had said. She turned to me, suddenly vulnerable rather than defensive, and asked me to tell her again about my experience. She put aside her reaction, focused on me, and a profound healing unfolded between us. I was able to voice feelings I'd had for a long time (and that had made me leave home at sixteen), and she was able to receive my experience without taking it personally and making it about her. I stepped across another threshold into adulthood, and she greeted me there.

When my mother became receptive and wanted to learn about my experience, I began to feel *seen and heard for my adult self*, not suppressed as I'd felt as child. I didn't need her to do anything else. I just needed her to hear me and do her best to understand. Eventually she apologized, not so much for creating the situation I lived through but for not asking about or being receptive to my point of view when I was a kid. That was a balm for me, and it brought us much closer together. This experience as an adolescent showed me that it was possible to repair relationships and evolve ways of communicating even if they'd been reinforced for many years.

Let's Start Close In

Evolving a family system in this way may be easier or potentially more difficult than communicating in ways that connect with people with different backgrounds, affiliations, and motivations from our own. My mother and I loved and appreciated each other, and this made it much easier for us to make our way through our conditioned behavior to deeper connection. Some people's families may be volatile, fragmented, or coercive. In this case, seeking connection may prove particularly challenging, as the wounds from early life bury deep inside the subconscious, often hidden from awareness yet ready to jump out and take over when touched upon.

Challenges arise in intimate relationships because *closeness brings someone near to the places inside you that are not yet healed*. When you fall in love, part of you imagines that finally! the person has arrived who will see, hear, and care for me the way I didn't experience when I was young. *This person will heal me,* you imagine unconsciously.

And yet anxiety, insecurities, fear, distrust, and self-criticism can arise as the younger and hurt-self (as we saw in Pillar Two) emerges and jumps into the driver's seat of your life. You may find yourself suddenly navigating aspects of your inner world as they emerge unbidden into your interactions. What was contained inside rises to the surface: raw, tender, angry perhaps, frustrated and sad almost certainly, and definitely in need of attention, compassion, and understanding. This can be very disturbing and confusing to everyone involved and needs to be handled with care and compassion.

Some people walk away from a relationship when this happens. If you don't understand what's going on and/or don't have the tools to navigate this kind of challenge, you may decide *this person isn't right for me* or *this relationship isn't worth it*. Yet this situation presents an opportunity for healing and growth of immense proportions. The hurt-self emerges because a container of love – or the hope for one – provides a safe place to show your vulnerable side, your unmet needs, and your deeper longings and desires. As author and "Mother of Rebirthing" Sondra Ray once said: "Love brings up everything unlike itself for the purpose of healing."

How that hurt-self expresses through you, and how you respond when someone expresses a hurt-self, determine whether your communication connects – or creates more distance and potential harm. As author, facilitator, and thought leader adrienne maree brown notes: "We are socialized, trained, encouraged and given permission to punish each other." We experience this early and carry the imprints forward until we intentionally interrupt this destructive pattern.

We can choose differently. You can choose differently. Lean into the power of the Gate 51, the Gate of Shock/Challenge we explored in Pillar Four, to break apart this cultural habit and initiate yourself into a more awakened and empowered way of being. Emotional wisdom teaches us to express without blame and witness without judgment, bringing us closer together.

Intimate relationships can be a crucible inside of which you build your capacity to speak up, listen, reflect, empathize, and truly connect.

Capacities built here create a foundation upon which you can spiral out into the world with other people with stability, compassion, and responsiveness. Unhealed wounds and trauma, conversely, can adversely influence your ability to be with and connect with people from different backgrounds and motivations. You may be prone to being triggered and fall into patterned behavior that you wouldn't consciously choose. Building your skills and capacities offered in earlier pillars ensures you won't tumble into this emotional morass – and if you do, you'll know how to get back out again.

As one wise friend of mine noted: "If you don't do your inner work on your own, it will come out in community. And no one likes that."

Spiraling Outward

All of this gains complexity as you spiral out of your family environment and close friendships to interface with other people. You're faced with how you've been conditioned to communicate in relation to how others have been conditioned to communicate. Yet for the most part *no one talks about this.* You just do your best to speak up and be heard, or stay quiet and not be noticed, or try to learn the rules of engagement inside an environment where no one fills you in. You might find yourself speaking up in a way that you feel embarrassed about in retrospect (more on this later). Or you might feel frustrated with yourself when you didn't say anything because you couldn't tell if it would be okay or not. You might feel stomped on because the person you're speaking with keeps interrupting you. Or maybe speaking over each other is part of your culture, and you can't understand why it bothers other people. And then there's that moment when you suddenly realize you've offended someone with something you said and you're not even sure why.

***Feminine* Sovereignty is *relational* rather than *individualistic*; this philosophy recognizes our interrelatedness and the interconnectedness of all things, including *each other*.**

Therefore Feminine Sovereignty calls us to perceive and acknowledge each other as sovereign beings: intelligent, capable, whole, and evolving, even though we've also experienced trauma and discrimination. Fostering communication that connects calls us to be aware of how power relationships influence meanings we may not otherwise be aware of so that we don't create harm unwittingly. Awareness enables us to unravel hierarchies rather than unconsciously replicating them. We can do this work in any relationship, any conversation, whether it's one-on-one, in an intimate group, or in a larger meeting of an organization or at work.

Historically women's voices, for example, haven't been heard as well as men's; sometimes women either haven't spoken up or were actively silenced. *To be seen and not heard* has applied to women as well as to children. In my work with clients one of the biggest if not the biggest wounds, especially among women, *is not feeling seen and heard*. This translates into feeling *you don't matter*. Many women felt invisible growing up. Sometimes we've effaced ourselves and focused our attention on more powerful family members, as did Jean who we learned about in Pillar Two. This can happen to such an extent that you lose touch with your own needs and opinions and never give attention to developing your own point of view.

Those with less cultural capital – e.g., BIPOC, LGBTQ, and immigrants as well as women – may mask our true feelings and points of view, sensing we're not welcome, safe, or understandable to people different from ourselves. We've experienced those with more cultural authority engaging in life as a finite game in which they play to win, as I did with my father and in the academy. Historically laws were written, for example, to exclude anyone who wasn't a white man from citizenship and voting. We continue to live with this legacy as systemic racism, xenophobia, misogyny, and homophobia are imbedded deep in the structures of our society. This legacy characterizes the culture of many of our institutions, organizations, laws and policies, real estate practices, access to education and capital, and so on. Many assumptions and expectations operate unspoken inside these cultures, influencing and often undermining our ability to communicate and connect across lines of difference.

Our programming teaches us to focus outside on those with more power to stay safe and avert persecution, punishment, and betrayal. A woman with a narcissistic partner may placate him, for example, or a worker may agree to do something against their beliefs when their boss insists that they do so. I've had younger people agree to do something simply because they thought that's what I wanted to hear – and then they don't do it but don't tell me. This kind of subterfuge is so common that we take it for granted simply as *just the way things are*. Our inability to feel safe and confident saying what's true for us mucks up our ability to communicate to the point where we're on the same page.

Can you think of a time when you felt caught in a dynamic like this – on either side – and you found it difficult to break out? What was that like for you? What's your perspective now on what happened? What role did you play? What would you do differently now? Write up or imagine a self-correction, as discussed in Your Daily Date with the Divine, *if that would feel good to you.*

Affinity groups provide an environment based in commonality, typically a vector of identity, such as gender and gender-spectrum or race or religion or age or combinations thereof. Inside these groups certain experiences may be assumed, such as having been subjected to "mansplaining" or "whitesplaining" or "wealthsplaining." Inside affinity groups vulnerability and transparency may be easier, as some degree of trust and support is assumed. I've participated in and facilitated many women's groups over the years. I've felt and witnessed much support being offered and received inside those groups. I've heard something similar from men about their men's groups, for example, and experienced this inside my yoga community. We all need groups where we can relax, remove the masks, and feel understood. Yet even here we need to be aware of our heterogeneity as, for example, women are very different from each other, especially when you factor in other aspects of identity plus our backgrounds, ages, values, and so on.

Growing yourself into a sovereign being in the world with other sovereign beings includes being able to step outside your own perspective, your default lens, and being receptive to new possibilities and points of view. This is particularly true for those who have more privilege, as our privilege tends to create blind spots in our understanding of ourselves and people with backgrounds different than our own.

George Floyd's murder in 2020 awakened vast numbers of white people both to the systematic abuse that Black people, especially Black men, experience on a daily basis and to their own, our own, race privilege. Being assigned the race "white" based on our skin color grants us race privilege without us having to do anything. Having privilege doesn't make you a bad person; in fact you can leverage your privilege to work for greater equity and unwind systems of domination. It's *entitlement* – this sense that you and people like you deserve certain things that others don't – that's a problem. Entitlement reinforces the power-over attitudes and behaviors of those with more resources or cultural capital and authority – sometimes overtly, sometimes unwittingly. For some working-class white men (and women), for example, the entitlement they feel based on their race privilege makes them feel powerful in a system that otherwise exploits them economically.

Pause here and reflect on the forms of privilege you have and how that's influenced your perception of the world and the ways you communicate. Do you find that in certain situations you have more privilege than other people, and the reverse in other situations? How does this influence your expression and your listening? How does your body feel in these different groups or conversations? What kind of beliefs influence your behavior? Are you aware of any default lens? This can be uncomfortable, so please take the time you need, breathing deep, to become present to what's arising; no judgment here, just awareness. Make a few notes or a drawing before moving on.

Growing Your Communication Abilities

The Gift of the Throat Center: Human Design + Yoga

So far we've explored how familial, cultural, and power dynamics influence our communication without us even realizing it, at least some of the time. In a few moments we'll dive into specifics of how we can evolve ourselves so that we connect rather than divide and harm each other. But first we'll look at how one key aspect of your Human Design and your understanding and command of it may be influencing your communication. As we explore an example from my life, let me reiterate that what's important isn't so much the particulars of your design as your response to and relationship with it.

I mentioned in Pillar Four that before I discovered my Human Design I judged certain behaviors in myself as character flaws. *Sigh.* Fortunately or unfortunately, I know I'm not alone in this. I'm grateful that understanding your Human Design can lead you away from harmful self-criticism and into greater self-understanding, acceptance, and appreciation.

Among the most significant of these are what I came to understand as traits associated with the "open" Throat Center in Human Design. I felt perplexed about why sometimes I had trouble getting words out of my mouth and felt uncertain about what to say. Then at other times I'd be quite articulate, even saying things I'd never thought of before and definitely hadn't rehearsed. At still others, I'd blurt things out inappropriately or lose track of what I was saying and go on and on and on. I didn't feel in command of these experiences, and this undermined my confidence. I discovered that when I was in a situation in which people had come to hear me speak, like when I was teaching or giving a talk, I was fine. These were moments when I felt most articulate and at ease.

In other situations, like at a dinner with colleagues, I might alternate between feeling stifled or unsuccessfully trying to get people's attention who weren't listening. As you might imagine, these traits influenced my ability to communicate and my confidence in doing so. I'm usually pretty confident, yet this variable uncertainty about my ability to express myself caused stress and confusion and reduced my effectiveness. I found it virtually impossible to track what was happening and pinpoint the cause, so I wasn't able to resolve the situation.

As it turns out, those are all known traits of someone with an open Throat Center in their Human Design! *Who knew?*

Let's recall that the areas in your chart that are defined (colored in) are the energies to which you have consistent access and a way of expressing them. I call these your *core energies*. The parts that are open (white), you've experienced many times and in many different ways, and the way you express them may vary tremendously. I call these your *variable energies*.

So for me, with an open Throat, I've experienced my ability to express myself in many different ways depending on who I've been around. This helps explain my inconsistent experience! This also helped me understand why, when I'm with a group of people, sometimes it's much easier for me to express myself, especially when I have their attention. In this case, I'm recognized by them and pick up and amplify their definition.

This is just one example of several about how your Human Design, and that of those around you, may influence your communication without you even realizing it. For those who have their Throat Centers defined, their way of expressing themselves will be relatively consistent based on the specifics of their chart. All of us may learn to express in different ways, emotionally, for example, or from the Heart, or through storytelling, or rationally. Yet for those with a defined Throat, you'll tend to have one mode that's more predominant depending on what channel(s) connect your Throat to other centers.

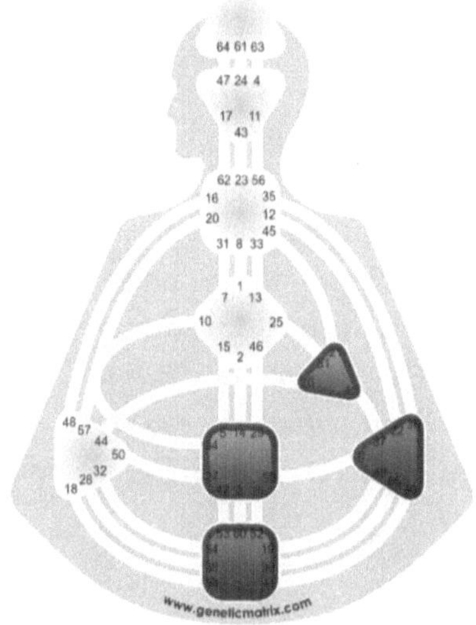

A third possibility arises when you have what we call a "motor to the Throat"; this is potent, activating, manifesting energy from an energetic engine or motor sending its energy to the Throat Center. Manifestors and Manifesting Generators have this configuration. This fast, powerful energy directs these Types through the creative impulses that come from the motor(s) they have connected to their Throat Center. The motor(s) fuel their ability to express, activate, and manifest.

Have you ever experienced or witnessed a situation in which someone who's usually quiet suddenly blurts something out or becomes talkative, perhaps even eloquent? In this case, the person speaking most likely has come into contact with someone(s) who, simply because of their design, has provided the speaker with access to energy they don't have on their own. This is one of the beautiful ways we energetically support each other without even trying or knowing what's happening. When I was first practicing reading charts, I noticed that a good friend of mine and I both have open Throats, but when we're together our Throats become defined because of how our designs interface and interact. When I shared that with her, she said: "Ah, maybe that's why when we're together we like to talk so much! And some things are so clear to me when we're talking, then we're apart it's harder for me to remember!"

Because most of us are unaware of these energetic interactions, we don't know how to use this to our advantage or how to avoid the potential pitfalls.

I spent years being confused and frustrated by my inconsistent ability to express myself. When I learned about my open Throat and explored how this attribute could be advantageous for me, *everything changed.*

The short version is that I began to pay attention to how I felt when I was teaching or speaking. I began recording everything so I could capture expressions I channeled directly through my open Throat, bypassing my thinking mind. When I wasn't in that kind of role, I practiced sensing the energy exchange happening at that moment. I stepped away from the ping pong communication style I grew up with by not trying to assert my point of view as I had in the past. Instead I paid more attention to right timing and readiness. *Is this the right time to speak up?* I'd ask myself. *Are they ready and interested in hearing what I have to say?* I learned to speak up only when the answer to both was a clear YES. I've become much more attuned to the degree of listening and receptivity in a room, avoiding situations in which people are jockeying for attention.

The piece that really empowered me was learning to recall for myself what it feels like energetically to have my Throat defined, even motorized. My Kundalini Yoga practice refined my ability to memorize the quality and intelligence of my energy when I'm in an elevated state. Now before I record my YouTube videos or begin writing for the day, I do my energy work to uplift and power my auric field. Then I imagine I'm speaking to you, my dear reader, and this makes me better able to express myself. I remember *what it feels like* to be articulate and for a time *I can recreate it.* That energy won't be sustainable, but I can invoke it for a time. *Pretty cool, huh?*

Layers of Complexity

Spiraling back to what we explored earlier in this pillar, I hope you're beginning to perceive the layers of complexity that influence our ability to communicate in ways that connect rather than divide. Whatever the specifics of your Human Design or your identity and background, you can develop your capacity to become aware of your own default tendencies, and also to the energetics of a conversation or meeting. Just one person's powerful presence and listening can set the tone or redirect the quality of a gathering or meeting. As you get to know yourself better and build your inner power, *you can become that person* even in challenging situations.

Before moving into more practical recommendations and practices, I want to note two points from Kundalini Yoga and the chakra system. First, trauma often causes you to hold your breath and close your throat. This is a survival response to a dangerous situation. This may be shock or the desire not to make a noise, to stay safe. Depending on the intensity of the trauma, such an experience may create an imprint of freeze and silence in your energy body until it's recognized, released, and healed. Sometimes these imprints come with you into this life from other lives; sometimes you may inherit them through your ancestral lineage. Supporting clients as a breathworker, I've witnessed imprints of being strangled or hung rise to the surface out of the subconscious and release out of the cells of the body. Other times trauma imprints come from being punished, abused, or neglected in early life.

Whichever the case, energy practices such as we do in Kundalini Yoga can help release these imprints, relaxing the nervous system and opening the throat chakra. As the practices energize and clear the heart and lungs, they facilitate greater ease in expressing yourself. Indeed the ease of your breathing greatly influences, well, *everything*, and most certainly the command of your voice.

If you've habitually suppressed your voice for whatever reason, when you first begin speaking up you may find you speak with much intensity. Understandably those who've felt suppressed may feel anger when they get a chance to speak. I've witnessed this in women, beginning with my mother and her friends and colleagues as feminism awakened them and continuing to this day with some of my mentoring clients. It's as if a pressure valve has been loosened, and what's been building inside finally has an outlet. If you witness this or you find yourself doing this, cultivate your compassion for the speaker and hold space for their communication as best you can. My experience is that as we liberate ourselves from our conditioning and own our inner power and authority, our communications may be particularly intense, especially at first. Remembering this can support you in the face of someone else's intense communication to not take it personally and to listen for the deeper truths as they emerge. Usually as the pressure lessens, in the presence of a compassionate witness, intensity will wane and possibilities will become available.

Communication that Connects Rather than Divides and Harms

For us to build capacity for communicating in ways that connect rather than divide and harm, we need to be alert, engaged, and purposeful. If we're going to learn to live together effectively and (relatively) harmoniously, we need to create ways of bridging divides that often have long and painful histories behind them. Creating these bridges is vital, whether in an estranged thirty-year marriage, or between parents and children, or between people of different political parties, ethnic or religious affiliations, economic and educational backgrounds, national origins, abilities, and/or different racial and gender assignments. Ping pong communication has so long been the accepted and anticipated norm; we can change this, yet it's not an *easy* or *obvious* practice.

So few of us had this modeled for us that we may not even know it exists or what it looks and feels like. Marshall Rosenberg, creator of Nonviolent Communication (NVC) as I noted in Pillar Two, observes that most of us automatically translate whatever other people say into criticism. This is why identifying your default lens is so vital, so you can gain perspective on the ways you filter and interpret what you hear. NVC teaches us how to tune in to another person, listen and take in what they're saying, and not take things so personally. It also teaches us how to express ourselves in nonjudgmental ways that both cultivate our connection with ourselves and invite others into our inner world.

One of the most empowering and liberating tenets of NVC is that you don't have to agree with what another person is saying to listen to them with the intention of understanding their point of view.

Many people don't even know this is possible! You think if you take in someone's perspective you're automatically annihilating your own. Yet the true magic comes when you've built the capacity to hold yet put to one side your own perspective and *need to be right* so that you can hear and try on how someone else feels and what they need – without believing you then need to fix anything. NVC is a *powerful presence practice* in which the *quality of the listening* of those involved does much of the connecting and the healing. I highly recommend studying at least its fundamentals if you sense you'd benefit.

In addition to each person feeling heard and seen, communication that connects can also help us create *a new shared perspective* that's greater than each individual's point of view. I had a profound healing with a friend with whom I'd had a brief romantic relationship. Our time didn't end well, and I was confused about why our communication had gone so sideways. Fortunately he became willing to meet with me and a woman facilitator who had profound listening and empathy skills. Through our conversations with her we became able to share more transparently, and each of us learned things about the other that we hadn't known. We had many moments of *ah, that's why you felt that way* or *that's why you acted that way.* The overlap in our perspectives grew and grew so that we created a new shared perspective greater than either one of us could have created on our own. This brought us deep healing individually and together, and our relationship has been easy and close ever since.

Key to this healing was our *willingness to be influenced* by what we heard from each other. It's an advanced practice to put down your defenses or opinions and be willing to be influenced by what they say. Now we'd been friends for years before we explored having a romantic relationship, so that certainly helped in our case; underneath the hurt we still had trust. Being influenced doesn't necessarily mean you're going to change your opinion or decide your position is wrong and you have to take on the other person's, although that may happen. When you focus on connecting and reconciling conflict rather than winning the game, you can repair misunderstandings, navigate difficult truths, and build trust based on truth. Your emotional wisdom, embodiment, energetic adeptness, and faith in Spirit all bolster your ability to engage in challenging conversations and come out the other side more connected.

Circling back together with the intention to understand more deeply, share with greater self-awareness, and listen more intently will enable you to repair rifts wrought by conflict. Indeed *repair is a keystone practice* of communication that connects. Every relationship, especially between empowered sovereign beings, will experience friction and dissonance in feelings and needs. That's normal and predictable, not a sign that's something's wrong. Instead conflict offers the opportunity to understand yourself and others more deeply, and to create greater connection and intimacy through truth-telling and powerful listening. Repair arising from difficult conversations characterizes healthy relationships among sovereign beings.

Suggested Guidelines for Communication that Connects

- Listen to understand without taking what's said personally.
- Be patient and receptive, discerning the right time, the right situation, and the right person(s) for your communication to be well received and heard.

- Assume the best of other people; unravel your *conditioned suspicions*.
- Pause to digest what you hear without needing to respond right away.
- Be open to new perspectives even if you don't agree with them; stop taking things so *seriously*.
- Be willing to let go of the need to be right (and to step away from the finite game).
- Be willing to change, to give up or modify your agenda for a better one.
- Appreciate anger and intensity for their honesty and build your capacity to be with it and foster safety without reacting.
- Articulate what's true for you as best you can, taking a hundred percent responsibility for your own experience and point of view (including your default lens), and *no more*.
- Speak from your heart more than from your mind; be willing to be humble and vulnerable.
- Be willing to make mistakes, to not know what to do or say yet be willing to *stay in*.
- Notice if fear arises; breathe to move the energy and regulate your nervous system. Don't let fear control you.
- Be willing to admit error, to see how you may unconsciously perpetuate hierarchies you don't believe in.
- Apologize and offer to make amends when appropriate. Apology, like listening, is a *balm* in stressed relationships and a key component of repair. This is *not* the same as admitting fault.
- Initiate repair after a conflict or misunderstanding; don't wait for the other person(s) to do this.
- Tap your intuition and creativity to come up with new possibilities and invite others to do the same.
- Seek/create common ground without erasing difference and complexity, fostering a *we're in this together* attitude to help guide new choices.

Additional Points for Purposefully Disrupting Cultural Patterns of Hierarchy

Depending on who's present, individuals will have different kinds of privilege in relation to each other. As a female-identified woman (known as cis) I may have more privilege than a trans or nonbinary person in a group of all genders – or less than a male-identified man. In a multiple racial group, I'll have white privilege. Becoming aware of your own vectors of privilege will support you to be sensitive to the often unspoken power dynamics in a room and to account for them accordingly.

For those with *more privilege* in a given situation, here are more specific guidelines:

- Facilitate trust by listening without reacting; check to see if unconscious entitlement or defensiveness are at play inside you.
- Be curious about perspectives that may feel challenging, especially from those with less privilege than you in this conversation.
- Develop your ability to ask clarifying questions and reflect what you heard with the intention of true understanding.
- Build your capacity to hold space for distress (not blame) to be expressed so that intensity diminishes and healing begins.
- If you feel distress, consider taking it to your affinity group for processing rather than expecting those with less privilege to help you in this way. *Really important.*
- After you've allowed yourself to be influenced by other people's points of view, circle back around and express your new understanding once you've taken in and integrated what you've heard. Acknowledge your growth without seeking approval.
- Speak less; listen more.

For those with *less privilege* in a given situation:

- Empower yourself by speaking truthfully in ways that invite understanding without diminishing your point of view.

- Be willing to name power dynamics that may be clouding the conversation without making individual(s) wrong.
- Learn to *stay in* even if you're afraid or offended and use your tools to regulate your nervous system so you can stay present and still listen.
- Assume the best of others until proven otherwise, even if they're from a group that's historically been oppressive.
- Keep in mind that systems of domination have distorted our perceptions and behavior for thousands of years and mistakes will be made as we unravel them.
- Invoking the power of the pause (Pillar Two) slows things down and gives everyone a chance to digest what's been said without the imperative (or even the invitation) to respond right away.
- Step away as needed if you feel those with more privilege have shut down, are pushing back, starting to seek your approval, or breaking down. If you're willing, let them know you're okay resuming when they've had a chance to do more of the inner work they need to do.

With these guidelines in place, imagine that:

- You could relax knowing that you and each person will have their turn to speak and everyone else has agreed to listen to the speaker. No cross talk. No interrupting. No getting on your phone and checking your social media and no watching someone else do that while you're talking.
- Someone reflected back to you what you shared so you knew you were heard. Then they asked you to go deeper with what you're sharing and helped draw you out so that you could discover more for yourself through the act of speaking.[18]
- You're open enough, curious enough, and engaging yet unattached enough that you could revise your point of view because you've taken in that of someone else.

---

18 This is particularly important for Projectors and people with open throats because they need to talk things through to get to clarity.

- You challenged yourself to grow beyond your conditioned ways of interacting and communicating, whatever they might be, and were willing to risk stepping into the unknown with others without guarantees of success.
- You could co-create an expanded and shared perspective that includes aspects of everyone's point of view, building trust, connection, and greater possibilities for the future.

How would that feel?

Practice for Communication that Connects in the Face of Conflict

In a classic ping pong communication game, no one is listening, people are taking pot shots at each other, and everyone alternates between defensive and aggressive. We see this mirrored everywhere in public discourse among politicians, commentators, advertisers, lawyers and more. This legacy of empire has become the norm, so if you're experiencing it, it's not your fault and you're not alone. But now that you know, it's your responsibility to change it. Here's one way how:

Step One

Interrupt the pattern. Before engaging with the other(s), tune inside to what you're feeling under the defensiveness, bravado, or hiding. Stop focusing on the other person(s) and what they're doing or not doing. Stop trying to negotiate or prove your point for a bit. What are you feeling? What do you need? What does this remind you of?

Step Two

At an agreed-upon time when everyone's ready in either order: a) Share your feelings and needs. Be vulnerable, revealing bits of your inner world. Let down the barricades; or b) Listen and take in what other(s) share without the pressure to respond.

Step Three

Take turns reflecting back to each other what you heard. Empathize if you can. Receive the other person's additions or adjustments to the reflections you offer. Sometimes you might not get it right the first time, and that's okay. The point is to aim to understand, not to never make a mistake. Sometimes you'll need a few back and forths so that everyone feels heard.

Step Four

On your own, reflect on how this new information influences your point of view. What can you see, feel, or know differently now as a result of receiving this other person(s)?

Step Five

Reconvene, and each share your new awareness. See what else arises from this sharing. Be open to something unexpected emerging as you go deeper together. *Welcome the mystery.*

Step Six

How would you characterize the new, shared perspective that's emerged from this process? How do you and the other(s) feel as a result? How will this guide you as you go forward in relationship with each other? Are there any new agreements you'd like to make to help solidify your new understanding?

Take Time to Assess, Integrate, and Apply What You've Learned

I'm so glad you've made it this far, as communication that connects is vital for healing and regenerating our world! I don't know about you, but I know I still have important communication capacities I need to keep developing! I think this is a lifelong endeavor. If you're feeling you need to do this, too, you're in very good company, LOL. Mine!

As usual, this section guides you through exploring your relationship to the themes of this pillar. You're an old hand at this by now, so go ahead and dive in! Below you'll find:

- **Self-Assessment**
- **Spectrum of Expression**
- **Pause, Reflect, and Review**
- **New Desired Capacities**
- **Questions for Reflection**

Self-Assessment

Ahhh, a moment to stop *taking in* and start *tuning in* …

Instructions

Give yourself a number 1–5 for each statement. Five means it's totally true for you, one means it's true occasionally. Leave it blank if it doesn't speak to you at all. Add up the numbers from A and B and subtract B from A. This gives you your Sovereignty score for this pillar.

(A) Strengths and Capacities Developed

[   ] I feel confident, clear, and comfortable expressing what's true for me without trying to convince anyone.

[   ] I'm curious about other people's point of view even when I don't agree with them. I listen and take in what they have to say and am open to being influenced by what they share.

[   ] I discern when it's the right time for me to speak up and when it's better for me to listen (or leave). I'm able to hold onto what I have to share until I have a receptive listener/audience.

[   ] I modulate the ways in which I speak so that others can hear and take in what I'm saying, especially when I sense disagreement or conflict is possible. Sometimes this requires that I carefully craft what I have to say while also maintaining the essence of my message.

[   ] When misunderstanding arises I focus on creating a receptive
        mode to help calm the energy, and seek to co- create a new,
        expanded point of view that includes everyone's perspective
        rather than simply arguing my case.

(B) Wounds or Lack of Capacity

[   ] No one hears me when I speak up. It's like I'm not even there.
        I feel invisible.
[   ] I find it difficult to say what's true for me. Sometimes I don't
        know what that is, and at others I can't find the words. I get
        tongue-tied.
[   ] I'm afraid of other people's reactions so I try to say what I think
        they want to hear. That way we can get along and avoid conflict.
[   ] When someone is talking, sometimes I miss what they're saying
        because I'm preparing what I'm going to say when I can get a
        word in edgewise.
[   ] I find it impossible to listen to someone talk about something
        I disagree with. I either shut my ears or I interrupt to talk over
        them. Being right and having the last word are important to
        me in these situations.

A = _____   B = _____   A – B = _____

This is your Sovereignty Score for Pillar Six.

If you have a positive score, this means that you've developed capacity in this area. The higher your score, the greater your strengths.

If you have a negative score – more checked from (B) than (A) – then this is a pillar where you'd benefit from building more capacity. The lower the score, the less in touch you are with the beneficial attributes of this pillar.

Spectrum of Expression

The Spectrum of Expression outlines three ways of expressing the themes, energy, and power of the pillars. Collectively we're evolving out of the power-over/disempowered paradigm that characterizes western civilization. Nevertheless we're still subject to expressing power in these ways, often without even realizing it. The three aspects of the spectrum will help you identify your tendencies and, I hope, reveal to you unconscious patterns, beliefs, or behaviors so you can become at choice about whether to continue or change them. Consider this an exploration in understanding power in the service of building your *power within*, the foundation of your personal sovereignty, and the inner support for your sovereign self.

Awakened/Empowered Expression

When you feel equally confident, clear, and capable when expressing yourself well and listening to others, you're embodying the awakened themes of Pillar Six. You're able to focus on what someone else is sharing, reflect what they're saying, ask clarifying questions, and empathize or relate to their emotional tone. You wait to be asked for your opinion or ask if they'd like to hear it before sharing. You realize that timing is everything, and you only want to provide input if the other(s) want and are ready to hear it.

Similarly you're able to express your perspective with enthusiasm and confidence in ways that are accessible to your best listener. You modulate your tone, words, and body language to match the message you're sharing so that all aspects of your communication are in integrity with you and each other. You know when to be assertive and when to pause and tune in. You have a good sense of what's needed when, and you don't require other people's attention to feel okay about yourself. You're comfortable with silence and waiting for the time to be right to share.

Shadow Expression

When you can't wait for the other person(s) to stop talking so you can assert your point of view, you're in the shadow expression of Pillar Six. You might interrupt, talk over the others, not listen to what they're saying, or challenge them outright. You may enjoy the ping pong, finite game of communication and play to win, as this is how you've been taught to be seen as an expert, to be respected and successful. You view communication as a way to position yourself with authority and are okay with bending the truth and omitting some of the facts if it seems that will help you. Being right and having the last word makes you feel powerful and respected. You're okay listening to experts you think you can learn from, but otherwise you're not very interested in what others have to say. You don't want to be *distracted*.

Disempowered Expression

If you find it difficult to speak up when you have something you want to say or if it seems people don't listen to you when you do speak up, then you're experiencing the disempowered expression of Pillar Six. You might hold back because you were taught to be seen and not heard or because you felt shut down when you were a young person in your family or by peers. You might not have a good sense of right timing (yet!) and so try to get people's attention when they're focused elsewhere, not receptive, or too lost in their own thoughts or feelings. You may try to take control of a conversation now and again only to feel frustrated, ignored, or rejected.

Pause, Reflect, and Review

Take a few moments as you read through the Spectrum of Expression to feel into what's true for you. You might want to write about your current understanding, how your relationship to these possibilities has changed over time for you (if it has), and if so what your journey has been like.

Now go back and review your self-assessment.

- Do you think or feel any differently now that you've dug in a bit deeper?
- Do you want to change any of your answers?
- Or do you want to add to the lists offered noting what's been especially true for you?
- At this point are you aware of wanting to develop new capacities in this area? If so start a list of your own or continue reading for my suggestions that might help you get started.

New Desired Capacities

To help you think and feel your way through this, I've created a list of potential capacities you may feel drawn to. This list is suggestive and far from exhaustive. Some may appeal to you while others may not. (Feel free to add your own!)

Now rank this list in the order of significance to you, one meaning this is a high priority for you, and five being "not relevant to me, at least not now."

[   ] I'm learning that listening and reflecting aren't the same as agreement. I can put aside my point of view long enough to gain understanding of where someone else is coming from. I want to create an environment in which the other person(s) feel they can be forthcoming about what's true for them.

[   ] I'm becoming more aware of when I emotionally and energetically react to something someone says. I'm becoming more able to pause rather than either challenge or dismiss the other person and their perspective.

[   ] I'm building my confidence that what I have to say matters. I'm practicing expressing myself with people I know want to hear what I have to say and that helps. *Good training wheels.*

[   ] I'm seeing and hearing my habitual assumptions and expectations with new eyes and ears, and I'm doing my best to expand beyond them.

[   ] I remind myself that really connecting with someone oftentimes means I have to step out of my desire to be right so that something new can emerge. I can't expect someone else to let go of their desire to be right if I won't.

Once you've ranked these possibilities, name your top two priorities. What can you do this week to begin to develop this valuable skill? You'll find helpful suggestions to support you with this in the next section.

Reflection Questions

I invite you to review and ponder these questions in any way that works for you. Feel free to respond to the ones that speak to you and leave the rest. You may write about them in your journal (highly recommended), take them into meditation or on a walk with you, make a sketch or painting about how they make you feel, or some other way that works for you. Writing down your reflections provides you with a record of your experiences, which can be very helpful later. As we evolve, we tend to forget where we were and that makes it difficult to appreciate how much we've grown.

> What did you discover about yourself through the self-assessment and Spectrum of Expression? Did you feel affirmed in some way? Did anything surprise or disturb you? Are you inspired to develop any new capacities?

> What can you do this week to begin to develop this valuable new capacity? What resources do you need? What do you need to prepare? What kind of support do you need? Is there any resistance you need to face and overcome? Who in your life can you partner with that will help hold you accountable?

> What was conversation like in the family you grew up in? Were you supported to express yourself? Did you feel heard? Were you accepted even when your opinion differed from that of the adults around you?

> How do you feel about your ability to communicate? Are you comfortable about speaking up for yourself when it's important to do so? Do you feel able and willing to wait for the right time to speak?

> How are your listening skills? Are you able to put aside your own thoughts and agenda and really tune in to what someone else is saying, even and especially when you don't agree with them?

> Are you willing to be influenced by what you hear from other people so that together you can create a shared understanding? What would become available in your life if you were able and willing to do this?

> Apply what you learned or realized in Pillar Six to your Learning Question. What does this teaching add to your inquiry? What was your Learning Question(s) for this specific pillar? Make a few notes about what's arising for you including how this feels in your body.
> With six pillars your Temple of Sovereignty is becoming larger and more stable. How are you imagining their forms, colors, textures, and arrangement? What kind of a whole are they creating?

Mutually Beneficial Collaborations

The ability to creatively partner with others to develop reciprocal, win-win scenarios that benefit all humans and the living world.

"Biodiversity leads to stability –
it leads to resilience, and it's easy to see why.
Species collaborate. It's a synergistic system."

—Suzanne Simard, author, researcher, forest biologist

"We close the divide because we know to put our future first,
we must first put our differences aside.
We lay down our arms so we can reach out
our arms to one another.
We seek harm to none and harmony for all."

—Amanda Gorman, National Youth Poet Laureate

"As a species, humans are wired to collaborate."

—Beronda Montgomery, professor of biochemistry

How well do I work with others?

**What excites me and what do I resist
about collaborating?**

Being in THIS Together

You've been striding under the midday sun, and it takes a moment for your eyes to adjust. The center of the "fairy-ring," created by the interlocking roots of redwood giants, is dim by comparison. Your feet sink into the layers of redwood detritus inside this stand of ancient ones, our primordial ancestors. You lie down and look up, marveling at the trunks reaching to the sky, a hundred million leaves open to receive moisture when the fog rolls in at night. Your body relaxes as you feel the earth pushing up underneath you, embracing and supporting you.

Under the surface, roots grasp one another, arms interlocked, holding the ring in place even in the highest winds. Bacterial partners drink in sugars shared by the redwoods as they send water and nutrients into the roots to feed the trees. Your mind softens and expands as you imagine the highways underneath you pulsing with life force and generosity: a whole world out of sight.

You're decompressing from a rich and sometimes difficult meeting with partners from around the globe. Each person Zooming in from their home office had shared their intent to support the new project with whatever knowledge, resources, and creativity they have. Excitement skittered along the airwaves as you explored what might be possible when working together. Speaking in rounds did take more time than you were used to, as you'd been warned. Yet instead of being impatient you found the focus on each person in turn to be relaxing, especially compared to other meetings you're more accustomed to when everyone speaks at once trying to claim the floor.

Speak. Listen. Take in. Digest. No hurry. Contemplate. Listen. Speak.

You'd been particularly surprised and inspired by your colleague in Belgium offering to send you her unpublished research notes. Feeling her trust and generosity, you said yes to working on the phase of the project when it came to California. You said you'd even host anyone who wanted to come in person, knowing how connecting it can be to be together in real time. Smiles all around at that, some eager and others wistful. That prospect was a year or more in the future, so perhaps you could find funding by then to bring you all together.

It was only during one moment, an important one, that tension rose, and with it a small but detectable sense of separation. The woman from Nigeria had pointed out what seemed to be a shared assumption among the westerners that selecting locations only in Europe and the United States would make the most sense since resources were more easily attained there. She suggested that following this route would perpetuate the westerners' ignorance of the rest of the world that *supply* much of what were being called "resources." Instead, she encouraged, let's have several locations in Africa and at least one in Latin America.

The tension rose, not because of her recommendation. Everyone could appreciate its value as soon as she offered it. It was more your sudden awareness of how your privilege limited your perception and assumptions, *like blinders being taken off,* that bothered you and the other westerners. You knew, feeling into your own belly, how easy it would have been, how seductive even, to be defensive, subtly argumentative. But you knew better by now, recognizing this tightness as residue from trauma mixed with entitlement. A couple of deep breaths and it passed. Within moments the energy began flowing again.

And you wonder, lying under the redwoods: *do the mycelium and roots and worms ever get tense with each other or fight? I wonder what they do then?*

We Humans Are Communal, Collaborative Beings

Inside and all around, beings great and small collaborate and cooperate in creating the fabric of their lives, our lives. As we explored in Pillar One, on the *soul level* we know we're all connected and are part of the Web of Life, which reverberates with each action we take whether we can feel or see it or not. In Pillar Two, we learned that being with people we trust helps us regulate our emotions and our nervous system. In Pillar Three, we discovered our seventy trillion cells humming together to create our human form, human and bacterial DNA working together to fuel, cleanse, and rebuild the body. In Pillar Four, we explored how energies inside and between us engage and interact with each other, bringing us new experiences. In Pillar Five, we looked at our drive to engage with life and to contribute to making a safer, more equitable, more regenerative world. In Pillar Six, we realized we're always communicating with each other and our environment, energetically as well as verbally and physically.

We spiraled inward to our most intimate inner landscape, meeting our humanness up close. We've been spiraling outward into the larger world, exploring our relationships with others: how we show up, how we relate, and how we can upgrade our perspectives from a vantage point that includes the Web of Life. Here in Pillar Seven we again aim to *remember what's true to our nature as human beings*. Spiraling back into our earlier evolutionary journey, we remember that we're primates, deeply communal beings designed to live together. And no wonder! We come into the world utterly dependent on the adults around us for years to come. Human babies take a couple of years to be able to run from danger (sort of), much less fend for themselves. (Just ask any parent.) We grow and thrive *interdependently*, not independently. A couple of centuries ago being banished from a community was the equivalent of a death sentence.

Take my hand as we spiral even further back in our evolutionary development, stripping away intellectual detritus as we go. Were you taught, as most of us were, the doctrine of "the survival of the fittest" as if it were *obviously* true? Actually this doctrine justifies the nineteenth-century Age of Empire during which Europe spread its control across the planet rather than being a scientific truth. *Poor Darwin*, saddled with a phrase he didn't even invent and a theory with which he didn't agree. Turns out that instead Darwin thought: "Those communities which included the greatest number of the most *sympathetic* members would flourish best and rear the greatest number of offspring" (emphasis added). Echoing this sentiment, Fulbright scholar, political scientist, and author Christopher Kukk suggests that *compassion* rather than *competition* lies at the heart of our achieving.

When we head even further back we find that cooperation spurs evolution forward. According to Jeremy Lent, climate activist and visionary author of *The Web of Meaning*: "When scientists now look at the richness and complexity of life over the billions of years there's only been a few big stages when life jumped [in complexity] ... [and] every one of those jumps ... came about ... *through increases in cooperation between different species in life. We now know that life evolved through cooperation*" (emphasis added). According to systems biologist Lynn Margulis, "Life did not take over the world by combat but by networking."

As far back as we know about here on our beautiful planet, life in all its forms has unfolded on the principle that *we're in this together.* We human beings have been around for hundreds of thousands of years, yet this is *barely a blip* on the evolutionary scale. Archeologist, professor, and author Marija Gimbutas discovered remains of peaceful, egalitarian societies in Old Europe (pre-Roman), approximately 9000–5500 years ago. She found many tools and painted clay artifacts but *no weapons* or other evidence of violence (like a dungeon) or hierarchy, like wealth concentrated in the homes or graves of one or a few people. Based on this research, Gimbutas suggests that this type of social organization characterized human communities for at least two millennia and possibly much longer. *Something relaxes inside me when I consider being a part of society in which people supporting each other and working together is assumed, expected, and part of the norm.*

How interesting when we consider that most of what's considered *history* dates back only about 5000 years at most, when *civilization* began in Mesopotamia and North Africa. Eisler draws on Gimbutas's research as she maps the ways in which "dominator societies" invaded and colonized earlier "partnership societies," in which cooperation and collaboration were more the norm. Eisler reframes the Greeks and Romans, credited with founding western civilization as we know it, as proponents of "dominator society." I remember when I was a first-year student in college I had to take *Humanities*, the first semester of which was Greek and Roman culture and history. I was taught to focus on their artistic and architectural achievements, obscuring especially the true violence of empire, including slavery and the subordination of women. *Is that what you learned too?*

As I unpack my conditioning and education, I've longed to have a better sense of what these more peaceful, egalitarian societies were like. As a person of Celtic heritage, I was delighted to discover the *Boudica* series by author and thought leader Manda Scott, which I mentioned briefly in the *Introduction.* In these four historical novels, Scott portrays the lives of Celtic people in what's now the United Kingdom when they lived in tribes during the period before Romans invaded and took control of the land and people. *The Boudica* was the warrior queen who helped fend off the Romans for a generation. In the thoroughly researched world Scott describes, Celtic tribes lived more or less harmoniously with each other, deeply connected to the land and the living world, and in service to the aliveness in all things. Although the Celts were warrior people who fought each other on occasion, they weren't *imperialistic* and they didn't seek to take each other's land or enslave each other's people. Indeed adolescent Celts, during their "long nights" of initiation, reach out to their gods, guides, and spirits and make a special bond with one of them. Scott's *Dreamers* (Druids) often discover, bond with, and become one with their animal guides. This series has spurred my imagination and perhaps my remembering of my indigenous roots and the ways in which my ancestors lived in community and with little impact on the Earth.

Although she's not represented in the *Boudica* series, the Sovereignty Goddess of the ancient Celtic world now comes to mind. Let's remember that she, representing the land, chose the man who would be king. Ceremonially she mated with him, ritualizing and authorizing his kingship provided that he acted as protector (not rapist or exploiter) of land and people. Sometimes she became queen and sometimes she remained the high priestess, in either case taking her place of authority alongside his. Deep in this history we have examples of balance and shared power and authority. Indeed Michael Newton, professor of Celtic Studies, remarks that if the *king* were unkind or otherwise didn't do his job of caring for people and land, his *subjects* would leave and join another clan. Leaders were chosen from a pool of candidates rather than enshrined by virtue of birth. The candidate chosen, according to Newton, had to prove his worthiness or he'd be replaced. This sounds like a reasonable scenario to me. How about you? Those of us of Celtic heritage can lean into our ancestral legacy to taste right relatedness to land, and selected and tested, rather than forced, leadership.

Roughly a thousand years ago on the other side of the world, people indigenous to what's now the northeastern United States developed a sophisticated governance structure that honored feminine and masculine energies and women and men. The Haudenosaunee, known to the French as the Iroquois, formed a confederacy of five and later six nations based on the *Great Law of Peace*. We'll revisit the Haudenosaunee and their *Great Law* in Pillar Eight when we explore stewardship. Here let's appreciate the reverence and respect with which the women of these nations were – and still are – held in positions of great authority. The *Great Law* established the structure of the confederacy: the females of the family have ownership of the chieftainship title, the 'lineal descent' running in the female line. The women select one of their sons to be chief, a trustworthy, honest man of good character who takes care of his family and has proven to be faithful to his nation. If he doesn't prove himself capable to the task, the women may remove him and choose another candidate from among their sons.

The *Great Law* includes intricate and specific measures to ensure that their leaders are steady, emotionally intelligent, wise, and "filled with a yearning for the welfare of the people of the League." In this case, the roles of women and men are designed to work together to balance and complement each other inside a code of ethics that prioritizes peace and harmony. Coming out of many years of tribal wars, the *Great Law* lays out a governing system so impressive that Benjamin Franklin and other founding fathers borrowed from it when framing the US Constitution. Not surprisingly though, given their patriarchal lineage, they left out the part about the women choosing and being able to replace the leaders if they weren't living up to their assignment. They also left out the parts about the men needing to exhibit emotional intelligence and prioritizing peace. *Oh well, I guess.*

The overculture teaches us that it's "human nature" for us to dominate each other, to have social hierarchies, and to have wealth accrue to the most powerful, who are backed by violence. How do you feel when you imagine what life may have been like prior to or apart from the Age of Empire? Does this help disrupt your programmed ways of perceiving and being? Certainly does for me. We don't need to hold ourselves hostage to the now-debunked idea of "the survival of the fittest." We can free ourselves to affirm our compassionate, cooperative, and caring characteristics.

The further back we step to take in a larger perspective, the more clearly domination becomes a *worldview* or *belief system*, not something innate or natural to human beings.

Indeed despite our programming to compete with and dominate each other, I see so many examples of people helping each other, especially when crises or disasters arise. In my area in Northern California, for example, I've seen – and participated in – so much sharing with people in need when fires have destroyed their homes. I heard stories from Oregon, when fires swept through huge areas in a matter of hours, of people who'd been politically at odds with each another nevertheless seeking each other out, taking care of each other's horses, goats, and dogs, and making sure their neighbors weren't trapped.

In the brilliant, visionary film *Arrival,* beings called "heptapods" visit Earth and descend their ships on twelve locations around the world all at the same time. What becomes clear over the course of the film is that the heptapods have come to Earth *in this particular way* to spur the major powers of Earth to work together because they – political and military leaders – are faced with what they perceive to be *a common threat.* The heptapods aren't actually a threat, and once they see that humans have united across their nations, languages, and cultures, they leave, that purpose fulfilled.

Simon Sinek reports that in his work with Marines he's heard over and over again stories in which someone jumped into the line of fire or similarly dangerous situation to rescue a fallen comrade. Asked why they did so, their response consistently was: "He'd do it for me." I wonder, do we really need wartime – or wildfires or flooding or tornados — to bring out this quality in us? Will it take facing massive Earth changes, breakdowns in supply chains, or the collapse of the monetary system for us to learn to cooperate and collaborate again?

Okay, I know, that's a pretty apocalyptic thing to say. Yet there does seem to be some truth to us needing real and present danger of a huge scale to get us to overcome our differences. Is it possible for us to tap into and cultivate our innate desire to cooperate and collaborate, despite our conditioning, without having to be faced with annihilation first?

Could there be another way?

Collaboration in the Living World

Turns out that *trees talk*. That's not a metaphor. It's just that they communicate in very different ways than we do, and mostly it's out of our sight. According to forest biologist and author Suzanne Simard, forests act like a single organism with their own intelligence. Trees are "super cooperators," both with each other and the vibrant and radically diverse lifeforms active below the surface. Trees produce more sugar than they need through photosynthesis and then share the extra with their fungi partners who need it. The fungi then send water, nitrogen, and phosphorous back up the tree's roots, creating a mutually beneficial cycle of exchange.

Trees and fungi together create mycorrhizae networks that enable the trees to communicate and share resources with one another. "Mother trees" constitute the largest hubs in this underground network through which they share nutrients with seedlings. These mother trees also send alerts through the network of an invasive insect or harmful bacteria, for example, so that other trees can protect themselves by secreting substances that repel these dangers. According to Simard, this back-and-forth communication – communication that connects! – increases the resilience of the whole community, giving it an enormous capacity to heal itself.

Sounds like we could learn a lot from trees, right, or rather from forests.

In the *New York Times* best-selling novel *The Overstory*, a character similar to Simard is called before a judge in a legal suit being brought against a logging company in an effort to halt clear-cutting of forests and replacing them with tree farms. The judge leans over his desk, looking over his glasses, and says to her skeptically, "Are you telling me that forests aren't the same as trees?"

"No sir," she responds, "they most definitely aren't."

This conversation characterizes what happens when *statistical mentality* (based in Newtonian physics) meets *animus* (Earth-based spirituality), the understanding that not only is everything alive but *everything has consciousness*.

You've probably seen lichens on stones and trees. Did you know they're actually two beings, not just one? In *Braiding Sweetgrass*, author, professor, and citizen of the Potawatomi Nation Robin Wall Kimmerer explores this ancient relationship, noting: "Some of Earth's oldest beings, lichens are born from *reciprocity*" (emphasis added). Geese who fly in their signature "V" formation trade the front position, where the work is most difficult, so that they share the work of migration. Peas are revered as nitrogen fixers for their ability to make nitrogen available to hungry plants. But it's *not the peas* that do this. It's *rhizobium bacteria* that latch onto the peas' roots that fix nitrogen in the soil. *Who knew?*

Coming closer to home, our own bodies rely heavily on reciprocal relationships with friendly bacteria. I knew I had gut bacteria, but when I first discovered the extent of our relationship with bacteria I was astonished! "Human beings have about 22,000–23,000 functional genes in our chromosomes," notes research microbiologist Kiran Krishnan, "which is not very many when you consider an earthworm has about 38,000." Current estimates are that the number of microbial cells match that of human cells, and the synergistic relationships among them "are what allow us to have become these sophisticated organisms … at the top of the evolutionary ladder." Of those seventy trillion cells humming in harmony that we first saw in Pillar Three, *we're as much bacterial and fungi as we are human.*[19] Wow, can you imagine?! *Maybe think again before you use that antibacterial soap on everything.*

Pause for a moment and notice how you feel and what you notice as you take this in. Maybe close your eyes, take a deep breath, place your hand on your heart, and tune in. Imagine the thousands of processes all those different kinds of cells are humming with, exchanging substances, nourishing and detoxing, and working together to create YOU. Try drawing an image or symbol of what this inspires in you.

---

19 Scientists are just beginning to understand the microbiome in and on the skin. New technologies have made it possible to study of what's going on inside, but this field is in its infancy and data and interpretations continue to evolve.

What's at Stake, What We're Facing

If reciprocity and collaboration have always organized the living world of which we're a part, then why is this often so difficult for we humans today? Through the pillars, we've dipped into our collective history to help us gain perspective on where we are now, including our own attachments to the Story of Progress.

A power-over system relies on its ability to *control the identity* of its people as part of its ability to dominate. Rigid gender roles, for example, create two groups, with one granted power over the other. Racial hierarchies stratify people's access to resources, opportunities, and self-determination. Multinational capitalism exploits the land and the people of the Global South for the wealth and technological benefit of the Global North. In each case the group that benefits from the hierarchy identifies with the role created for it, so that it continues to not only receive the benefits but *feel good about it.* This keeps people committed to maintaining the hierarchy, even if they're uncomfortable with it or whether they realize it or not. As Professor Vanessa Machado de Oliveira notes: "It is extremely difficult to interrupt the satisfaction we have with modernity's rewards, and it certainly doesn't happen overnight."

For example men reproduce the notion that women should be responsible for childcare and homemaking, even though women are also working full-time. White people reproduce the notion that their neighborhoods are safer because they're better people and BIPOC are *naturally* more dangerous. Westerners reproduce our identity as consumers – *retail therapy,* anyone? – and ignore the human and environmental costs of mining lithium and other precious earth metals so we can enjoy buying a new phone every year or two. The overculture continues to spew out media and entertainment that reinforce these perspectives, while giving us the release valve – relief valve? – of, for example, *Star Wars'* Rebellion against the Empire. No wonder this mythological universe has been so incredibly popular.

We're facing highly sophisticated mechanisms of control and coercion that we're entangled in and perpetuate, often without knowing what else to do. *It's like we're wrapped up in webs of modernity tougher yet more invisible than that of any spider.* This is the magnitude of what we face as we choose to think, feel, and live differently. This is the *bad news*, and I imagine for you it's *not news* at all.

The good news, and this is the premise of the 8 Pillars, is that we have the opportunity and the capacity to become and create the change we envision for the world. We can take command of our consciousness to build our inner power and grow ourselves into the people who can communicate, collaborate, and cooperate in creating a world we'd be proud to leave to future generations, a more beautiful world our hearts know is possible.

We're being called to resist the imperative of modernity to homogenize people and culture, creating sameness through consumer culture. Yet we've come to rely on a sense of sameness (or at least similarity) to provide us with a sense of safety. In Pillar Six we looked at affinity groups and their premise that a common characteristic, typically a vector of identity, provides the organizing principles of the group. When I was younger, I participated in and helped run several groups organized either by identity or interest. None of these groups was particularly good at honoring diversity and often experienced difference as disruption rather than wealth. We were more focused on the identity vector or project/interest that was the basis for the group, relying on that to create cohesion and assuming we had shared experiences and interests.

My experience is that sometimes this worked better than others, and that often we did not well understand the dynamics that would make or break a group. These groups were peer led, and none of us had had training or modeling about how to organize and facilitate groups. Reflecting now, I think we were pushing back against the dictates of the overculture by organizing as women, for example, or as LGBTQ people, or as people who love to dance and be in conscious community. We found an immediate sense of camaraderie that arose from an assumed sameness but that also became troubled if too much difference entered the mix. Do you include the trans woman? Or the lesbians who're into BDSM? Or the people who want to play a kind of music you think is noise? Or why don't the women of color want to participate in our feminist events? Or the white people who don't get how privileged they are? *I think you get the idea.*

We didn't have the skills to navigate these complex dynamics. Even worse, we didn't *realize* we didn't have the skills. Too many unspoken assumptions and expectations roiling beneath the surface, stimulating triggers and creating offense. Most often these were never acknowledged or addressed, but they nevertheless created fissures that eventually split the group apart. The result was that either the group ended when a specific project or timeframe was completed (like with my feminist writers' group when I was at Columbia – it ended when I left!), or the group tended to become more homogeneous over time, if it wasn't homogeneous to begin with. The challenge before us now is to explore ways of organizing ourselves and our work together based on principles that honor both commonality and diversity, the tribe and the individual.

The Story of Progress: Our Common Threat

As we've seen, a common threat or enemy tends to galvanize a group. Of course, dictators have used this tactic to brainwash the populace into supporting their efforts. Remember Hitler? We see this today among reactionary forces demonizing transgender people and LGBTQ folx in general, or migrants or, as always, Black men. The benign heptapods in the movie *Arrival* understood this human tendency and offered themselves as a perceived threat to help humanity recognize our common interests.

The premise of this book is that we do have a common threat: the Story of Progress, the extractive, exploitative practices that characterize it, and the systemic inequities that perpetuated and continue to perpetuate it. All of these features are mutually supportive, reinforcing and replicating each other.

Climate emergency, economic disparity, and chronic debilitating illness among living beings of all kinds are symptoms and outgrowths of the Story of Progress. With fewer and fewer *resources* available, the monstrous forces of modernity intensify their efforts to maintain control of our minds, as well as of land, food, water, air, and medicine. We're already in a dangerous dance for our very consciousness, in addition to the necessities of life.

What are different ways of organizing ourselves than those that have grown out of the Age of Empire and its Story of Progress?
Feminine Sovereignty calls us to adopt a cooperative and collaborative approach with whatever forms we experiment with, focusing on our work together being reciprocal and mutually beneficial for all of life. We need to mature ourselves out of self-interest, an adolescent quality, to focus on how we create ways of being and being together with each other and the living world that foster the well-being of all, while also honoring individual diversity. For that, we do well to turn to the teachings of indigenous people for whom this way of being has been the way of life for thousands of years.

How Do We Connect Again?

Given the forces that program and divide us, pitting us against each other and even against our world, how can we connect again, cooperate and collaborate again? As legal expert, author, activist, and member of Penobscot Nation Sherri Mitchell notes: "The people targeted for colonization were self-sufficient, and most often living in harmonious balance with the living world." We all have in our shared memory what it was like to live more connected and in balance. Indigenous peoples live among relatives of every kind in what Enrique Salóm calls "kincentric ecology." An author and professor of American Indian Studies, Salóm coined this term to explain to outsiders how an indigenous worldview works through *relatedness*.

Native peoples experience themselves as part of the larger ecosystem in which all things are beings and relatives, "all my relations." They don't see themselves as separate from the living world and often don't even have a word for *nature* in their native languages.

An indigenous worldview, according to the *First Nations Development Institute*, feels "that humans are directly related to everything around us. The trees are us, we are the trees. I am the rain, the rain is me. The rain is all around me, it aligns inside of me." Similarly Kimmerer devotes a chapter to "Maple Nation," who her people call "standing people."

The closest I've felt to this is while practicing Continuum, as I shared with you in Pillar Three. While I've known for a long time that trees breathe in carbon dioxide and breathe out oxygen, and we humans do the opposite, it was during Continuum practice that *I consciously felt* the reciprocal breath of the green living world and me and we, the human world. This has helped me develop an inner awareness of and appreciation for my tree elders and all that they are and provide.

How would you see the world differently, what different choices would you make, if you were to cultivate this worldview inside yourself? (I bow to you if you're an indigenous person for whom this is the norm. Most of the rest of us have some work to do to even begin to reconnect.)

I need to pause here for a moment to acknowledge that as a descendant of colonists, I've always had mixed feelings in relation to indigenous American wisdom traditions. I know that I and other westerners have much to learn from indigenous Americans; in fact our survival probably depends upon implementing similar ways of relating to our landscapes and the living world. My intention has been to be respectful and honoring and not culturally appropriative, though I'm not always sure how to do that. Those of us who aren't indigenous Americans need to be aware of our tendency to romanticize, pigeonhole, and appropriate from these native peoples. As Salóm notes, we westerners have a habit of cherry-picking the aspects of spirituality that appeal to us without bothering to learn the context and the meaning of the whole. (Reminds me of what I said a few moments ago about how the founding fathers left out of the US Constitution the bits about women's authority and emotional wisdom because they didn't fit into their revolutionary agenda.)

For example I learned from the Gabrielino-Tongva, indigenous peoples of Southern California, that white sage is being poached and offered for sale in ways they find harmful to the plants, the ecosystem, and their spiritual power. They ask all of us not to use their traditional ways of smudging with white sage, with an abalone shell and a raptor feather, unless we're an active member of a tribe that's done that historically. And when we do smudge, to do so only for major life events, not because your house feels heavy or someone you don't care for just left. My head is hanging remembering all the ceremonies I've attended with mostly white people smudging in precisely this way, and even the days I've lit a smudge stick to *clear the energy* in my house. *Oh my.*

Fed by endless westerns and products of consumer culture, we tend to speak of indigenous people as if they were one people, homogenizing them into "Indians," a native "other." Yet thousands of tribes have existed throughout the Americas for millennia, and today there are 574 tribes recognized by the Bureau of Indian Affairs in what's now the United States alone (and many more unrecognized). Westerners have been exploitative, violent, and dishonest in the extreme in relation to America's First Nations; it's on us to unravel any voyeuristic or appropriative tendencies even as we respectfully and humbly seek to learn from them. We will stumble and make mistakes, and we need to build the inner mettle to handle embarrassment and shame rather than expect others to make us feel okay about ourselves and our history.

Having said that, I'm inspired by Mitchell's explicit offering of "sacred instructions" from her own heritage to help us "find some solid ground [we] can stand on." Indeed her book *Sacred Instructions* generously offers people like me a window into the communal tribal life of her people to help us disrupt the programming of the Story of Progress that still haunts us. She demonstrates what's possible, and her work helps bring to the surface memories of my own indigenous, Earth-based roots. Kimmerer's *Braiding Sweetgrass* similarly offers westerners gems of wisdom from her archive of tribal knowledge, inviting us to throw off the blinders of modernity so we can see, feel, and experience the living world. She even wonders about we immigrants, why we haven't settled down and *become indigenous.* Honestly when I first read that, I thought: *Is that okay?*

Wouldn't that be appropriative? But now I receive her words as an invitation to cast aside our extractive and exploitative ways and to rediscover our birthright of interconnectedness with land, wind, water, sun, and the living world they create.

I love and appreciate the invitations; they've helped me do this work. Yet as a highly educated white person who grew up and has lived in cities most of her life, I wasn't brought up in a community that honored the oneness of all of life, and no one taught or modeled for me how to feel and know my place in creation. I never resonated with the Judeo-Christian origin story or its instructions for how to live other than "do unto others as you would have them do unto you." *That's a keeper.* Unfortunately Christians are not historically well-known for actually living this way. As I shared in Pillars One and Four, my Kundalini Yoga practices help me feel *energetically* connected to the Flow of Life in the Great Cosmic Womb, the unified field, as the quantum physicists call it. Yet my most profound experiences of connection have happened through Continuum.

Continuum has taught me ways to connect through my consciousness (we call it *diving*) with, for example, the waters of the planet, our stone brethren, and our primordial nature. Continuum uses subtle movement, breath, sound, images, and radical perspectives to "open portals of exploratory consciousness."[20] We practice expanding our *kinesphere* (technically the space around us demarcated by the reach of our limbs) by using our senses to exchange information and energy with the living world and offering our attention, appreciation, and blessings as we become present to what's being offered to us. This enables us to soften our individual identities and ego structures, shedding, dissolving, and melting our inner armor; grieve and lament what we've lost; praise and honor the elements and living world; and experience the grace of being moved and breathed by creation. In this way I purposefully generate a breakthrough in my default androcentric

---

20 About Susan Harper from her website, ContinuumMontage.com: "Susan has the ability through personal demonstration of sounds, breaths, and movement to transmit a primal and spiritual fluidity that inspires participation resulting in embodied innovative discoveries. Her students call her a moving storyteller, a dream weaver, one who opens portals into the vast space of creativity, which is available in all human beings."

(human-centered) point of view and stimulate wonder to help open my perception. I'm in the process of growing myself into someone who can increasingly be aware of the living world so I can make new choices that honor more life for all, a critical aspect of any Thrutopian future.

One of my first steps to expand my practice of connecting to the physical world has been to start growing my own food in collaboration with others. A couple of years ago I finally gave up on trying to do so on the property where I live, as I just don't have enough sun to grow food for people. (I switched to cultivating food for bees, hummingbirds, and butterflies.) Instead I committed to working with a friend in her garden, where she's been growing food for a number of years now. This has been incredibly grounding and nourishing for me on many levels, and I'm grateful. We humans collaborate with each other in cultivating brassicas, celery root, beets, snap peas, and all manner of greens and flowers for salad. We also collaborate with the sun, moon, rain, and soil, tuning in as best we can to what's available and what's needed. Ironically, as I've been increasingly aware of the life teeming below the surface, I've begun to question some of the ways I've learned to garden, like weeding, pulling out roots, and even how to use mulch! Recently I pulled up straw mulch I'd laid down last fall to transplant a perennial. I discovered a mycorrhizae network spreading out in thin white tendrils all over the underside of the straw and I immediately thought: *Oh no! I've killed it!* I flipped it back over and patted it down with an apology, a prayer, and some water.

Is it dead? Will it recover? Only the mycelium know for sure.

---

*Pause for a moment to consider your perspective on
and experiences with the living world. Do you garden?
Do you steward land? Do you feed birds? Do you sit with
your back against a tree and tune into the highways inside
running water and nutrients up and down the trunk, in
and out of the roots, light pouring in through the leaves?
How does that feel in your body, heart, mind?*

Creating Mutually Beneficial Collaborations

We've been exploring the rich tapestry of mutually beneficial collaborations that characterize the living world and our place inside it as human beings. We've been unraveling our attachments to power-over and shadow strategies based in separation and domination. A key place for us to continue this work is in our relationship to leadership. We carry millennia of scars and sometimes still seeping – or gushing – wounds from coercive, violent forms of leadership.

Though the United States was founded on the revolutionary (and extremely radical in its time) notion that "all men are created equal," we've been woefully inconsistent and hypocritical in actualizing that in our lived experience. We'll dig more into the antecedents of this in Pillar Eight. Here let's hold this as *context* for considering our complex and often vexed relationship with leadership.

A couple of years ago I offered a short course called *Light-Worker Leadership Codes* that was based in Human Design and the 8 Pillars of Feminine Sovereignty. I heard from participants and others with whom I raised the topic that they felt uncomfortable with the prospect of being a leader and leadership. Consistently people expressed their dislike of and alienation from leaders they see in the media, from politicians to CEOs, entrepreneurs, activists, influencers, and thought leaders. What turned people off was the sense of leaders having *power over* them, even if in an unclear way, and that they're subjected to policies, financial situations, and hierarchical forces they didn't agree to and don't feel they can change.

Sounds like the legacy of the Age of Empire, right?

The Pillars of Feminine Sovereignty aim to give you a clear path to empower yourself on the inside and in your life so that you can positively influence what's happening in your world, in our world. This is a form of evolutionary leadership.

At the same time I understand this reticence toward leaders and becoming a leader if what you think is required is becoming akin to someone you don't respect or admire. Yet this book calls you to grow yourself into the person you have the potential to become and to make the contribution that best expresses your heart. This is a kind of *individual, personal leadership*. We know by now that this is *necessary yet insufficient*; we can't stop there.

We're in the process of evolving what leadership means, what it looks like, how it operates, who can lead, and how we can work in ways that decentralize and democratize power. How do we become leaders together? How do we share power and rotate power, have power among and between us? How do we best build collective as well as individual power so that opportunities and responsibilities are well distributed and kept juicy and alive? How representative or decentralized do leadership and power need to be?

Many exciting and provocative projects seeding the New World call for moving away from a democratic republic, for example, which is the form of government we have in the US, and call for governing structures to become more local so ordinary people can play a bigger role in making decisions that impact them. Similarly various forms of cryptocurrency aim to decentralize our relationship to money by creating currencies not controlled by the current banking system and governments. While this is an enormous topic that we can just touch on here, let's take a look at three lenses through which we can explore potential models for *shared leadership, reciprocity, and collaboration* mapped in the Human Design system.

Human Design and Evolving Leadership

Interestingly Human Design offers three primary expressions of leadership, one in each of the major circuits: tribal, collective, and individual. We need new definitions and felt experiences of what leadership can mean so that more people of varying backgrounds and compassionate attitudes can feel they have access to this potential.

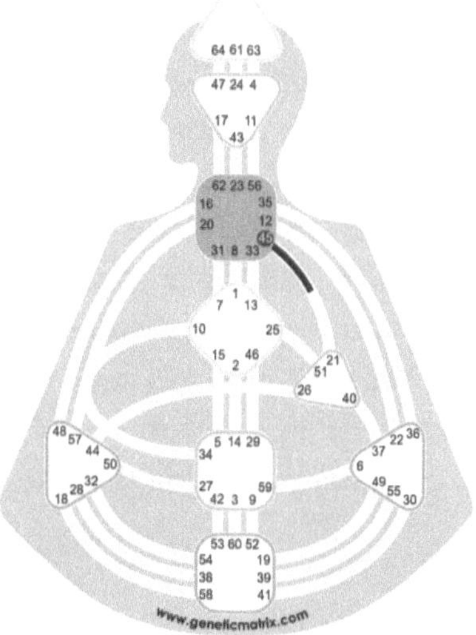

The tribal leadership of the Gate 45 in traditional Human Design (THD) is known as the *King/Queen* or *Sovereign* gate, and in Quantum Human Design (QHD) has been renamed *Distribution*. This is where we find the grace and generosity of the mythological rightful ruler and also the shadow of dictatorship and authoritarianism. In its awakened, most empowered expression, the Gate 45 receives and then distributes resources for the highest good of the community. It's radiant, regal, attractive, magnetic, and generous.

This is the energy of the King as chosen by the Sovereignty Goddess of the Celtic traditions that we explored earlier in this pillar. As a warrior-king he understood his role to be to protect the land and the people. His powerful masculinity that honored and protected women and children was channeled into the service of the whole. In this way the Sovereignty Goddess *collaborated with* the man she chose to be king, sometimes joining him as Queen and sometimes maintaining her role as High Priestess. Either way their collaboration was designed to support the well-being of the people and the lands he/they governed.

The shadow of this energy expresses itself as self-interest, greediness, favoritism, and violence for the sake of pleasure and self-aggrandizement. Unfortunately our historical examples of royalty have too often exhibited this shadowy power-over expression in which coercion rather than collaboration was the norm. Modern-day authoritarianism often expresses itself this way as well. This is the old style of leadership out of which we're evolving.

As we grow our personal sovereignty the awakened expression of this energy can be both appealing and supportive. As you step into this archetypal energy by building your power within, particularly your energetic hygiene and radiance (Pillar Four), you can feel your spine lengthen, your head lift, your heart expand, and a sense of purposefulness and contribution come alive in the cells of your body. This regal quality enhances your confidence, your beauty, and your attractiveness. You shape your expression of sovereignty to suit your values, desires, cultural heritage, and your chosen domain(s). Yet now, rather than being a queen (or king) *over* your subjects, you're a sovereign *among* sovereigns, working together for the greater good, honoring and protecting the land and the people.

Let's turn to the primary leadership energy in the Collective Circuit of the Human Design system, as it complements this more traditional tribal leadership energy.

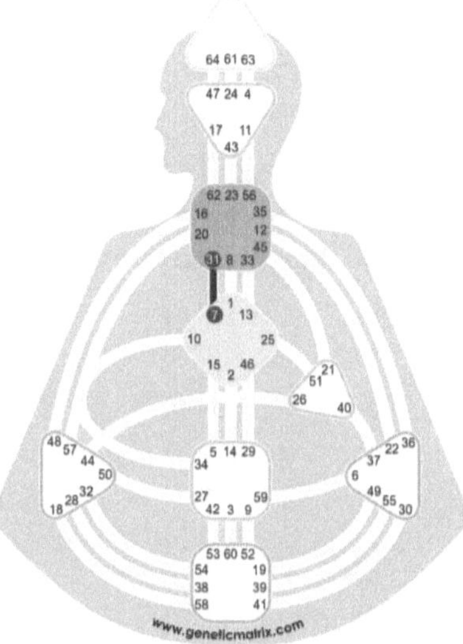

The Channel 31/7 lies in the Logic subcircuit of the Collective Circuit and in THD is known as the "Channel of the Alpha." The Gate 31 parallels the Gate 45, also being on the Throat Center, and therefore is an energy for activation, expression, and manifestation. It's known as "Democracy" in the THD, and the "Leader" in QHD. Being Collective Circuitry, this energy includes and addresses larger organizations and infrastructures such as modern-day governments. Being part of the Logic circuit, one of its primary superpowers is the ability to perceive and work with patterns – in this case really big patterns.

Interestingly enough the Gate 7, which lies on the G-Center (the Heart), is considered in THD to be the Chief of Staff, the one who knows everything that's going on and is actually in charge behind the figurehead of the Gate 31. In QHD, the Gate has been renamed "Collaboration," the partner of the "Leader" in Gate 31. I love the way the revisioning of these energies demonstrates our evolution from a shadowy if not fully power-over relationship between the parts – president and chief of staff – into a more egalitarian relationship both between these two energies and also between these energies and the larger populous they serve.

In my work with the six *Feminine Sovereign Archetypes,* I associate the Gate 31 with the New World Leader (NWL) as I define it. The NWL works through collaboration, listening to all voices, taking account of the needs of the many, and creatively working toward solutions for the highest good of all. The NWL does not act alone but instead recognizes their relationship to the whole and engages with others in collaboration with intention that's arising from the G-Center, the center for love, lovability, identity, and direction. As such this leadership is infused with compassion and love that we'll explore more in the next chapter on compassionate stewardship.

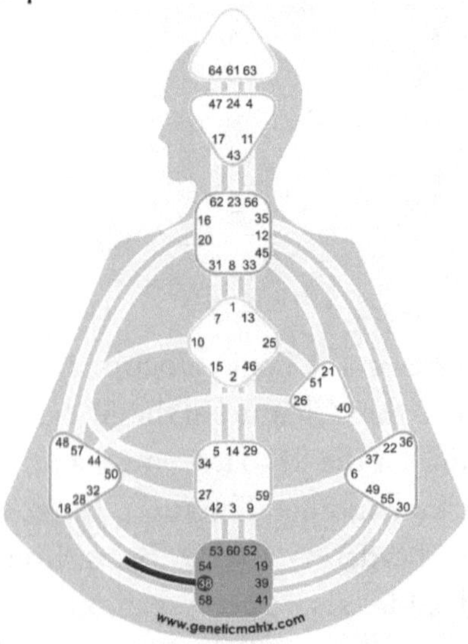

We can also find a form of leadership in the Knowing Circuit (see in Pillar One), which is part of Individual Circuitry, in the Gate 38. The Gate 38 is colloquially called the Martin-Luther-King gate, and officially called "The Fighter" in THD and "The Visionary" in QHD. I like to call this *stake in the ground* energy that calls you to step forward and act for what you believe in. This energy is nonviolent, despite its traditional name, and relies on its ability to invoke and inspire to gain followers and make change. Because it's Individual Circuitry, the Gate 38 embodies the evolutionary impulse of humanity and is a potent and mutative force for change.

The leadership of the Gate 38 works out in front, thinking in new ways through leading-edge, out-of-the-box possibilities and breaking traditional and conventional assumptions and expectations. It's brave, committed, and evolutionary in the extreme.

These three forms of evolving leadership may spark in you new possibilities for forms of leadership that share and rotate power. If we imagine decentralizing government and money, for example, and cultivating more localized currencies and ways of making decisions, clearly we'll need to develop our skills in creating mutually beneficial collaborations. The ideas of the Gate 38 open new possibilities, the generosity and distribution of the Gate 45 help ensure that everyone gets what they need, and the collaborative spirit of the Gates 7 and 31 honors everyone's voice and expressed needs.

Biomimicry: Relationship Ecosystems[21]

As we explored above part of our challenge is honoring individuality and cultivating diversity inside a sense of wholeness and interrelatedness. We noted that modernity tends to homogenize, the better to control our identities and aspirations. Healthy ecosystems beautifully demonstrate how biodiversity plays a critical role in the functioning and well-being of the whole.

The next steps for us include learning to honor and navigate diversity by embracing our differences as part of our cultural wealth rather than as a challenge to our common identity.

Relationships can be thought of as an ecosystem to which everyone contributes. Relationship ecosystems need some of the same primary elements ecosystems in the living world do if they are to thrive. They need to be nurtured and protected, especially in their early stages while

---

21 The term "biomimicry" has been criticized by proponents of an indigenous worldview as replicating the separation of humans from our ecosystems such that we "mimic" them rather than become a part of them. I also think that people who didn't grow up in a community that lived this kind of relatedness, like myself, may benefit from taking steps in that direction. Biomimicry helps me break out of the ways I've been programmed to relate to other people and the world around me and to explore what I can discover from learning about and imitating living ecosystems.

they're just getting established. Ecosystems already occur inside each of us. Pillars One through Four have taught us much about how to build our own thriving inner landscape with its own ecosystem. Thinking in terms of ecosystems can support couples, families, neighbors, co-workers, and other collaborators to imagine and create outside of their self-interest alone and in service to the communal ecosystem. This places integrity and sovereignty of the individual inside a larger context that acknowledges our impact on and responsibility to each other.

Healthy ecosystems share a few common needs, among them movement, nutrition, decay, and detoxification. In wetlands or forests, for example, many different beings do different tasks that contribute to the whole. When we apply this to our social relationships, we can appreciate how complex and dynamic working and being together really are. Using this model for a couple or a family can reveal what often goes unseen and unappreciated as one or some members of the group take on more responsibility than others for the health of the whole.

I drew on this model with a partner I was living with to help us make apparent the many ways in which I was cultivating and nurturing our relationship and living situation that weren't visible to him. I think many women experience something similar with men they live with, where our cultural programming leads us to do many tasks that men rely on without even knowing it. Doing so may give us a sense of power and authority, as this is the way that patriarchy has taught us – insidiously so – that we gain value in a relationship. Yet too much of this will spark resentment, especially if the woman is working full-time as well. In conversation with my partner, I underscored that *we didn't need to do the same things*, simply rotating tasks, although that's one approach. Another option, and one that worked better for us, was to encourage each of us to do what we did and loved best, then share the tasks that neither loved. I happily agreed to be the primary cook provided that he cleaned up and also planned vacations for us. I love to cook, and shopping goes with that. He's a world traveler and understands the ins and outs of international travel. And he's fine with cleaning up. That felt like equal contributions to us. The main idea here is that each contributes in ways roughly equal in value in terms of contributing to the health and well-being of the ecosystem, according to their abilities and interests.

Below are aspects to consider in relationships, whether that's a couple, family, team, organization, or work crew. The main categories include bringing in nutrients to ensure freshness and aliveness, eliminating toxins and waste to keep the environment clean, and sparking movement when stagnation sets in.

Bringing in Nutrients

- Fresh energy, vitality, optimism, enthusiasm, and a can-do attitude
- Expertise in needed areas
- New perspectives, possibilities, and potentials
- Labor – chop wood, carry water
- Money – the least interesting factor though still vital
- Connections – people, resources, opportunities, support
- Brainstorming/heart-storming
- Imagination/creativity exercises – exploring what else is possible
- Life experience/wisdom
- Witnessing, listening, being "present," being a supportive sounding board
- Attending to what's needed even if it's not *your turn* or *your job*
- Humor, play, fun, lightness of being
- Emotional maturity, emotional wisdom
- Compassion and love
- Sensuality and sex (if appropriate to the relationship)

Eliminating Toxins and Waste

- Honesty – saying what's true for you in ways others can hear it
- Emotional- and energy-release techniques and practice (Clarity Breathwork, kriya practice, EFT)
- Self-reflection, adjusting, atoning as needed
- Reflecting and adjusting together
- Clearing "withholds" and getting up to date
- Holding space for tension and conflict; being tolerant and resilient
- Seeking the generative aspect of conflict – what needs tending to, what can we learn, where can we grow?

- Being transparent about your prejudices, stories, stereotypes, conditioning, projections
- Rituals for letting go – regular maintenance – *take the garbage out*
- Forgiveness practice

Sparking Movement When There's Stagnation

- Asking questions that spark and generate new possibilities
- Heart-storming out-of-the-box, even outrageous, possibilities
- Acting differently – listening if you usually talk; speaking up if you usually listen
- Role-playing, empathy, trying on someone else's point of view
- Somatic exploration – move your body!
- Breaking up routines and doing something different
- Literally get moving – go outside, take a walk, go away for the weekend or longer

---

Pause for a moment and choose an important relationship to consider. At present, what are you contributing? What nutrients are you bringing in? How are you helping to eliminate toxins and waste? Are you sparking movement to prevent stagnation from happening or helping to get things moving if they've become stale? Does the current arrangement feel equitable to you? If so congratulations! If not what shifts could be made to create more balance? Notice if programmed roles are interfering with your ability to collaborate reciprocally in ways that benefit everyone involved. Do you feel able to have a conversation, even if it's a difficult one, that would bring more clarity to the situation? What do you need to grow inside yourself so that conversations like this became routine and obvious rather than negatively activating? Make a sketch of what would feel good to you.

Decentralized Models for Working Together

Diversity in our human ecosystems makes us stronger and culturally wealthier.

Yet navigating our differences isn't always so easy. The overculture teaches us to compete and distrust each other rather than cooperate and collaborate. Even though working collaboratively together may be innate to us, so much programming to the contrary has disrupted this inner knowledge. According to the *Harvard Business Review*, the more specialized and expert someone becomes, for example, the less likely they are "to share knowledge freely, to learn from one another, to shift workloads flexibly to break up unexpected bottlenecks, to help one another complete jobs and meet deadlines, and to share resources – in other words, to collaborate. They're less likely to say that they 'sink or swim' together, want one another to succeed, or view their goals as compatible." How different this is from what we heard from the Marines Sinek talked about who would put their own lives in danger to save a comrade!

So we need to (re)learn how to work together; we need practice, structure, and help. Otherwise we're likely to create experiences like the ones my kid had when told to work in groups without instruction or support: they ended up doing most of the work because they were the one who cared about school – and they resented it. That's not what we're going for here.

Inca Mohamed, internationally recognized facilitator and consultant, notes that: "A lot of social justice groups have seen collaborations that didn't produce results. They realize that to be really effective, they have to work together, but working together is quite challenging. We have so glorified the term collaboration that we obscure what it really takes."

Indeed collaborating among people with differently assigned and differently designed identities may prove to be particularly challenging, as these are likely not "like-minded" people. A diverse population has different histories, different roles in social and economic power dynamics, different levels and forms of privilege, and so on. Trust and camaraderie will need to be earned and should not, cannot, be assumed or expected, especially at first.

Will you polarize or will you seek common ground? Will you act out of default thinking and programmed behavior, or will you seize the opportunity to step out of your patterns, to be influenced by what others share, and to learn and co-create something new? Will you foster curiosity and inquiry, opening up possibilities and staving off habitual opinions and conclusions? Or will you defend your position against all comers, determined to have things go "my way"? Will you play a finite game to win, focused on getting what you want just for yourself and "yours"? Or will you play to keep the game going, focused on fueling the synergy that arises from the dynamic interaction of different players?

Facilitation: To Make Easy

To help you understand the conditions that support a mutually beneficial collaboration, I spoke with Jes Montesinos (them/they), Senior Director at the San Francisco Foundation. Montesinos has been working in the community development field for almost thirty years, supporting community-based organizations to envision and then implement the developments that are most critical for their residents. Montesinos has provided technical assistance, facilitation, and other support for capacity building in BIPOC, lower-income neighborhoods working on affordable housing, healthcare, education, and climate justice. A child of Latinx immigrants, they grew up in the Mission District of San Francisco and currently live in the Bay Area's most culturally diverse city of Oakland. I asked them what in their experience brings people together who have different backgrounds and different interests and who represent different communities. What they shared echoes some of the key elements we discussed in *Pillar Six: Communication that Connects*. Here are their main points:

What inspires people to collaborate?

- Having a shared vision of what's possible.
- Recognizing that this shared vision can't be created by a single person or entity and that there's power in numbers.

- Seeing the benefits to a larger community than maybe you can reach on your own.
- Recognizing that funding and other resources may be more forthcoming from foundations, government, and other agencies when collaborations bring together multiple stakeholders and a broad and diverse constituency.
- Wanting to make changes at the policy and systems level by dismantling old dysfunctional ways and building new constructs that support greater equity and the inclusion of diverse and underrepresented voices and concerns.

What are the key ingredients for a successful collaboration?

- Passion for the project. It has to be meaningful and compelling.
- Make a commitment to doing the work and working through challenges together.
- Be able to listen, to take in other people's points of view and priorities.
- Expressing what matters to you and your organization in ways that invite others to participate and at the same time being willing to let go of your own agenda in the service of the larger vision.
- Being clear about what you bring to the table, what you have to offer the whole.
- Every participant has a stake in the success of the project; everyone has a role and a responsibility.
- Having agreement about what constitutes success and how you measure success.

What support is needed to create a successful collaboration?

- Excellent facilitation that:
  - Invites participants to bring their full selves, recognizing that everyone has their own experience and expertise to bring and all of you is welcome. This is particularly meaningful for those from marginalized communities because they've often felt they had to mold themselves to fit into the overculture's version of what's acceptable and to cloak the rest.

- Helps participants be their best selves and manages potential hot spots.
  - Builds trust through helping people get to know each other beyond their title or mission of their organization.
  - Helps develop strategies that build toward specific desired outcomes.
  - Helps people stay accountable for their part.
  - Keeps everyone focused on the agenda (created and distributed ahead of time).
  - Helps participants navigate tense moments when perspectives or agendas appear to be in conflict.
  - Promotes participation by everyone, not just the most resourced, loudest, or most confident.
- Having sufficient resources, such as a meeting space, translation, research and data, and funds for an experienced facilitator.
- Learning sessions can be very helpful in building rapport, as everyone learns together and can be curious and newly informed together.

Sociocracy: The Ninth Brain

Did you know that octopi have a ninth brain? According to author John Buck, *an octopus has a brain in each of its eight limbs* and also a ninth brain that helps them all work together. Buck offers this as an analogy for a system of collaboration and governance developed in the Netherlands called "Sociocracy." Sociocracy offers a decentralized model based in interlocking circles of influence. A group can create as many circles as needed depending on the size of the main group, the different domains involved, and the number of tasks at hand. Mostly I've seen this at work among people who live in some form of intentional community, although a similar system named "holacracy" (from the Greek world for "whole") now is being utilized in the business sector. Sociocracy, like other forms of collaboration, benefits from skilled facilitation, especially at the beginning as people are learning to engage with each other in this way. Here I'll share a few key points of the system, and you can explore more on your own if this way speaks to you.

Circles

The larger group differentiates itself into circles of no more than ten people based on a particular subject or domain. Each circle learns about, makes decisions about, and is accountable and responsible to their domain. Each circle is authorized by the whole to move forward as that group sees fit without having to gain permission or approval from everyone. This fosters responsibility, efficiency, and guardianship of the circle's mission and purpose.

Rounds

Circles function through rounds during which each person has the opportunity to share their perspective without interruption or conversation. This practice reminds me of the "talking stick" meeting structure of some indigenous American nations where the person with the talking stick receives the full attention of those gathered. Everyone relaxes, knowing they'll have their chance to speak, which makes it easier to truly listen to each person. Rounds continue as long as participants have something to share.

Consent

Decisions are made through consent. You consent if you don't have an objection to what's proposed. If you do have an objection, you can share it during the rounds, and others can respond. In this way the group dialogues about their ideas and concerns, listening to each other and seeking common ground. Consent is reached when everyone agrees that the proposal is "good enough for now" and "safe enough to try," recognizing that every decision will be revisited when they engage in feedback.

Feedback

Decisions are revisited once a project has been underway for a time to discern if learnings suggest a shift, what changes need to be made, and what's been working well and may be expanded. Feedback closes the creation loop so that the group can grow from what's been tried and can build from there.

Interlocking Circles

Each circle includes two people who also participate in another circle with pairs from other circles. This way the different groups can be kept informed of decisions being made in other circles.

We Are Collaborative Beings, Yes We Are

We are by nature collaborative beings, yet we've had this innate intelligence programmed out of us, at least to some degree. Examples and models of mutually beneficial collaborations abound all around us when we pause long enough to notice. We use the tools we've learned in Pillars One through Six to be able to participate cooperatively with others even when we don't agree about everything. We can ground and breathe when something triggers us, calming our nervous system so we can still listen. We can speak up purposefully and passionately about what matters most without laying blame on others. We can grow our capacity to question our blind spots and become aware of other perspectives that haven't been as visible or well understood. We can remember the bigger picture that includes all perspectives so that we can make fully informed decisions, rather than ones that arise out of our default lens.

Let us take lessons from our bacterial allies and create reciprocal ways of interacting and supporting each other that benefit everyone in different and compatible ways. In our eighth and final pillar, we'll explore our next step of growing ourselves into the compassionate, sovereign stewards our hearts desire and our world so needs us to become.

Take Time to Assess, Integrate, and Apply What You've Learned

Octopi have nine brains, and we're as much microbe as we are human. Who knew!? I don't know about you, but that really made me pause and consider my assumptions about, well, many things. This is where you get to pause and consider, reflect on your assumptions and expectations, and bring yourself up to date now that you've read through the themes of Pillar Seven. Exciting!

Take a moment to breathe, ground and center yourself, and then tune in to see what's true for you. As always, below you'll find:

- **Self-Assessment**
- **Spectrum of Expression**
- **Pause, Reflect, and Review**
- **New Desired Capacities**
- **Questions for Reflection**

Self-Assessment

Instructions

Give yourself a number 1–5 for each statement. Five means it's totally true for you, one means it's true occasionally. Add up the numbers from A and B and subtract B from A. This gives you your Sovereignty score for that Pillar.

(A) Strengths and Capacities Developed

[   ] I enjoy the creative synergy that arises when brain- and heart-storming with others as we craft our collaborations. Working and playing together is more fun too.

[   ] I seek opportunities to co-create with others with whom I have common interests even if we don't agree about everything.

[   ] We're stronger, more effective, and more impactful together even if sometimes creating and maintaining agreements is challenging.

[   ] I believe that we can find and work from common interests if we're willing, creative, and flexible. I find it very helpful to keep the big picture in mind.

[   ] I enjoy the challenge of collaborating with others because it calls me into my most creative and best self.

(B) Wounds or Lack of Capacity

- [   ] Everyone is focused on what's in it for them, so it wouldn't be wise to rely on others for support.
- [   ] It's faster and easier to do things myself.
- [   ] I barely have enough energy for myself and what I need to do. I don't have enough time and energy to negotiate and create with others.
- [   ] Every time I work with others, I end up doing most of the work. So I don't bother any more.
- [   ] I'm afraid that other people will steal my ideas if I collaborate with them.

A = _____   B = _____   A - B = _____

This is your Sovereignty Score for Pillar Seven.

If you have a positive score, this means that you've developed capacity in this area. The higher your score, the greater your strengths.

If you have a negative score – more checked from (B) than (A) – then this is a pillar where you'd benefit from building more capacity. The lower the score, the less in touch you are with the beneficial attributes of this pillar.

Spectrum of Expression

The Spectrum of Expression outlines three ways of expressing the themes, energy, and power of the pillars. Collectively we're evolving out of the power-over/disempowered paradigm that characterizes western civilization. Nevertheless we're still subject to expressing power in these ways, often without even realizing it. The three aspects of the spectrum will help you identify your tendencies and, I hope, reveal to you unconscious patterns, beliefs, or behaviors so you can become at choice about whether to continue or change them. Consider this an exploration in understanding power in the service of building your *power within*, the foundation of your personal sovereignty, and the inner support for your sovereign self.

Awakened/Empowered Expression

When you feel empowered around the themes of Pillar Seven, you'll look forward to connecting with others as you co-create projects together. When needed you're willing to take on a leadership role for a time and you're interested in growing your capacity in this area. You're comfortable taking the time needed to hear everyone's point of view, their intentions and concerns, so that everyone is included in decision-making. You're willing to adjust or even let go of your initial agenda or proposal if it becomes clear to you that someone else has a better idea, the energy of the group is moving in a different direction, or you can see it's not the right time (yet?) to pursue your proposal. You're excited to learn from others and you're happy to share responsibilities with others you've come to trust. You now welcome tension and disagreement because you're confident that something creative and better for everyone will come out of addressing differences directly. You recognize that your circles include people with very different backgrounds and life experiences, and this calls all of you to grow beyond where you've been before. As stressful as this can be at times, you relish the realness of your rich dialogues and the new possibilities that emerge as a result.

Shadow Expression

If you try to persuade others of your point of view without truly listening to theirs, then you're in the shadow expression of Pillar Seven. In this case you may participate in circles or coalitions or other groups, but you're committed — albeit unconsciously perhaps — to directing action and even emotions toward your desired outcome. You're certain that you're right or other people's points of view are super triggering for you; either way you want to ignore, squelch, silence, or subordinate views that run counter to your own. Manipulation may feel natural or necessary to feel safe and in control of the situation. You won't agree to a proposal that doesn't show a direct way of benefiting you and yours, though you may be practiced at invoking other reasons for your objection.

Disempowered Expression

If you're feeling disempowered in relation to collaborating, you may just decide not to engage at all. You may isolate yourself believing that you're better off this way. You don't have to deal with other people's agendas and you don't even have to articulate, much less defend, your point of view. If you do participate in a circle or group, you may stick to yourself and not truly engage. Or you might agree to do what others propose even if you don't truly agree because you want to avoid the tension of different opinions and potential conflict. You may feel overwhelmed by different ways of looking at issues and projects and you just want things to be simpler and easier.

Pause, Reflect, and Review

Take a few moments as you read through the *Spectrum of Expression* to feel into what's true for you. You might want to write about your current understanding, how your relationship to these possibilities has changed over time for you (if it has), and if so what your journey has been like.

Now go back and review your self-assessment.

- Do you think or feel any differently now that you've dug in a bit deeper?
- Do you want to change any of your answers?
- Or do you want to add to the lists offered, noting what's been especially true for you?
- At this point are you aware of wanting to develop new capacities in this area? If so start a list of your own or continue reading for my suggestions that might help you get started.

New Desired Capacities

Now that you've had a chance to familiarize yourself with the Spectrum of Expression for Pillar Seven, go back and review what you checked in the self-assessment above. Has your perspective shifted at all? Are you aware of wanting to develop new capacities in this area?

To help you think and feel your way through this, I've created a list of potential capacities you feel drawn to. This list is suggestive and far from exhaustive. Some may appeal to you while others may not. (Feel free to add your own!)

Now rank this list in the order of significance to you, one meaning this is a high priority for you and five being "not relevant to me, at least not now."

[   ] I'm curious about collaborating with others because I can see that I can only do and create so much on my own. I'm open to putting aside past experiences and trying something new.

[   ] I'm excited about partnering with others, as I'm seeing that coming together can increase our impact. I'm really wanting to make a difference and I'm just one person.

[   ] I'm willing to face my fear of being taken advantage of and build my ability to discern when someone would be a trustworthy and beneficial collaborative partner. I'm open to assuming the best of others until proven otherwise.

[   ] Even though I've had negative associations with leadership in the past, I get that for our world to evolve to be more equitable, sustainable, and regenerative we need new forms of leadership and new people to fill those roles. I'm going to look for how I can participate in my community.

[   ] I love the idea of working hand in hand and shoulder to shoulder with others who are also focusing on creating the New World we long for, beyond the Age of Empire. I can't wait to read Pillar Eight and get more recommendations about what I could do!

Once you've ranked these possibilities, name your top two priorities. What can you do this week to begin to develop this valuable skill? You'll find helpful suggestions to support you with this in the next section.

Reflection Questions

I invite you to review and ponder these questions in any way that works for you. Feel free to respond to the ones that speak to you and leave the rest. You may write about them in your journal (highly recommended), take them into meditation or on a walk with you, make a sketch or painting about how they make you feel, or some other way that works for you. Writing down your reflections provides you with a record of your experiences, which can be very helpful later. As we evolve we tend to forget where we were, and that makes it difficult to appreciate how much we've grown.

> What did you discover about yourself through the assessment and Spectrum of Expression? Did you feel affirmed in some ways? Did anything surprise or disturb you? Are you inspired to develop any new capacities?

> What can you do this week to begin to develop this valuable new capacity? What resources do you need? What do you need to prepare? What support do you need? Is there any resistance you need to face and overcome? Who in your life can partner with you and help hold you accountable?

> Apply what you learned or realized in Pillar Seven to your primary Learning Question. What does this teaching add to your inquiry? What was your Learning Question(s) for this specific pillar? Make a few notes or doodles about what's arising for you, including how this feels in your body.

> What have been a few of your more memorable experiences with collaborating? Were they more positive or negative at the time? What do you feel about them now?

> Did you ever receive training in school or anywhere else about how to work with other people? Or have you been thrown into situations where you were expected to work with others, weren't quite sure what to do, and found it less than satisfying?

> Have you had nourishing, stimulating, and satisfying experiences collaborating with others? What made the difference in these situations? What made the collaboration work?

> Have you ever collaborated with people who have very different backgrounds from yours? What was that like? What made the collaboration work? Were you able to find common ground that you could create from? What were the tension points if any? What did you learn from this experience? Do you feel this is an important growth edge?

> Have you ever collaborated with people who you disagreed
  with about something important? Did you have a facilitator
  to help you to connect and work together or did you try to do
  it on your own?
> How would our world evolve if we all committed to creating
  mutually beneficial collaborations every chance we get?
> Your Temple of Sovereignty is nearing completion. How are
  you feeling now? What does this pillar look and feel like? And
  your temple, what does it look and feel like? When do you
  visit it and for what purposes?

Compassionate Sovereign Stewardship

*Reciprocal caregiving for
the living world that sustains us.*

"Humans are a keystone species."

—Enrique Salmón

"We have changed climate so rapidly that
forests will need help to survive and reproduce.
We need to become active agents of change –
productive agents instead of exploiters."

—Suzanne Simard

"Ultimately, the reason why love and
compassion bring the greatest happiness
is simply that our nature cherishes them
above all else. The need for love lies at the
very foundation of human existence."

—His Holiness, The 14th Dalai Lama of Tibet

What am I stewarding?

What are my principles of stewardship?

Helpful Burning, Harmful Burning, Cultural Burning

You're pitching wood into the stove, grateful that you'll soon be warm. You close the door, open the vent just a bit, and watch while the blaze grows before your eyes. Light pours out of the window on the door and in a few moments, heat radiates out into the room. Your body relaxes and you begin to ponder, gazing out the window, coffee mug in hand.

Prometheus stole fire from the gods, so the old Greek stories say, for which he was tormented by Zeus. *Typical brutal beginning to western civilization*, you muse. *Well I, for one, am glad he did, because otherwise I'd be mighty chilly on this winter morning. Though I'd rather he hadn't been tortured for doing so.* You remember learning how to build a fire from your father while camping in the summer. He was always up before everyone else, and usually the fire was already going by the time you zipped open the tent door. But some mornings you got up in time to watch him build the bundle of twigs and shavings, then toss in the match, hoping it would light in one try. Sometimes he succeeded, but more often, especially if it was wet out, it would take many more. Then he'd have to use the newspaper he'd bought on a water run the day before to get the blaze going. You still use his methods, but you'd also learned that wood stoves are different from campfires and you'd had to learn a new method. *Nothing like the smell of a campfire*, you recall nostalgically.

Except of course when it's a wildfire. You're grateful you didn't smell that smell this last summer and fall, but oh man is it ever emblazoned in your senses. The sky gray and thick with smoke that billowed and cleared a bit depending on the wind. You'd never been in real and present danger yourself (except to your lungs), though you'd been evacuated and had your power turned off a number of times. Even this last year wildfires had ravaged the Sierras, though you hadn't been affected by smoke. The entire town of Paradise, poof, burned to the ground overnight. And fires in Colorado, and southern Canada, and Australia, and the Amazon.

You take a few deep breaths, grieving all the loss and lamenting the human choices that fostered the conditions wildfires love. Years of drought caused by our extractive energy practices weakened whole forests of trees, making them susceptible to beetles that then eat and destroy them. Across the landscape dead trees stand amidst the merely struggling ones, ready tinder for any fire. You remember being stunned and heartbroken on your camping trip last summer, seeing brown trees almost as numerous as the green ones, and then farther on only trunks left standing with black bark and no branches where wildfire had swept through. Big breath and a deep sigh. *Fortunately,* you note to yourself, *there are some benefits to fire even in the landscape and even in the wild ones. But it would be so much better if we just got smart and started listening to the people who stewarded this land for so many generations before we came.*

You'd learned about "cultural burning" the summer before on a webinar about fire readiness. The authorities in your area had been offering a lot of education about safety zones around your house, what to do if wildfire came close to your home, and where to go and what to take with you if you're evacuated. The fire chief had alerted you that this summer cultural burning would be happening in certain areas to help reduce the potential for out-of-control wildfires, and not to be concerned if you saw smoke from them. That got your attention and you'd done some research on cultural burning, as you'd never heard that term before. You'd learned years ago that indigenous people used to light fires to clear brush and stimulate new growth, but you really didn't know much about it. You discovered that some indigenous people still did this – when they could – and many more would if it weren't illegal.

The fire crashes in the stove as the smaller bits are consumed and the bigger bits fall to the bottom. You turn to face the stove, your face lit by its glow, and give a moment of thanks for the fire, its heat and light, and also to the stove as its trusty container. *We sure do need to get smarter about fire,* you muse. You take a moment to bow to the original stewards of the land and say a silent prayer that they may guide us out of our folly. *If we'd only ask and humbly listen,* you think. *If only.*

We Humans Are Compassionate, Stewarding Beings

We in the west have had the great good fortune to receive the philosophy and blessings of Tenzin Gyatso, The 14th Dalai Lama, the spiritual leader of the Tibetan people. He's brought us the uplifting and connecting perspective that "kindness is my religion" and compassion is our primary role. And how remarkable that he and other Tibetan spiritual leaders and teachers have continued in this vein even though they've been forcibly exiled from their homeland for many decades now, as has happened to so many indigenous people around the world. I grieve the circumstances that led them to come teach in the west even as I'm also so grateful for their teachings. They've brought us such a welcome departure from the Story of Progress and its sovereign citizen, out for himself whatever the cost.

Compassion and kindness arise from the heart and a deep sense of our interconnectedness. They inspire an ethic of care, a way of being that honors the waves of life and the understanding that *there but for the Grace of God go I.* Challenge and misfortune come to all of us, to some more than others, to some more often than others. The question is: *How do we respond?* If we have more privilege and the relative safety and stability that affords, do we see those with less as deficient, deserving of their fate, or not as competent as we are? Do we see them as victims that need us to rescue them? Do we think, *oh how unfortunate,* yet continue to walk on by, maybe throwing a dollar or two into their cup? Or can we at least pause, soften our armored way of moving through the world, and let ourselves feel? Can we imagine what it's like to walk in someone else's shoes, even for a few moments, letting our fixed perspective shift as we turn to look out through their eyes? How does the world appear now? What stories and experiences brought us to this time and place, to these circumstances, to these hard times?

What especially do we see and feel when we remember that grain can rot in warehouses while people starve outside because they can't afford to pay for it? As Robin Wall Kimmerer notes, "The shortage isn't due to how much material wealth there actually is, but to the way in which it is exchanged or circulated." How have profit-driven forces much larger than any of us orchestrated the circumstances of so many people's lives, with such unfairness, callousness, and even brutality? How can we judge each other harshly when truly we know so little about what each other has faced, what our ancestors faced, and what our people continue to face? As one friend of mine often says, *have mercy.*

The Tibetan Buddhists understand impermanence and the ups and downs of life. Their medicine is kindness, compassion – and laughter! We can heal ourselves with this medicine, which they offer so freely, a capacity for which we all have inside of us. Starting close to home, how can you be kinder and more compassionate with yourself? Western culture teaches us to criticize and belittle ourselves even as we're supposed to project an identity of confidence and authority. How can you take yourself and the circumstances of life less seriously, and even laugh a bit at foibles close in and farther way? Not because you don't care, but because you care enough not to be disabled by despair, cynicism, or overwhelm, and laughter is surprisingly good medicine to prevent or heal those ills. As you ground yourself in compassion and kindness, you become more and more able to see through this lens and apply it to others as well.

We are *innately* kind and compassionate beings. As we strip away the conditioning that teaches us to pit ourselves against one another for personal gain, we open the door to becoming sovereign not just of our own lives, but as sovereign stewards of our world.

We do this, not so we can dominate the world, as did leaders of empire, but so we can use our intelligences in the service of life, the living world. Our ability to dominate, extract, and consume has seduced us into believing in our own superiority. Yet now the consequences of this folly are all around us. The way out requires us to drop our human-centered ways of being and *take our rightful place as one species among many*, all of whom deserve life. Indigenous people understand that we humans are the youngest species and that we do well to observe, honor, and learn from the plants, our ancestors. Plants, after all, magically create food from sunlight and water alone for themselves and the rhizomes, fungus, and bacteria with whom they partner. It's well past time for us to direct our considerable power to compassionately caring for the living world as its sovereign yet servant stewards. Doing so paradoxically requires us to mature ourselves into responsible adulthood while simultaneously bowing our heads and our hearts to the magnificence and magnitude of creation.

Where We've Been. Where We're Going

Let's pause for just a moment and situate ourselves inside our spiraling journey through the 8 Pillars. In Pillars One through Five, you explored how you can grow your capacities in your creative relationship with Spirit, your emotional wisdom, your physical vitality and connection with the living world, your energetic adeptness and radiance, and your feeling of being on purpose. As you alight on each of these aspects of your inner landscape and seek to heal and grow them, you're *stewarding yourself* into more fully expressing your potential. Your personal sovereignty relies on and grows out of your ability to well steward your personal resources: your thoughts and beliefs; your heart and vision; and your creativity and intuitive intelligences as well as your emotions, physical and energy bodies; and sense of purpose and possibility. Doing so builds a stable base that supports you as you move through the world with other people. As an evolving and integrated self, you're able to listen well, speak up at the right time with the right people, and work together with others in collaborative ways that benefit everyone.

Pillar Eight spirals you back to Pillar One and your relationship with the Great Web of Life. It invites you to upgrade your relationship with it by asking: what's the quality of your relationship with people who are different from you, who have different backgrounds, differently assigned races and genders, whose belief systems and life experiences vary from yours? What's your relationship to the vast living world? What beliefs do you hold? What values are at play informing your decisions and actions? How can you make a shift to think, feel, and act more compassionately in some way toward yourself, someone in your life, or an aspect of the living world?

Pillar Eight invites you to continue down this path of development so you can take on the larger mantle of stewardship as a caretaker of our living world. As Sherri Mitchell says: "In this effort, everyone is required to show up. No one can afford to sit this one out, or wait and see what might happen." Doing so requires a quantum shift in our thinking and perception as if we're *moving from wave to particle*, a difference in kind. It's as if we're turning the kaleidoscope of our lives, moving out of what's been normal to us and into ways of seeing and being that may feel new and unfamiliar, too, yet also reverberate with ancientness inside of us.

Unpacking Stewardship

To give us some context, let's unpack what *stewardship* has meant historically in western culture, as it's meant very different things at different times and in different contexts. Then we'll draw on what Human Design has to say as a starting point before turning to the paradigm shift into which *compassionate sovereign stewardship* calls us. Compassionate stewardship grows us beyond our narcissistic self-absorption, our privileges and entitlements, our attachment to comfort, our fears and anger, our despair and desire to control. Compassionate stewardship grows us beyond even cooperation and collaboration, calling us to stand tall, powerful yet humble, facing the tasks before us with determined optimism and a willingness to truly *become the change*, becoming the agents of change that our world is calling us to be.

Steward and stewardship are old words in English. In feudal Europe, a steward was a position of authority. A steward could be extremely powerful, being appointed to represent the monarch, like a regent, to rule the country until the monarch came of age or until the monarch returned from a journey. In modern times you may best know this position as that of Denethor in *The Return of the King*, the third book and film of *The Lord of the Rings*. Denethor is the Steward of Gondor, as the line of kings of Isildur had been lost until Aragorn, the rightful King, returns (thus the title). Unfortunately Denethor is maniacal and cruel, not a great example of a steward. But then he mirrors the attitudes and behaviors of royalty. *This isn't what we're after.*

Or a steward might have acted more like an ambassador, representing the monarch to other monarchs and empowered to make agreements or confirm alliances. More simply a steward might oversee and manage a sizable household, manor, or even a castle. These are all powerful positions within a given sphere that center on managing resources – relationships, alliances, grain and meat, horses and sheep and cows, who does what, who gets to wear what, where people sleep and shelter, and so on. This is a hierarchical position of authority with a form of *sovereignty over* their given domain.

Stewardship also has a history in the Catholic Church. Christian Stewards are charged with taking care of the ill and elderly, the young without family, and the destitute. While I'm sure some Christian stewards have carried out their role with compassion and care, we all know how representatives of the church could turn care into control and coercion. When I mentioned to a friend of mine that in my work on Feminine Sovereignty I'm writing about stewardship, her face wrinkled in discomfort. "What?" I asked.

"Reminds me of church," she replied with a shiver.

I don't have that association so I don't have that reaction, *but maybe you do?* Let's see if we can decouple stewardship from these unfortunate associations, as they're not inherent to it.

The Gate 21: Stewardship for a New World

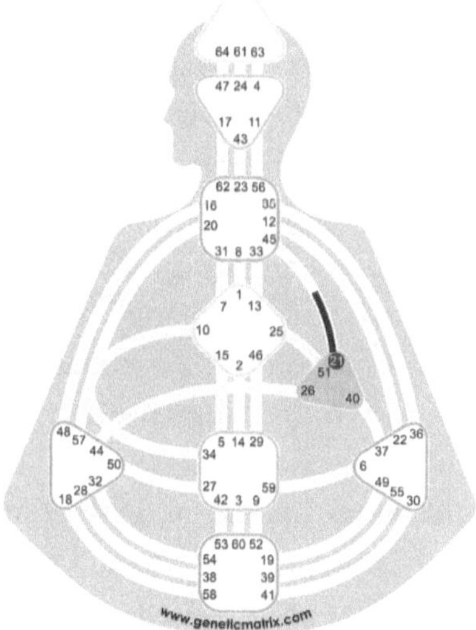

The Gate 21 in Human Design is my primary gate, like your Sun sign in astrology, because this is where the Sun was when I was born. I know this energy well and have worked with it unknowingly and then more purposefully for most of my life. In my view this is an energy of Stewardship, the right management of resources of all kinds, including one's personal energy, finances, connections, and opportunities, but also the resources of the community. This is "tribal energy" in the Human Design system, so it's also about our relationships and how we understand each other and function as a community. In traditional Human Design the Gate 21 is called the "Treasurer," denoting its role in tracking, distributing, and accounting for resources. In Pillar Seven, we took a look at the Gate 45, the Sovereign or King or Queen gate. The Gate 21 is its mate, in the feudal world managing the resources of the monarch. As we're evolving leadership in all its forms, the Gate 21 also is evolving into a nonhierarchical position similar to one that's imbedded equitably and horizontally in the Web of Life.

What does it mean to steward the resources of the community in the New World we're longing for and bringing into being? Part of that depends on how we define "community," of course, who and what are included. In the old world *community* was defined as the monarchs and their subjects, royalty and the aristocracy demanding resources from *commoners* who served to feed the royal machine. In the New World, stewardship paradoxically focuses more specifically and expands infinitely at the same time. We return to organizing ourselves more locally – a key aspect of well-managing resources – and in smaller groups.[22] Small towns, hamlets, or villages would become more the norm, where people likely know each other, food and energy are produced nearby and consumed locally, and we know and care well for our water and watersheds. We benefit, too, by focusing more on our proximate landscape and ecosystems, and give less authority to the human-made borders of private land ownership, municipalities, and states.

As we do, the world seems to change, with relationships among forests, rivers, creeks, watersheds, and the rise and fall of hillsides suddenly appearing differently. A view of the Web of Life emerges, inviting us

---

22 Transporting food, energy, and other goods and resources greatly increases their cost and their impact on the living world. Decentralizing services to reduce both of these will likely be forced upon us as supply chains break down unless we proactively reorganize ourselves in different ways.

to step outside of our habitual, confined ways of seeing and knowing into interconnectedness that spans the world. In this we have much to learn from people all over the world who've lived this way for untold generations, and who are doing their best both to keep stewarding their ancestral lands and to wake the rest of us out of the Story of Progress and into our true nature.

Indigenous Sovereignty and Stewardship

Indigenous leaders from many tribal nations speak of sovereignty and stewardship. For them, sovereignty means their ability – especially but not exclusively legally – to have authority and command of their ancestral lands and all the "natural resources" that live within them. In particular many tribes want to at least be at the table when governmental decisions are made regarding actions like drilling, (oil and water) fracking, mining, logging, and building oil pipelines on their ancestral lands. Even better would be for them to have the ability to *decide for themselves* and have their decision be honored legally. The Vatican's *Doctrine of Discovery*, still a legal precedent today, gave European monarchs legal authority to claim lands deemed either vacant or simply "unoccupied by Christians." *You get the idea.* Laws based on this doctrine continue to legally (not morally) grant authority to the US and Canadian governments, for example, to lease rights to mine and drill and log to multinational profit-driven forces against the expressed concerns and wishes of the indigenous stewards of those lands, even on their own reservations. For Indigenous Americans, *land sovereignty* asserts their legal rights to their ancestral lands as *sovereign nations.*[23]

Like sovereignty, stewardship means something very different in an indigenous world view than in a western one. Indigenous stewardship understands we humans as being *responsible to* the land and all living

---

23 In *Sacred Instructions* Mitchell presents four types of sovereignty needed for self-determined communities: water, food, energy, and education to break our dependence on systems of domination and control.

beings, as one important species among many. Our role is to care for the Earth that sustains us. Hundreds of tribal peoples for thousands of years developed and practiced ways of being with their specific landscapes, some of which you'll discover later in this chapter. In doing so people and the living landscape evolved together, the people *stewarding* the land based on specific, time-tested principles. They knew that they needed to take the lives of plants and animals to live. Yet they also knew that for there always to be plenty, taking must be moderate and something potent must be given in return. So goes the ethic of "reciprocity." This stewardship is grounded in understanding that everything is alive and "all our relations," meaning our extended family. It centers on our role as a "keystone species" to compassionately care for the living world of which we're a part and upon which we depend.

Pretty different from the western version, right?

Let's pause for a moment to consider what compassion, care, sovereignty, and stewardship have meant for you in your life. What associations do you have and what's been your experience? What have you been stewarding in your life and based on which principles? What kind of stewardship is calling you forth? Write or draw in your journal to capture your awareness while it's fresh.

To move forward, let's spiral back through time to uncover what's unfolded and led us to where we are today. With eyes wide open we can better meet the present and the future.

Rights and Responsibilities

Human rights. It's the language we use here in the US and internationally to name the fundamental principles upon which our version of civilization is based. Some have been enshrined in our Constitution: the right to free speech, the right to bear arms, the right to an attorney and to be judged by a jury of your peers. Many more have been included in the United Nations' *International Bill of Human Rights*. Some are hotly debated: the right to have command of one's body, for example, the right to food and housing, or the right to healthcare. Others have been named by only a few: the right to clean air, water, and soil. And even more, organizations like the Global Alliance for the Rights of Nature (GARN) seek to "create a system of jurisprudence that sees and treats nature as a fundamental, rights-bearing entity and not as mere property to be exploited at will" to ensure that members of the living – and *more-than-human* – world have places to live and thrive.

The United States was birthed into and out of debates about "natural rights" in France and England in particular, a new concept that disrupted what had been the divine right of kings to largely do whatever they pleased. Ironically the doctrine of natural rights – the foundation of human rights philosophy – arose in Europe *in response to* Europeans witnessing the lives of peoples indigenous to the Americas. Europeans oppressed by royalty and aristocracy felt intrigued and liberated looking at the lives of these tribal peoples so different from their own. They took for themselves the aspects of aboriginal life they felt drawn to, invoking them to wrest power away from the royals and grant it to themselves.

Yet these Europeans only took the parts that spoke to them, that they could use to empower and authorize themselves, and excluded other aspects that are critical to the whole. As we explored in Pillar Seven the *Founding Fathers* discarded the balance of masculine and feminine energies and women and men laid out in the *Great Law of Peace,* although they did incorporate a different kind of balance of power among the three branches of government. Because they were positioning themselves against hierarchical structures of domination and control, the founders were more concerned about defining and checking the authority of leaders and government than they were about laying out an ethic of responsibility for the "all men" who "are created equal." They assumed, perhaps, that when liberated from tyranny, "all men" would respect each other's rights and behave in reasonable ways, which is the basis of individualism's version of personal sovereignty.

These European men didn't appreciate sufficiently the depth and persistence of the social conditioning into brutality, coercion, and dominance that their people had already been subjected to and which they were reproducing. They didn't realize, perhaps, that men liberated from tyranny would need guidance and support to grow themselves into members of a more egalitarian society. What they didn't see in the indigenous communities that inspired them were the cultural systems (similar and different among the many nations) that *grew native children into responsible adults*. To the Europeans, the indigenous peoples appeared to be "in a state of nature," not members of ancient, thriving cultures with sophisticated forms of education. Their default lens cracked enough in the face of indigenous people's ways of living to let the light of equality shine into their oppressive worldview. But that lens didn't shatter enough for them to see the whole picture of indigenous life, including their codes of conduct, requirements for leadership, and ethic of care for the living world. Assuming to be superior because of their technological and philosophical differences, the Europeans didn't see the greater *maturity* of the indigenous populations.

This lack of awareness followed us into the twentieth century and rears its head in the *Universal Declaration of Human Rights*, first formulated by the United Nations in the aftermath of World War II. Almost all of this document focuses on human rights as *protection for humans from each other*. Only one brief statement mentions that we humans may have a responsibility beyond honoring other people's expression of their rights, called "the just requirements of morality, public order and the general welfare in a democratic society."

Can't argue with that, but it sounds pretty vague to me. What does it mean to you?

Certainly the doctrine of human rights pushes back against the forces of authoritarianism and misuses of power inside democracies and multinational capitalism that seek to reduce people to pawns. Detailing these rights has outlined values upon which *civilized society* organizes, many of which speak against slavery, torture, and arbitrary detainment, all tools of oppressive regimes. Yet even here we don't receive guidance about how you or I or anyone is to behave as functioning, contributing members of society. We know far more about what *we're not to do* than *what we are to do.* Driven by generations-old fear of tyranny, we've been reluctant to curtail the rights of individuals. But what about the behavior of individuals? Religions teach morality and right behavior; that's not the business of government. Well yeah, I agree it's not the business of government. Especially now that we're witnessing the rise of the radical Christian right's attempt to enforce their version of morality on the majority of the population, who don't share their views, through governmental actions. A new kind, yet also an old kind, of religious tyranny. *That's not what we want either.*

What if the larger we, humanity that is, have become an oppressive regime to the living world? What if we've become the dictators, taking whatever we want without concern for the impact on other living beings?

What if we've been perpetuating slavery and torture, as in the commercial treatment of cows, chickens, sheep, and bees? Yes, *bees.* You probably already know about the toxic travesty of cattle and chicken farms. But did you know that bees are routinely housed in mobile hives, fed antibiotics, shipped around the country, and forced out of their natural rhythms so they can pollinate almond trees? *Who's the tyrant now?*

> *"Demanding rights without taking responsibility*
> *for creating and maintaining those rights for others*
> *creates a warped sense of entitlement that often*
> *leads to violence, injustice and chaos."*
> —Sherri Mitchell

For most of us food is grown, harvested, packaged, and shipped out of our sight. We buy it in grocery stores with little to no recognition of where it came from, how the animals or plants were treated, the people who were involved, and the conditions under which they worked. We've become dependent upon this *industrial food system* to deliver what we need at *a price we can afford.* Yet we're not paying the true costs of commercially grown food, as these prices are subsidized and politically manipulated. Plus we're not accounting for the damage done to the soil and microorganisms that industrial agriculture causes. Ignorance of how that system operates and the damage it causes helps us feel innocent and content with how things are. *Out of sight, out of mind. I mean, you can't be responsible for something that's out of your control, right?*

In emphasizing rights and not including responsibilities, we perpetuate our *adolescence*.

Rights without responsibilities is for the young who don't yet have the capacity to be fully responsible. Maturing into adulthood includes accepting the responsibility to see and act beyond personal gain toward the greater good of the community. Ironically the ability to control impulses and the understanding of the consequences of one's actions takes place in one of the last areas of the brain to develop in our mid-twenties. For we westerners the appropriate period of adolescence expired long ago, and we need to mature our emotional and moral development to match our ability to impact the world. *Empowered men – empowered people – without responsibility to the whole are dangerous to themselves and the community.* Even a moment spent considering the rising numbers of mass murders in the US from those using assault weapons designed for war illustrates the point.

Rites of Passage – or Lack Thereof

The march of empire has done its utmost to wipe out the rites of passage of the tribal peoples who were colonized. This act strikes at the heart of a people in an attempt to destroy their culture. At the end of the nineteenth and early-twentieth centuries, for example, governments in the United States and Canada forced children from indigenous and First Nations peoples into boarding schools where they were physically and emotionally abused and their languages, customs, and ways of being were forbidden. Their motto: *Kill the Indian. Save the man.* Disrupting the maturation process of a community through which new adults are cultivated and recognized aims to make colonized people subservient and dependent on the colonial power, a kind of *domestication* if you will. Fortunately this strategy, while devastating, harmful, and deadly to many, wasn't entirely successful. Some people escaped having to go to the schools, while others were able to maintain or regain their inner identity as a tribal person.

An outgrowth of this strategy is that we descendants of colonizers no longer have meaningful rites of passage either. Rather than being an apprentice with a master and taught a trade, for example, now we're taught to be workers and consumers. Getting a driver's license and being old enough to vote and drink are about it. Living on your own, getting a bank account, and making your own money mark stages of independence that call for a level of *individual* responsibility. Typically we follow the track laid out for us by the Story of Progress: go to school, get a good-paying job, get married, have some kids, buy a house, save for retirement. This path to adulthood requires you to assimilate, fit in, and do what "works" financially. Saving for retirement, for example, means pouring money into the stock market in the expectation that it will grow over time. This path doesn't support your individuality (even though it's based in individualism), your self-knowledge and self-acceptance, or your awareness of your own unique role, purpose, and contribution to the whole.

Maturing in western culture calls for accumulating wealth and resources and bringing up your child to do the same. It teaches "getting ahead" (ahead of what? Debt, right?!), becoming an expert (specialization), and enjoying and displaying your success through exotic vacations, sending your kids to private colleges, and a home on a tree-lined street with a BBQ on the back deck and hard liquor in the cabinet next to it. *Ironically the freedom Europeans envied in the peoples of the Americas hasn't been realized.* Instead conformity and consumerism condition us to desire these benefits, which run deep in our psyches and obscure our ability to be in the world differently. *And yet we must.* It's time for us to grow our capacity *to be responsible to the living world* as the compassionate stewards we have the potential to become.

Also ironically the *Great Law of Peace* includes, as we saw in Pillar Seven, an elaborate system for selecting chiefs and removing them if necessary. *The colonists loved that part.* But it also includes very specific guidance and instructions for the appropriate behavior of chiefs, especially their calm, grounded, humble demeanor and the priority they place on the well-being of the people of all the confederated nations. This kind of oversight grew out of lifetimes of proximity, people living in tribal groups inside of which children would be seen and tracked as they grew, and at adolescence would be guided to develop their gifts and inclinations. Members would be well known to each other, hiding neither possible nor desirable. The women selecting chiefs would have observed the boys growing into men, then determining which had the character and temperament suitable for the role.

I wonder what my country would be like today if a council of post-menopausal women were able to remove arrogant, overly emotional, and demeaning men from office and replace them with ones who truly live with compassion and the desire for the greatest good for all?

Uprooted. Unrooted. Re-Rooted?

I've moved over twenty times in my lifetime. I've lived in four states on the west and east coasts. My parents moved from Amherst, Massachusetts, where my father was teaching, to Seattle when he got a job at the University of Washington. They both grew up in different parts of New York State, and in my mother's words *were happy to get as far away as possible from the culture of the Northeast.* Like other Euro-Americans before them, they went west in search of a better life. Both my grandfathers were from the South and moved north to New York state as young men. I believe they were both from Louisville, Kentucky. Most likely I have slaveholding in my heritage.

My mother's family was from Evanston, Illinois. My grandfather was a successful *businessman* (in what?) who was politically progressive, didn't support Jim Crow laws, and taught my grandmother to drive a Model T in the early 1900s when she was a teenager. Both my grandmothers earned advanced degrees in the 1920s during a brief period when women from monied families were allowed to do so. My father's mother came from a dysfunctional wealthy family, the father of which was so controlling that my grandmother and her younger brother, who was gay, walked away and never turned back. This grandmother married my brilliant, controlling, and dour grandfather, moving from her family home in Dunkirk, New York, a small town on Lake Erie, to the college town of Ithaca, New York, where my grandfather was a Samuel Richardson scholar of great report. Although we didn't have much money when I was growing up, still a patina of wealth colored our lives with jewelry, linen, and silver inherited from an earlier age.

I'm related by marriage to the infamous Zachary Taylor, twelfth president of the United States, who was a military hero for his multiple campaigns against indigenous peoples. *Ouch.* And I'm descended from Louisa White, whose ancestor Peregrine White became known as the "first born child of New England," having been born on the Mayflower when it was docked at Cape Cod in 1620.

Even though branches of my family have been in what's now the United States for *a long time*, I don't feel rooted to any particular place. Moving around seems to have been more the norm for my family, like so many of us European immigrants. I feel even more unrooted when I read about and talk with people, especially Indigenous Americans, who grew up connected to a landscape and ecosystem, sometimes for generations. I feel sad as I realize I will never experience that kind of relatedness, as I didn't grow up learning to cultivate it or having it modeled for me. My father loved his garden; in the summer he could be found on his knees weeding and planting. But the way our environment was carved up into little lots where we could have a few feet of grass and garden didn't inspire connection to the land. I take walks in the parks and green spaces where I live, yet my head is full from so many years of intellectual practice that I go there primarily to decompress. My family lineage and strong mind have enabled me to be successful in the terms of the overculture – to a degree. My education and family prepared me to use my mind to create my life. These have given me privilege because I know how to make systems work for me and because of my assigned race I'm granted a certain amount of authority and safety.

Yet this privilege masks my unrootedness and dissociation from land, landscape, and ecosystems. I've moved around, contributing as I go yet never settling for more than a few years. *I don't have a home to go back to.* The city I grew up in – Seattle – has changed beyond recognition to me under the force of Amazon.com. I'm more *at home* in Sebastopol than anywhere else I've been, yet I know this isn't my last destination.

I approach the material and perspectives of Pillar Eight with curiosity and trepidation. This isn't in my domain of knowing from my lived experience as the earlier pillars have been. It may be that you'll walk ahead of me with more understanding from your heritage or life experience. Or it may be you'll walk beside me as together we look clearly and compassionately at our lineages and our relationship to land. I can feel inside how embracing this material reveals my trained and now habitual disconnection from the land where I live. *I feel loss and a hole in my consciousness where rootedness would be.* This awareness stirs a deep longing that at times I've fulfilled, at least partially, as I've nestled into a place for a time.

My child's father and I stewarded the home we bought in Oakland (the one with the powder-post beetles), upgrading its structure and appearance in many ways. We replaced the foundation, built a weight-bearing wall (one had been removed), built a new kitchen, and redesigned the yard, small as it was, with bricks from the former foundation. We left that home immeasurably better off than when we bought it. The part of me that's still hooked into the Story of Progress wishes we hadn't sold it when we did, as it's now risen in value significantly. The part of me that's free from the need for my financial situation to grow feels satisfied with the way we stewarded that home and land, passing it on healthier and more sustainable than it was when we received it. I get to notice these different perspectives alive inside me with their different aspirations, values, priorities, and emotions.

The part that's still hooked thinks: *That was a stupid move, to sell the house. I'd be wealthier today if I hadn't. Isn't that the way my parents accumulated wealth, through their home appreciating over forty years? They stayed in one place, and look what it got them.*

Yes, that's true, the appreciating value aspect, the other part admits. *But the situation was very complex in 2011 when we decided to sell. The decision wasn't made lightly, and it made the divorce much easier in 2015, which was its own blessing. But even more, we did the job we set out to do, which was to heal and strengthen that home, which had been neglected, so that it would be well and provide more than shelter for decades to come. We've always had what we needed when we needed it, so let's rest in knowing that and unhook ourselves from the need for growth, shall we?*

I've chosen to give my attention and energy to this second point of view; yet even a decade later I can still feel the pull of the other, *the one who mourns the loss of potential wealth.* After all, this is how I was conditioned and shown that the middle class passes on and accumulates wealth. My parents gave my family funds for a down payment. My mother's parents had done that for them, so my parents did it for me (and my brother too). Walking away from our home in the aftermath of the housing disaster of 2008 wasn't easy, even knowing we were among many were hit hard by the crash. We didn't foreclose, but we left with zero funds, not even our initial investment.

The kid and young adult inside me who grew up believing in this part of the American Dream still gets tight in the chest and belly when I consider this, so deep does this conditioning go. I'm taking a few deep breaths as I notice the regret and disappointment that lingers even now; the western cultural imperative to accumulate – as a way to create safety and security – dies hard.

I've lived in three places since I moved north fourteen years ago. In the first place I discovered how limited my experience was about gardening, as I'd only done it in cities. I prepared and filled a garden bed with eager seedlings only to discover they'd all been eaten by deer overnight. When my marriage ended, I moved onto a piece of land where a friend of mine was living, excited about the prospect of gardening together. My then-teenager and I moved into a tiny place (500 square feet) situated on three acres with dozens of mature fruit trees, a beautiful pond, and plenty of garden beds. The property was already fenced so deer weren't a problem; for some unknown reason we didn't have many gophers there either. We grew enormous collard greens, cabbages, tatsoi, and celery far too bitter to eat. We made apple cider, dried jar upon jar of Asian pears, and gave away bowls of Santa Rosa plums. I felt closest to that land, but the property was sold and we had to move on – a common occurrence where I live.

My kiddo and I then moved into a duplex in town that gave us a lot more room inside but without the rich land outside. I've missed living on more open land ever since. The small yard I have stewardship of now has little sun in the back and too much sun in the front. My landlord laid down landscaping cloth across the backyard and covered it with wood-chips. It feels dead back there. I've added three raised beds and many pots and filled them with shade-loving plants from which bees love to eat. I've successfully grown lettuce, but all my other efforts at growing food have yielded slow-growing, lanky plants that look at me and murmur: *Really? You want me to grow with that big house in the way of the Sun?*

Grandmother Oak spreads her arms overhead, her legs and feet extending underground undeterred by that landscaping cloth. Her body-trunk lies on the other side of a fence, a bizarre and unfortunate example of humans' artificial boundaries. Every day I gaze at Grandmother Oak out my office window or from my deck, wishing her body was inside my yard so I could sit at her feet with my back against her. Her body lives in a parking lot on the other side of the fence. One day I remarked to her, slightly annoyed, that her leaves are prickly and they hurt my feet. *If you hadn't built your house so close to me,* she replied, *then it wouldn't be an issue. You're the one who came into my "yard."* I smiled, a bit grimly. *True that,* I silently replied. *True that, indeed.* So I joined my friend and a few others at her garden where we grow much of our food for most of the year.

Pause for a moment, taking a deep breath, and reflect.
What's your family's history in relation to land and
colonialism? We've all been affected by this larger history,
yet we often ignore it, especially if we've benefited from
it. Where did your people come from and how and why
did they get here? How rooted do you feel to the landscape
where you live? Have you stewarded a home or landscape?
What's that experience been like for you? Make a few notes
or drawings in your journal before moving on.

During this last year I've learned so much about different farming methods, land stewardship, and what contributes to healthy ecosystems.

I've discovered contradictory world views and their differing approaches, and see in them, on the one hand, residue from the Story of Progress, androcentric perspectives of human dominance, and a focus on productivity. In others, I see restoring landscapes as something similar to what they were before Europeans brought their own plants and farming and building methods, such as oak woodlands. These woodlands would have been and still are in areas where indigenous people are stewarding the land, cared for by regular burning of the understory, which deposits nutrients back into the soil, stimulates new growth, and activates those plants who need fire to germinate.

Historically the indigenous people in the area where I live – the coastal Miwok, Pomo, and Wappo peoples – weren't agricultural in the western sense. They hunted, fished, foraged, and cultivated based on principles and wisdom developed over millennia of observing and experimenting rooted in reverence and respect for all living beings and their understanding of a specific landscape. While they understand that living requires taking life, whether that's of an animal or plants, they do so according to a *code of ethics* that ensures both right relationship between the human and living world and also plenty for all.

Fortunately indigenous people from many different places with different tribal affiliations have begun generously sharing aspects of their wisdom traditions. Many ancient prophecies foretold this time when the animals would die and the Earth would suffer and the immigrants/colonizers would know they needed to change and would become receptive to their ways of knowing. These first peoples have long embraced their role as the caretakers of the world, what today we're calling "land stewardship." As Chief Seattle once said: "The Earth does not belong to man, man belongs to the Earth." As a powerful species we're obliged to use our perception, innovation, and abilities in ways *responsible to* the well-being of plants, forests, and ecosystems, as well as for ourselves. As it turns out plants and ecosystems in the Americas evolved with humans acting as what Salóm calls "a keystone species" in a "kincentric" world, active participants who worked with them and cared for them. Let's explore a few examples together.

Reciprocity and Stewardship

Sweetgrass and basket weavers need each other. Kimmerer describes a study by one of her grad students that yielded *scientific proof* of this. The initial investigation sought to determine which of two different traditional harvesting methods were the best for the sweetgrass. As it turned out, both harvesting practices benefited sweetgrass; it was when there was *no harvesting* that the sweetgrass died out. Over many generations of practice, sweetgrass and basket makers developed a reciprocal relationship in which they became dependent on each other. The careful harvesting – taking only what you need and never more than half – stimulates growth by removing just part of the plant. This opens the remaining plant to light and air, making space for new growth. The basket weavers get what they need: sweetgrass for their baskets. The sweetgrass gets what it needs: grooming to make space for and to stimulate growth. This discovery went directly against accepted scientific truth as espoused by the head of the biology department, who was on this student's dissertation committee. He said: "Everyone knows that it weakens a plant to harvest from it." *Hmm, maybe not so much.*

This reminds me of basket maker, dancer, and member of Wappo nation Clint McKay talking about how indigenous peoples burn the understory at any time of year for different purposes. We're out on a walk at the Pepperwood Preserve, the tagline of which is "Viewing the landscape through an Indigenous lens." McKay, the Pepperwood's Indigenous Education Coordinator, is descended from several important local culture bearers and is himself a culture bearer with extensive Native historical knowledge not only of Pepperwood but of the entire region.

McKay is looking to a hillside opposite where we're standing, noting how covered it is with fir trees, straight and narrow conifers. "Those don't belong here," he says. "If it were up to me, I'd take them all down and burn them. These hills belong to the oaks. The conifers are choking out the oaks, creating an environment for the massive fires we've been having. The naturalists used to scoff at these ideas, asserting the best forest management is to leave the forest alone. But after the Tubbs Fire my phone hasn't stopped ringing. They're coming around now, open to learning indigenous ways because they're seeing that their way isn't working. They're learning to do cultural burns, and they're seeing how this benefits the land and animals in so many ways."

This is an example of indigenous stewardship from which the rest of us can learn.

Western environmentalists typically recommend that the best thing we humans can do is leave a landscape to itself, the idea being that this is how it will best recover and thrive. This has led to large areas being *set aside* as nature preserves or, in the US, national parks and monuments. Compared to drilling for oil, strip mining, or clear-cutting, setting land aside is a step in the right direction. This creates a pause in the march of empire over the landscape, which otherwise would leave toxic waste and devastated ecosystems in its wake. Even so, mining, logging, and other extractive practices are still allowed inside these parks under certain circumstances, so being *set aside* doesn't always mean what it seems.

Even more this desire to protect the land has meant that people indigenous to it have been ousted as a threat, as solutionist, filmmaker and environmentalist Nicola Peel notes. In her work in the Equatorian Amazon, Peel has worked with many indigenous people who face either having to cut down their forest to raise funds to feed their kids or get kicked off their land when it's being "protected." She's created a project called "Pay to Breathe" that calls for giving indigenous people a living wage to be "guardians of the forest," as they've always been. She advocates "direct payments to farmers who have Key Biodiversity Areas so they can be the caretakers, the seed savers and tree nurseries of the future." In this way forests need not be cut, the people who know best how to care for the forests are supported to do that work, and the rest of the world receives the massive amounts of oxygen and carbon sequestering that the Amazonian forests provide.

Some (white) environmentalists don't support this, arguing that indigenous people *can't be trusted* to steward the land and not cut down the trees. *Now that's what I call gaslighting!*

Plus kicking indigenous people off their ancestral lands to *protect* it mirrors the mindset that fueled the colonial notion that the Americas were virtually empty when Europeans arrived. The *logical* solution, then, is to *return* the land to an unpopulated state. Yet as many indigenous people have pointed out, millions of people were living in and stewarding the lands of the Americas when Europeans arrived. Forests, plains, meadows, all were tended in myriad ways, including burning, harvesting, and cultivating (but not in the European agricultural sense). They developed principles of reciprocity that enabled both them and the living world they depended on to thrive. Principles such as "take only what you need, never take more than half," and "always honor the lives you must take" guided their harvesting and stewardship. These principles and methods were and are so different from a western mindset that initially they were *invisible* to the colonists.

Europeans were accustomed to more open land where forests had been leveled and divided by fences. Part of the reason common people of Europe emigrated to the Americans is that land that had been held in common and upon which they'd once grown food and hunted game had been *enclosed* to direct wealth to royalty and the aristocracy. Many people were driven into the cities where the plague and smallpox thrived. Fleeing starvation and impoverishment, they unwittingly brought with them pestilence that spread over the "new world," devastating the indigenous peoples who had no immunity to these super diseases bred in the overcrowded, polluted, and toxic *grand* cities of Europe. The early newcomers interpreted land that hadn't been enclosed or fenced in as being unoccupied, not seeing the land stewarding practices of the original peoples. Later newcomers did discover, in some places, land where indigenous people once lived but were no longer, so extensive were the epidemics that ravaged the native peoples.

My heart hurts when I face this. How terrifying it must have been to discover not just yourself or your family but virtually everyone in your community dying suddenly and nothing you could do to stop it. And to know, for me, that most likely my ancestors were among those who brought those diseases here, and in some cases spread them on purpose.

In recent years, we outside the tribes have begun to perceive and value ancient and proven ways of the original peoples beyond our voyeuristic, romanticized visions.

Regenerative agriculture recognizes that we humans have done so much to damage our ecosystems that setting aside areas is insufficient and perhaps even harmful. Much of the land in northern California where I live has been *protected* by the Bureau of Land Management (BLM), which means it's been left alone. Yet this policy has led to increasingly damaging wildfires so hot that they burn even the older trees, which under indigenous stewardship would be scorched but not burned. These fires are fueled by undergrowth and the proliferation of conifers, which, as McKay notes, don't belong here in such numbers. We do well to listen to and follow the guidance of peoples who for thousands of years developed healthy, respectful, sustainable, and reciprocal relationships with plants, rivers, forests, animals, and birds of their shared ecosystems. It's difficult to overestimate the value and significance of such ancient wisdom and knowledge.

Embracing compassionate stewardship, even as a concept at first, helps shifts us out of the shadow of power-over perspective of androcentrism (the world revolves around we humans and exists for our purpose) to the empowered and awakened understanding of being a member of the living world. Our intelligence and strength confer on us the responsibility to use our power wisely within a "kincentric" world.

Reflections and Longings

I'm lying in bed just about to turn off my light. I've been reading *Braiding Sweetgrass*, and the last chapter I read is about Kimmerer working with others to save salamanders as they awkwardly waddle across the road on their way to their breeding grounds in the ponds nearby. Like so much of her work, this story stirs in me a deep sense of loss – who knows how many thousands of salamanders die under speeding car tires? – and an aching sense of beauty at the way she and her companions stay up most of the night grabbing salamanders and taking them to the other side of the road. I think about my own loss, never having been immersed in our living world in the ways she describes. This story about the salamanders recounts an attempt to undo harm that roads are doing.

In another chapter Kimmerer shares about a trip she took one of her classes on during which they spent a few days deep in marshy wetlands. She shows them how cattails can provide most everything they need from shelter to food. All the way through I thought, *Oh I'd so love to be in that class!* Although I've never been drawn much to the science I've been presented with, I love her practice of biological field science informed by her indigenous wisdom. I consider the plants I have in my home, my little gardens, and the bigger garden I'm helping to steward at my friend's home. I feel how ignorant I am, how not really connected I am. There's that hole in my heart again where a deep sense of belonging might have been.

I'm wondering if I can find some people who are helping salamanders near where I live?

Cultivating Your Capacity for Compassionate Stewardship

Each one of us really can make a difference. Each one of us matters. You know what cultural anthropologist Margaret Meade reportedly said: "Never doubt that a small group of thoughtful, committed citizens can change the world. Indeed, it's the only thing that ever has." We quote it often, like that quote attributed to Mahatma Gandhi's "Be the change you wish to see in the world." Yet we don't necessarily know *how* to put that statement into action in our everyday lives. By now it's abundantly clear that we need to evolve our big systems, like government and finance, and yet each move forward begins with the actions of one and then a few and then more.

The ancient yogic traditions offer ahimsa अहिंसा as a foundational ethical concept meaning "nonharming." Ahimsa rests upon the understanding that we're all connected, indeed we're all one, in the great Flow of Life. Given this, harm done to others is harm we do to ourselves as well. This reminds me of that phrase from the Hippocratic Oath taken by medical doctors: *First, do no harm.* This ethic reverberates across time and space, resonating at the frequency of compassion, love, and acceptance that characterize the spiritual realm. Unfortunately our society isn't organized on this principle and currently we often do harm without meaning to or even realizing it.

Stepping into stewardship means we need to become aware of the harm caused by our actions and to do what we can to end it.

We've become so accustomed to everyday harm and violence that we've become a bit numb to it – *maybe a lot numb.* I know it's difficult to stay present to the ways in which violence and harm occur moment to moment as part of our daily lives. For example the computer upon which I'm writing to you right now relies on precious earth metals that are mined in conditions that are horrendous for the miners and the landscape. The miners' below-subsistence experience lies outside my view unless I go looking for it; we privileged ones of the Global North are *protected* by this lack of knowledge so we'll continue to consume a new phone, for example, as often as possible. I don't really know what to do with that knowledge, but I try not to be oblivious of it and I don't get a new phone every year (or even often). When I remember I say a prayer for the women and small children who at this moment are digging so that I can write to you in this way. My prayer doesn't eliminate the harm the miners are experiencing, but *it does help keep me on track* with what I feel I can do in my life right now. Some things are so imbedded in the big systems that you may feel you can't make a difference, and then acknowledgement and a prayer may be what you can offer, at least right now.

Yet I believe – *I know* – that you and each of us can begin where we are and take a step toward reducing if not eliminating harm. You can review your everyday behavior and challenge yourself to make changes that may be uncomfortable or inconvenient but move us all in the right direction. You can also look around and see what others are already doing in your community to reduce the harm we've collectively been doing to the Earth and contribute to creating new ways of being based in ahimsa. Yeah, I know, there's so much that needs to be done. The key, as I've discovered along with a lot of other people, is to stay out of overwhelm and despair by choosing and beginning actions you can take *right now* in areas you're passionate about. Maybe you're drawn to how animals are treated, or children in need, or grief work, or survivors of sexual abuse, or planting trees and stewarding forests, or making *wake-the-fuck-up* art, or registering voters, or advocating for renewable energy in your town, or holding a circle of elders to offer sage advice to younger people, or getting your local golf course to stop spraying herbicides, or teaching people how to shop at the farmers' market, or … the possibilities are literally endless.

Let yourself be inspired and guided by the seven generations principle held by indigenous people to not only do no harm now but intend to do no harm for the generations that come after you. *The Great Law of Peace* calls on the selected, governing chiefs to "have always in view not only the present, but also the coming generations, even those whose faces are yet beneath the surface of the ground – the unborn of the future nation" (Article 27). Don't let this principle simply be an eco-friendly brand of household goods (though we need those too). Let this principle inspire, stimulate, and even provoke you as you make choices about where to spend your money, your time, your energy. Expand your view out beyond your phone and computer screen, and even your family, work, home, and community, out into the future. We've become so accustomed to fast internet, immediate streaming, instant gratification, and getting what we want *right now* that our sense of time has become warped. We've gotten disconnected from the rise and setting of the Sun, the turn of the seasons, and the passing of the years, awash in a 24/7 culture that isn't really culture so much as an insatiable, never-ending marketplace.

Quick! Stand up and move your body around. Oh my, even just writing that I started going into a consumer-induced trance, thinking about the next episode of the series my kid and I are currently watching ...

Many years ago, on a trip between undergrad and graduate school, a friend and I visited the town of Autun in France, home to the Saint-Lazare cathedral. We could see the spire from miles away reaching up into the sky, a pinnacle of craftsmanship of the twelfth century. As we walked toward the town of 13,000 people, I turned to my friend and remarked with awe, "Oh my, no wonder they believed in God."

Known for its *Romanesque* architecture, the cathedral was largely built over about twenty-five years but continued to be added to for up to eighty years. Can you imagine being one of the stone masons, laying stone by stone, year after year, never seeing it completed? What sense of time and labor would be required to dedicate your life to a project you'd never see finished? In a world of rapidly created digital art, you may find it, as I did, difficult to imagine spending a life this way. I suspect that faith and dedication to craft inspired them and kept them going.

We could use more of that as we look out into our future and envision the new, more beautiful world our hearts know is possible. Let's not be dissuaded by not knowing how things will unfold or the outcome of our efforts. Let's refuse to be deterred by uncertainty, doubt, or weariness, or give victimhood or cynicism a seat at our table. Let's set places instead for creativity, camaraderie, intuition, grace, and determined optimism, filling their plates with our intention, attention, and energy. Let's nourish ourselves with possibility and support one another as we create *a small group of thoughtful, committed citizens* even when we know many of our efforts will fall on deaf ears and fail to create the outcomes we desire. The truth is, we'll never know the full impact of the actions we take today. So let's commit and keep going, remembering that, as Maya Angelou once said: "Now I know better, I can do better." And so can you and I. *And so we will.*

Everyday Compassion and Care

Changing the trajectory we're on will take many of us turning the wheel toward compassion, nonharming, sustainability, and restoring our planet and ourselves. Let's focus first on recommendations for *what you can do right now* to make shifts in your choices and behaviors through a transformative, Thrutopian, seventh-generation, and restorative lens. After that we'll explore a series of collaborative projects large and small that I hope will inspire you to join with others on a project with which you resonate. Each of us can make efforts to change our habits to be more beneficial for our environment, our ecosystems, the people around us, our own bodies, and truly all of life. *Never underestimate the significance of what you can do through your own efforts.* Bring along your primary Learning Question and consider how these examples relate to it.

Provocative Questions for Inquiry as We Explore Our Next Steps

- Where does your food come from?
- Where does your garbage go?
- Where does your water come from?
- Where does your sewage go?
- How do you get around?
- What kind of power and how much do you use?

Many of us are privileged enough that we don't have to think about these factors very much. We just head to the grocery store, take out the garbage, turn on the faucet and the light switch, and jump in our cars when we want to go somewhere. Yet *most people in the world* can't take these fundamentals for granted. We're insulated in ways that diminish our awareness of our common humanity, enabling us to do harm without our conscious intent. But we can change that. *You ready?*

My family and I have adopted many of the practices that I share below, and we aspire to all of them. Some will be familiar to you, and you may already be practicing them, and no doubt others will not. Consider which of the practices listed you'd like to adopt for yourself. Please add to this list practices that you're already doing or intending to do toward stewarding care and fostering compassion in your spheres of influence. I also invite you to share with me practices that you don't see listed here. I'm always open to creative and innovative possibilities that can positively impact our world.

Notice resistance as it comes up. I'm sure that it will at some point! *Welcome resistance.* Welcome it and spend a few moments going inside to reflect on what's going on in that resistance. Some of it may be habitual, some may be cultural, and some might feel inconvenient or even outlandish. *That's a-okay.* We know we need to decondition and reprogram ourselves to new normals, right, if we want to change our world for the better.

Some of this has been easy for me. I grew up in Seattle where recycling came in early. I remember taking out both ends of a tin can so we could stomp on it and collapse it. We drove boxes of bottles, paper, and cans to recycling centers once a month. This has become so ingrained in me that I can't throw anything that can be recycled into the garbage. Call me weird, but I'll throw an empty bottle in my bag and carry it home to recycle it if I have to.

In 1986 my brother convinced me to start exclusively eating organic food. I was in graduate school and didn't have a lot of money. Plus it wasn't easy to find. I had to drive on the freeway to another town to a natural food store that had organic produce. When I lived in New York City I took the subway from where I lived on 119th Street all the way down to Greenwich Village to get organic food. It wasn't easy or cheap, but by that time I was so committed to buying and eating organic that it was *just what I did.* I did it for my own health. I did it to support the farmers. I did it for the soil and the earth. The benefits are many, many, many.

I recommend that you give yourself a pat on the back for what you're already doing from the list below and select a few that you've been meaning to do but haven't yet. Finally pick at least two that are new to you, or that you're particularly resistant to, and give them a try. Of course this list is far from exhaustive, so if you've got other ideas go for it! This list mirrors the one in Pillar Three that offered ways of caring for your physical well-being. Here we're expanding to how we care for the larger

Planetary Body of which we're a part. The suggestions are organized into three levels or stages of difficulty and investment. Begin where you are and keep moving.

Start Here

- **Buy organic food.**
  I know I mentioned this in Pillar Three, and it's well worth emphasizing here. Refuse to buy or eat food that's been poisoned. Yep, if it's commercially grown it's been poisoned. I know that might sound extreme but it's really true. From chemical fertilizers, herbicides, and pesticides, at every stage commercially grown food is subject to being inundated with substances harmful to your health. Even grains that aren't GMO (genetically modified) are now routinely sprayed with Roundup®, which has been shown to cause cancer, to "ripen" the grain. Basically the chemicals kill the plant and in its last gasp the plant sends all the nutrients it can into the grain, its fruit, yet the poison remains.

  Also organic food is more nutritious than commercially grown food. Commercially grown food may be bigger and free from most blemishes, but it's not going to have the nutrients you need because the soil in which it's grown has been dramatically depleted by agricultural practices that have become the norm in the last sixty to seventy years. And commercially grown food is one of the most harmful industries, destroying the life of the soil, using increasing amounts of chemicals to produce yields from depleted soils, and making it extremely difficult for smaller family farms to even exist. *Vote with your dollars, and just say no to industrially grown food.*

- **Support your local farmers at farmers' markets.**
  Farmers' markets will have the freshest produce you can get after growing your own. Purchasing direct from the farmers supports small farms, ideally organic or biodynamic, in your area. As supply chains become increasingly challenged, being able to get locally grown food will help protect you from shortages while also supporting a healthier system as well as a healthier you. When you buy direct, the

farmers get more for their produce. Farming is difficult, risky work, and we've been insulated from the real costs of real food by legislated protections for the industrial food industry. Let's support these key members of our community! Plus you'll discover what's in season (and what's not) and you can learn a lot about food by speaking to farmers. A friend of mine just shared a story with me about asking a farmer how to tell which peaches are better. He was amazed at the depth and detail the farmer shared with him. Another option is to join a CSA – Community Supported Agriculture – where you pay for a box of fresh produce (weekly or monthly). Farmers are assured of a certain income and people to eat their crops.

- **Reduce your own food waste.**
  According to Food Rescue US (more on them below), *we waste forty percent of our food here in the US.* As one friend of mine exclaimed: "That's staggering!" I practice reducing waste in two ways. First, I save vegetable cuttings of all kinds and bones and keep them in a plastic bag in my freezer. When the bag seems full enough I make stock and then compost the remains. Second, I'm doing my best to not let food spoil in my refrigerator. This one has been harder for me. I've had to really focus on getting only the amount of food my kiddo and I can consume before it goes bad, and also eating leftovers right away. While the issue is much bigger and more complex than what's happening in my refrigerator, they're related. In fact my kid and I just had a conversation about committing to eating whatever we bring into the house as part of how we honor the abundance of the Earth that we're fortunate enough to enjoy.

- **Compost, either on your own or with your city/town.**
  Many cities and towns now will pick up yard waste and fruit and vegetables scraps. Some will pick up bones and meat scraps as well. Check with your local waste management service. Composting yourself isn't that easy unless you have the right setup. It can be a great source of compost for your garden if you have the attention, energy, and setup needed to do it well. Lomi Composter is an option for

those who live in apartments and/or cities or places where their towns don't provide this service.

- **Reduce water usage.**
  Water is far more precious than gold, yet we flush it down, let it run, and even wash our sidewalks with it as if it were limitless. Here in California we've had drought for years, and many of us have adopted water-saving habits as a result, such as flushing toilets only when *really* necessary, taking short showers, avoiding baths, not watering lawns (even better taking out lawns), putting gardens on drip, and watering when the sun isn't out. Use a high-quality dishwasher – it uses less water than handwashing. Only wash full loads of laundry and full loads of dishes. Use a car wash that recycles their water. Never use water to clean your deck or driveway. Say a blessing of gratitude for your water. Having it piped into your house really is miraculous.

- **Be mindful of what you flush and drain into the sewers, septic, and ground water.**
  Flushing something down your toilet or sink doesn't mean it *goes away*. It goes into the sewer or septic and often out into the groundwater, creeks, rivers, lakes, and ultimately the ocean. Medications in particular harm our water and make their way back into our bodies in detrimental ways. Protect yourself, your family, and our waterways and oceans by properly disposing of toxins like antibiotics and oil. Our local police station, for example, has a place to safely dispose of medications.

- **Refuse, reduce, reuse, refill, repair, pass it on, and only then recycle.**
  Single-use plastic can be found in the stomachs of birds far out at sea. Why not just refuse to use it as much as you can? Wash your plastic bags and reuse them until they fall apart. Take your own plastic bags to the grocery store. Don't bag things that don't need it, like bananas or onions or potatoes. As big an advocate of recycling as I am, I acknowledge that many things can't be recycled. The whole industry is a very mixed bag (is plastic recycling really a thing?), and it takes

a lot of energy to break down and remake things. I hate putting perfectly good glass bottles and jars in the recycle because I know they could be reused instead. *We need better systems to make reuse and repair easier.*

As I'm sure you know, many things are designed to break or stop working, and they can't be repaired or upgraded. Electronics are definitely this way, yet so, so many of the items we purchase and use regularly aren't built to last. I always ask myself: *Will this end up in the landfill and if so, how soon? How much use can I really get out of it?* If I can't repair it when it breaks, what will happen? Sorry, but this means fewer balloons, gift bags, and kitchen gadgets you use once a year (or less). Balloons, as fun as they are, are notoriously dangerous to wildlife, turning up in the bellies of birds and littering the ocean. Best to stop using them, especially outside where they have a tendency to drift away.

My requirements for gifts now are they need to be consumable (meaning they'll disappear, like food or candles) or wearable, hand-made (especially art), or compostable (will break down in a relatively short period of time).

- **Reduce or eliminate as many *disposables* as possible. Use refillable and reusable items instead.**
  Buy a great water filter and a heavy glass or metal bottle and take your own bottled water with you. Carry a reusable mug with you when you go get coffee, and have your own knife, fork, and spoon so you don't need to pick up disposable ones at the hot bar. If you do pick up disposable utensils, clean them and keep them in your car so you have them for next time. I've reused a paper cup until it literally fell apart in my hands. Never, no not ever, get to-go items in Styrofoam. That substance will be around for millennia and not in a good way. Use rechargeable batteries. They cost more but they last a long time. Properly dispose of all batteries, as they're toxic.

- **Recycle whatever and whenever you can.**
  If you can't stop using it, then recycle it. Choose things you can recycle. Check what your local recycler will and will not take. I see

people put things in the recycle bin all the time that aren't recyclable – like plastic packaging or to-go containers and cups, even clothing and wood. Anything that's wet or has food on it can contaminate an entire load of recyclables! Recycling paper, cans, and glass works pretty well, but that's about it. Plastic recycling only applies to bottles and not even that is consistent or guaranteed. Make sure to recycle your electronics! Electronics contain rare and precious minerals that can be reused in new electronics. The better we get at reusing rare metals, the less they need to be mined. See if you can find an organization in your area working on *zero waste* or one that offers education online.

- **Reduce electrical and natural gas usage.**
  Hang your laundry. Turn out lights when you leave the room or your home. Put a hat and a sweater on when the temperature drops. Wrap a wet bandanna around your neck when the temperature rises. Even better, allow yourself to get used to changes in temperature with the seasons. Your body is designed to adapt to seasonal changes and it will if you let it! Too many of us have become accustomed to keeping our homes at seventy-two degrees all year around. Doing that lowers your adaptability and negatively impacts your immune system. You'll save money too.

- **Use either recycled paper or paper made from bamboo or sugar cane.**
  You can find printer paper, toilet paper, paper towels, and tissues all made from recycled or truly renewable sources. Don't be fooled by paper made from *sustainably managed forests*. Yes, this is better than paper made from old growth forests, which unfortunately is still made especially for magazines. But these tree farms don't replace actual forests. Let's stop cutting trees for our paper. I like Reel Paper; their motto is *Sit down for what you believe in.* Always good to have a sense of humor. Even better, get a bidet and skip the paper altogether!

- **Stop using chemicals in your yard.**
  Herbicides, pesticides, and even chemical-based fertilizers cause harm to the ecosystem in which you're living. Bees suffer, the microbiome

of the soil suffers, and some of those so-called pests play an important role in the living world. In fact we're facing the extinction of many insects that are crucial to the well-being of the whole. When I was a kid the windshield of our car would be covered with dead insects on road trips. Are you old enough to remember that? That doesn't happen anymore. Why? *Because of the decline in the insect populations.* The largescale use of these human-made chemicals in commercial farming and on golf courses and in city and state parks have done the greatest damage. Yet what you do in your own yard does make a difference. Make an ahimsa choice.

Dig Deeper

- **Grow your own food whenever possible.**
  If you have a garden with some sun you can grow food. If you have a lawn you can tear it up and plant a vegetable garden instead. This reduces water usage considerably and turns an often unused piece of land into a living ecosystem. (Lawns are monocultures, not ecosystems.) If you even have a pot on your porch, patio, or balcony, you can grow herbs and a surprising number of vegetables. Check out *The Vertical Veg Guide to Container Gardening* to discover how to transform a small space – like a balcony or patio – into an abundant container garden filled with herbs, fruit, veg, beauty, and life.

- **Purchase eggs and meat from local farmers.**
  For several years I've been getting a whole lamb twice a year from a farming family in Mendocino. Their lambs live outside, eat grass, frolic in the sun, and I'm told are even serenaded by elk on occasion. I feel great supporting this family and also supporting the lambs to have the best if rather short life. I also feel great providing this nutritious food to my kiddo and myself. I also buy eggs from local farmers most of the year. They're fresher and tastier; the chickens roam outside during the day eating bugs and worms as well as organic feed. These foods are more nutritious, usually aren't poisoned with antibiotics and growth hormones (be sure to check), and are grown

in ways that benefit rather than harm the landscape. A few companies are sprouting up where you can buy such foods from small farms and have them delivered to you.

- **Reduce or eliminate packaged food.**
Pre-packaged food is typically filled with sugar and sugar substitutes plus stabilizers, preservatives, and God knows what else. Refuse to eat foods that have ingredients you can't pronounce or that weren't around a hundred years ago. Also packaging creates a lot of garbage, most of which isn't recyclable. That means it goes in the landfill and much of it ends up in our oceans. Not good and definitely avoidable.

- **Buy organic cotton clothes and linens.**
Okay, I know you're not going to eat cotton and linens. I include cotton here because it falls into a similar category as a cash crop that's been genetically modified and is one of the most heavily sprayed with pesticides of all crops. People who harvest commercially grown cotton typically live in poorer countries in the global south and often have significant health issues. Yes, it's more expensive and not always easy to find. Organic cotton sheets and pillowcases are especially important, as you're touching them and breathing next to them one third of your day every day.

- **Switch to renewable and low-impact energy.**
See if you're eligible for any government support for switching to renewable, low-impact sources of energy. Depending on where you live, your best choices may be solar or wind power. Where I live we have power captured from geysers! These new sources are an investment in ahimsa – and a key aspect of well stewarding our world.

- **Reduce petrol usage. Drive less. Fly less.**
We, myself included, take gas for granted. We pretty much assume that we can go and get it when we want to, though we complain about its price rising. We've become accustomed to hopping in our cars and heading to wherever we want whenever we want. We're pretty

attached to the convenience and comfort of having our own cars. So much so that many people see electric cars as the solution to the gas crisis because we don't want to give up our cars! Yet electric cars aren't the solution – there's not enough lithium in the world to create enough cars for all of us, plus mining lithium devastates the miners and the landscape. Hydrogen for fuel may become a viable option in the future. Even better is to unhook ourselves from our attachment to this individual form of transportation and begin to invest in much more efficient and sustainable forms of public transportation. *Having your own car is a marker of wealth that masks the real cost of individual transportation for the environment.*

- **Get an electric bike!**
  If you're still committed to having your own way of getting around, get an electric bike (e-bike)! They use very little power and give you extra oomph for getting your groceries home from the store. E-bikes are becoming increasingly popular. The technology is improving, and the initial costs are coming down. I'm looking forward to either a solar panel or the ability to recharge the battery with pedaling, both of which would eliminate the need to get power from the grid. Nice!

- **Use zero-VOC paint inside and out.**
  Paint and glues from carpets and flooring can outgas toxins *for years*. When my child was small, I did a lot of research on this, as I love to paint my environments. Fortunately more brands of eco-friendly paint are now available. Yes, sometimes they cost a little more. Isn't it worth it to *not be poisoning the air* you and your family breathe every day? If you've moved into a place that's recently been painted or carpeted, get a high-quality air filter to protect your and your family's health.

- **Build your relationship to a place.**
  In the spirit of re-rooting, choose a place in the living world to get to know and appreciate. This could be a tree, a turn in the river, a meadow or top of the hill, a strip of beach, or even your own yard. Re-rooting

invites you to step out of the statistical mentality inside of which many of us spend our days and into a dynamic, reciprocal, respectful, and honoring relationship with an aspect of the living world.

Fresh home from a Continuum workshop, I sat on a rickety wooden bench in my backyard to gaze at the bees drinking from a sprawling, wildly blooming lavender plant. The first day just two bees were circling and diving into the lavender. I admired their beauty and their intent focus with gratitude for their pollinating and the splendor of their dancing. I invited them to bring their friends, as I have plants that will bloom all summer that I chose as food for them. And you know what? Within a few days the lavender became covered with bees! Just this morning I sat with them, sharing my delight at their presence and encouraging them to keep coming back. I'm happy I can provide meals for this vital and endangered species.

Get Creative

- **Make eco-bricks with single-use plastic.**
  A friend of mine taught me how to make eco-bricks, and now making them has become a regular part of my kitchen routine. We've reduced our plastic garbage to virtually ZERO. Yes, really. I've been hearing about more and more people using these, so if you do some research in your local area you may just find someone building with eco-bricks who would be happy to take yours off your hands. Or you can make things yourself with the bricks. Check out EcoBricks.org for more info. Nicola Peel has a video about people in the Amazon creating eco-bricks to deal with their "rubbish," as she says, and as sturdy building materials. Start a trend!

- **Recycle your clothes – start a clothes swap.**
  Clothing swaps are fun! Here in my town we have one twice a year, and everyone looks forward to it. It's a cool community gathering as well as a great way to pass along clothes you're not wearing and receive ones new to you. We've also started bringing household goods, books, and other items we're ready to pass on. I'm always

amazed at how much we all have to give away! This is an excellent way to experience the wealth of your community and what's available to you without having to spend even a dime. All it takes are people willing to organize.

- **Set up a water catchment system.**
During the twenty-five years I've been living in California we've had years of drought and other years with more rain that we could handle, leading to flooding and landslides. We're now having "atmospheric rivers" that can drop many inches, even feet, of water in a matter of hours. Some of that water goes to replenish our reservoirs, lakes, and ground water. But as much as eighty percent (!!) simply runs into the creeks (and streets), then out into the ocean. In a study of what the county where I live will be like in 2050, the primary recommendation was for as many people as possible to have water catchment systems, as we'll continue to have more and more atmospheric rivers and longer, hotter summers. Catching water at your home enables you to use that water in your garden for much of the summer. Some systems can keep water fresh enough that it can be filtered and then drunk by humans and animals.

Even if you live somewhere with abundant rain, catching water takes pressure off your local water system and honors the gift of water falling from the sky. Build your relationship with water beyond turning on a faucet. Water is life, and unfortunately much of the world is being turned into desert by climate change. The more we can all contribute to honoring and caring for water, the better off we'll all be. These are pretty easy systems to set up.

- **Set up a graywater system.**
These systems are more complex to set up than water catchment, yet it could well be worth the effort depending on your situation. Much of our water could be reused for the garden. Graywater comes from your kitchen sink and washing machine, and if you're using nontoxic, eco-friendly soap, the used water can be directed to your garden. (Blackwater is what goes down through your toilet, and, no,

you don't reuse it!) Some places have made using graywater illegal, but that's changing as we've been coming to realize how we're wasting this valuable, life-giving element. Check the regulations in your locale.

Pause for a moment. Close your eyes and take a big breath. How are you feeling in your body right now? Take out your journal and make a few notes or doodle about what you've been discovering. How are you feeling emotionally? Reviewing a list like this might trigger different responses – excitement, overwhelm, curiosity, confusion, possibility, despair. Give yourself the gift of your attention, not trying to change anything, just noticing and tending. Spiral back into the earlier pillars as needed to support you as you also spiral out into the world and the challenges we and our beautiful world are facing.

Need Inspiration and Motivation?

Are you feeling more optimistic about what's possible and how you can contribute? We just explored actions you can take right at home, and I hope you've selected a few new things you can begin right away. This is a start! And what about how we work together? I've found great medicine in collaborating with others on projects that are doable and close to home. In this section, you'll find examples of what people are doing in their neighborhoods, cities, and even across their countries to build the New World they long to live in and leave to future generations. Rather than getting depressed or angry watching the news, why not give your precious life force energy to something that lights you up?

I've curated a series of projects from the thousands currently happening. Check out the bibliography for links to find out more. As you read through these pay attention to how you feel in your body and your energy. What do you feel drawn to? What activates your imagination?

What do you think is cool but you'd never want to do yourself? What do you not relate to? Do you feel inspired to join or start something? *Notice if resistance or doubtfulness creeps in and send them off to the beach with a cocktail!* Remember from Pillar Five that doing what makes you feel *on purpose*, what makes you feel alive and energized, is your inner wisdom helping to guide you. Maybe none of these projects feel like something you'd like to do, but reviewing them awakens a desire, even a passion, inside you that you didn't know you had.

Take a look, go check out some websites and videos, and *unleash your imagination* about what could be your *compassionate stewardship project*. What will support you in growing yourself into deeper relationship with other people and aspects of the living world for the benefit of all?

Stewarding and Healing Your Neighborhood

Sometimes it's easiest to begin in your own backyard! You might be surprised by the ripple effects of new choices you make and how they influence the people around you. Read through these short descriptions of transformational, restorative projects and check the bibliography for links if you want to find out more about them.

Ron Finley Project in South Central Los Angeles

Ron Finley changed the character of his neighborhood by one simple yet mighty act: *growing food*. Frustrated that he had to drive forty-five minutes to get an organic tomato, he started growing vegetables in his parking strip. Finley grew up and lives in South Central Los Angeles, a lower-income, under-resourced, and primarily African American neighborhood and food desert where diabetes is five times higher than in the neighboring Beverly Hills. Taking over his parking strip might not seem like a radical act, but get this – he got a citation and a warrant for his arrest for planting a garden! Fortunately he was able to overcome this attempt to suppress his creativity and purpose. Finley has started a movement and he now collaborates with community members to make many more gardens grow in South Central LA. Finley enjoys putting a shovel into the hands of young people and teaching them how to be "garden gangstas."

"We envision a world where people know nutrition and where it comes from. Where all ages embrace the act of growing, knowing and sharing the best of the earth's fresh-grown food. We envision and want to facilitate a world where gardening is gangsta! *Gangsta:* projecting strength on one's own terms, hip, cool, innovative, revolutionary, resolute, vital, the cutting edge."

The Ron Finley Project teaches communities how to transform food deserts into food sanctuaries and teaches individuals how to regenerate their lands into creative business models. It's not just about food, it's about people.

Canfield Consortium of Detroit, Michigan, founded by Rhonda and Kim Theus

Sisters Rhonda and Kim Theus were fed up with what had happened to the neighborhood where they grew up. The East Canfield neighborhood of Detroit, Michigan, was once a "very thriving and self-sustaining community." But like other Detroit neighborhoods, disinvestment led to a decline. "We deserve a nice quality of life, and we deserve a beautiful neighborhood in which to live. So that is the foundation of our organization," Rhonda Theus says. The sisters started Canfield Consortium with the intention of eradicating issues associated with blight, such as substandard infrastructure, rundown buildings, and idle space. They received a $50,000 grant to "activate" an alleyway by removing garbage and creating a rain garden, council circle, and community toolshed to start. The sisters intend to incubate small businesses in the alleyway in unused garages. They're also working on creating a greenway for walkers and bikes that will connect different parts of the community.

Their approach has been called "urban acupuncture," where a whole landscape and community can be activated and enhanced by making small, targeted changes that can have big impact. The Theus sisters partner with Professor Paul Draus and Korey Batey, who both work on alley activations more widely and see them as key points for urban renewal.

These efforts represent a departure from relying on urban planning coming out of city government. This is *grassroots urban renewal* driven by residents themselves.

Take Heart, Take Action with Trathen Heckman of Daily Acts of Petaluma, California

In the small city just south of where I live, Daily Acts has been helping residents transition their lawns with water-wise plants or a vegetable garden, capture rainwater for later use, reuse graywater, and work together to influence policy at the city, county, and state levels.

This organization grew out of the inspiration and vision of Trathen Heckman, who started close in with teaching people how to take command of the land they live on. He was influenced by the Bioneers organization and by the Transition Movement, both of which highlight and engage leading-edge changemakers focused on climate change, systemic inequality, and the potential of individuals to create positive change. Organizing community workdays, educational workshops, and climate activism brought together *residents who wanted to contribute but didn't know how to*. His passion inspired others, and over time his organization grew in volunteers and impact, eventually influencing policy at the city, county, and state levels.

Many of their events are now offered online, a positive outcome of the Covid era, which means you can take advantage of their programming wherever you are in the world.

Transition Towns – Global and Local

In 2006 a group of people in Totnes, a small town in the United Kingdom, decided they wanted to explore what they could do now to face the big issues in the world in their local community. They called their projects *Transition*. The experiment was so successful that the idea quickly spread to other parts of the UK, then Europe and across the world. Transition is now "a movement of communities coming together to reimagine and rebuild our world" focused on creating a low-carbon, socially-just future with resilient communities, largely self-governed with a culture of care.

I'm particularly impressed by the Transition Town in Liege, Belgium, where the local community held a large, community-wide planning process focused on the question: "How do we manage, in 25–30 years, to transform the local food system to make it more democratic, local and ecological?" They created small farms around their city to reimagine the local economy as well as their food system. Produce is available at the farms, is sold in town at a grocery store created for that purpose, and supplies restaurants and schools as well. Chefs, farmers, gardeners, shopkeepers, families, schoolteachers, and students all get in on the act!

You can now find Transition Towns in forty-eight countries, with thousands of groups focusing on all kinds of projects, including building local currency, repair cafes, free stores, and restaurants that provide meals for free as part of a gift economy. Daily Acts, above, started as a Transition Town project.

Regenerating Food Ways

Food, land, people, and health are at the center of all restorative projects. We're just coming to see the entangled interconnections of depleted soils and poisoned produce, packaged and fast food, our current chronic diseases crises, rise in extinctions, and the collapse of ecosystems. These aren't isolated issues but ones that are bound together as the consequences of the Story of Progress.

Deep Medicine Circle + Tree Leaf Farm
with Rupa Marya and Benjamin Fahrer

In the heart of the Temescal neighborhood of Oakland, a one-acre rooftop farm provides their produce free to people in need in the local community. Last year the project gave away two thousand pounds of greens. *That's a lot of greens!* I had the opportunity to visit the farm and it's amazing, all 187 rows of it. The farm sits atop a new six-story building with a Whole Foods at the ground level and apartments in between. The farm is a partnership of *Tree Leaf Farm*, whose mission is to reimagine our cities with a thousand new urban rooftop farms, street farms, and community food hubs by 2030, and *Deep Medicine Circle*, a Women of Color-led nonprofit organization dedicated to repairing critical relationships and healing the wounds of colonialism through food, medicine, story, learning, and restoration. The project breaks down the transactional relationship most of us have with our food, both by providing opportunities for staff and interns to grow food in an urban environment, and by giving away their produce to community-based organizations that distribute it to people in the community.

Rupa Marya and Benjamin Fahrer co-founded Tree Leaf Farm and work together at a thirty-eight-acre farm and land restoration project called Te Kwe A'naa Warep (honoring Mother Earth) that's returning the land to the Ramaytush, the indigenous people of the San Francisco Bay Area Peninsula. Both the rooftop and the indigenous land project assert that food is medicine, and even more, "farming is medicine." We create medicine and heal ourselves and our world as we re-story our relationship to land. They're piloting ways of evolving the urban landscape and restoring ecosystems that could be modeled by others similarly seeking to steward our world into a regenerative future.

Turtle Lake Refuge in Durango, Colorado, founded by Katrina Blair

Katrina Blair eats weeds and can teach you to do the same! She's passionate about wild foods and wild lands, and she can live off the land in the Rocky Mountains and has done so for months. Turtle Lake Refuge includes a two-acre regenerative farm that supplies food for the lunches they provide twice a week and also to local restaurants, schools, stores, and individuals. They provide classes in wild foods, living soil, and wild plant permaculture. They'll even go to your place and help you regenerate your land through their organic land stewardship project, Bee Happy Lands project. They promote sustainable practices honoring the wild wisdom of nature and the health of the community.

Not only that, Blair spearheaded a project to end chemical treatments – fertilizers and herbicides – in Durango's city parks. Did you know that these chemicals are harmful to pollinating insects, birds, and bats, as well as to small children playing there (not to mention the rest of us)? Blair reached out to the City of Durango's Parks and Recreation Department to see what could be done. The first step was to stop using chemicals in Brookside Park as a test project and start using organic fertilizers instead. Turtle Lake Refuge and a Fort Lewis College Environmental Justice class led the way by applying compost tea for two years, and thereafter the city continued to manage it with organic fertilizers. The result of continued advocacy, seven parks are now organically managed, one third of the city's parks. What a wonderful change spearheaded by the vision and efforts of a local resident in collaboration with other residents and city government.

Food Rescue US – Nationwide

As previously mentioned, we in the United States *throw away or otherwise waste forty percent of our food supply.* Shocking, right, when an estimated forty-two million people will experience food insecurity at the very same time. And did you know that *food waste* creates methane as it decomposes, negatively impacting our air? A few empowered souls got together to found Food Rescue US, an organization that connects still viable, extra food with organizations that can use it and distribute it to people who need it. It's a win-win-win-win scenario! Originally based in Detroit, Food Rescue US now operates in twenty-four states and is expanding to new states and locations all the time. In addition to serving their community, Food Rescue also has developed instructions and support for those who want to become site directors of similar operations in their own communities. They always need volunteers to help with their work, so reach out to them if this calls to you.

Regenerating Community Relationships

Down to Earth Derby with Jamie Quince-Starkey in Derby in the United Kingdom

Jamie Quince-Starkey, a self-proclaimed pirate gardener, could see how despondent his community was feeling, so he started a garden and invited people to work with him. They discovered as they spent time with their hands in the soil that their spirits lifted and a sense of possibility emerged. *Starkey's garden project has grown to include 3000 people.* Down to Earth Derby blossomed into a community interest company that connects people with nature, themselves, and their communities with the intent to make living with nature a part of everyday life. They're now working on the Eden Project, which will include a large community garden in the heart of the city, along with restaurants and an outdoor event space, and have plans for as many as nine city centers that bring gardens, wetlands, and people together.

"Imagine having the largest rooftop garden in the UK, in Derby, connected to an urban farm right next to it, connected to another proper space for kids to play and learn. We want to revolutionize this city just like they did back during the Enlightenment. This can be a new enlightenment, driven by us all getting properly connected with nature," says Quince-Starkey. Now that's an interesting twist on the Enlightenment, right?

Folded Map Project in Chicago, Illinois, created by Tonika Lewis

Photographer Tonika Lewis has created one of the most innovative and creative projects I've ever seen. Lewis grew up in Chicago, Illinois, and experienced the city's segregation firsthand when she took the bus as a teenager from the southside where she lived to the northside where her art-focused high school was located. She says she enjoyed getting to know people from different backgrounds, but the economic disparity between the sides of the city bothered her. So she decided to investigate what urban segregation looks like and how it impacts Chicago residents through a photographic study called the *Folded Map Project*, which visually connects residents who live at corresponding addresses on the North and South Sides of Chicago. Residents are invited to connect with those who live on their same street with the same number simply marked north or south, what she calls "map twins." The project invites participants to dialogue about how everyone's impacted by social, racial, and institutional conditions that segregate the city and the historical conditions that created the situation. Lewis challenges everyone to think about how change may be possible and to contribute to creating a solution. She's creatively used her photographic skills to produce a visually illustrative experience that piques curiosity and fosters connection among Chicagoans who otherwise would never have met. In this her project weaves people together and supports them to get to know each other as neighbors, breaking down unconscious social segregation.

Bay Area Green Tours with Marissa LaMagna

As a fourth-grader, Bay Area Green Tours (BAGT) Executive Director Marissa LaMagna attended a field trip to a wastewater treatment plan in New York City. She wondered, "Where does all the waste go?" This experience sparked curiosity in her about how our systems are set up and operate and how they impact the larger environment. BAGT is the most recent project in her life focused on eco-activism, synergistically connecting people and resources, and fostering collaboration for community good. BAGT moves education out of the digital world and presentation mode to expose participants firsthand to projects happening in the larger Bay Area. Having an experience inspires and opens possibilities in ways that information alone can't accomplish.

On a tour with her I got to visit Urban Tilth, an urban farm and community corridor project in the multicultural and underserved community of Richmond. We walked through a massive green house and shade house bursting with new life, with rows of beds being prepared for seedlings. Urban Tilth has a farm-to-table CSA that serves the local community, offering pay-it-forward pricing for those who can afford it and either low pricing or free for those who need it. I was so impressed by the young people running the farm and their vision for the future, for which they just received funding to begin building. Marissa's desire to make real projects such as these for people like me was fully realized on this tour. I loved seeing what they're doing and hearing from them rather than just reading about them on their website or hearing a presentation on what they're up to. I took photos to bring back to the garden I'm working on with friends so we can learn from them.

HeartMath Institute Global Coherence Initiative and App

This one has a global rather than local focus, although you can create a local group if you want to. We explored the work of HeartMath in Pillar Four on developing the energetic power of the heart center. HeartMath has many programs and events, as well as the technology, to support you to create Heart Coherence. Their Global Coherence App enables you to practice getting into heart coherence (they have a device that teaches you how) and connecting with others around the globe to focus on bringing peace, love, and compassion to a given hot spot.

You can join with others in the Global Coherence Network, a community of people who strive to awaken the higher mental, emotional, and spiritual capacities in themselves and the global community through genuine love, care, and heartfelt compassion. They hold regular sessions during which people around the world focus on uplifting the frequency in parts of the world where there's conflict. This is a good option if you want to contribute but for whatever reason you want to do that from your own home.

What Will Be *Your* Project?

In the examples above I highlighted the work and imagination of individuals who joined with others in projects great and small to help reestablish our relationships with our food, the land, and each other in community. I'm hoping they'll inspire you to either begin a project or join one that's making a meaningful contribution to your community in ways that resonate with you.

Take Time to Assess, Integrate, and Apply What You've Learned

Congratulations! You've made it to Pillar Eight, where everything we've been exploring comes together. How are you feeling right now as you consider what you've been learning? When you consider your project? While yes, absolutely, we need systems change, you have agency now to begin something new and different that affirms your values and commitment to helping bring into being the world you'd be proud to leave to future generations. I'm excited to hear about what you come up with! You can let me know in our Feminine Sovereignty online community.

One more time you'll get to reflect on your own experience, values, and attitudes and see if you'd like to upgrade anything and/or grow yourself in a particular area. This is your final pillar before you gather all of your responses so far and create a guide for your next steps. As always, below you'll find:

- **Self-Assessment**
- **Spectrum of Expression**
- **Pause, Reflect, and Review**
- **New Desired Capacities**
- **Questions for Reflection**

Self-Assessment

What's your relationship with compassionate stewardship so far in your life? Let's find out.

Instructions

Give yourself a number 1–5 for each statement. Five means it's totally true for you, one means it's true occasionally. Add up the numbers from A and B and subtract B from A. This gives you your Sovereignty score for that pillar.

(A) Strengths and Capacities Developed

[   ] I use the privilege I have due to my race, gender, economic status, education, sexuality, or country of origin to create greater equality and respect for all.

[   ] In making choices, I do my best to consider the long-term impact on our younger generation and generations to come. I don't want to be controlled by the trance of consumer culture and consensus reality that focus on short-term outcomes.

[   ] I live and act inside the inquiry: What can I do to consume less, pollute less, and support healthier, more regenerative, more life-giving/supporting ways of being?

[   ] Although resources maybe limited in this physical earth
     plane, I refuse to be ruled by scarcity and lack consciousness.
     I live in the awareness that in fact we do have all that we
     need and that we have enough for everyone, we just need to
     change how it's distributed.

[   ] I devote time, attention, and financial resources to help
     build an aspect of the New World that inspires and lights
     me up. Doing so, I feel on purpose, guided from within,
     hopeful and well used by the Flow of Life.

(B) Wounds or Lack of Capacity

[   ] I focus on taking care of my family and don't have time or
     energy for thinking about anyone else.

[   ] I know it's terrible about what's happening for people
     around the world, but it really doesn't have anything to do
     with me. I'm focused on my own community.

[   ] I find it really overwhelming and depressing to think
     about poverty, racism, sexism, and what's happening to
     our environment. So mostly I don't pay attention to what's
     happening. Easier that way.

[   ] I really don't like this New Age crap about how we're all
     connected. Clearly we're not.

[   ] I worked hard to buy this property. I can do what I want
     with it.

A = _____   B = _____   A - B = _____

This is your Sovereignty Score for Pillar Eight.

If you have a positive score, this means that you've developed capacity
in this area. The higher your score, the greater your strengths.

If you have a negative score – more checked from (B) than (A) –
then this is a pillar where you'd benefit from attending to building your
capacity. The lower the score, the less in touch you are with the beneficial
attributes of this pillar.

Spectrum of Expression

The Spectrum of Expression outlines three ways of expressing the themes, energy, and power of the pillars. Collectively we're evolving out of the power-over/disempowered paradigm that characterizes western civilization. Nevertheless we're still subject to expressing power in these ways, often without even realizing it. The three aspects of the spectrum will help you identify your tendencies and, I hope, reveal to you unconscious patterns, beliefs, or behaviors so you can become at choice about whether to continue or change them. Consider this an exploration in understanding power in the service of building your *power within*, the foundation of your personal sovereignty, and the inner support for your sovereign self.

Awakened/Empowered Expression

In the awakened expression of Pillar Eight, you're increasingly aware of the ways western society is organized that create harm for people, animals, the landscape, and the living world. You tap this awareness to guide your choices, doing what you can to reduce or eliminate harm. You've explored what's happening in your local community and you're now collaborating with a group in developing a project that's meaningful to you. You're practicing being aware without getting overwhelmed. And when you do feel overwhelmed, you know what to do: sit with your back against a tree, or do some breathwork, or share with a friend who can hold space without trying to fix you.

You're committed to being optimistic in the face of challenging situations, looking for the possibilities and opportunities that those challenges provide. Even though it's not easy at times to be informed, you know that the best medicine is to take the next best actions, whether that's to give yourself time and space to grieve or to get out to an event with others with whom you resonate. You're not naïve about the breakdowns that are underway, but rather than numbing yourself out with television, sugar, or alcohol, you focus on tending your relationship with the land where you live and helping others do the same. You join with others as you explore how individually and together you can better steward both your own energy and resources and that of the living world.

Shadow Expression

If you're leveraging the fear people have about climate change to sell products or services, then you're expressing the shadow aspect of Pillar Eight. You're aware of the climate reports and you're not convinced they're accurate. But you can still use people's fear to your advantage and for your personal and professional gain. As far as you're concerned, you might as well make the best of a deteriorating situation by making products to help people ignore what's happening and focus on their ease, comfort, and pleasure. Or you realize that yes, we're at "peak oil," so you figure you should travel as much as possible, enjoy your eighteen-foot mobile home, and keep updating your electronics often *while you still can.*

Disempowered Expression

In the disempowered expression of Pillar Eight, you ignore what's happening in the living world, preferring to live in the digital world. You love the endless entertainment that's available to you 24/7 and you're always on the lookout for what to watch next. You prefer being inside where you can control your environment, the temperature, the light, the humidity, and the noise. You don't watch the news and you'd rather not know about climate change because it's too depressing. You don't see any value in being better informed and in fact think it's harmful to your health. Ahimsa to you means watching out for number one.

Pause, Reflect, and Review

Take a few moments as you read through the Spectrum of Expression to feel into what's true for you. You might want to write about your current understanding, how your relationship to these possibilities has changed over time for you (if it has), and if so what your journey's been like.

Now go back and review your self-assessment.

- Do you think or feel any differently now that you've dug in a bit deeper?
- Do you want to change any of your answers?

- Or do you want to add to the lists offered noting what's been especially true for you?
- At this point are you aware of wanting to develop new capacities in this area? If so start a list of your own or continue reading for my suggestions that might help you get started.

New Desired Capacities

To help you think and feel your way through this, I've created a list of potential capacities you may feel drawn to. This list is suggestive and far from exhaustive. Some may appeal to you while others may not. (Feel free to add your own!)

Now rank this list in the order of significance to you, one meaning this is a high priority for you, and five being "not relevant to me, at least not now."

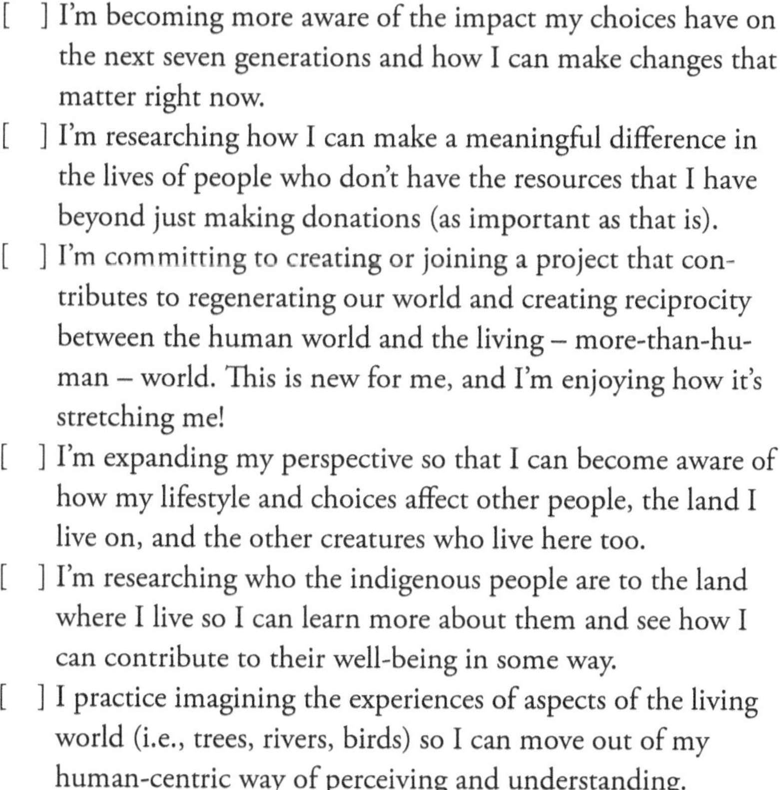

[   ] I'm becoming more aware of the impact my choices have on the next seven generations and how I can make changes that matter right now.

[   ] I'm researching how I can make a meaningful difference in the lives of people who don't have the resources that I have beyond just making donations (as important as that is).

[   ] I'm committing to creating or joining a project that contributes to regenerating our world and creating reciprocity between the human world and the living – more-than-human – world. This is new for me, and I'm enjoying how it's stretching me!

[   ] I'm expanding my perspective so that I can become aware of how my lifestyle and choices affect other people, the land I live on, and the other creatures who live here too.

[   ] I'm researching who the indigenous people are to the land where I live so I can learn more about them and see how I can contribute to their well-being in some way.

[   ] I practice imagining the experiences of aspects of the living world (i.e., trees, rivers, birds) so I can move out of my human-centric way of perceiving and understanding.

Once you've ranked these possibilities, name your top two priorities. What can you do this week to begin to develop this valuable skill? You'll find helpful suggestions to support you with this in the next section.

Reflection Questions

I invite you to review and ponder these questions in any way that works for you. Feel free to respond to the ones that speak to you and leave the rest. Remember that writing down or drawing your reflections provides you with a record of your experiences, which will be very helpful when you head into the next chapter: *What Now; What's Next?* As we evolve, we tend to forget where we were, and that makes it difficult to appreciate how much we've grown.

> What did you discover about yourself through the self-assessment and Spectrum of Expression? Did you feel affirmed in some ways? Did anything surprise or disturb you? Are you inspired to develop any new capacities?

> What can you do this week to begin to develop this valuable new capacity? What resources do you need? What do you need to prepare? What support do you need? Is there any resistance you need to face and overcome? Who in your life can you partner with who will help hold you accountable?

> Apply what you learned or realized in Pillar Eight to your Learning Question. What does this teaching add to your inquiry? What was your Learning Question(s) for this specific pillar? Make a few notes about what's arising for you, including how this feels in your body.

> What's your relationship like with the living world? Do you feel connected to the land, animals, plants, and/or ecosystem, or is that difficult for you? How's your perspective changed as a result of reading this book?

> Do you agree it's time for us to develop more respect for all of life, not just human life? If so what might this mean for you in your daily life?

> What does compassion mean to you? How do you express it in your life?

> What would your life – and our world – be like if you and all of us had a compassionate approach to all of life? What would become possible? Wow!

> What are you already doing to help reduce the burden on the planet? (Give yourself a pat on the back for that.) What else could you do from the list above that you haven't tried yet?

> What're you doing or can you do to help heal and cultivate ecosystems in your area?

> Are there projects you'd like to plug into that are helping us transition from where we are now to the world we'd be happy to leave to future generations? Make a commitment to get started now.

> Now that you've been creating your own 8 Pillars, what does your Temple of Sovereignty look like? What does it feel like? Does it move? When do you visit? What kind of support does it give you? What messages do you receive when you're there?

What Now, What's Next?

Wow, we've been on quite a journey, haven't we? We're on our last leg, and it's time to reflect on where we've been and decide where to go from here.

You've explored your inner landscape, focusing on your intuitive, co-creative relationship with the Flow of Life, your emotional wisdom, your physical vitality and connection with the living world, and your radiance and energetic intelligence. You've also dug into what makes you feel on purpose, how you communicate, your experiences with collaborating, and your life experience in relation to honoring and stewarding the living world. And you've had the opportunity to reflect on your life experience to date; what experiences have led you to feel, think, and believe; and where you may want to heal and/or grow yourself beyond what you've known so far.

So much richness here, yet this is also just an introduction! What really matters is what you bring with you from your experience of reading and reflecting into your life and your world and *let it change you.* To facilitate that process for you, this chapter invites you to gather your thoughts, feelings, and aspirations and guides you into creating a way forward to becoming your sovereign self and a sovereign steward of our living world.

Recall that the 8 Pillars of Feminine Sovereignty offer you a structure inside of which you're invited and supported to evolve your consciousness and, influenced by that, your ways of showing up in the world.

As you engage the energetic construct of the pillars, you step through a portal into a new world, a New World, one of your own making that shimmers and shifts as you gaze and move through it. You're sovereign of this domain, in a dynamic, compassionate relationship of reciprocity with your life experience, your Human Design, your desires and aspirations, other sovereign beings (people), and the living world.

You have command of what this New World looks and feels like. You're intuitively co-creating this environment with the Flow of Life as you tune in during your daily date with the divine. You're open to receiving guidance from within and from there moving out into the world with other people infused with possibility and potential. You choose inspired optimism as your demeanor as you engage your own evolutionary process. You reach out through the *inner-net* to energetically connect with others who are also developing their Feminine Sovereignty wherever they are in the world, and from now forward into time. You're aligned, connected, and ready for your next steps.

Your Learning Questions

Review what you've written, drawn, or contemplated so far regarding your main Learning Question. Gather your thoughts and feelings and create three or more key insights you've gleaned from your inquiry. How do you feel meeting these insights? Make a few notes or drawings about your inner experience. Repeat this process with the learning questions for each of the pillars.

Your learning questions enable you to create your own curriculum in relation to the themes and teachings offered in the 8 Pillars. Inviting your questions to stimulate and grow you gives you more command of your evolutionary journey. Ultimately Human Design always leads you back to your own inner guidance and the gems of your life experience. *What are you gleaning now?*

Your Self-Assessments

Your self-assessments along the way are designed to give you traction on the themes of each pillar based on the Spectrum of Expression. I've discovered that most of us range in our expressions across the spectrum depending on the specifics of our life experience, myself included. By bringing your assessments into relationship with each other, a map of your personal sovereignty will emerge, revealing where you're already strong, where you may be acting unconsciously, and where you've got gaps in your development. With this map you can make informed choices about where you next want to invest your time, energy, attention, and finances. Here we go!

Step One

Go back and review your self-assessments from each of the pillar chapters. First list the pillars and your Sovereignty Score (A-B) for each.

What do you notice? Do you have more strengths in the first four pillars that focus more on the inner landscape and fewer in the second four pillars? Or the reverse? Or are your scores pretty consistent across the pillars? Or do they vary widely? Do you see any pattern? How do you feel in your body as you review your scores? Does anything in particular jump out at you?

One	Two	Three	Four	Five	Six	Seven	Eight	Total

Now add up your Sovereignty Score (A-B) from all eight pillars. Do you have a positive or negative score, or does it balance out closer to zero? This could mean many different things depending on how your scores are distributed across the pillars. How do you feel in your body as you review your total score? What thoughts and emotions are arising? Write or draw for a bit before moving on.

Step Two

Collect the statements under *(A) Strengths and Capacities Developed* in each chapter that you checked as being true for you. You may choose to keep them as they're currently written or revise them so that they feel more specific and compelling for you. Together these provide you with an inventory of your strengths in relation to the themes raised by the 8 Pillars. Do you see any recurring themes? Does anything in these statements jump out at you as being particularly affirming, inspiring, and/or valuable?

If you like select one or two statements that particularly inspire you, rewrite them on a notecard or make a drawing, and post it where you can see it often. Color and decorate this card in ways that delight and inspire you. Make a collage with images representing these attributes to reflect back to you how far you've already come on your journey. *Celebrate!*

Step Three

Now repeat the process of gathering the statements you checked in each of the pillar chapters for (B) Wounds or Lack of Capacity. Again revise any of the statements so they'll be more specific and true for you. Be aware if you want to ignore or reject any of these statements because they feel uncomfortable to you or if *you don't want them to be true* for you. See if instead of leaving them out you can begin an inner inquiry about your relationship to this statement. Be gentle and compassionate with yourself and aim to create awareness rather than self-judgment. Together these statements provide you with an inventory of life areas that may need healing or development for you to feel more empowered and sovereign of your life.

Do you see any recurring themes? What emotions are rising up, and how do you feel in your body as you review these statements? Lean into what you're feeling and open space inside yourself for greater awareness to emerge. Breathe. Expand. Take your time. Be kind, compassionate, and forgiving.

Which of these statements/themes jump out at you as particularly needing your more immediate attention and care? What can you do in the next week to attend to what's calling to you most?

Step Four

Return to the sections on (C) New Desired Capacities. Similarly gather the statements you checked in each of the pillars. Do they tell a story about you? Who is the new you that emerges from these aspirations? Breathe deep into possibility and refuse to be confused or overwhelmed. Which new capacities shimmer as you look at them? Which call to your heart and soul? Pick two or three to begin focusing on right away.

Step Five

Finally, review what you wrote in response to the Reflection Questions at the end of each pillar. Take some time simply to absorb what your journey's been.

Do you see any themes emerging?

What have been your greatest growth areas? Does this surprise you?

Where have you felt resistance? How did you respond to your resistance?

Do you want to do anything differently now that you've come to the end of the book?

Project Invitations

Now that you have a clear picture of where you've been, what you've experienced, and where you want to go based on the 8 Pillars, I invite you to create two projects for yourself. Projects help you focus your intention and your attention so that you can move forward inspired and with integrity. This book has presented you with many, many themes, perspectives, provocative ideas, and stimulating possibilities. *Don't try to take it all in at once or make too many changes at the same time. That's stressful and ineffective.* Far better is to choose specific next steps and follow your intuition and inner guidance as the steps after that, and after that, and after that unfold before you on your journey to developing your sovereignty.

I recommend that you design two projects, one focused on your inner landscape (Pillars One through Four), and one focused on being in the world with other people (Pillars Five through Eight).

Inner Landscape Project

Your project for your inner landscape could be as simple as creating your personalized *Daily Date with the Divine*. You can emphasize any specific aspect of the first four pillars that's particularly relevant and beneficial for you.

For example during the pandemic my regular practice of dancing two or three times a week halted. Even though I walked every day and rode my bike, my body locked up from too much sitting and not enough spiraling. So for six months or more I've been focusing on bringing more flow back into my body and *getting my spiral back*. I've been working with a physical therapist with a dance background who has her own highly effective technique based in the Pilates method. She showed me what to do, and I've been practicing at home and at the studio *every day*. This has been my devotion to my physical form (Pillar Three) that I unknowingly damaged during lockdown. I shifted what I included in my daily date with the divine based on a new situation that called for healing attention.

Being in pain (I'd been having excruciating pain in my knee especially at night) and limited in my range of movement were disrupting my life in myriad ways, and my body was screeching at me for attention. I no longer have pain, I can spiral as I dance again, and my overall well-being has improved immensely. This inner landscape project is now diminishing in significance because I've developed the new desired capacity – to be free, fluid, and happy in my body again – and I've integrated into my daily life what I need to do to stay that way. Soon I'll be ready for a new focus on my inner landscape so that I continue to develop my personal sovereignty, a never-ending journey.

What speaks to you as your best next step?

Create a doable project that also stretches you beyond your normal and out of your comfort zone. Specifying a specific time frame may be helpful, such as you'll dig into this for a week or a month or six months. That can help the part of you resistant to change relax and agree to participate. Seek out the support and camaraderie you need to move forward with this. You don't have to do this alone. Consider joining our growing Feminine Sovereignty online community space to connect with others doing this work.

Suggestions for Inner Landscape Projects

- Commit to experimenting with your Human Design Type, strategy, and authority for at least thirty days. (Pillar One)
- Identify thoughts and beliefs that limit and inhibit you and work with releasing them purposefully with regular energy practices. (Pillars Two and Four)
- Practice the Power of the Pause, giving yourself time and space to discern and work with your emotional energy so that you can respond rather than react to other people. (Pillar Two)

- Take time each day to meet the living world, blessing the trees and actively fostering your relationship with the beings in the ecosystem where you live. (Pillars Three and Eight)
- Shift what you're eating in ways that support your vitality and clear-mindedness and show love for our Earth. (Pillar Three)
- Explore a few Kundalini Yoga kriyas. Select one to do every day for forty days. (Pillars One and Four)
- Work with your Temple of Sovereignty in a creative way. You may want to use the program I created for you for this purpose. Access it here: FeminineSovereigntyBook.com/templegift. When you create a sacred object with intention, it will hold that energy for you so you don't have to use so much of your own energy. Try it!

Out-in-the-World Projects

Your project for being in the world with other people ideally will involve you communicating and collaborating with others in ways that make you feel on purpose. I've already included in Pillar Eight examples of projects people are currently engaged in. You may choose to join one of these, look for similar projects in your area in which you can participate, or create a new project of your own.

For example, as I already shared with you, I started collaborating with friends in a shared garden. This has fostered my relationship with the living world, required me to communicate with my co-gardeners, and given me the opportunity to reflect on my relationship with land, soil, mycelium, plants, sun, rain, and water.

Writing this book has been a major collaborative project in which I communicate with *you* and all those drawn to this work. I've learned new ways of writing, exposed myself to and digested challenging points of view, and questioned how my own attachments have been influencing the way I show up in the world.

Bringing this book out into the world requires me to communicate and collaborate on a bigger scale than I've done before. Even though I've worked with thousands of clients and students in my programs over the years, this particular project is of a different nature and requires me to build new capacities in areas such as podcasting, book distribution, and joining with other writers to cross-promote our work. I'm also creating avenues for my readers who want to dive deeper together to be able to do that. In all of this, I feel deeply on purpose, excited to be making my best contribution, and delighted to be collaborating with others for the mutual benefit of us and our world.

What speaks to you about a doable project that stretches you out into the world with other people in ways that are different from what you've done in the past? How can you join with others outside your zone of comfort and convenience to learn new perspectives, grow your communication skills, and co-create an aspect of the more beautiful world your heart knows is possible? What lights up for you when you feel into something that matters to you and you decide to do something about it?

Suggestions for Out-in-the-World Projects

- See if there's a climate action organization in your area that you can learn from and possibly participate in. Discover what's already happening and join in or address a gap you see that's important to you.
- Join or help create a community garden, a beach or neighborhood clean-up project, or a group working on bringing clean, renewable energy into your area.
- Learn about the watershed and ecosystem of where you live. Find out who the original inhabitants of your area were and what their situation is today. How can you join with others to bring greater awareness to the natural contours and requirements of the landscape and create change to support its well-being? For example advocating for a moratorium on building in wetlands and flood plains or regulating commercial use of the communal water supply. How can you contribute to greater equity for indigenous people in your area?
- If you're politically minded, join one of the many organizations that focus on voter registration and voter rights, such

as Postcards to Voters, The States Project Giving Circles, or Markers for Democracy. These provide focus, camaraderie, and specific actions toward specific goals to support democracy in the US.
  - Research if field biologists are working in your area and explore how you might work with them (saving salamanders?). Local to me, Pepperwood Preserve provides educational field days, workdays where participants contribute to their research (fun!), and programs to becoming a naturalist or a nature steward.
  - Join or start an organization focused on policy changes at the city, county, or state level that impacts something meaningful to you and that's part of the New World you're imagining.

Would you like to connect with others who are also creating projects of their own? Would you like to be part of a community of those who are exploring what actions they can take to make a Thrutopian difference? If so, please join our Feminine Sovereignty community in our Becoming Sovereign Quantum Retreat Center and Global Community. (The QR Code to join us is on the Resources Page.)

You Matter

Whatever you decide to do, wherever you decide to focus, know that your actions and intentions *matter*. Yes, you live inside a world influenced by larger forces at play, but you need not become a victim or collapse into denial and despair. That's not helpful, and it doesn't feel good either! Instead choose to be part of a small group of committed citizens making a dent in the world. Even if your efforts don't immediately yield what you're hoping for, every step, every movement, and every shift in the direction of wholeness and respect for each other and our living world contributes beyond what we can currently understand.

Engaging with the big challenges we and our world face right now takes faith. If you were to simply believe the climate crisis science, you might lose heart because yes, the news is dire. I'm not suggesting you ignore the numbers. I'm suggesting you digest that information inside your Temple of Sovereignty, leaning into the pillars that speak to and support you, discerning your best path. Optimism requires faith as fuel to propel us out of doomsday predictions and into our Thrutopian future.

Remember. Always. You're at choice about where to focus, how to respond, what you think, what you do, and what you create. You have a role to play, and it's a vital part of the whole, even if you can't see it right now. Cultivating your personal sovereignty, step out into the world with other sovereign beings, evolving together into compassionate sovereign stewards of our mother, our beautiful planet Earth.

Bless you, Dear One, bless you.

Epilogue

Another broken nail. You dust off your hands and take another swig from your water bottle. Your lips taste slightly salty, sweat dried on your skin. It's been an especially scorching day. But you're happy. The snap peas are almost over, but the zucchini is fruiting, the kabocha squash is flowering, and your harvest basket is full. You have an extra bag of veggies you're going to drop off at the multidenominational food bank down the street from you. *Feels good to have more than enough to share.*

You wave to your co-gardeners as you walk back to your e-bike. You made sure you got paniers big enough for harvest, farmers' market, and grocery shopping, though you don't do much of that this time of year. Men love your e-bike, and you pause to answer their questions and encourage them to get one themselves. "It's the wave of the future," you encourage, *"everyone needs to get one."*

As you head home, you remember the day you were out under Grandmother Oak, dreaming into your Temple of Sovereignty, walking among the pillars, feeling into their solidity and sense of purpose, when Pillar Seven lit up right in front of you. You'd stepped forward, placing your hands and forehead against its shimmering form. Earlier you'd heard about that community in Liege, Belgium, that recreated their local food system as part of Transition Town and an epiphany downloaded into your imagination about what you could do.

And now you've got to get home and cleaned up in time for your weekly meeting with *Healthy Hometown*, the Transition Town project you helped form that focuses on uplifting and supporting younger people in your area. When you learned about the sky-rocketing suicide rates and attempts among teens and twenty-somethings, you knew this was something you wanted to meet and help transform. Public mental health services are overwhelmed, inefficient, and ineffective; something else needed to be done. After all, the youngers are bearing the brunt of decades of short-sighted choices by the olders, and they need and deserve support.

So you'd reached out to the healers, coaches, artists, gardeners, and street performers you knew and invited them to explore ways of inspiring, encouraging, and surrounding with care the adolescents in your community. Together you've already offered a *Day in the Garden*, where they get their hands in the soil, learn what's happening in the garden, eat a delicious (free) lunch, and take home a harvest basket. A *Ranting Afternoon*, where they each get a dedicated listener for up to an hour to rant about anything they want to with no advice given unless they ask for it. And a *Storytelling Evening*, during which olders share challenging adventures and interesting experiences that have influenced their direction in life and respond to any questions or curiosities the youngers have.

Although attendance has been uneven, you're inspired by the willingness of the adults to show up and experiment to see what works. Some of the kids have been very appreciative while others have been more reserved, so it's difficult to know what's landing for them. As of now there've been as many grownups at the events as youngers, but that's to be expected, especially at the beginning. Most of the kids are referrals from people you and your collaborators know. You've got plans for a theater game experience facilitated by someone who's done street actions with Extinction Rebellion. You participated in direct action when you were younger and loved the feeling of *doing something meaningful* it gave you at the time. Right now the group's focusing on incubating projects and seeing what works. You plan to increase your outreach to youngers beyond your current sphere of influence who are particularly under-resourced and at risk.

The meeting goes well, with a new arts teacher joining in who wants to offer a body-painting day. That sounds fun and edgy. She's got a lot of energy, and you love to see people take an idea and run with it. One thing you know for sure: you feel good co-creating and playing with vibrant people in your community and exploring what supports the youngers. The more beautiful world you're focused on creating is for them, and they need attention and support to be able to move into the future.

You hope they'll see beyond the blinders already being placed on them by the overculture and refuse to take the bit and bridle too early offered them. You want to open hope into possibilities they'd like to live into. You don't know how viable that is or what you'll need to learn and grow inside yourself to be capable of this. But you're willing to try, and that's really the most important thing.

And so, my friend, shall we take hands and walk into the future – together?

Resources

FeminineSovereigntyBook.com
Visit us at the book's website to discover more about the process of writing this book and creating the painting that graces its cover. You'll also find additional recommendations, including websites to dive deeper into specific themes and topics covered in the 8 Pillars, resources on Human Design and Kundalini Yoga, and supports for integrating what you've been learning into your daily life.

Your Temple of Sovereignty Program
Receive Your Gift @
FeminineSovereigntyBook.com/templegift
Create your own sacred space for your journey through the 8 Pillars with Maggie's Temple of Sovereignty Program, our gift to you. Receive this creative and potent guide that walks with you step by step, inviting you to make the journey, the pillars, and the temple your very own.

Your Temple of Sovereignty

**Becoming Sovereign Quantum
Retreat Center + Global Community**

Join us for Free @ BecomingSovereign.mn.co
Join us in our Feminine Sovereignty exclusive collection in our virtual retreat center. You'll be able to connect with Maggie and other readers, gain access to additional practices and tools, and participate in live events and study groups as you choose. I hope you'll come participate in our kriya practice, explorations into embodying your Human Design, and other topics in Feminine Sovereignty.

Explore Maggie's YouTube Channel:
YouTube.com/@maggieostaraphd

Dive deep with Maggie in over 300 videos from getting started with Human Design to advanced special topics, and a growing collection of videos exploring the 8 Pillars of Feminine Sovereignty.

To use the QR Code, point the camera in your smart phone at the image and click to be taken to the appropriate website.

Bibliography by Chapter

Introduction

Curry, Karen. 2013. *Understanding Human Design: The New Science of Astrology: Discover Who You Really Are*. San Antonio, TX: Hierophant Publishing.

Davidson, Zahra. "How to Find Your Learning Question (and Why You Should)."

Huddlecraft. October 20, 2022. https://medium.com/huddlecraft/how-to-find-your-learning-question-and-why-you-should-645fe62b7904.

Eisenstein, Charles. 2013. *The More Beautiful World Our Hearts Know Is Possible*. Berkeley, CA: North Atlantic Books.

Eisler, Riane. 1987. *The Chalice and The Blade: Our History, Our Future*. Cambridge, MA: Harper & Row.

Estes, Clarissa Pinkola. "The Overculture." Facebook. March 4, 2015. https://www.facebook.com/29996683634/photos/a.391385543634/10152805542223635/?type=3.

Gilbert, Elizabeth. 2015. *Big Magic: Creative Living Beyond Fear*. New York: Riverhead Books (an imprint of Penguin Group).

Green, Miranda. 1995. *Celtic Goddesses: Warriors, Virgins, and Mothers*. London: British Museum Press.

Feminine Sovereignty Online Community. https://BecomingSovereign.mn.co.

Menakem, Resmaa. 2017. *My Grandmother's Hands: Racialized Trauma and the Pathway to Mending Our Hearts and Bodies*. Las Vegas, NV: Central Recovery Press.

Ostara, Maggie. *Getting Started with Human Design* and *The Reflection Journal* e-book series. https://YourFreeHumanDesignChart.com.

Parker, Karen Curry. 2022. *The Encyclopedia of Quantum Human Design™*. Colorado Springs: Human Design Press (a subsidiary of Grace Point Publishing).

Proctor, Bob. 1997. *You Were Born Rich.* Steamboat Springs, CO: LifeSuccess Productions.

Read, Rupert. "Transformative Connection: Mapping the Way through with Thrutopia's Originator: Rupert Read." Interview by Manda Scott. April 13, 2022. https://accidentalgods.life/transformative-connection/

Read, Rupert. "THRUTOPIA: Why Neither Dystopias Nor Utopias Are Enough to Get Us Through the Climate Crisis, and How a 'Thrutopia' Could Be." Huffpost UK. November 6, 2017 https://www.huffingtonpost.co.uk/rupert-read/thrutopia-why-neither-dys_b_18372090.html/.

Tanner, Linnea. "Celtic Sovereignty Goddess." Apollo's Raven. June 11, 2008. https://apollosraven.wordpress.com/2018/06/11/celtic-sovereignty-goddess/.

Thich Nhat Hanh. 2020. *Interbeing: The 14 Mindfulness Trainings of Engaged Buddhism,* 4th ed. Berkeley, CA: Parallax Press.

Watson, Jules. "Mythology." http://www.juleswatson.com/myth.html.

Wilbur, Ken. "Superhuman Operating System Program." https://actualizeos.com/.

Pillar One

Taylor, Jill Bolte, PhD. 2021. *Whole-Brain Living: The Anatomy of Choice and the Four Characters that Drive Our Life.* New York: Hay House.

Buhner, Stephen Harrod. 2010. *Ensouling Language: On the Art of Nonfiction and the Writer's Life.* Rochester, VT: Inner Traditions International, Limited.

"Nature Search Online Etymology Dictionary." www.etymonline.com. https://www.etymonline.com/search?q=nature&utm_campaign=sd&utm_medium=serp&utm_source=ds_search.

Morus-Baird, Gwilym. "Gwilym Morus-Baird Interview." Interview with Sharon Blackie. This Mythic Life Podcast. Episode 14. https://sharonblackie.net/podcast/.

Merchant, Carolyn. 2013. *Reinventing Eden: The Fate of Nature in Western Culture,* 2nd ed. New York: Routledge.

Mitchell, Sherri L [Weh'na Ha'mu' Kwasset]. 2018. *Sacred Instructions: Indigenous Wisdom for Living Spirt-Based Change.* Berkeley, CA: North Atlantic Press.

Ostara, Maggie. Updated 2020. *Use Your Breath to Free Your Life Featuring Clarity Breathwork.* https://Clarity-Breathwork.com.

Ostara, Maggie. "Maggie Ostara | Human Design | Feminine Sovereignty YouTube Channel." https://www.youtube.com/@maggieostaraphd

Sri Swami Satchidananda. 2012. *The Yoga Sutras of Patanjali.* New York: Integral Yoga Publications.

Pillar Two

Taylor, Jill Bolte. 2021. *Whole Brain Living: The Anatomy of Choice and the Four Characters that Drive Our Life.* Carlsbad, CA: Hay House.

Castellino, Ray. "About 'Womb Surround' Process Workshops." https://castellinotraining.com/process/.

Heller, Diane Poole, PhD. 2019. *The Power of Attachment: How to Create Deep and Lasting Intimate Relationships.* Boulder, CO: Sounds True.

Hicks, Esther and Jerry Hicks. 2004. The Teachings of Abraham. *Ask and It Is Given: Learning to Manifest Your Desire.* New York: Hay House.

Hicks, Esther, and Jerry Hicks. 2008. *The Astonishing Power of Emotions: Let Your Feelings Be Your Guide.* New York: Hay House.

Kessler, Steven. 2015. *The 5 Personality Patterns: Your Guide to Understanding Yourself and Others and Developing Emotional Maturity.* Richmond, CA: Bodhi Tree Press.

Lipton, Bruce H. 2008. *The Biology of Belief: Unleashing the Power of Consciousness, Matter & Miracles.* Carlsbad, CA: Hay House.

Ostara, Maggie. Update 2020. *Free Your Breath, Free Your Life with Clarity Breathwork.* https://Clarity-Breathwork.com.

Rosenburg, Marshall B. 2003. *Non-Violent Communication: A Language of Life.* Encinitas, CA: PuddleDancer Press.

Pillar Three

"The Dirty Dozen: 12 Foods You Should Buy Organic." EatingWell. https://www.eatingwell.com/article/15806/the-dirty-dozen-12-foods-you-should-buy-organic/.

Finley, Ron. "A Guerilla Gardener in South Central LA." *TED Talk*. March 6, 2013. https://www.youtube.com/watch?v=EzZzZ_qpZ4w&t=6s.

Goodenough, Ursula. 2023. *The Sacred Depths of Nature: How Life Has Emerged and Evolved*, 2nd ed. Oxford: Oxford University Press.

Harper, Susan. Interview with Susan Harper. Interview by Lamara Heartwell. Body Intelligence Summit. February 19, 2015. https://youtu.be/vI3Ehot_g1k.

Hawkins, David R. M.D., PhD. 1995. *Power vs Force: The Hidden Determinants of Human Behavior*. Carlsbad, CA: Hay House.

"Indigenous Calendars Mark Much More than the Spring Equinox." MUSKRAT Magazine. March 18, 2016. http://muskratmagazine.com/indigenous-calendars-mark-much-more-than-the-spring-equinox/.

Kessler, Steven. 2015. *The 5 Personality Patterns: Your Guide to Understanding Yourself and Others and Developing Emotional Maturity*. Richmond, CA: Bodhi Tree Press.

"Men's Community for the 21st Century." ManKind Project. https://MankindProject.com.

"Home – ManKind Project USA." http://mkpusa.org.

Menakem, Resmaa. 2017. *My Grandmother's Hands: Racialized Trauma and the Pathway to Mending Our Hearts and Bodies*. Las Vegas, NV: Central Recovery Press.

Meyers, Nikki. October 2020. Radiant Body Yoga 200 Hour Teacher Training, Guest Speaker.

Roman, Sanaya. "Overcoming the Self-Destruct." Guided Meditation. https://www.orindaben.com/catalog/singles_downloads/#SI060.

Schwartz, Richard. 2023. *Introduction to the Internal Family Systems Model*. Boulder, CO: Sounds True.

Smith, Laura. "53 Sleep Statistics: What Percentage of the Population Is Sleep Deprived?" The Good Body. December 10, 2018. https://www.thegoodbody.com/sleep-statistics/.

Smith, Laura. "68 (Surprising) Sleep Facts: Scary, Important, Interesting, Fun!" The Good Body. Updated August 17, 2023. https://www.thegoodbody.com/sleep-facts/.

Pillar Four

Devi, Nischala Joy. 2007. *The Secret Power of Yoga: A Woman's Guide to the Heart and Spirit of the Yoga Sutras.* New York: Three Rivers Press (an imprint of Harmony Books).

DiAngelo, Robin. 2018. *White Fragility: Why It's So Hard for White People to Talk About Racism.* Boston: Beacon Press.

Childre, Doc, Deborah Rozman, Howard Martin, and Rollin McCraty. 2022. *Heart Intelligence: Connecting with the Heart's Intuitive Guidance for Effective Choices and Solutions.* Cardiff by the Sea, CA: Waterside Productions.

Miller, Kia. Radiant Body Yoga. https://KiaMiller.com.

Shimshai. "I Sense Your Presence." "Lyrics | Shimshai | Old World Wisdom with New Messages & Inspiration." 2004. https://shimshai.com/lyrics/i-sense-your-presence.

Swami Satyananda. Quoted in *Radiant Body Yoga 200 Hour Teacher Training Manual* by Kia Miller.

Your Daily Date with the Divine

Chodron, Pema. "The Freedom to Choose Something Different." https://product.soundstrue.com/freedom-to-choose-something-different.

Dispenza, Joe. "Being Positive Won't Help| Let Go of Control | Life Can't Be Controlled." June 26, 2023. https://www.youtube.com/watch?v=38rza4bDQ0I.

Miller, Kia. 40-Day Sadhana Practices. https://www.youtube.com/playlist?list=PLrO8wbA49lMJHfm5uLh8ghM410P7AaBtB.

Ostara, Maggie. Kundalini Yoga ~ Awaken and Upgrade Your Energy and Your Purpose. https://www.youtube.com/playlist?list=PLyUVR3COLjluOxy3j-hI_yhqSJwtx63g7.

Shaw, Martin. "Codes from the Old World." School of Mythopoetics
    Livestream Event. May 15, 2023.
    https://streamofconsciousness.ca/event/codes-from-the-old-world.

Pillar Five

Bush, Zach. "A Path for Healing People and Planet." OneCommune
    Course. https://www.onecommune.com/products/a-path-for-healing-
    people-planet-hosted-by-zach-bush-md-and-farmer-s-footprint.
Martyn, Steven. "Agents of Cultural Regenerations – Steven Martyn
    (The Sacred Gardener)." Interview by Ian MacKenzie. March 2,
    2022. Mythic Masculine Podcast #49.
    https://www.themythicmasculine.com/episodes/steven-martyn.
McCloud, Shiloh Sophia. https://Musea.org.
Menakem, Resmaa. 2017. *My Grandmother's Hands: Racialized Trauma
    and the Pathway to Mending Our Hearts and Bodies.* Las Vegas, NV:
    Central Recovery Press.
Mitsumatsu, Kayoko. https://YogaGivesBack.com.
Off the Mat. https://Offthematintotheworld.org.
Winship, Samantha Foxx. Mother's Finest Urban Farms.
    https://www.mothersfinesturbanfarms.com/
Zippia. "20 Stunning Great Resignation Statistics: Why Are Americans
    Leaving Their Jobs?" Oct. 12, 2022.
    https://www.zippia.com/advice/great-resignation-statistics/.

Pillar Six

brown, adrienne maree. 2021. *Holding Change: The Way of Emergent
    Strategy, Facilitation, and Mediation.* Chico, CA: AK Press.
Rosenburg, Marshall B. 2003. *Non-Violent Communication: A Language
    of Life.* Encinitas, CA : PuddleDancer Press.
Sinek, Simon. 2019. *The Infinite Game.* New York: Penguin Books.

Pillar Seven

Buck, John. "Sociocracy: Thinking Smarter Together." TEDxUMD.
  April 25, 2018. https://www.youtube.com/watch?v=K3s6Ak-iCug.

Chin, Alana. "Redwood Trees have two types of leaves, scientists
  find – a trait that could help them survive in a changing climate."
  The Conversation. April 13, 2022. https://theconversation.com/
  redwood-trees-have-two-types-of-leaves-scientists-find-a-trait-that-
  could-help-them-survive-in-a-changing-climate-179812.

Darwin, Charles, quoted in Kukk, "Survival of the Fittest Has Evolved:
  Try Survival of the Kindest."

Eisler, Riane. 1987. *The Chalice and The Blade: Our History, Our Future.*
  New York: HarperCollins.

Gabrieleno (Tongva) Band of Mission Indians. "White Sage Is Being
  Poached." 2021. https://www.gabrieleno-nsn.us/whitesage.

Gimbutas, Marija. 1991. *The Language of the Goddess: Unearthing the
  Hidden Symbols of Western Civilization.* New York: HarperCollins.

Gimbutas, Marija. 2001. *The Living Goddess.* Berkeley: University of
  California Press.

Gorman, Amanda. "The Hill We Climb." January 20, 2020.
  https://www.youtube.com/watch?v=Wz4YuEvJ3y4.

Gratton, Lynda, and Tamara J. Erickson. "Eight Ways to Build
  Collaborative Teams." *Harvard Business Review*, November, 2007.
  https://hbr.org/2007/11/eight-ways-to-build-collaborative-teams.

Harper, Susan. Continuum Montage. https://ContinuumMontage.com.

Kimmerer, Robin Wall. 2013. *Braiding Sweetgrass: Indigenous Wisdom,
  Scientific Knowledge, and the Teachings of Plants.* Minneapolis:
  Milkweed Editions.

Krishnan, Kiran. "Your Friendly Bacteria Are Your Greatest Ally."
  Interview with Jeffrey Smith. Healing from GMOs Online
  Conference. Produced by Maggie Ostara. July 2018.

Kukk, Christopher. "Survival of the Fittest Has Evolved: Try Survival of
  the Kindest | Even Charles Darwin thought 'survival of the fittest'
  was misinterpreted. Instead, consider 'survival of the kindest.'" Better
  by Today. March 7, 2017. https://www.nbcnews.com/better/
  relationships/survival-fittest-has-evolved-try-survival-kindest-n730196.

Lent, Jeremy. 2021. *The Web of Meaning: Integrating Science and Traditional Wisdom to Find Our Place in the Universe.* Gabriola Island, BC, Canada: New Society Publishers.

Machado de Oliveria, Vanessa. 2021. *Hospicing Modernity: Facing Humanity's Wrongs and the Implications for Social Activism.* Berkeley, CA: North Atlantic Press.

Mantooth, Katie. "Pre-Columbian Native American Civilizations." Updated January 7, 2022. https://study.com/learn/lesson/native-american-civilizations-pre-columbus-tribes-facts-cultures.html.

Mitchell, Sherri L. [Weh'na Ha'mu' Kwasset] 2018. *Sacred Instructions: Indigenous Wisdom for Living Spirit-Based Change.* Berkeley, CA: North Atlantic Press.

Mohamed, Inca A. Change Elemental. https://changeelemental.org/people/inca-a-mohamed/.

Montesinos, Jes. Interview with Jes Montesinos. Interview by Maggie Ostara. 2022. https://montesinosandassociates.com/about.

Montgomery, Beronda L. "Plants Thrive in a Complex World by Communicating, Sharing Resources and Transforming Their Environments." The Conversation. https://theconversation.com/plants-thrive-in-a-complex-world-by-communicating-sharing-resources-and-transforming-their-environments-156932.

National Institutes of Health. "The Teen Brain: 7 Things to Know." National Institute of Mental Health. 2020. https://www.nimh.nih.gov/health/publications/the-teen-brain-7-things-to-know.

Newton, Michael. "Solar Session: The Sovereign." Interview by Ian McKenzie. School of Mythopoetics. August 8, 2022. https://mn.schoolofmythopoetics.com/posts/solar-session-the-sovereign-with-michael-newton-recording.

Ostara, Maggie. "Feminine Sovereign Archetypes." https://SovereignQuiz.com.

Powers, Richard. 2018. *The Overstory: A Novel.* New York: W.W. Norton & Company.

Romero-Briones, A-dae, et al. 2020. *Recognition and Support of Indigenous California Land Stewards, Practitioners of Kincentric Ecology.* Longmont, CO: First Nations Development Institute and California Foodshed Funders.

Read, Donna and Starhawk. "Signs Out of Time: The Story of Archeologist Marija Gimbutas." Belili Productions. March 30, 2016 YouTube release. https://www.youtube.com/watch?v=BjE2-H1R9Zs&t=2s.

Salmón, Enrique. "Enrique Salmón: Ancestral Foodways That Enrich Local Landscapes." Interview by Kamea Chayne. Green Dreamer podcast. Episode 391. https://greendreamer.com/podcast/enrique-salmon-eating-the-landscape.

Scott, Manda. 2003. *Dreaming the Eagle*. Book One of the Boudica Series. New York: Delacorte Press.

Seneca-Cayuga Nation. *The Great Law of Peace*. https://sctribe.com/sites/default/files/2022-10/Great-Law-of-Peace.pdf.

Simard, Suzanne. 2021. *Finding the Mother Tree: Discovering the Wisdom of the Forest*. New York: Alfred A. Knopf.

Sociocracy for All. "What Is Sociocracy?" March 7, 2019. https://www.youtube.com/watch?v=b6r3-s2p7eI&t=4s.

Pillar Eight

Bloom, Isabella. "Meet the Three Women Behind an Indigenous Land Back Effort to Reclaim an SF Peninsula Farm." 2022. https://www.kqed.org/news/11911817/meet-the-three-women-behind-an-indigenous-land-back-effort-to-reclaim-an-sf-peninsula-farm.

"Canfield Consortium." https://www.canfieldconsortium.org/.

Colvin, Rukiya. "Canfield Consortium Awarded $50,000 to 'Activate' a Previously Abandoned Alleyway on Detroit's East Side." Planet Detroit. October 14, 2021. https://planetdetroit.org/2021/10/canfield-consortium-awarded-50000-to-activate-a-previously-abandoned-alleyway-on-detroits-east-side/.

Deep Medicine Circle. https://DeepMedicineCircle.org.

"Down to Earth Showcase Vision for Derby's Nature Based Regeneration." Down to Earth Derby. April 21, 2022. https://www.dtederby.org/down-to-earth-showcase-vision-for-derbys-nature-based-regeneration.

Finley, Ron. "A Guerilla Gardener in South Central LA." *TED Talk*. 2013. https://www.youtube.com/watch?v=EzZzZ_qpZ4w&t=6s.

The Ron Finley Project. "Ron Finley: Gangsta Gardener in South Central LA | Game Changers." https://www.youtube.com/watch?v=owDCnGmhdAs&t=22s.

"Food Rescue US – the Simple Solution to Ending World Hunger." https://foodrescue.us/.

Garrity, Mike. "Big, Bad Forest Clear Cutting Continues: Daines, Gianforte Mislead Public About the Practice." Daily Montanan. June 12, 2021. https://dailymontanan.com/2021/06/12/big-bad-forest-clear-cutting-continues/.

Global Alliance for the Rights of Nature (GARN). October 20, 2020. https://www.garn.org.

Gyatso, Tenzin, The 14th Dalai Lama. "Compassion and the Individual." 2019. https://www.dalailama.com/messages/compassion-and-human-values/compassion.

HeartMath Institute. "Add Heart. Uplifting Global Consciousness." Global Coherence™ App. https://www.heartmath.org/gci/global-coherence-app/.

Heckman, Trathen. 2023. *Take Heart. Take Action. The Transformative Power of Small Acts, Groups, and Gardens.* Petaluma: Daily Acts Press. https://DailyActs.org.

Indigenous Values Initiative. "What Is the Doctrine of Discovery?" *Doctrine of Discovery Project* (30 July 2018). https://doctrineofdiscovery.org/what-is-the-doctrine-of-discovery.

Johnson, Tonika. "Folded Map Project." https://foldedmapproject.com.

Kimmerer, Robin Wall. 2013. *Braiding Sweetgrass: Indigenous Wisdom, Scientific Knowledge, and the Teachings of Plants.* Minneapolis: Milkweed Editions.

LaMagna, Marissa. Bay Area Green Tours. https://www.bayareagreentours.org/.

Mitchell, Sherri L. [Weh'na Ha'mu' Kwasset] 2018. *Sacred Instructions: Indigenous Wisdom for Living Spirit-Based Change.* Berkeley, CA: North Atlantic Press.

US National Park Service. "Mining Claims." December 14, 2020. https://www.nps.gov/subjects/energyminerals/mining-claims.htm.

Peel, Nicola. "Building Houses from Garbage." December 22, 2011. https://youtu.be/2F5K6m4qKcQ https://Ecobricks.org.

Peel, Nicola. "Saving Chocolate! And Finding Solutions to the
     Meta-Crisis. Interview by Manda Scott. Accidental Gods podcast.
     Episode 167. February 14, 2023. https://accidentalgods.life/
     saving-chocolate-and-finding-solutions-to-the-meta-crisis/.
Pepperwood Preserve. https://www.pepperwoodpreserve.org.
Words of Chief Seattle. https://www.goodreads.com/quotes/
     845732-the-earth-does-not-belong-to-man-man-belongs-to.
Salmón, Enrique. "Enrique Salmón: Ancestral Foodways That Enrich
     Local Landscapes." Interview by Kamea Chayne.
     Green Dreamer podcast. Episode 391.
     https://greendreamer.com/podcast/enrique-salmon-eating-the-landscape
Seneca-Cayuga Nation. *The Great Law of Peace.* https://sctribe.com/
     sites/default/files/2022-10/Great-Law-of-Peace.pdf.
Shiffman, Richard. "'Mother Trees' Are Intelligent: They
     Learn and Remember | And ecologist Suzanne Simard
     says they need our help to survive." *Scientific American.*
     May 4, 2021. https://www.scientificamerican.com/article/
     mother-trees-are-intelligent-they-learn-and-remember/.
Sidhu, Jatinder. "What is a keystone species and why do they matter?"
     World Economic Forum. Sept 16, 2021.
     https://www.weforum.org/agenda/2021/09/what-is-a-keystone-species/.
Smith, Mark Ridsdill. 2022. *Vertical Veg Guide to Container Gardening:
     How to Grow an Abundance of Herbs, Vegetables, and Fruit in Small
     Spaces.* White River Junction: Chelsea Green Publishing.
Sproul, R.C. "What Is Biblical Stewardship?"
     https://www.ligonier.org/learn/articles/what-biblical-stewardship.
"Stewardship." https://ministrydesigns.com/stewardship/.
Global Transition Movement. https://TransitionNetwork.org.
Transition Town. "The Essential Guide to Doing Transition." 2016.
     https://transitionnetwork.org/wp-content/uploads/2018/08/
     The-Essential-Guide-to-Doing-Transition-English-V1.2.pdf.
Tree Leaf Farm. https://TreeLeafFarm.com.
Turtle Lake Refuge. http://www.turtlelakerefuge.org/chemical-free-parks.
United Nations. "The International Bill of Human Rights Fact Sheet."
     Article 29. https://www.ohchr.org/sites/default/files/Documents/
     Publications/FactSheet2Rev.1en.pdf.

Webpage with List of Nonprofits Supporting Restorative Projects.
  https://welovetheearth.org/nonprofits/.
Zero Waste North Bay. https://zerowastenorthbay.org/.
Front Image of Cultural Burning from their press kit.
  https://climatechange.ucdavis.edu/climate/news/rethinking-wildfire.
  Attribution in the endnote and on copyright page.

Acknowledgments

So many incredible people have influenced and supported me along the way of growing myself into the person who could create this body of work. I especially bow to:

- Frances Smith Foster for guiding my young mind into uncharted territory and taking me with her as she excavated the literature of slavery and African American women's writing of the nineteenth century.
- Olivia Corson for demonstrating and teaching me how to express and heal myself through movement, sound and story, by becoming deeply embodied.
- Ashanna Solaris, Dana Dharma Devi, and Peter DeLong for first teaching me about the power of the breath.
- Sue Hoya Sellers and Shiloh Sophia for being my Intentional Creativity mentors.
- Susan Harper and Stephen Buhner for opening my senses to the pulse of the living world and giving me language for expressing from the imaginal realm.
- Karen Curry Parker for teaching me traditional and Quantum Human Design in ways that truly support our awakening and empowerment.
- Manda Scott for helping me feel into the ancient roots of my ancestors and for opening my eyes to see that the future truly is here now, we just need the will and mettle to bring it all the way into being.
- Kia Miller for guiding me along the path left by the ancient yogis and so generously making their technologies available to so many of us in this time.

In addition much gratitude goes to all the many wayshowers, visionaries, teachers, writers, activists, and provocateurs who appear in these pages, helping to guide us into what's possible beyond the bridle and blinders and into the living world.

I thank Maggie McReynolds and the staff at Un-Settling Books for their care in editing, designing, and producing this book. I'm particularly grateful for Maggie's support during the writing process and her reflections on the strengths in the writing that led me to write a better book.

I'm grateful for the presenters and participants in our Thrutopian Seminar. My heart and perspective have been greatly enhanced by your visions and work in the world.

Thank you to the presenters and participants in my Women Evolving the World conference and seminar. Your passion for the 8 Pillars affirmed the significance of this work at a critical point. Thank you also to all of my clients, students, and colleagues who've inspired me and helped keep me going when sometimes I doubted myself.

I thank my dear friend, Susan Rutherford, for her encouragement through the years of working through this material and for providing cogent and inspiring feedback on earlier drafts. Thanks go to Christine Arylo for being my visionary soul sister and always reminding me what's most important. I'm particularly appreciative of the loving care and attention I received from Deb Root Grant and Elizabeth Lakin during periods of difficulty while writing this book.

To my parents, Roger Sale and Dorothy Young Sale, I owe my deepest debt of gratitude for not only schooling me in the life of the mind and always supporting me along my wayward path, but for demonstrating how possible it really is to grow yourself into the person you have the potential to become.

Finally, for my dear Sam, your presence, humor, insight, and passion have meant more to me than you may ever know. This book is for you, Beloved, and for your generation, that we olders may do the work that's ours to do so you youngers may have a world in which to do yours. I love you.

About the Author

Maggie Ostara, PhD, left her prestigious job as the Director of Women's and Gender Studies at Columbia University when she realized she wasn't meant to work for anyone else. (Now she knows that's part of her Human Design.)

She's a multiply published and #1 Amazon best-selling author, an arousing speaker, beloved teacher, and highly intuitive and skilled mentor-coach. She's the creator of the *8 Pillars of Feminine Sovereignty* and the six *Feminine Sovereign Archetypes*.

Maggie says: "Now is the time for those of us who've been clearing our outdated belief systems and building our skills and wisdom in the energetic and emotional realms to step forward and take our place among the leaders of today. For too many years, those who claim leadership in our world have valued profit and personal gain over the well-being of most of humanity and the Living World. We're transforming and upgrading what it means to be a leader in alignment with the More Life principle: more life to all and less to none. I invite you to take the next step forward – whether that's simply in your own life, or in your family, community, neighborhood, or in your work in the world – shining out your values, your radiance, your compassion and your vision of the world you want to live in. Together we truly can make a difference!"

Maggie has a thriving YouTube channel, teaches online courses, works 1:1 with clients and in groups, provides business consulting and relationship guidance, and particularly loves guiding change-agents to develop their Feminine Sovereignty and make the contribution and impact they came here to make. She lives in northern California on the traditional lands of the Pomo people, with her 20-something non-binary kiddo and her black feline familiar. Find ways to connect with Maggie on the Resources Page.